POSTMODERNITY AND THE CREATION OF THE ANTHROPOCENE

How our current period evolved out of history and where it is going

NEIL PITTS

Dynasty Press Limited
12 New Broadway,
Worthing,
England,
BN11 4HP

First published by Dynasty Press 2021

ISBN 978-1-916131-75-0

Cover Design by Rupert Dixon

Printed in Great Britain

CONTENTS

The Mongol Empire receded in the late 1200s, and the European Renaissance began. However, the Bubonic Plague decimated populations in the 1300s. Reunited by Timur, the Mongols converted to Islam in the 1400s, while Ottoman Turks sacked Byzantium, closing the land trade routes into Asia and forcing Europe to explore sea trade routes.

As Europeans developed maritime trade, the Age of Discovery led to the recolonisation of the Americas and European global empires linking the Americas, Africa, India and the Far East. However, in Europe itself, the Protestant Reformation led to a series of wars over the balance of power.

The Industrial Revolution enabled the rise of democratic governments and Modern Capitalism. However, it also inspired political revolutions, such as U.S. independence, the French Revolution and later Communism. In 1914 Europe collapsed into WWI, leading to the Russian Revolution, League of Nations, rise of Fascism and WWII.

In 1945 the UN began its mission to ensure a lasting global peace. Despite localised conflicts between the Communist block and the West (known as the Cold War) and political instability leading to the problem of terrorism, geopolitics is moving forwards into a new period.

List of the sources cited in this work.

INTRODUCTION

This book describes how our current period, Postmodernity, has come into existence, and the Anthropocene, or 'Human Age', has been proposed as the name for the next. As all historical periods are named according to the effect of progress on society, we must understand them in terms of how one has evolved out of the last. Henceforth, this book takes the reader through each period of human history, one step at a time. It explains how today's world was created, where we are in terms of our current period, and how we can see events leading towards the next.

Starting with the first societies of Prehistory, it then takes us through the series of empires and religions which appeared in the Ancient world, the events which went back and forth between East and West during the Middle Ages, then the rise of scientific ideas and democratic government in the Modern periods; these events are used to explain the world which created Postmodernity. Its dictionary definition is 'the state of affairs which exists after modernity', thus giving us the problem of its subjective nature, which we have been addressing throughout this period, but how are we coping with the way the world is heading towards the next?

With the rise of computers, this is creating a shift to the more objective, scientific worldview we need, and nations are heading increasingly towards an objective reality due to the increasing ability to share complex information, but the Digital Age can hardly be the name for this new period. The term Anthropocene has thus been proposed by scientists as a concept which supersedes Postmodernity by incorporating all our previous periods into a single history. Currently, the rise of this term is largely being fuelled by ecologists who are saying the effect we are having on the environment means we need to take more responsibility for our actions. Other scientists have argued that nuclear technology has created that need, regardless of our impact. However, as this book shows, we can already see a new age emerging from within the structure of global civilisation itself.

CHAPTER 1

Prehistory

Due to scientific breakthroughs in the 20ᵗʰ century, including the deciphering of ancient texts, DNA testing and radio-carbon dating, we can now trace the course of human history back into its origins. Starting with hunter-gatherer society, six 'Cradles of Civilisation' were created by settled farming, which then generated their own language and writing systems. The first major society to unite was Egypt, around 2700 BC, from settled farming and cattle herding...

Part 1: The Original Spread of Humanity

The people of early civilisations knew much more than many people think. They had myths, science, philosophy and religion. So, why does it seem that we are only now beginning to see what they did? The problem with this would appear to be that later civilisations were built upon the sites of earlier ones, so many pieces of evidence were destroyed which held the key to understanding what had gone before. For many centuries, whole periods were lost to the archaeological record, known only through scriptures like the Bible, and as new civilisations appeared they re-wrote history in their own image. However, owing to scientific breakthroughs in the 20th Century, it is now possible to see how the world order developed through every stage.

Starting in prehistory, we can now see how people spread across the world, into various regions which had seen earlier waves of migrating hominids. Many sources state there were several variations in early humans and, until relatively recently, there was more than one human species. Philip's Atlas of World History says that around 100,000 years ago two hominid species existed in the eastern Mediterranean, 'One was the Asian representative of the Neanderthals . . . who inhabited Europe and West Asia from some time after 200,000 B.C.; the other was an early form of Homo sapiens (modern humans) who had first appeared some 20,000 years earlier in southern Africa. By 40,000 B.C. modern humans were to be found throughout the previously inhabited world...'[1]

It continues to say that, 'Whether they interbred with the hominids they displaced or simply extinguished them is unclear, but almost certainly, Homo sapiens was the only surviving hominid by about 30,000 BC.'

The next map shows the direction in which Homo sapiens spread out of Africa and across the world: in the red area (1) Homo sapiens, in the yellow (2) Neanderthals, and in the green (3) were other early hominids.

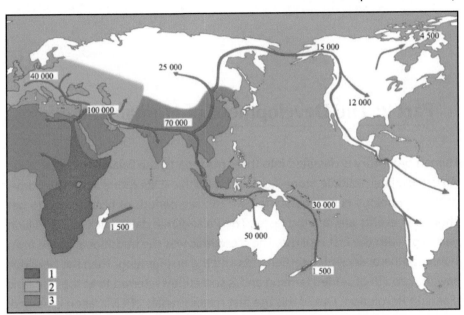

One thing you may have noticed about this map is that the Americas were originally colonised from the east. It is only in later periods that the Europeans recolonised them from the other side. Obviously, the shape of human society has changed massively since then, and to understand how this has occurred we must look at how societies evolve.

Part 2: The Development of Human Societies

Human prehistory is classified into three main parts, the Palaeolithic (Old Stone Age), Mesolithic (Middle Stone Age) and Neolithic (Late Stone Age). Over time, as the technology curve accelerates, we can see periods of history tend to get shorter as events are moving faster. The Palaeolithic dates back to 3.3 million years ago with the first tool use. The Mesolithic was the transitional phase from hunter-gatherer society to settlements and the first farming. Then the Neolithic saw the growth of settled farming and is sometimes referred to as the Neolithic 'Farming Revolution'. Out of this the first major Cradles of Civilisation emerged, which between them created the first great empires, along with their languages and writing systems. Following this, we have written records and are into history itself.

The timescale for all this has been discovered by archaeologists who have found that early hominids began to spread out of Africa approximately 2 million years ago. Until then, they were found mostly in east Africa, east of the Great Rift Valley. Most known fossils dating earlier than one million years ago are found there, in Kenya, Tanzania, and Ethiopia. Between 2 and 1.5 million years ago, groups began leaving Africa for southern Europe and Asia. The Southern Caucasus were occupied at 1,700,000 years, and northern China by 1,660,000. By the end of the Early Palaeolithic, people were also living in western Indonesia and Europe (around the Mediterranean and migrating north into England, Germany and Bulgaria). However, studies of cave settlements in Europe indicate there was not even the regular use of fire as late as between 400,000 and 300,000 years ago.

By the Middle Palaeolithic, people were wearing clothes (around 170,000 BC); beaded seashells have been found at Taforalt in Oujda, Morocco (dated around 80,000 BC); in Blombos Cave in South Africa there were engraved ochre, beaded marine shells, engraved bone and stone tools (70,000 BC); after this, the bow and arrow replaced the spear thrower in Africa (around 64,000 BC).

In the Late Palaeolithic, a sewing needle made by the Denisovans has been found (dated to around 50,000 BC); a flute in Germany and deep sea fishing equipment in East Timor (42,000 BC). Aboriginal culture reached Australia, as travel by sea increased (between 40,000–30,000 BC); a figurine carved from mammoth ivory was found in Germany (35,000 BC); and a small hamlet consisting of huts built with rocks and mammoth bones was discovered in the Czech Republic (25,000 BC).

Hence, the Mesolithic period began to appear and more advanced tools were created (for example, smaller lithic tools rather than the heavier chipped tools of the earlier period). This finished as the larger settled farming civilisations began (around 12,000 BC). In the Near East, the transition from one to the other occurred much earlier (20,000 to 8,000 years ago), while Europe was later (between 15,000 to 5,000 years ago). Evidence of the first social systems organised around a temple has been found at Gobekli Tepe in Anatolia, southern Turkey, which was in the north of the Fertile Crescent at the time (around 9,000 BC). Various stone circles show two human figures carved into monoliths surrounded by a circle of local animals, all similarly carved onto smaller pieces of stone. This temple indicates that people began domesticating wild plants and animals as settlements enabled culture to be organised through primitive religion.

Various stones in this and other early temples, such as Stone Henge, were aligned with the stars, and are assumed to have functioned like a giant clock which mapped out the course of the seasons, which could also be used as a directional compass to spread their culture to other places on Earth. Out of this emerged a type of society which became more aware of its own direction, purpose, and relation to others. In this way, early networks of societies created the foundations of the later civilisations which developed myths and religions.

The establishment of organised societies then meant they could create storage systems, build more advanced shelters and gradually learn to record information, hence they could explore, create basic maps describing things like mountains and rivers, and develop more advanced technology. Following this, various metal-ages appeared as people discovered that ores heated to specific temperatures would produce liquid metal which could be shaped as it cooled. Copper, Bronze and Iron were produced (in that order) and people went from having stone spear and arrowheads to cutting tools and basic machinery. However, while there was an abundance of Gold, Silver and Copper in the Americas, Iron ore was not so common on the surface, and it is generally thought this was the reason they became trapped in the Stone Age. These occurred in various places at different times, with most metalworking periods happening between 6,000–2,000 BC.

By around 3,000 BC six 'Cradles of Civilisation' were beginning to appear: in Egypt, Mesopotamia, the Indus Valley, China, Mexico and Peru. These are places where independent civilisations evolved complete language and writing systems. People in these places developed distinctive cultural identities which influenced the direction of their societies. As they grew, they began to fill up all the territory around themselves and this brought them into closer contact with each other. No longer was it a case of the original spread of humanity, and a new phase emerged.

H.G. Wells comments on how they were interconnected, [2]'In the neolithic period there was a remote connection between Central and Western Asia and Europe. . . It is quite clear from Chinese records that there were southern as well as northern beginnings of a civilisation, and that the Chinese civilisation that comes into history 2,000 years B.C. is the result of a long process of conflicts, minglings and interchanges between a southern and a northern culture, of which the southern may have been the earlier and more highly developed. The southern Chinese perhaps played the role towards the northern Chinese that the Hamites or Sumerians played to the Aryan or Semitic peoples in the west, or that the settled Dravidians played towards the Aryans in India.' As this new level of society appeared, writing and mathematics began to record dates, events and financial transactions.

Part 3: The Development of Language, Writing and Mathematics

They started as early symbolism which conveyed ideas in pictorial terms. Georges Dean says in 'Signs, Symbols and Ciphers', [3]'The invention of writing was a long, slow, complex process. Yet writing was neither the first nor the only means our earliest ancestors found to record ideas. Long before the appearance of this form of expression, figurative and non-figurative images were used in pictorial systems of communication.' He adds that (on page 12) 'more than 30,000 years ago, in the upper Palaeolithic period, in the heart of the European regions now called France and Spain, people began to make "useless" objects: ornaments, jewellery and especially decorated pieces of stone and bone. These tokens were marked with sequences of incisions, rhythmic lines, and dots, arranged in a certain order and with regular spacing. Such marks also began to appear on the walls of caves and shelters at about the same time.

Perhaps they were simply exercises, the hand of an artisan or artist practising dexterity. Yet we call these marks signs and are confident that they once conveyed specific meanings, though the first systems of writing were not invented until between 10,000 and 5,000 BC. We can no longer decipher their long-hidden messages; nor can we guess the reality to which they once referred. A sign, in this sense, is a line, dot, bar, rectangle, or other geometric or repeated shape thought to have a symbolic value. Between 35,000 and 8,000 BC Palaeolithic craftsmen made great drawings, paintings, relief sculptures, and engravings on the walls of caves — Lascaux in France, Altamira in Spain, and many other sites in Europe, Africa and Asia.' He says (on pages 15–17) that these images 'speak' of animals, objects, the hunt, the god of the mountain, etc. without actually using words. Over time these ideas developed into symbols which described human activities such as the plough, cart and ox-goad. Eventually they grew into languages which could describe more abstract legal, religious and philosophical ideas.

Mathematics appeared around the same time as writing. Richard Mankiewicz says in [4]'The History of Mathematics' (on page 10), 'The earliest evidence of numerical recording was excavated in Swaziland, southern Africa, and consists of a baboon's fibula with 29 clearly visible notches, dating from about 35,000 B.C.' He adds that a wolf 's radius from 30,000 BC was found in Western Europe with 55 markings in groups of five, and another from 20,000 BC indicates a link to the phases of the moon. He also holds the view that ideas develop along with society and says (on page 8), 'Rather than taking the reader through a sequence of 'great theorems', I wanted to illustrate how the mathematical sciences were intimately linked to the interests and aspirations of the civilizations in which they flourished.'

He says that, since its invention, people have been calculating things like the distance between places, the length of days, the time between changing seasons, angles, weight, velocity, the properties of physical materials, then how to construct buildings and make machinery. Next, he says, people attempted to work out what was happening in the heavens. One example he gives of this is the Mayan civilisation, which accurately calculated the lunar month to three decimal places. He adds that periods in the history of mathematics generally correspond with the models we have of the solar system and stars.

Hence, people began devising myths from the relationships which existed between the stars. They also used features which made up their local environment, such as animals and plants, in sculpture, art, pottery and jewellery, to create gods like those of the sea or sky, thunder and lightning. Jack Tresidder says, in his [5]'Dictionary of Symbols', 'Traditional symbols form a visual shorthand for ideas — and yet their functions and meanings extend to something much more than that. For thousands of years they have enabled sculptors, painters and craftsmen to embody and reinforce deep thoughts about human life in single, immediate and powerful images.' He continues to say that (on page 6), in the beginning, the most important symbols represented attempts to give 'order and significance to human life in a mysterious universe.' He adds that (on page 7) 'Familiar features of the earth or the visible universe — animals, birds, fish, insects, plants or stones — are all included in the symbolic repertoire. These, like humans themselves, were once seen as reflections of a greater reality, having qualities expressive of laws and moral "truths" inherent in the cosmic order.' By using elements of their environment, they could explain life from the viewpoint of their own society, according to its place in the world. This functioned as a tool which enabled members of these societies to understand who and where they were, like an early form of education.

Part 4: The Cradles of Civilisation

Now we can see enough about the development of early human societies to take a look at the situation which led to the creation of the six distinctive cultures from which we can see then the large empires of the Ancient world develop. Going back to the first map, we can see that a separation appeared between the civilisations in the Americas and those on Africa-Eurasia, which eventually led to the European recolonisation of the Americas. I shall start by examining the societies in the Americas, before taking a look at how the early world order we know today emerged on Africa-Eurasia.

Native American Culture

Originally, the first people to set foot on the Americas crossed over the piece of land between Alaska and Siberia. Known as Beringia, it was exposed during the last Ice Age when large amounts of the Earth's sea water was trapped in the ice. Large numbers of people may have even lived on it for up to 10,000 years before the American ice-sheets melted enough to allow them across, around 13,000 BC. That is, as the permafrost on the ground receded, it meant that the land corridor into the Americas could support a human migration. Various animals like the horse, antelope and woolly mammoth were able to cross earlier. However, as the ice melted further, sea levels rose and the Americas became separated from Africa-Eurasia around 10,000 BC.

It included the region which is now the Chukchi Sea, Bering Sea, Bering Strait, Chukchi and Kamchatka Peninsulas in Russia and Alaska in the United States. At 620 miles wide, its area totalled 620,000 square miles. Scientists have recently drilled down into the ocean floor and found samples of pollen and vegetation which indicate a steppe-tundra landscape with a large variety of grasses and herbs. A common language root has also been found between the people in the Americas and those who lived in Siberia. The Yupik tribe, for example, lived on both sides. The land bridge theory was established as far back as 1590 and has been generally accepted since the 1930s. In 2012 the governments of Russia and the United States finally announced a plan to formally acknowledge a 'transboundary area of shared Beringian heritage' through a joint project linking the Beringia National Park in Russia to the Bering Land Bridge National Preserve in the United States.

What happened to their original culture is not too difficult to see, as it changed relatively little over time. DNA testing of modern Amerindians indicates a large-scale migration from a single source which then separated into two groups. Firstly this spread eastwards, into North America, then one group migrated more directly south towards Central and South America, reaching its southern tip around 9,000 BC. Large regional centres developed into major cities in Mexico and Peru while the northern tribes remained mostly nomadic.

Agriculture developed from around 8,000 BC in Central America and, by around 4,000, maize and tomatoes had become a staple food source. The first agricultural villages appeared around 3,000 BC and, by 2,000, ceremonial temples, pyramids and palaces. The first complex society there was the Olmec, which arose around 1200 BC and fell around 400.

The Archaic period of the Mayan civilisation (up to 2000 BC) had the first agriculture and village settlements. The Pre-classic period (2000 BC to AD 250) saw more advanced societies who cultivated maize, beans, squashes and chilli peppers. The first Mayan cities developed around 750 BC and Hieroglyphic writing was in use by the 3rd Century BC, the only fully developed writing system in the Americas before their re-discovery by the Europeans. Geographically, they occupied territory in southeastern Mexico, Guatemala, Belize, Honduras and El Salvador.

The Aztec Empire had a similar system of developing the agricultural crops which were typical of central America, although it was a triple alliance which arose much later. Around AD 1427, Tenochtitlan, Texcoco and Tlacopan joined forces in the Valley of Mexico. Their economy was feudal and highly centralised, as 5% of the population were nobles who controlled the land on which the others worked. The social system was a hierarchy which limited the interaction between outlying areas and heavily controlled the distribution of luxury goods.

The Incan Empire was later still, one of the largest in the 16th Century AD. They had roads, agriculture and a religion which spoke of their chief as the son of the Sun god, Inti. At one point it connected Peru, Argentina, Colombia, Ecuador, Bolivia and Chile, but they lacked the wheel, metalworking and even a writing system. Their economy functioned largely without money and has been described as a Socialist slave system whereby taxes were paid in the form of labour to the empire. As a reward, rulers would provide access to land, resources and celebratory banquets. Hence, we can see the larger civilisations of Central and South America created both left-wing Socialist, and right-wing Feudal societies, but all were limited in terms of technology.

Those in North America remained nomadic. C.F. Taylor and W.C. Sturtevant say in their book, [6]'Americans', that some elements were common to all, yet different themes emerged within the various parts of North America. Matters of tribal importance, such as who were friends and enemies were dealt with by the Chieftainship. A central concept in their religion was the idea of a 'spirit-world', to which only proper initiates could relate. Their spiritual Shamans (tribal priests) sat on the boundary between this world and the next, and played an important role in advising society. Major decisions involving multiple societies were made at large meetings involving many tribes, or 'Confederations'.

The Basin Area, for example, featured ideas about death, regeneration and immortality. They add (on pages 213–14) that the people of the Arctic, the Yup'ik, spoke of the material and spiritual as two different worlds, visible and invisible, which occupied the same space at the same time. At certain times the 'Veil' between them grew thin and it was important to conduct ceremonies to ensure that rites of passage took place properly, so evil spirits were not released at the point of change. Issues like the formal passing from youth into adulthood, for example, were dealt with in public rituals attended by the whole tribe. Like in many other cultures, they functioned as a social confirmation of changes in role and responsibilities. The Yup'ik also believed that all objects, animate and otherwise, had Yuas. That is, they could be seen and described in human form. This enabled the Shaman to see the spirit of the forest, the mountain, or even whole nations, the hunter to communicate with his prey, or the Chief to see good or ill-meaning from other tribes.

They say that the tribes in the northeast (on page 227) were especially strong on the rights of the individual and liberty. They founded the Confederacy of the League of the prophet called Deganawida, who had a vision of a great spruce tree which reached through the sky to communicate with the Master of Life. Its roots represented the tribes of the Confederacy: Seneca, Mohawk, Cayuga, Onodaga, and Oneida. The tree represented their sisterhood. It was constructed in 1570 as a response to continual warring between the tribes in the region, with the aim of creating a new era of unity and prosperity. An eagle lived on top of the tree, symbolising their awareness.

Despite the official surrender of their main chiefs to Washington, many still perpetuate this indigenous culture on 'Reservations' (areas of land they managed to preserve through treaties with the United States government).

Africa–Eurasia

Now, if we look at events in the rest of the world, what happened there which led to the Europeans recolonising the Americas from the other side? This is obviously a huge subject and takes place through many stages. But, through them, we can see the shape of human society change, and this is what ultimately brings us to the idea of Postmodernity as a period of history.

Both Africa-Eurasia and the Americas were in the Neolithic period at the same time (10,000–5,000 BC) and, as the world began to move out of that period, people in the Americas began experimenting with large amounts of plants and various styles of land-management, leading to the development of the larger civilisations. In a similar way, Ancient Egypt (the first Cradle of Civilisation to become part of the early world order) was just beginning to emerge from the pre-dynastic period (5,500–4,000 BC), through settled farming and cattle herding, uniting some time after 3,000 BC.

The people there settled in two main regions, the Nile Delta in the north and the mountains to the south. Unification occurred through the conquest of Lower Egypt by Upper Egypt and their first king, Menes, wore the crown of both. This created three major periods known for stability and three Intermediate Periods were society broke down before re-emerging in a new form. The Old Kingdom (2686–2181 BC) was the time when the king established the title of divine ruler, and included the 3rd to the 6th dynasties. Then, in the First Intermediate Period, the economic system began to break down, to the point where the king could no longer support the economy in times of crisis. Various regions broke down into famines and minor civil wars before the kingdom was reunited by a war between Herakleopolis and Thebes.

In the Middle Kingdom (2050–1710 BC) the new system which emerged was more focused on rich landowners who made up the aristocracy. As it was more decentralised it was more politically unstable, but people had less of a state to pay tax to, and it was more financially secure. At the same time, its society moved forward to the point where texts were written for entertainment and educational purposes. Therefore, it is regarded as something of an economic and cultural renaissance, perhaps caused by the fact that its society was no longer focused on the absolute power of the king. It included the 11th and 12th dynasties before breaking down into the Second Intermediate Period (of the 13th dynasty, which was actually a series of unrelated kings).

Its kings became known as the Pharaohs during the New Kingdom (1550–1070 BC), its most prosperous time, and when it expanded to its greatest extent. Diplomatic relations existed with Mitanni, Assyria and Canaan. They extended themselves into Mesopotamia, fought the Hittites for control of Syria and also expanded south into Nubia. By this point, larger civilisations had arisen in Mesopotamia and other places around the world.

There was then a long period of slow decline known as the Third Intermediate Period, firstly in relation to the growing powers in Mesopotamia, but also to rival kingdoms in Africa. Because of its long history, we can see the periods involving many of the societies which appeared in the Ancient world reflected in Egyptian history. Over the next millennia, they were attacked by the Hyksos and Libyans, conquered by the Nubians (728 BC), attacked by the Assyrians (671 BC), conquered twice by the Persians (525–404 and 343–332), then by the Greeks. It was subsequently ruled over by the Ptolemaic kingdom which was established after the death of Alexander the Great, then became a Roman province in 30 BC under Cleopatra.

Egyptian Culture

We can begin to see the emergence of an early world order here, as the development of mass religion served as a means of social organisation. In Ancient Egypt, the myths of various regions were assimilated following unification, as the cult of the Pharaoh became the focus of its culture. Until this point they worshipped different sets of deities who represented natural laws, or forces of nature. Each area had its own creation myth, yet they all share a common theme: the birth of a new world.

Lucia Ghalin says, in 'Egypt. Gods, Myths and Religions'[7] (on page 50), that 'Several explanations as to how the universe came into being survive from Ancient Egypt. Each major centre of religious belief had its own version of the myth of creation, with a different main creator deity who was self-engendered and who went on to generate the other gods and goddesses before creating humankind.'

For example, she says, in 'The Creation Myth of Memphis', Ptah is the self-engendered creator-god who is referred to as the 'father of the gods from whom all life emerged'. She says that he brought the universe into being by conceiving the aspects of it in his heart, then speaking his thoughts out loud. First he created the other deities, then towns with shrines in which to house them. He provided wood, clay and stone statues to act as bodies for the spirits or divine power (ka) of the deities, and offerings to be made to them. All things, including people and animals, were then brought into being by Ptah declaring their names.

In 'The Creation Myth of Elephantine' she says the creator god of the southern cataract region, Khnum, was the ram-headed god who made all the other gods and created the Egyptians (and people who spoke other languages). He then made the animals from clay on his potter's wheel. He placed particular importance on creating the skin, bone and internal organs, and watches over their conception and labour.

'The Creation Myth of Hermopolis Magna' first describes the vital elements necessary for the creation of human society. She says, 'The fundamental factors were arranged into four male-female pairs: primordial water (Nun and Naunet); air or hidden power (Amun and Amaunet); darkness and light (kuk and kauket); and (on page 51) formlessness or infinity . . . (Huh and Hauhet)'. The four male gods were all frog headed, the four female gods were snake headed. At one point, all eight interacted to create the universe. There are then two versions of what happened as the universe actually came into being. In one, the god Thoth (in the form of an Ibis) rose up out of the waters and placed a cosmic egg on a single patch of earth (the Isle of Flame). The Sun hatched out of it and rose immediately into the sky. In the other, the Sun hatched out of a lotus flower floating on the water, personified as the deity Nefertem. The Sun then became the god Horus.

In the creation myth of Heliopolis, before creation, there was endless, lifeless water personified as 'Nun', and the self-engendered creator-god appeared on a mound of silt which emerged out of it. Atum, 'the All', or 'Complete One' created two other gods out of his own bodily fluids, Shu (air) and Tefnut (moisture). This male-female pair were able to reproduce together and their children were Geb (the earth) and Nut (the sky). Isis, Osiris, Seth and Nepthys became their offspring.

In the creation myth of Thebes, Amun was the creator-god. He was beyond the sky and deeper than the underworld. His act of creation broke the stillness of the primeval waters and created the Ogdoad (eight primordial deities) and Ennead (nine manifest deities: the sun god, Amun; his children, Shu and Tefnut;

their children, Geb and Nut; and their children, Osiris, Isis, Seth and Nephthys). Amun was separate from this world, even to the point where his nature was hidden from all the other gods. Because he represents the source of all creation, all other gods can be regarded as aspects of him. He became the supreme god of the Egyptian pantheon, due to Thebes' political position after it unified the Upper and Lower kingdoms. Thebes was also thought of as the location of the emergence of the primeval mound at the beginning of time.

Ghalin sums up 'The Creation Myths in Context' (on page 52), saying the one thing they all have in common is order emerging from Chaos. The water and the mound of silt represent the key event in society, the annual flooding of the Nile. This produces the fertile silt, but it needs the Sun for this to take place. Thus, she concludes, all the explanations tend to hinge on the fertility of the land and the heat of the sun. But, how did they combine these multiple versions into a single, national culture? It seems this was through the national religion which emerged after unification.

The idea that a fully centralised conceptuality evolved within Egypt is supported by many sources, one of which is [8]'The Egyptian Book of the Dead'. It describes nearly two hundred spells contained within the Egyptian Religion, claiming that the mysterious connection they saw between the different parts of the universe was diffused through their laws of physics. The way that they resolved the issue of having multiple creation theories in the same place at the same time was by speaking of people appearing to live many lives in different times and places, which were separated by a mysterious veil. Thus the aim of the religion is to realise how we are one person throughout space and time. Dr. Ramses Seleem, in [9]'The Illustrated Egyptian Book of the Dead', describes the concept of the 'Veil' as an invisible barrier between the different worlds. He quotes from the Papyrus of Ani (on page 10), written by the chief scribe of the Pharaohs,

'See, is it not written in this scroll? Read, you who will discover it in future ages, if God has given you the power to read. Read, children of the future, and learn the secrets of the past, which are so distant to you and yet in reality so near. Men do not live once, in order to vanish forever. They live several lives in different places but not always in this world, and between each life there is a veil of shadows. The doors will finally open and we shall see all the places where our feet have trodden since the dawn of time. Our religion teaches us that we live for eternity. Thus, since eternity has no end, it cannot have a beginning. It is a circle. If, therefore, the one is true, namely that we live eternally, the other must also be true, namely that we have always lived. In the eyes of men, God has many faces, and each swears that he has seen the true and only God. Yet it is not so, for all of these faces are merely the face of God. Our Ka, which is our double, reveals them to us in different ways. By drawing forth from the bottomless well of wisdom, which is hidden in the essence of every man, we perceive grains of truth, which give those of us with knowledge the power to perform marvellous things.'

The Egyptian religion thus provided a framework within which people could resolve conflicting experiences of the world by synthesising them into a whole. It did this by creating a complex social system in which its religion functioned through the worship of its various gods. Each had their own literature, temples and priests who created magical inner-worlds which enabled people to 'interact' with them.

Hence, Egypt produced a socio-religious system by which the priesthood managed the population's development. They maintained regional social structures and involved people in the interaction with the various deities (who were believed to be present in the forces of nature). The priesthood had additional roles, such as teaching in schools and performing public rituals. Hence, the system relied on having an elite priesthood class who oversaw the daily affairs of the state and maintained social order. Therefore, the main criticism of it is that it created a large degree of political and social control, and kept a large portion of the population poor and subservient, by reserving formal education for only those families who could afford it, but we can now see this being in proportion to the way the world worked at the time.

CHAPTER 2

Sumeria–Akkadia

Also ruled over by a divine monarchy and adjacent to Egypt in the Fertile Crescent, Mesopotamia started to produce a slightly more advanced type of society. Starting from around 5500 BC, its temples emerged around 3500 and writing around 2700. Here we can see progress in terms of law codes, civil rights and a myth describing the early 'world order'. The first major civilisation there was the Sumerian, which began as a series of city-states in the south and grew northwards up the Euphrates river. Following this, Semitic tribes migrating from North Africa and western Mesopotamia merged with and assimilated the Sumerians, creating the world's first real empire, Akkadia, around 2100…

Part 1: Sumeria

For a long time, the history of events there was lost to the archaeological record. But, over the last century or so, multiple excavations have discovered thousands of stone tablets and other artefacts, which have been deciphered and analysed to reveal a large amount of information about the development of civilisations in the region. This includes a consistent growth in population, the city-states which became characteristic of the Ancient world empires, writing and language systems, financial records, royal letters and a myth describing the relationship between early kingdoms.

Susan Pollock describes the region, saying that ''Mesopotamia is geologically speaking a trough created as the Arabian shield has pushed up against the Asiatic landmass, raising the Zagros Mountains and depressing the land to the southwest of them . . . Within this trench, the Tigris and the Euphrates Rivers and their tributaries have laid down enormous quantities of alluvial sediments, forming the lower Mesopotamian plain (also known as the alluvial Mesopotamian plain).' She says that the water from the two rivers flowed all the way down the plain, meaning that irrigation channels could be dug as far as it was possible to find soil to grow crops on. Thus, the perpetuation of whole empires came to depend on the ability to dig and maintain them.

She quotes William Kenneth Loftus (on page 28), one of the first archaeological writers to visit there. He says, 'In former days the vast plains of Babylonia were nourished by a complicated system of canals and watercourses, which spread over the country like a net-work. The wants of a teeming population were supplied by a rich soil, not less bountiful than that on the banks of the Egyptian Nile . . . The land was rich in corn and wine. How changed is this aspect of that region at the present day! Long lines of mounds, it is true, mark the courses of those main arteries which formerly diffused life and vegetation along their banks, but their channels are now bereft of moisture and choked with drifted sand; the smaller offshoots are wholly effaced . . . . All that remains of that ancient civilisation — that "glory of kingdoms,", "the praise of the whole earth" — is recognisable in the numerous moulding heaps of bricks and rubbish which overspread the surface of the plain. Instead of the luxuriant fields, the groves and gardens, nothing now meets the eye but an arid waste — the dense population of former times is vanquished...'

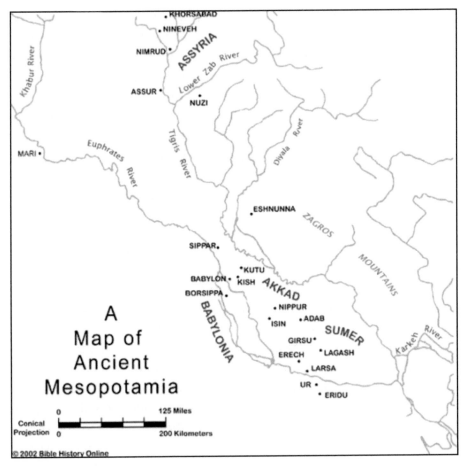

In the bottom right of this map, we can see the first towns in Sumeria, Eridu and Ur. Subsequent settlements, such as Nippur, spread up the river to create the region before it became part of the Akkadian Empire, due to the influx of Semitic tribes. In the next chapter we shall see how this all became part of Babylonia, while the far north grew into Assyria, with its capital at Nineveh.

Samuel Noah Kramer, described as 'the greatest Sumerologist of the twentieth century'[2], describes what life was like there. He says, in his book 'Sumerians'[3], that 'Sumer, the land which came to be known in classical times as Babylonia, consists of the lower half of Mesopotamia, roughly identical with modern Iraq from the north of Baghdad to the Persian Gulf . . . an area of approximately 10,000 square miles, somewhat larger than the state of Massachusetts. Its climate is extremely hot and dry, and its soil, left to itself, is arid, wind-swept and unproductive . . . In spite of the land's natural drawbacks, they turned Sumer into a veritable Garden of Eden and developed what was probably the first high civilisation in the history of man.'

Kramer says its name meant 'Land of the Lords of Brightness', and that the people there 'devised such useful tools, skills, and techniques as the potter's wheel, the wagon wheel, the plough, the sailboat, the arch, the vault, the drone, casting in copper and bronze, riveting, brazing and soldering, sculpture in stone, engraving and inlay. They originated a system of writing on clay, which was borrowed and used all over the Near East for some two thousand years.' He adds that they were also remarkable for their ideas, clear-sighted and level-headed, rarely confused fact with fancy, or mystery with mystification. Also, they evolved a faith which 'gave unto the gods what was the gods', and recognised the inevitable moral limitations of humankind, especially that of 'helplessness in the face of death and divine wrath.'

We can see progress in terms of the type of society they had, when compared with the Egyptian model. Kramer adds, 'the Sumerian was deeply conscious of his personal rights and resented any encroachment on them, whether by his king, his superior, or his equal. No wonder that the Sumerians were the first to compile laws and law-codes, to put everything down in "black and white" in order to avoid misunderstanding, misrepresentation and arbitrariness.' He additionally says, 'While the Sumerians thus set a high value on the individual and his achievement, there was one overriding factor which fostered a strong spirit of co-operation among individuals and communities alike: the complete dependence of Sumer on irrigation for its well-being — indeed, for its very existence. Irrigation is a complicated process . . . Canals had to be dug and kept in constant repair. The water had to be divided equitably among all concerned. To ensure this, a power stronger than the individual landowner or even the single community was mandatory: hence the growth of governmental institutions and the rise of the Sumerian state . . .'

They expanded by developing large-scale farming techniques. However, as Kramer says, 'Sumer, because of the fertility of the irrigated soil, produced a vast surplus of grain but had practically no metals and very little stone and timber, and the state was forced to obtain the material essential to its economy through trade or by military force. So that by the third millennium B.C., there is good reason to believe that Sumerian culture and civilisation had penetrated, at least to some extent, as far east as India and as far west as the Mediterranean, as far south as ancient Ethiopia and as far north as the Caspian.' From this we can see the ability to organise people had grown by this time into a powerful force which could exert great influence on others, as civilisations developed their own states, workforces, religions, militaries and cultures.

Sumerian Myth

One of the few myths surviving from this period is known as 'Enki and the World Order'. At first glance it describes the Sumerian gods but, upon closer examination, it shows how they saw themselves in terms of their position in the world. The reason why the idea of the world order appears here in literature seems to be because of the growing need for each society to have a clear idea of its identity and relationship to others. In terms of the way societies have grown since the end of the Stone Age, this is the point at which their technological, trading and language abilities are starting to grow stronger, and also their territories are literally starting to fill up all the physical space around themselves.

Kramer describes Enki as a fertility god who presides over individual souls, which are referred to as the 'me's'. The narrative builds up a picture of him riding around in his boat and guiding events. Kramer says it is [4]"An excellent illustration of the Sumerian mythological imagination . . . one of the longest and best preserved of the extant Sumerian narrative poems. Its text consists of approximately 460 lines, of which about 375 are preserved entirely or in large part . . .' Here are a few extracts to demonstrate the type of language they used:

[5] "My father, the king of the universe,
Brought me into existence in the universe,
My ancestor, the king of all the lands,
Gathered together all the me's, placed all the me's in my hand.
From the Ekur, the house of Enlil,
I brought craftsmanship to my Absu of Eridu.
I am the fecund seed, engendered by the great wild ox,
I am the first born son of An,
I am the 'great storm' who goes forth out of the 'great below',
I am the lord of the Land.
I am the gugal of the chieftains,
I am the father of all the lands,
I am the 'big brother' of the gods,
I am he who brings full prosperity,
I am the record keeper of heaven and earth,
I am the ear and the mind (?) of all the lands,
I am he who directs justice with the king An on An's dais,

I am he who decrees the fates with Enlil in the 'mountain of wisdom,'
He placed in my hand the decreeing of the fates of the 'place where the sun rises,'
I am he to whom Nintu pays due homage,
I am he who has been called a good name by Ninhursag,
I am the leader of the Anunnaki,
I am he who has been as the first son of the holy An." '

This is the first declaration by Enki about who he is and, instantly his role as a god is apparent. While he is subordinate to Enlil, he is also an important cultural figure who can act autonomously. He then speaks of his shrine:

'I built my [house], a shrine, in a pure place,
I called it with a good name,
I built my Abzu, a shrine . . .
I decreed a good fate for it.
My house — its shade stre[tches] over the 'snake'-marsh,
My house, its . . . wears a beard among (?) the 'honey'-plants (?),
The ca[rps] wave the tail to him in (?) the sm[all gizi-reeds],
The sparrows chirp in their . . . ,
The weapon-carrying . . . ,
Came into my, Enki's,
The abgal's,
. . . [into my] . . . . ,
The enkum (and) [ninkum] . . . ,
Sacred songs and spells filled my Abzu.'

From this we can see that he cares about his duty, the good name of his shrine and its divine purity. The spells in his Abzu suggest he can use his supernatural powers. It continues:

'My magur-boat, the crown, the 'ibex of the Abzu'-
In its midst there is a great rejoicing.
The lofty marshland, my favourite spot,
Stretches out its arms to me, bends (?) its neck to me.
The kara's drew (/) on (?) the oars in unison,
Sing sweet songs, cause the river to rejoice. . .

Loaded the Magan-boat sky high;
The Magilum-boat of Meluhha
Transports gold and silver,
Brings them to Nippur for Enlil, the [king] of all the lands.

To him who has no city, to him who has no horse,
The Martu — Enki pre[sent]ted cattle as a gift,
To the [great] prince who came forth in his [land],
The Anunnaki pay due homage:
"Lord who rides the great me's, the pure me's,
Who has charge of the universe, the widespread,
Who received the lofty 'sun-disk' in Eridu, the pure place, the mo[st prec]
ious place,
Enki, lord of the universe, praise!"

Nippur, also known as Enlil City, was the holy city of the Sumerian civilisation and home to the wind-god Enlil (who was subordinate only to An). It was found to contain the archaeological remains of the shrine of Enlil and could grant the kingship onto other cities in the region. The myth then describes the set of relationships which existed between the different parts of the region. However, it proceeds to denounce Elam and Marhashi:

'....Elam and Marhashi....
Were (destined) to be devoured like ..-fish;
The king (presumably Enki) upon whom Enlil had bestowed might
Destroyed their houses, destroyed their walls.
Their (precious) metal (and) lapis lazuli (and the contents of) their
storehouses,
He brought to Nippur for Enlil — the king of all the lands.'

Hence, the relationships between the different areas of the region are the Sumerian interpretation of the 'world order', as it existed at the time.

The Sumerian King List

Archaeologist Paul G. Bahn writes, in 'The Story of Archaeology', [6]'The earliest traces of human occupation in the Tigris–Euphrates river valley of southern Mesopotamia date to around 5500 B.C., when villagers using a particular style of painted pottery first appeared in the archaeological record. From this time, until the first written texts, the community of occupation remained unbroken. By around 3500 B.C., these people were building elaborate temples, which they filled with stone and metal objects. At about this time, the need to keep track of more complicated financial transactions led to the invention of a primitive writing that developed into a literary instrument within the next thousand years. Around 2700 B.C., kings began leaving inscriptions boasting of their deeds, priests began recording their myths, and accountants kept track of the finances of palaces and Temples. These Sumerians laid the foundations of the Mesopotamian civilisation.'

A famous document known as The Sumerian King List shows the major dynasties in the area up to the time of Babylonia. David Rohl describes it in his book, 'Legend, The Genesis of civilisation'. He says, ''...the most important source for the chronology of early Mesopotamia is the famous Sumerian King List (SKL) which was meticulously compiled by Thorkild Jacobsen in 1939 from his study of the remains of around fifteen different fragmentary copies.'

It reads as follows:

'THE FLOOD ???? – ????
KISH I (b) ???? – ????
KISH I (a) ???? – ????
URUK I ???? – 2223
KISH II ???? – 2175
UR I 2348 – 2173
KISH III 2173 – 2165
AKSHAK 2238 – 2140
URUK II 2221 – 2114
LAGASH ???? – 2113
URUK III 2112 – 2088
UR II 2171 – 2043
KISH IV 2163 – 2033
AGADE 2100 – 1920
GUTIUM 1988 – 1889
URUK IV 1922 – 1885
URUK V 1891 – 1885
UR III 1900 – 1793
ISIN 1805 – 1569
LARSA 1798 – 1536
BABYLON I 1667 – 1381'

Rohl adds that the ideas behind it extend back 400,000 years, into dynasties of deities and angels. Sumerian legends claim that the Anunnaki (gods of the sky) came to Earth from Nibiru, a tenth planet in our solar system, when it last passed by, and this world will have ended by the time it comes around again. Led by Enki, Enlil and a pantheon of other gods, they mixed the souls of gods together with primitive humankind to create the people who did their work.

Hence we can see the idea of religious believers existed at this time, and also religious prophecies.

Part 2: The Akkadian Empire

To understand the story of the Sumerian King List in terms of actual events, we must now look at the emergence of the Semitic tribes in Mesopotamia, as this led to the creation of its larger empires. Migrating from the west, they merged with and assimilated the Sumerians, before the Semitic empires finally took over the region.

In the time of Sumeria, the Semitic tribes occupied three main areas. The southern one stretched across Northeast Africa into the Middle East, the Central area included parts of present day Saudi Arabia and the U.A.E., the western half of Mesopotamia (including Israel and Syria), the Sinai peninsula, Cyprus, and reached as far north as southernmost Turkey. The eastern area intersected the Central in northern Syria and stretched all the way eastwards through northern Iraq and down its eastern side, into the Sumerian region. Thus they separated Egypt, in North Africa, from the Sumerians in the Middle East. However, as they expanded eastward, gradually absorbing the Sumerian territory, the regions of North Africa and Mesopotamia became interlinked. This is the reason why the whole region known as the Fertile Crescent is also referred to as 'The Cradle of Civilisation' when it comes to talking about the early world order and, over time, it became transformed into a larger region known as the Levant.

There is evidence that the Semites had influence in Mesopotamia before the Sumerians arrived, or at least existed on a contemporary basis. H.W.F. Saggs says in his book, 'Everyday Life in Assyria and Babylonia', [8]'One reason for guessing that there may have been Semites in South Iraq when the Sumerians first arrived is that some of the earliest Sumerian inscriptions contain words undoubtedly taken over from Semitic speech. Unfortunately, such evidence is not conclusive, because we do not know whether the period of contact between Sumerians and Semites, which resulted in such borrowings, was a matter of a few years or of centuries. The earliest certain movement of Semitic peoples into Iraq began in the second quarter of the third millennium (i.e. after 2750 B.C.), from which period there is evidence of a group, whom we know as the Akkadians, moving into northern Babylonia from the Jebel Sinjar areas in East Syria. The growing strength of the Semitic element in the population culminated in the coming into power of an Akkadian dynasty. In northern Babylonia the greatest Sumerian centre was the city of Kish, and the last King of Kish had as chief minister a man whom we know under the Semitic name of Sharrum-kin or Sargon, meaning 'true king', though this could hardly have been his original name. Sargon had founded a city called Agade (exact whereabouts still unknown), and when the King of Kish was overthrown by a Sumerian ruler from farther south, Sargon took over the reigns of government and gained control of the whole of the land later known as Babylonia (2371 B.C.). Sargon's descendants reigned for over a century and we refer to this dynasty as the Dynasty of Agade, or, using the Semitic spelling of the name, the dynasty of Akkad.'

The significant contribution it made was in bringing the idea of centralised government to areas which were clearly beyond the boundaries of its original territory. Hence, it is seen as the first real empire, and a milestone along the way to the larger empires of Assyria and Babylonia, which were the largest before Persia, Greece and Rome.

Saggs continues to say that, 'Sargon ultimately extended his conquests up the Euphrates to North Syria, and possibly even into Asia Minor. He also conquered Elam to the east of Babylonia, and gained control of northern Iraq, the area later known as Assyria . . . Sargon's economic and political control of this unprecedentedly large area produced a marked rise in the standard of living in Babylonia, so that this period was remembered in tradition as a golden age.

The other great ruler of the Dynasty of Agade was the fourth, Sargon's grandson, Naram-Sin. According to tradition, supported to some extent by archaeological evidence, Naram-Sin controlled an empire from central Asia Minor to the southern end of the Persian Gulf . . . The achievements of the Agade dynasty were of lasting importance despite its relatively short duration (2371 to 2230 B.C.). Especially significant was the introduction of new administrative methods, in particular the attempt at centralised government from a single city . . .'

Following the fall of Agade, the situation continued to develop further, mainly owing to the way earlier economic stability was created by sustained population rise, the spread of mass farming techniques and the establishment of administrative centres. Saggs says northern Babylonia was occupied by the Gutians, but southern Babylonia was still largely under Sumerian control. The kingdoms of Sumeria then rose to prominence once again, this time as the Third Dynasty of Ur, but this was to be relatively short-lived, as more Semitic tribes came into the southern region.

Saggs says 'This dynasty collapsed after about a century, leaving Babylonia in temporary chaos. The main factor in the collapse was a fresh movement of Semitic peoples, this time the group called the Amurru or Amorites.' He adds that (on page 36), 'A people called the Amorites are well known to readers of the Old Testament, where the term is used for one of the main groups of inhabitants of Palestine before the final entry of the Hebrews under Joshua.' He continues to say that they were the descendants of the tribe who were known earlier (in cuneiform script) as the Amurru, who lived in the Syrian desert and threatened all the fertile lands from Palestine to Iraq.

He says the first evidence we have of them comes from 'the year in which Sharka-lisharri [Naram-Sin's son and successor] defeated the Amurru in Basar' (Basar is a mountain in the Syrian desert). References to these Amurru become more frequent during the period of the Third Dynasty of Ur. One passage shows the contempt of the city-dwelling Sumerian for the savage desert dweller, who is described as 'the Amurru, . . . who eats raw meat, who has no house in his lifetime, and after he dies lies unburied. . . Quickly, though, these Amurru ceased to be despised desert savages and became a threat to the security, and finally to the very existence, of the third Dynasty of Ur. Some of the rulers of that dynasty built fortifications against these people. Such measures did not, however, succeed in holding back the mounting pressure, and the ancient cities first of the Middle Euphrates and then of Babylonia proper, gradually fell under the domination of these people.' He says (on pages 36–7) that, at this point, there is an increase in names, god-names and institutions of Amorite origin. Thus began the complete takeover of Mesopotamia and the creation of its larger empires.

CHAPTER 3

Assyria–Babylonia

As Mesopotamia grew, Babylonia and Assyria became the world's most powerful empires. While they came to occupy the eastern side of Mesopotamia, other important Semitic empires emerged in Mitanni and Syria while Media grew to the east, Judah was created around 1400 BC and Europeans entered the scene from the northwest. Egypt was also involved in the area which was no longer known as the Fertile Crescent, as it had become the Levant...

Part 1: The Growth of the Mesopotamian Empires

In this chapter we shall see how human activity in Mesopotamia came to fill up the entire region. Assyria became the large region in the north like Babylonia was in the south, Syria grew to the west and Media to the east. Egypt remained from the earlier period, and we can see how big it all is now compared to the size of Ur (on the bottom right of the map).

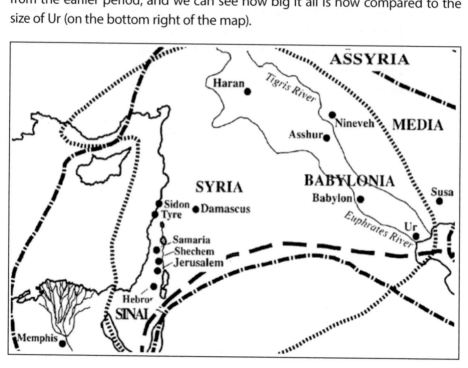

Continuing the story from the last chapter, as the Third Dynasty of Ur was destabilised by the Amorites, Saggs says ''In other cities, some of the earlier peaceful Amorite settlers actually became officials in the service of the Third dynasty of Ur . . . . The Third Dynasty of Ur finally crumbled under the pressure of the Amorite invaders, city after city ceasing to acknowledge the sovereignty of Ur.' However, he continues to say, the final overthrow of the dynasty was not actually the work of the Amorites, but of the Elamites (from southern Persia). Following this, he says, 'With the breakdown of central control by Ur, dynasties arose in other cities, the two most prominent at first being Isin and Larsa. For this reason the century or so after the overthrow of Ur is often known as the

Isin–Larsa period (2006–1894 B.C.). The Larsa dynasty gradually increased its influence at the expense of Isin, but was finally itself overthrown (1763 B.C.) by the sixth ruler of the Dynasty of Babylon, the great Hammurabi (1792–1750 B.C.).'

Babylonia

M. P. Bahn's book, 'The Story of Archaeology', says [2]'Babylon was a small town until around 1900 BC. The famous law-giver Hammurabi (1792–1750) . . . made it the capital of his imperial kingdom and elevated the city's god, Marduk, to the national god. Hammurabi's success had established the city as the political centre of Babylonia, and over a thousand years later Babylon hosted another powerful dynasty that overthrew Assyrian domination and created an empire. Its king, Nebuchadnezzar (604–562 BC), completely remodelled the city and erected a massive palace, the Hanging Gardens, the ziggurat and the Temple of Marduk.'

He adds that the German archaeologist Robert Koldewey excavated many of Nebuchadnezzar's buildings between AD 1899 and 1917, and the 'excavation showed that Babylon was not one but two cities. The outer city spread over $7km^2$ (3 miles^2) and was surrounded by a massive triple wall with towers placed at regular intervals. As Herodotus described it, the wall was wide enough for a chariot pulled by a team of four horses to turn around. The outer city wall merged with two other compounds. The northeast corner held a palace whose modern name, Tell Babil, reflects the ancient name. The western side was given over to the inner city, itself covering over $5km^2$ (2 miles^2) and divided into two parts by the Euphrates river . . . Most of the monumental buildings lined a major avenue, the Processional Way, that stretched southward from the Ishtar Gate through the inner city. The Ishtar Gate, named after the goddess of love and of war, was a high arched affair decorated with figures of animals . . . a group of underground rooms with vaulted ceilings and equipped with wells and water-proofing may represent the foundations of the Hanging Gardens of Babylon . . . nearly 1km (0.6 mile) farther south along the Processional Way, two adjacent plazas contained the city ziggurat and the Temple of Marduk. The ziggurat, the characteristically Mesopotamian stepped tower and prototype of the Tower of Babel . . . was about 91m (298ft) on each side, though its original height is unknown. The temple of Marduk, who the Greeks call Bel, also contained shrines to other gods.' Babylon was twice the largest city in the world (and one of the first to exceed a population of 200,000).

Following the rule of Hammurabi, it superseded Nippur as the region's holy city, signifying a regional transition from one period to the next. The Babylonian Creation Myth describes how the new god, Marduk, was added to the Sumerian pantheon (of An, Enlil, Enki etc.), and became the principle deity of Babylonia. In the myth he wins an epic battle against the old order within the gods, then appoints Babylon as the centre of the universe. It is quite long, written on several tablets, and I have only been able to comment on selected passages.

[3] 'Tablet I

When skies above were not yet named
Nor earth below pronounced by name
 Apsu, the first one, their begetter,
And maker Tiamat, who bore them all,
Had mixed their waters together,
But had not formed pastures, nor discovered reed-beds;
When no gods were manifest,
Nor names pronounced, nor destines decreed,
Then gods were born within them.

Lahmu (and) Lahamu emerged, their names pronounced.
As soon as they matured, were fully formed.
Anshar (and) Kishar were born, surpassing them
They passed the days at length, they added to the years. . .

As we have seen, the religions of Mesopotamia are different to Egypt, but they still speak of the creation of a new world when explaining the emergence of their society. They use a hierarchy of gods, who correspond with the state of affairs on Earth.

'Anu their first born son rivalled his forefathers:
Anshar made his son Anu like himself,
And Anu begot Nudimmud in his likeness.
He, Nudimmud, was superior to his forefathers:
Profound of understanding, he was wise, he was very strong at arms.
Mightier by far than Anshar his father's begetter,
He had no rival among the gods his peers.
The gods of that generation would meet together
And disturb Tiamat, and their clamour reverberated . . . .
Apsu could not quell their noise,
However grievous their behaviour to her,
However bad their ways, she would indulge them.'

As new gods appear, they seem to upset the order in the heavens. Apsu wishes to quell their behaviour, while Tiamat has sympathy for them. The next extract shows how this led firstly to arguments, then conflict between the gods. From the new situation emerged the new god-form, Marduk.

'Finally Apsu, begetter of the great gods,
Called out and addressed his vizier Mummu,
'O Mummu, vizier who pleases me!
Come, let us go to Tiamat!'
They went and sat in front of Tiamat,
And discussed affairs concerning the gods their sons.
Apsu made his voice heard
And spoke to Tiamat in a very loud voice,
'Their ways have become very grievous to me.
By day I cannot rest, by night I cannot sleep,
I shall abolish their ways and disperse them!
Let peace prevail, so we can sleep.'
When Tiamat heard this,
She was furious and shouted at her lover;
She shouted dreadfully and was beside herself with rage.
But then she suppressed the evil in her belly . . .
'How could we allow what we created ourselves to perish?
Even though their ways are so grievous, we should bear it patiently.'
(Vizier) Mummu replied and counselled Apsu;
The vizier did not agree with the counsel of his earth mother.
'O father, put an end to (their) troublesome ways,
So that she may be allowed to rest by day and sleep by night.'
Apsu was pleased with him, his face lit up
At the evil he was planning for the gods his sons.
(Vizier) Mummu hugged him,
Sat on his lap and kissed him rapturously.
But everything they plotted between them
Was relayed to the gods their sons.
The gods listened and wandered about restlessly;
They fell silent, they sat mute.
Superior in understanding, wise and capable,
Ea who knows everything found out their plot,
Made for himself a design of everything, and laid it out correctly,
Made it cleverly, his pure spell was superb.
He recited it and it stilled the waters.

He poured sleep upon him so that he was sleeping soundly,
Put Apsu to sleep, drenched with sleep.
Vizier Mummu the counsellor (was in) a sleepless daze.
He (Ea) unfastened his belt, took off his crown,
Took away his mantle of radiance and put it upon himself.
He held Apsu down and slew him;
Tied Mummu up and laid across him.
He set up his dwelling on top of Apsu,
And grasped Mummu, held him by a nose-rope.
When he had overcome and slain his enemies,
Ea set up his triumphal cry over his foes.
Then he rested very quietly inside his private quarters
And named them Apsu and assigned chapels
Founded his own residence there,
And Ea and Damkina his lover dwelt in splendour.
In the chamber of destinies,
The hall of designs,
Bel, the cleverest of the clever, sage of the gods, was begotten.
And inside Apsu, Marduk was created;
Inside pure Apsu, Marduk was born.
Ea his father created him, Damkina his mother bore him.'

What this shows is how this new god represents change in the social order, which correlates with the way Babylon established itself as the capital of the region.

'Proud was his form, piercing his stare,
Mature his emergence, he was powerful from the start.
Anu, his father's begetter beheld him,
And rejoiced, beamed; his heart was filled with joy.
He made him so perfect that his godhead was doubled.
Elevated far above them, he was superior in every way.
His limbs were ingeniously made beyond comprehension,
Impossible to understand, too difficult to perceive.
Four were his eyes, four were his ears;
When his lips moved, fire blazed forth.
The four ears were enormous.
And likewise the eyes; they perceived everything.
Highest among the gods, his form was outstanding. . .
Anu created the four winds and gave them birth,

Put them in his (Marduk's) hand, 'My son, let them play!'
He fashioned dust and made the whirlwind carry it;
He made the flood-wave and stirred up Tiamat.'

Tablet II describes the confrontation which then began between the old and new gods.

'Anshar listened, and the report was very disturbing
[He twisted his fingers (?)] and bit his lip;
[His liver was enflamed(?)], his belly would not rest.
His roar to his son Ea was quite weak.
'You must be the one who declares war!
Keep brandishing what you have made (as arms) for yourself.
[You are the hero, (?)], you slew Apsu.
Where else (will we find) someone to face Tiamat when she rages uncontrollably?"
Anshar addressed Anu and said that he should go and face Tiamat, and that if she will not listen to these words then to speak his own.

When he returned without success, Marduk volunteered (Tablet III–IV).

'He spoke his words to me:
"If indeed I am to be your champion,
To defeat Tiamat and to save your lives,
Convene the Council, name a special fate,
Sit joyfully together in Ubshu–kinaki
And let me, my own utterance, fix fate instead of you.
Whatever I create shall never be altered!
Let a decree from my lips never be revoked, never changed!"

So, they built for him a shrine, and declared that his words had the power of Anu. Thus Marduk became leader of the gods.

' "O Marduk, you are our champion!
We hereby give you sovereignty over the whole universe.
Sit in the assembly and your word should be pre-eminent.
May your weapons never miss (the mark), may they smash your enemies!
O Lord, spare the life of the man who trusts in you,
But drain the life of the god who has espoused evil.'

Marduk was then armed and readied to do battle.

'They set up in their midst one constellation,
And then they addressed Marduk their son,
'May your decree, O Lord, impress the gods!
Command to destroy and to recreate, and let it be so!
Speak and let the constellation vanish!
Speak to it again and let the constellation disappear!'
He spoke to it and the constellation vanished.
He spoke to it again and the constellation was recreated. . .'
They gave him an unfaceable weapon to crush the foe.
'Go, and cut off the life of Tiamat!
Let the winds bear her blood to us as good news!' '

He then had to face Tiamat in person. In the myth, he fashioned a bow, carried a mace, harnessed lightning before him, made a net and marshalled the four winds so that no part of her could escape.

'The Lord raised the flood-weapon, his great weapon,
And mounted the frightful, unfaceable storm chariot.
He had yoked to it a team of four and had harnessed to its side 'Slayer',
'Pitiless', 'Racer', and 'Flyer';
Their lips were drawn back, their teeth carried poison.
They know not exhaustion, they can only devastate. . . .
The Lord set out and took the road,
And set his face towards Tiamat who raged out of control.
In his lips he gripped a spell,
In his hand he grasped a herb to counter poison.'

Then there came a mighty battle between Marduk and Tiamat:

'The gods his fathers thronged about him . . .
The Lord drew near and looked into the middle of Tiamat:
He was trying to find out the strategy of Qingu her lover.
As he looked, his mind became confused
His will crumbled and his actions were muddled. . .
Tiamat cast her spell.
She did not even turn her neck.
In her lips she was holding falsehood, lies. . .
'[How powerful] is your attacking force, O Lord of the gods!
The whole assembly of them has gathered to your place!'
(But, he ignored her blandishments)
The Lord lifted up the flood weapon, his great weapon,

And sent a message to Tiamat who feigned goodwill, saying: 'Why are you
so friendly on the surface
When your depths conspire to muster a battle force?
Just because the sons were noisy (and) disrespectful to their fathers,
Should you, who gave them birth, reject compassion?
You named Qingu as your lover,
You appointed to him rites of Anu-power, wrongfully his.
You sought out evil for Anshar, king of the gods,
So you have compounded your wickedness against the gods of my father's!
Let your host prepare!
Let them gird themselves with your weapons!
Stand forth, and you and I shall do single combat!'
When Tiamat heard this,
She went wild, she lost her temper.
Tiamat screamed aloud in a passion.
Her lower parts shook together from the depths.
She recited the incantation and kept casting her spell.
Meanwhile the gods of battle were sharpening their weapons.
Face to face they came, Tiamat and Marduk, sage of the gods.
They engaged in combat, they closed for battle.
The Lord spread his net and made it encircle her,
To her face he dispatched the imhullu-wind so that
she could not close her lips.
Fierce winds distended her belly;
Her insides were constipated and she stretched her mouth wide.
He shot an arrow which pierced her belly,
Split her down the middle and slit her heart,
Vanquished her and extinguished her life.'

The remaining tablets describe how he then created the universe by making
the earth out of her body and created the constellations of stars.

'He fashioned a stand for the great gods.
As for the stars, he set up constellations corresponding to them. He
designated the year and marked out its divisions,
Apportioned three stars each to the twelve months.
When he had made plans of the days of the year,
He founded the stand of Neberu to mark out their courses,
So that none of them could go wrong or astray.
He fixed the stand of Ellil and Ea together with it,

Opened up gates in both ribs,
Made strong bolts to left and right.
With her liver he located the Zenith;
He made the crescent moon appear, entrusted night (to it)
And designated it the jewel of the night to mark out the days ...'

Marduk thus became the chief deity of Babylon. He took the 'Tablet of Destinies' from Quingu and, from the body of Tiamat, made the sky, moon and clouds. Springs which flow from her eyes became the rivers Tigris and Euphrates. Then, he appointed a sacred palace at the centre of the world, Babylon, in which he built a shrine for the other gods to come and visit him.

'Lahmu and Lahamu [ ]
Made their voices heard and spoke to the Igigi,
'Previously Marduk was (just) our beloved son
But now he is your king. Take heed of his command.'
Next they spoke and proclaimed in unison,
'LUGAL-DIMMER-ANKIA is his name. Trust in him!'
Marduk made his voice heard and spoke,
Addressed his words to the gods his fathers,
'Over Apsu, the sea-green dwelling,
In front of (?) Esharra, which I created for you,
(Where) I strengthened the ground beneath it for a shrine,
I shall make a house to be a luxurious dwelling for myself
And shall found his cult centre within it,
And I shall establish my private quarters, and confirm my kingship.
Whenever you come up from the Apsu for an assembly,
Your night's resting place shall be in it, receiving you all.
Whenever you come down from the sky for an assembly,
Your night's resting place shall be in it, receiving you all.
I hereby name it Babylon, home of the great gods.
We shall make it the centre of religion.'

Thus the myth thus announces Babylon as the new capital. Those who lived according to the previous traditions of Mesopotamia can see how things have changed. Over time, the Sumerians became barely recognisable as a distinguishable ethnicity and were absorbed into the Babylonian and other empires. However, in these myths and various other traditions, the Babylonians were to preserve Sumerian culture in a similar sense to the way in which the Christians preserved Latin.

Part 2: Assyrian Imperialism

Saggs says Babylon brought advances in terms of social systems and their administration, adding that 'The First Dynasty of Babylon (1894–1595 B.C.) is rightly thought of . . . as one of the highlights of ancient civilisation.' He adds that it was an age of material prosperity, particularly due to Hammurabi's 'aptitude for diplomacy, and to his administrative ability and concern for social justice throughout his land.' However, he says, Assyria, another kingdom of Amorite origin to the north, also exerted a 'considerable influence upon the regions to the south and south-west. Another powerful contemporary kingdom was Eshnunna and there were yet more Amorite power bases in north Syria.' He describes the situation as being summed up in a royal letter from this time:

'There is no king who of himself alone is strongest. Ten or fifteen follow Hammurabi of Babylon, the same number follow Ibal-pi-El of Eshnunna, the same number follow Amut-pi-El of Qatanum [in Syria], and twenty kings follow Yarim-Lim of Yamkhad [in North Syria].'

However, when the empire went into decline under Hammurabi's son, Babylonia then spent a long time under the control of the Assyrians, Cassites and Elamites. Saggs says, 'The actual political achievements of Hammurabi. . . in bringing all Babylonia, and some regions beyond, under the control of the city of Babylon, did not long survive him. In the reign of Hammurabi's successor the marsh country of the south broke away, and the same ruler came into conflict with the Cassites, from the mountains north-east of Babylonia. . . After this first evidence of Cassite pressure, the following century saw a gradual increase both of peaceful immigration of individual Cassites, and of organised movements of armed bands. This may be connected to pressure upon the Cassites themselves by a southward movement of Indo-European peoples and other people farther north. Amongst these peoples two of the most prominent groups were the Hittites and the Hurrians. . . The Hittites, an Indo-European people whose language was closely related to Latin, had begun to appear in northern Anatolia (eastern Turkey) early in the second Millennium and had established a powerful kingdom in Central Anatolia soon after 1700 B.C.'

The Hurrians had been centred in the region around Lake Van before the Agade period, but had been pushing southwards on a large scale by the early second millennium. He says (on page 40) that pressure from them made the collapse of centralised government in Babylonia inevitable, even though the actual overthrow of the city of Babylon came from the Hittites of central Anatolia. He continues to say that 'In 1595 B.C. the Hittite ruler made a sudden attack southwards into Syria, and then moved down the Euphrates to plunder Babylon. . .' Thus, he adds, the raid left Babylon unable to resist future attacks and, for this reason, the Cassites were able to take over north Babylonia and establish a dynasty which lasted around 400 years (1595–1150 B.C).

He adds that the Hurrians brought progress in terms of the military and, 'Associated with them at this time was an aristocracy of the race which we know as Indo-European or Aryan. The Aryans derived ultimately from the steppes of Russia, one of the original homes of the wild horse. Because of this, the Aryans were always found in association with the horse, and it was the Aryan migrants of the second millennium who introduced the horse-drawn chariot as an instrument of war.'

He says that this chariot-riding Aryan aristocracy, ruled by the Hurrians had, shortly before 1500 BC, established a powerful kingdom in the Habur area called Mitanni. Evidence shows at one point it ruled over Assyria and was even on an equal basis with Egypt. He says marriage alliances were made with Egypt involving several princesses who were sent as brides for its kings. But, he adds, by 1350 BC, internal problems had torn it apart and it was virtually a dependency of the Hittite ruler Shuppiluliuma. Assyria then saw this as an opportunity to re-assert its independence and, under Ashur-aballit I (1365–1330 BC), emerged as one of the great powers of Mesopotamia.

Assyria first secured itself against Babylon, then took over Mitanni. He adds (on pages 42–3) that this period of consolidation and expansion culminated in the capture of Babylon by Tukulti-Ninurta I (1244–1208), the significance of which was like a king of Scotland in the Middle Ages capturing London. However, he says, following this there was a sudden decline, partly because of its former expansion, but also because Mitanni was no longer keeping the Syrian area stable, and Egypt was so weak it was limited to operating within its own boundaries.

He says that, around 1200 BC, 'The Hittite empire which had formerly given stability to Asia Minor and northern Syria, thereby protecting the trade routes, had, under the pressure of people migrating from Europe, rapidly crumbled away until by 1200 B.C. it was nearly powerless.' He continues to add that 'This situation throughout the Near East was ultimately the result of a southward movement of peoples from Europe, of which the Greeks and probably the Biblical Philistines were a part. It was these people who ultimately broke up the Hittite Empire, destroyed Egyptian authority in Syria and Palestine, and seriously weakened Egypt itself by a direct attempt at invasion, which was beaten off by a great sea battle in about 1190 B.C.'

Assyrian Culture

Saggs says that (on pages 99–102) 'Amongst all the aspects of ancient Mesopotamian life, there have been few which have been more widely misunderstood and misrepresented than the nature of Assyrian Imperialism. Few historians or writers who touch upon Assyria in the period between 900 B.C. and its final fall just before 600 B.C. can resist the temptation to. . . add yet another shocked comment upon the barbarism, brutality and unmatched ruthlessness of the Assyrians. It is rare to find any look at Assyrian warfare and imperialism as a whole in its perspective. . . At most periods there was a very tight control of affairs by the central government at the capital, so that the King (or his ministers) frequently required very detailed reports from provincial officials on all aspects of administration. Nearly 2000 of the letters which passed between provincial officials and the authorities at the capital have now been found, and letters such as these often enable us to fill out the bare outline of events which the royal annals and similar documents give us.'

He adds that their typical official administrator 'was born of an Assyrian father who held land from the King in the district around the ancient city of Ashur, in former times the capital. The family had lived there for generations, and each new heir had the estates granted to him afresh (upon payment of substantial presents) by the reigning monarch. The members of the family had loyally performed their part in the royal service, and in the family burial ground there were regular offerings of food and beer at the tombs of ancestors who had died fighting for the King.'

He describes life inside the Royal Court, saying that, 'Though his duties all centred around the King, there was a good deal of variety in the things he and the other young men like him actually did. Periodically vassal rulers and their representatives made visits to the Assyrian King, and on these occasions Quirdi-Ashur-Lamur. . .' (his name for a typical Assyrian administrator) '. . .with some of the other young men, might be in attendance. Often these were routine occasions, but sometimes there were excitements, as when a ruler from a distant land sent presents of unusual creatures, such as an elephant, a crocodile, or two-humped camels. . . Another excitement would be when the victorious Assyrian army returned from campaign laden with booty. There would be a procession through the capital to the chief temple, and after the King had presented his report to the god and made dedications, some of the booty would be installed within the palace, perhaps fine gold or bronze vessels from Urartu (Armenia) or carved ivory furniture from Syria.'

He then adds that (on page 103) inside the palace it was likely that, among their other duties, the pages served the king at mealtimes. But, their really important task, as one king put it, was to be the 'brighteners of the royal mind . . . Exactly how they set about brightening the royal mind we do not know, but presumably their presence and liveliness served to counteract the possibly depressing effect of the ponderous Court ritual and the gravity of the leading religious functionaries and ministers.' He also says, the king himself was 'often put to great personal inconvenience. There were even occasions when the priests claimed to have seen menacing omens and the King might be made to fast for several days, be obliged to keep away from his women folk, or even have to be shaved all over.'

The Fall of Assyria

However, the empires of Mesopotamia were not to last forever as, in the 600s BC, the Assyrians were encountering problems with a group of tribes in the Zagros Mountains known as the Medes. Saggs says (on page 22) that, around the time of Shamshi Adad V, they were 'undertaking military action in the north and north-east to defend Assyrian interests against the Medes (an Iranian people who had recently migrated into North-West Persia)'. He adds that, from about 800 BC, the Urartu began to expand, especially in North Syria, while Assyria declined. In 746 BC there was a revolt in which all of its royal family were killed. Under their successor, Tiglath-Pileser III (745–727 BC), administrative reforms occurred which reduced the power of regional government, then Assyria rose again.

He says (on page 23), 'The story of the remaining period of the Assyrian Empire is one of continual expansion up to just after 640 B.C., and then a dramatic collapse'. He says this period is known as the Sargonic period, after its first king. Despite inventing new technology, creating a new capital city in Nineveh, and even conquering Babylon, the king Esarhaddon (680–669 BC) made two terrible mistakes: firstly, he tried to incorporate Egypt into his empire, and then he left the kingdom to two of his sons — the Assyrian part to one and the Babylonian part to the other — the result of which was that they went to war with each other.

Ashurbanipal of Assyria (680–626 BC) finally captured Babylon in 648 BC and, Saggs says, 'between then and 639 B.C. he was able to undertake a series of campaigns to overun Elam. There were, however, fresh factors in the world scene. In Iran, north of Elam, the Medes, a group of vigorous Iranian tribes (a branch of the Indo-European race) who had migrated into the area at about 900 B.C., were becoming a force to reckon with.' The Assyrians had previously been subjugating the Medes and extracting tributes from them but, at the same time, changes in the Far East meant they had been acquiring the ability to create an empire of their own.

CHAPTER 4

The Medo–Persian Empire

While the empires of Mesopotamia had grown, the Far East had developed its own civilisations, which had also been undergoing their own changes. In China, power had changed hands between north and south and, as this new order emerged, its great philosophers laid its new intellectual foundations. At the same time, Aryans brought the Vedic Scriptures into India and this created Hinduism. In northern India/ Eastern Mesopotamia, these two influences met to create the 'philosophical religion', Zoroastrianism. It empowered the Medes with a new vision of the world as a battleground between good and evil, and inspired them to challenge the Mesopotamian empires...

Part 1: The Transformation of China

This chapter involves the other two Cradles of Civilisation on Africa-Eurasia, India and China, which, until this point, had not been particularly influential in terms of world affairs. H.G. Wells says, in 'The Outline of History', [1]"between the eighth and fourth centuries B.C. "there were in the Hwang-ho and Yang-tse valleys no less than five or six thousand small states with about a dozen states dominating over them." The land was subject to perpetual warfare ("Age of Confusion"). In the sixth century B.C., the great powers in conflict were Ts'i and Ts'in, which were northern Hwang-ho states, and Ch'u, which was a vigorous power in the Yang-tse valley. A confederation against Ch'u laid the foundation for a league that kept the peace for a hundred years; the league subdued and incorporated Ch'u and made a general treaty of disarmament. It became the foundation of a new pacific empire.'

Wells continues to say that the rule of Shi-Hwang-ti, the first Universal Emperor, marked the end of this feudal and divided period. He built the Great Wall of China as a defence against the Huns and this had a permanently unifying effect upon the Far East. As this new stability appeared, China's most famous philosophers appeared from within the states of the second (Eastern) half of the Zhou Dynasty (1046–256), which had been at the centre of this nationwide conflict. P. Buckley-Ebrey writes in 'The Cambridge Illustrated History of China',

[2]'The intellectual foundations of Chinese civilisation were established during the Eastern Zhou dynasty (770–256 BC), a period of political fragmentation and moral crisis. The first half of this era is commonly called the Spring and Autumn period, after the name of a chronicle covering 722 to 481 BC.

During these centuries the Zhou kings continued to rule by default while their putative vassals competed against each other, making and breaking alliances, exchanging hostages, and sporadically taking up arms. Over time military conflict became more frequent and more deadly, and the second half of this period is conventionally called the warring states period (402–221 BC). By then the Zhou king was no longer a major player and one by one the smaller states were conquered and absorbed by the half-dozen largest ones.'

However, despite this seemingly chaotic transformation of China, there was enough stability in the system to prevent it collapsing completely. He adds that, 'During the Spring and Autumn period, a code of chivalrous or sportsmanlike conduct still regulated warfare between the states. For instance one estate would not attack another while it was in mourning for its ruler and during battle one side would not attack before the other side had time to line up. Perhaps out of the fear of the wrath of the ancestors of defeated rulers, efforts were made not to wipe out ruling houses, but to leave at least one successor to continue the sacrifices.' It appears they had been able to perceive the way in which change was occurring during this period and saw preserving key aspects of society as the way to survive it. This period is traditionally associated with the philosopher Confucius.

Confucius

As one of the most famous of many travelling sages, some of whom had been successful at making a living by advising wealthy and powerful government ministers, Confucius spent some time at the Lu court in Shandong. After that he went wandering through the neighbouring states, acquiring his own disciples and becoming China's first moral philosopher.

To add a comment of Wells' (on page 403), 'The teaching of Confucius centred upon the idea of a noble life which he embodied in a standard or ideal, the Aristocratic Man.' This seems to be the type of citizen he thought was best adapted to the society of the time, one who could lead its people through times of instability. He supported the idea of 'Filial Piety', the respect of children towards their parents — which was obviously designed to preserve the family itself. Ebrey describes extracts of his work (on page 46) from a collection known as the 'Analects',

'The Master said, 'Lead the people by means of government policies and regulate them through punishments, and they will be evasive and have no sense of shame. Lead them by means of virtue and regulate them through rituals, and they will have a sense of shame and moreover have standards.'

The Master said, 'The gentleman understands moral standards; the petty person knows about profit.'

The Master said, 'When you meet someone wise, think about becoming his equal. When you meet someone inferior, reflect on yourself.'

The Master said, 'I am not someone who was born wise. I am someone who loves the ancients and tries to learn from them.' '

His work shows how a conscientious person could lead society through this period, by being aware of what was happening and setting a good example of how to live.

Lao-Tse

Also known as Lao-Tsu, Laozi and Li Dan, he was a Chinese philosopher and author who is generally considered to be a contemporary of Confucius, although some historians place him slightly later, in the Warring States period. Reputedly the author of the Tao Te Ching, he is considered to be a divine figure in Chinese folklore. Both the Tang Dynasty and modern people of the Li surname claim he is the founder of their lineage.

If Confucius was focused on advising government, he represented the element of folklore and popular culture. His work has been used by various anti-authoritarian movements and in Chinese Legalism (a philosophical movement which promotes the transformation of chaos into order). A key figure in Chinese culture, he is worshipped under the name Supreme Old Lord, one of the Three Pure Ones, and was granted the title of Supremely Mysterious and Primordial Emperor.

Here is a short extract from the Tao Te Ching. It is written in a style where the reader must follow the meaning of what is being said, as it enlightens them through a progressive transformation. Taoism directs people towards finding their 'way' in life (Tao literally meaning 'way').

[3]'The world had a beginning
And this beginning could be the mother of the world.
When you know the mother
Go on to know the child.
After you have known the child
And to the end of your days you will not meet with danger.
Block the openings
Shut the doors
And all your life you will not run dry.
Unblock the openings, add to your troubles
And to the end of your days you will be beyond salvation
To see the small is called discernment

To hold fast to the submissive is called strength.

Use the light

But give up discernment.

Bring not misfortune to yourself.

This is known as following the constant.'

He gives advice to people from the point of view of a mystical sage, in a way which saves them from worrying about the complexity of politics and helps them to focus on everyday life. In contrast to the austerity of aristocratic rule, he appeals to people's own sense of self. Buckley-Ebrey quotes him (on page 48),

'Do not honour the worthy,

And the people will not compete.

Do not value rare treasures, and the people will not steal.

Do not display what others want,

And the people will not have their hearts confused.

A sage governs this way:

He empties people's minds and fills their bellies.

He weakens their wills and strengthens their bones.

Keep the people always without knowledge and without desires,

For then the clever will dare not act.

Engage in no action and order will prevail.'

His work and that of Zhuangzi led to the growth of Taoism as a relatively large religion which still exists today. It differs from Confucianism in the sense that, instead of prescribing a rigid social order, it promotes the state of mind which arises from a natural way of being. Wu Wei (action without intention) arises from human behaviour which is in balance with the alternating cycles of nature. Hence, naturalness simplicity, spontaneity, and the Three Treasures (compassion, frugality and humility) are at its core. Its roots go back to at least the 4th century BC and its cosmological concepts come from the Naturalist School of Yinyang. It was also deeply influenced by one of the oldest texts in Chinese literature, the I Ching. Some of its more devoted practitioners live in monasteries and practice the cultivation of stillness, a state of being which has become associated with inner peace and compared to the enlightenment of Buddhism.

Mencius

Mencius was concerned with the morality of the state itself and (on page 44) responded to a question from one of his rulers on how to regard the state,

'Why must your Majesty use the word "profit"? All I am concerned with is the good and the right. If your majesty says, "How can I profit my state?" your officials will say, "How can I profit my family?" and officers and common people will say, "How can I profit myself?" Once superiors and inferiors are competing for profit, the state will be in danger.'

Other famous quotes of his include:

'Only when there are things a man will not do is he capable of achieving great things.'

'Friendship is one mind in two bodies.'

'The great man is the one who does not lose his child's heart.'

'The feeling of right and wrong is the beginning of wisdom.'

Zhuangzi

Last of all, Zhuangzi was concerned with the philosophy of the workplace. He saw the worker's problem was that they did not have much formal education, but they still had to find a way of reasoning within a changing environment. He created a philosophy which they could feel with their hands and enabled them to simply 'go with the flow'.

'I see things in terms of my own work. When I chisel at a wheel, if I go slow the chisel slides and does not stay put; if I hurry it jams and doesn't move properly. When it is neither too slow nor too fast, I can feel it in my hand and respond to it from my heart. My mouth cannot describe it in words, but there is something there. I cannot teach it to my son, and my son cannot learn it from me.'

He does not concern himself with political issues, but instead shows them how to adopt the pragmatic philosophy of simply coping with the situation as it arises. Between them, the Chinese philosophers helped them to cope with social change, and created a new sense of continuity.

Part 2: The Transformation of India

The other major Cradle of Civilisation in the East was India. It was first colonised by humans as early as 70,000 BC and the primary settlement to emerge out of Prehistory is known as the Indus Valley culture (3300–1300 BC). During this time, waves of Dravidians migrated into the area (4000–2500 BC), before Aryans came from the north (1500–500 BC).

Veronica Ions states in her book, 'Indian Mythology' that, [4]'The Dravidian people who spread into almost every part of India and Sri Lanka were a mixture of native populations of India and Proto-Dravidians, who seem to have entered in waves from about 4000 to 2500 B.C.' She adds (on page 16) that the Indus Valley civilisation stretched all the way down into India, from Afghanistan down past Delhi and the Maheran coast of Baluchistan far down into Gujerat. But, the appearance of the Aryans led to, or at least coincided with the decline of the Indus Valley culture. She additionally says, 'The Aryans brought with them their own culture which for some seven centuries dominated the north Indian scene. Aryan beliefs and mythology, however, gradually absorbed native cultural traditions and, ultimately evolved into Hinduism.'

In Hindu mythology this is not the first universe. In the beginning there was neither existence nor non-existence. Then the One issued the breath of life by its own will. It was made by Lord Brahma the Creator. Lord Vishnu is the Preserver and Lord Shiva the Destroyer and Re-creator. They are all forms of the Supreme One which is behind and beyond all. Thus progress is regulated through these three abstract principles and, when one universe ends there is a void from which another arises. One version of this creation myth states,

[5]'Before this time began, there was no heaven, no earth and no space between. A vast dark ocean washed upon the shores of nothingness and licked the edges of the night. A giant cobra floated on the waters. Asleep within its endless coils lay the Lord Vishnu. He was watched over by the mighty serpent.

Everything was so peaceful and silent that Vishnu slept undisturbed by dreams or motion. From the depths a humming sound began to tremble, Aum. It grew and spread, filling the emptiness and throbbing with energy...

The night had ended, Vishnu awoke. As the dawn began to break, from Vishnu's navel grew a magnificent lotus flower. In the middle of the blossom sat Vishnu's servant, Brahma. He awaited the Lord's command. Vishnu spoke to his servant: 'It is time to begin.' Brahma bowed. Vishnu commanded: 'Create the World.' A wind swept up the waters. Vishnu and the serpent vanished.

Brahma remained in the lotus flower, floating and tossing on the sea. He lifted up his arms and calmed the wind and the ocean. Then Brahma split the lotus flower into three. He stretched one part into the heavens. He made another part into the earth. With the third part of the flower he created the skies.

The earth was bare. Brahma set to work. He created grass, flowers, trees and plants of all kinds. To these he gave feeling. Next he created the animals and the insects to live on the land. He made birds to fly in the air and many fish to swim in the sea. To all these creatures, he gave the senses of touch and smell. He gave them power to see, hear and move.'

Its scriptures are called the Vedas, meaning 'knowledge', and they are the oldest texts written in Sanskrit. Hindus consider the Vedas not to be of human origins, but to have been revealed by the consciousness of the Universe itself, Brahma. Hinduism has no central doctrinal authority and thus many practising Hindus do not claim to belong to any particular denomination. Four major traditions exist, for the purpose of scholarly studies: Vaishnavism, Shaivism, Shaktism and Smartism. Some focus more on Shivu, Vishnu or Brahma, or are shaped by the personal logic of a particular Guru. As the main difference is in the primary deity at the centre of the tradition, it has been referred to as Poly-centrism.

Brahmanism

As the religion which became known as Hinduism was created, it passed through a phase known as Brahmanism, as the power of the new priesthood emerged. Bowker says in the 'Cambridge Illustrated History of Religions', [6]. . . during the first millennium BCE Vedic culture became firmly established, especially in the north of the subcontinent. Although a minority of the population, the Brahmins were the most important social group who performed rituals for the aristocracy and governed the religious ideology of the community. Their place is expressed ... in the Rg Veda, the oldest of the Vedic collections ... ' He adds that one of these, below, describes the origins of the world and society. It represents people going through the stage where the system of Castes, or social classes was created, each coming from a part of the giant sacrificed-god, Purusa. Thus, it appears to point to the sacrifice of the old religion and beginning of a new period, through which a new division of labour was being created.

[7]'HYMN XC. Purusa.

1 A THOUSAND heads hath Purusa, a thousand eyes, a thousand feet.
On every side pervading earth he fills a space ten fingers wide.

2 This Purusa is all that yet hath been and all that is to be;
The Lord of Immortality which waxes greater still by food.

3 So mighty is his greatness; yea, greater than this is Purusa.
All creatures are one-fourth of him, three-fourths eternal life in heaven.

4 With three-fourths Purusa went up: one-fourth of him again was here. . .

5 From him Virāj was born; again Purusa from Virāj was born.
As soon as he was born he spread eastward and westward o'er the earth.

6 When Gods prepared the sacrifice with Purusa as their offering,
Its oil was spring, the holy gift was autumn; summer was the wood.

7 They balmed as victim on the grass Purusa born in earliest time.
With him the Deities and all Sādhyas and Rris sacrificed. . .

8 . . . He formed the creatures of the air, and animals both wild and tame.

9 From that great general sacrifice Rcas and Sāma-hymns were born:
Therefrom were spells and charms produced; the Yajus had its birth from it.

10 From it were horses born, from it all cattle with
two rows of teeth:
From it were generated kine, from it the goats and
sheep were born.

11 When they divided Purusa how many portions
did they make?
What do they call his mouth, his arms? What do they
call his thighs and feet?

12 The Brahman was his mouth, of both his arms was
the Rājanya made.
His thighs became the Vaiśya, from his feet the Śudra
was produced.

13 The Moon was gendered from his mind, and from
his eye the Sun had birth;
Indra and Agni from his mouth were born, and Vāyu
from his breath.

14 Forth from his navel came mid-air the sky was
fashioned from his head
Earth from his feet, and from his ear the regions.
Thus they formed the worlds. . .

16 Gods, sacrificing, sacrificed the victim these were
the earliest holy ordinances.
The Mighty Ones attained the height of heaven, there where the Sādhyas,
Gods of old, are dwelling.'

It is notable here that the Brahmins were the mouthpiece of the religion, the soldiers its arms, merchants the thighs (upon which the economy stands) and the servant class its feet. Each level of society thus has its own importance, without which the whole cannot function. Bowker adds (on page 30), that one of the most important functions of the Brahmins was to perform elaborate, public sacrifice. Thus we can see the practice of the religion itself brings it out into the open — leading to the mass-culture found in Hinduism.

Hinduism

Another name for Hinduism is 'Sanatana Dharma' or Eternal Law. Veronica Voiels[8] says Dharma comes from the Sanskrit 'Dhru' which means to hold, exist, remain or support. It relates to the ancient concept of Pta in the ancient Vedic Hymns. Dharma is the background of society. Pta is the harmony and order which must be maintained to prevent the collapse of society. It works on the principle that the law of cause and effect says nothing happens by accident. Thus, in acting with accordance to Sanatana Dharma (eternal law), people are ensuring that society works in a civilised fashion.

The term Hindu is ultimately derived from 'Sindhu', after the name for the river Indus. She says (on page 10) that it created a caste system in which there are four castes or social classes, the Brahmins (Priests), Kshatriyas (Warriors), Vaishyas (Merchants), and Shudras (Servants). 'Varnashramadharma' means to perform one's duties correctly for one's caste in life. She also asserts (on page 12) that the caste system was created through the Aryan invasion of north and west India from around 1500 BC. As they moved in, they converted people with religion and established rulerships using the military. After that the ability to trade produced merchants, which then created the servant as the last class.

In Hinduism, the idea of the individual human and the universe start off as being separate, and the practitioner aims to unite oneself with the universe through self-actualisation. That is, firstly to achieve Dharma, which is concerned with performing duties correctly, fulfilling responsibilities and creating the right lifestyle to cope with them. Then there is Artha, which is the concern of pursuing livelihood, obligations and material prosperity (and includes diplomacy, political life, social position and material security). Next is Kama, the enrichment of life which is brought by art, music, culture, food, sensual pleasure, or that which we would ascribe to a personal life. The intention is to build one's life so that one may live it to the full, while adhering to responsibilities and ethics. Finally there is the attainment of Moksha, the achievement of one's overall goal in life, which enables the realisation of the unity of everything and a selfless union with the cosmos.

Buddhism

Buddhism contains many schools of thinking, but it is focused mainly around the teaching of an Indian nobleman, Siddhartha Gautama. He founded a monastic order during the Mahajanapada era, during the reign of Bimbisara, the ruler of the Magadha empire (around 558 – 491 BC). He spent much of his life living in the luxury of his father's palace, but renounced material possessions, calling them 'transient', and sought spiritual enlightenment. After trying many methods, he realised while sitting under a Bodhi tree that it was not through trying, but by letting go that we realise we are perfect just as we are.

It is thus like a distilled form of Eastern religion which emerged during the time when the power of Hinduism was growing. During this time, there was somewhat of a religious rebellion, as many members of the Vaishya class spoke out about the injustices of the Caste system and the power of the Brahmins, but no-one could directly challenge the idea of the Vedic gods at the time. For this reason, it appears to be a breakaway sect which was created as an alternative. Rather than relying on the huge framework of society which Hinduism needs for people to reach their goal in life, it teaches that spiritual enlightenment is essentially the same experience for everyone, and can thus logically be achieved without necessarily achieving any physical goal.

Zoroastrianism

Finally, the effect of eastern culture worked its way back into the culture of the Aryan invaders. Some sources claim it was the eventual religion which appeared within the Aryan culture itself, as a reaction to the creation of Hinduism, others say that it was the result of Zoroaster reforming another part of the existing Aryan religion in the region to the west; the now Iranian part which bordered on Mesopotamia via the Zagros Mountains. Perhaps a combination of both, and a reaction to the oppression by the Assyrian Empire; it was adopted by the Medes and became the religion of the Persian Empire.

Zoroaster was both a philosopher and a prophet, and it thus became known as 'the philosophical religion'. Its teachings are focused on creating a new world order out of the old. One of its methods involves making sacrifices upon a fire and seeing the new arise out of the old through the release of matter. John R. Hinnels, Research Professor in Comparative Religion at the University of Derby, describes its ideas as creating a form of social progress through religion. He says various comments have been made in the West about its nature (in this case Schroff followed by Masani), [9]"Zoroastrianism, he says, 'is nothing but the Natural Law of Evolution . . . (p 37). On earth, he writes, there are different levels of souls according to their development. . . different religions are necessary for different souls in various stages of their spiritual and mental development . . . the Zoroastrian religion . . . can only be followed by the . . . souls that have already reached the foremost stage of human spiritual progress. . . The great prayers of religion, offered in purity by the necessarily advanced soul, have their great vibratory effects in removing and annihilating all the major evil forces in nature...'

He says (on page 133), 'The religious path is for the soul to unfold itself from the lower levels of physical matter and for it to develop its latent higher spiritual powers. This unfoldment takes many ages, or births. The esoteric teaching of Zoroastrianism leads to knowledge of all the laws of the universe . . . , to an appreciation of the forces seen and unseen. The rituals, not least the purity laws, help souls onward in their march in the unseen world. The understanding of science, especially the polarity of 'magnetism' and electricity . . . is used to explain how rituals work on unseen spiritual forces which the soul encounters as it progresses in the unseen world (page 135) . . . Similarly the emphasis on mantras whose efficacy depends on the holiness of the reciter's physical, mental, moral and spiritual constituents recalls much contemporary Indian thought.'

The fact that there is much similarity with the Hindu religion is particularly significant, if we consider the effect that establishing a new culture in India would have had on the Aryans. Hence, combined with the time and place in which it existed, it became particularly effective in helping the Medes, who were being subjugated by the Assyrians in the Zagros mountains. It enabled them not only to rebel, but to consolidate themselves and launch a counter-offensive.

Bowker adds more information about the relationship between the Aryans in the Indus Valley and those in Persia (modern Iran). He says that, as [10]'The Indus Valley culture declined between 1800 and 1700 BCE . . . groups of people calling themselves 'noble ones' (Aryans) migrated into or invaded southern Asia from the northwest and became the culturally dominant force. The most commonly accepted theory has been that some of these groups entered India through the northern passes from central Asia while others entered Iran. Indeed, there are close affinities between the Iranian Zoroastrian religion, with its scripture in the Avesta . . . , and the religion of the Veda, the sacred revelation of the Hindus.'

He adds that (on pages 214–219) 'Zarathustra's teaching related to the outlook of the Vedas, and especially Ra Veda in India, but, Zarathustra's under-standing of God (unlike the Vedas and brahmical religion) began with his conviction that he had seen God who had taught him personally.

His own teaching (of which little survives that has not been reworked) is contained in 17 hymns, or Gathas, found in a liturgical text known as Yasna. One of them asks: 'Who established the course of the sun and stars? Through whom does the moon wax and wane? Who has upheld the earth from below, and the heavens from falling? . . . Through whom exist dawn, noon and eve?' (Yasna

44.3–6). Zarathustra answered that it is the Father of Order, Ahura Mazda. Who then created evil and disorder? Zarathustra lived at a time of great strife and he believed that a war on earth reflects a war in heaven: there co-exists with Ahura Mazda a creator of evil and destruction, who he called Angra Mainyu, known as Ahriman in Pahlavi (Middle Persian) . . .'

In its mythological aspect it depicts the world as a battle between good and evil; Ahura Mazda is the 'good' spirit of the new (the life which we must consciously generate), while the evil Ahriman is the 'evil' spirit of the dark entropic forces which we must strive to overcome. Thus, it creates a mechanism which moves society forward. Thus, in religious terms, what he has done is to create a way for people to philosophically accept a mythological interpretation of their own existence, which we can see related to their collective position within global society.

Part 3: The Medes Empire

Tom Holland describes the Medes' rebellion in his book, 'Persian Fire'. He says the Medes tribes lived on the most famous road in the world, the Khorasan Highway. It joined Mesopotamia to the cultures of the East, leading from the Fertile Crescent to the Iranian plateau, through the Zagros mountains. He adds, [1]'Over the millennia, the Khorasan Highway had been followed by any number of travellers: nomads, caravans — and the armies of conquering kings. One empire, in particular, for centuries synonymous with cruel and remorseless invincibility, had sent repeated expeditions into the mountains, dyeing the peaks, in its own ferocious vaunt, 'like wool, crimson with blood.' The Assyrians, inhabitants of what is now northern Iraq, were city dwellers, a people of the flat, alluvial plains; but to their kings, warlords who had spread terror and extermination as far as Egypt, the Zagros was less a barrier than a challenge. Themselves the patrons of a proud and brilliant civilisation, sumptuous with palaces, gardens and canals, the kings of Assyria had always seen it as their duty to flatten resistance in the wild beyond their frontiers. This, the wilds being what they were, had proved a calling without limit. Not even with their incomparable war-machine could the Assyrians pacify all the mountain tribes — for there were some living in the Zagros who clung to the peaks like birds, or lurked in the depths of thick forests, so backward that they only subsisted entirely on acorns, savages hardly worthy of the royal attention. These too, however, with regular incursions, could be taught to dread the name of Assyria, and provide her with the human plunder on which her greatness had come increasingly to depend. Again and again, punitive expeditions would return from the mountains to their native plains, to the sacred cities of Ashur, Nimrud, and Nineveh, while in their wake, naked and tethered, followed stumbling lines of captives. Increasingly, the Assyrians had fallen into the habit of moving entire populations, shunting them around their empire, transplanting one defeated enemy into the lands of another, there to live in the houses of the similarly transported, to clear weeds from the rubble, or cultivate the abandoned, smoke-blackened fields.'

He continues to say (on pages 4–5) that, by the late 8th century BC, the people along this highway had been placed under an Assyrian governor, and the Zagros mountains had become famous for their slave-trade. He additionally says that the mountains were full of 'clover-rich pastures', and the Medes, a loose confederation of Aryan tribes, provided the best horses as tributes to the Assyrian Empire. He continues, 'No wonder the Assyrians came to prize the region. Their mastery of Media, as well as enabling them to control the world's most important trade route, permitted their armies to develop a new and lethal quality of speed. By the eighth century BC, cavalry had become vital to the ability of Assyria to maintain her military supremacy. The tribute of horse from the mountains had become the lifeblood of her greatness. The richest silver mine could not have been more precious to her than the stud farms of the Zagros. And yet, in Assyria's supremacy lay the seeds of its own downfall. The mountains were a mish-mash of different peoples, Aryans and aboriginals alike, even the Medes themselves ruled by a quarrelsome multitude of petty chieftains. Foreign occupation, however, by imposing a unitary authority upon the region, had begun to encourage the fractious tribes to cohere. By the 670s BC, menaced by the shadowy leader of a formal Median union, the Assyrians' hold on the Zagros started to slip alarmingly. Tribute dried up as its collection grew ever more challenging. Open revolts blazed and spread. Over the following decades, the scribes of the Assyrian kings, employed to keep a record of the victories of their master, ceased to make mention of Media at all.'

Holland adds that (on page 6), in 615, a king who claimed sovereignty over all the clan chiefs of the Medes, Cyaxares, subsequently joined in an alliance with the empire's other rebellious subjects and attacked the Assyrians eastern flank. Within three years they had conquered the Assyrian capital, Nineveh. He says, 'Four years later, all traces of the Assyrian colossus, which for so long had kept the Near East in its shadow, lay obliterated. To the victors, naturally, had fallen the spoils. Media, precipitately elevated to the rank of great power, seized a huge northern swath of the defeated empire.' From there they continued to expand, and conquered other territories in Mesopotamia, such as northern Syria in 610 BC and the Lydians in 585.

Part 5: The Persian Empire

As the Medes Empire had been created very fast, it was immensely forward-leaning and their new king, Astyages, suffered from tremendous superstitions. Holland says this was caused by the Zoroastrian prophecies. He continues to say that (on page 34) 'the most fabled of visionaries, Zoroaster, the prophet of the Aryans, the man who had first revealed to a startled world that it was the battleground in a relentless war between good and evil. Here in this war, was the great death struggle of things — for the prophet, continuing with his novel doctrines, had taught that the cycles of the cosmos would not keep revolving forever, as had always been assumed, but move instead towards a mighty end, a universal apocalypse in which Truth would annihilate all falsehoods, and establish on their ruin an eternal reign of peace. Presiding over this final and decisive victory, would be the Lord of Life, Wisdom and Light, Ahura Mazda himself — not, as other Iranians had always believed, one among a multitude of divinities, but the supreme, the all-powerful, the only uncreated god.'

The problem was that, as they became caught up in the idea of using the real world as a battleground in their war between good and evil, they had overlooked what would actually happen as they carried out this conquest. This seems to be what was causing Astyages such anxiety, as the question arose over where society would come to be in terms of the greater scheme of things. If they followed the prophecies to the end, where would that be? After the ultimate victory, what would come next?

While it was easy to conceive of life as a war which must be won when the Assyrians had been oppressing them, it became increasingly difficult to maintain this perspective as they had become the victors, and it was not long before the Medes empire became criticised for its inability to change. Holland comments on how (on page 8), 'Astyages, it was said, even amid all the proofs of his greatness, was haunted by prophecies of doom: strange dreams tormented him, warning him of his downfall and the ruin of his kingdom. Such was the value ascribed by the Medes to visions of this kind that a whole class, the Magi, existed to divine what their meaning might be. Skilled in all the arts of keeping darkness at bay, these ritual experts provided vital re-assurance to their countrymen, for it was a principle of the Medes, a devout and ethical people, that there was a shadow lurking beyond even the brightest light . . . All the world, it seemed to the Magi, bore witness to this truth. A fire may be tended so that it burned eternally, but there was nowhere, not beside the coolest spring, nor even on the highest mountain peak, where the purity of its flame might not be menaced by pollution. Creation bred darkness as well as the daylight. Scorpions and spiders, lizards, snakes and ants all crept and seethed, the visible excrescences of a universal shadow. Just as it was the duty of a Magus to kill such creatures wherever he found them so shadows had to be guarded against when they darkened people's dreams — and especially the nightmares of a king.'

He then describes the issue which arose with the Persians as (on pages 9–11), 'In 599 BC, while Astyages still ruled in Media, a young man came to the throne of this upstart kingdom. His name was Cyrus, and his attributes included a hook nose, immense ambition and quite limitless ability.' He adds that it was this person who had been 'prophesied as the bane of Median greatness.' Astyages had previously married his daughter to a Persian after having a dream that she had put the kingdom of Media in jeopardy. Cyrus was her child. According to legend Astyages ordered him to be killed, but he survived. Astyages then became paranoid about the way that the Medes empire was run. Its sense of maintaining order was very strict and, this became the source of many constitutional disagreements. A major one then emerged with the Persians over the way land was organised into areas (or 'Satrapies'), as it infringed upon the Persians in favour of the Medes. Cyrus took an interest in pursuing the case against the Medes which caused Astyages to regard him as a threat to constitutional stability and, as Holland says, this led to an armed response.

Holland says, 'Accordingly, in 553 BC, he mustered his fearsome horsemen and struck south. Heavily outnumbered, the Persians resisted ferociously. When it appeared that surrender was imminent, even their women took to the battlefield, to encourage Cyrus and his warriors to fight on. For three years, the conflict convulsed the Zagros — and then, suddenly, in 550 BC, it was over. . . Cyrus scattered the large armies of the Medes with his small army. And he captured Astyages, king of the Medes.'

He continues to say that, 'Not since the downfall of Assyria had there been an upset on such a scale . . . Yet, Astyages, with all the resources of a mighty empire behind him, would surely still have triumphed — had he not been grievously stabbed in the back . . . Harpagus, commander of the Median army, and most prominent of the clan chiefs, had deserted to Cyrus, leading a rebellion in mid-battle, and taking Astyages captive.' Holland says it was not only because

Harpagus could have command of far greater armies with the Persians than he could have ever had with the Medes, but there had also been a personal dispute between himself and Astyages, whom he had come to distrust.

John Curtis says, in his book on Persia published by the British Museum, that Harpagus was left behind in Lydia [12]'to consolidate the Persian position, and shortly afterwards Lycia, Caria, and even the Greek cities of Asia Minor were added to his newly founded Persian Empire. Cyrus built himself a capital in Fars, and for this he imported stone from Ionia and Lydia. . . Cyrus now turned his attention to the eastern domains: he certainly reached the river Jaxartes (Syr Darya) and may have got as far as the Indus. The time was ripe to add Babylonia to his conquests. Nabonidus, its fanatically religious king, was deposed, and Babylon was captured in 539 BC. With it came those parts of the Babylonian empire that had not already defected to Cyrus, and in this way much of Syria and Palestine fell into his hands. Cyrus was now master of an area stretching from the Mediterranean to eastern Iran and from the Black Sea to the borders of Arabia. It was with some justification, that in the so-called 'Cyrus Cylinder' — a barrel shaped (on page 38) clay cylinder inscribed in Babylonian cuneiform recording the capture of Babylon — Cyrus describes himself as the 'ruler of all the world'.'

Curtis describes how Cyrus repatriated various peoples, created the world's first multicultural empire, and solved the problem the Medes had in imposing order on Mesopotamia: its subject nations were allowed to keep their own religions and maintain order for themselves. He says that the Jews are not mentioned by name, but the book of Ezra (I, 1–3) says that this is the time when the captives who were deported by Nebuchadnezzar were allowed to return to Jerusalem and rebuild the temple. Ezra and Nehemiah of Persia were present at a massive ceremony around 430 BC called the 'Dedication of the Walls', which is said to mark the founding of Judaism as an organised religion. Thus, the Persian Empire was a step forwards in terms of creating a centre ground in world affairs, and a new era of peace based on inclusivity rather than domination.

The next map shows the Persian Empire around 500 BC, at the point where it stretched across Mesopotamia, Egypt, Libya, Turkey and even parts of Greece. While the Assyrian empire had perhaps occupied half of the world-centre, this was the first to visibly conquer the whole. It also represented the interaction of multiple Cradles of Civilisation, and thus we can see a whole new level of global society appear.

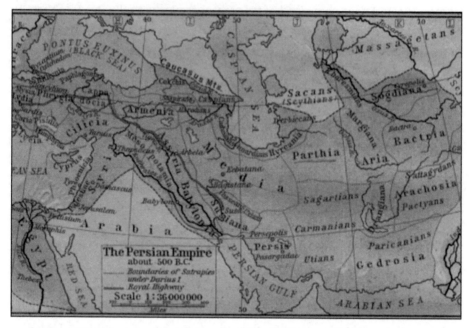

Curtis adds that (on page 38) Cambyses (r. 530–522 BC) was the elder son of Cyrus and his successor, but there was a revolt at the end of his reign. It was headed by two maji, members of the Median priestly class, one of whom pretended to be his murdered brother, Bardiya. On his way from Syria to deal with the revolt, Cambyses was accidentally killed, and the imposter was in power for some time. He was eventually killed by a group of conspirators and one of them, Darius, became the next king (522–486 BC).

He also adds that (on pages 39–40) '. . . two campaigns from Darius' reign stand out. His expedition to India resulted in an annexation of Sind and also possibly the Punjab, but a campaign against the Scythians to the north of the Black Sea was less successful, owing to the mobility and elusiveness of the enemy. Nevertheless, under Darius, the Achaemenid empire reached its greatest extent, embracing Egypt and Libya in the west, and extending to the river Indus in the east.'

Its territories, like those of the Medes, were also called 'Satrapies', assessed for tax purposes and required to generate a fixed annual tribute. Curtis adds that he was the first king to mint coins and built a canal between the Red Sea and the Mediterranean, which was like an early version of the Suez canal. He finishes the story of Darius by noting the reaction his empire was causing in Greece, as a conflict of interests was developing over the Ionian Isles.

CHAPTER 5

The Creation of the Greek Empire

Following Minoan Crete and the Mycenaean civilisation, the Athenian period of Greek democracy emerged from the Greek Dark Ages. Its mythology emerged in the 800s BC, followed by the Pre-Socratic philosophers, then growth in the economy occurred and folklore gave way to philosophy and proper science. However, wars with Persia led to calls for them to have an empire of their own and, as the power of Athens wavered, there was not enough stability to prevent a Macedonian takeover. Hence, the next great empire appeared in the form of Alexander the Great...

Part 1: The Athenian Period

Now we come to see the contrast which came to exist between the religious empires of the East and the fledgling democracies of Europe. Greece was on the route by which farming spread to Europe from Mesopotamia and was home to its earliest settlements, around 7000 BC. The first civilisation in the area was the Cycladic, which existed on the islands in the Aegean Sea (around 3200 BC). Then there was Minoan Crete (2700–1500 BC) and the Mycenaean civilisation which grew on mainland Greece (1900–1100 BC).

Charles Freeman says, in his book 'Egypt, Greece and Rome', [1]'The island of Crete occupies a central position in the eastern Mediterranean. It is accessible from Egypt, the Near East, mainland Greece, and from the west. The island is fertile and well-wooded and towards the end of the third millennium was able to sustain several urban settlements. In some of these, around 2000 BC, large 'palace' complexes appeared. The 'palaces', which have large central courtyards and a series of public rooms, acted as centres for the storage of surplus grain, wine, oil and other produce. Whoever controlled the 'palaces' recorded the goods stored on clay tablets, first in hieroglyphic script and later in the island's own syllabic writing, known to scholars as Linear A . . . It is known as Minoan, after a king, Minos, reputedly the son of Zeus, who, according to later legends, was given Crete to rule . . . Minoan civilisation was rediscovered when an English archaeologist, Arthur Evans, intrigued by carved seal-stones from the area, started digging at the site of Knossos in 1900. It was here that he discovered the grandest Minoan palace of all and evidence of a sophisticated civilisation. . . working on other sites, among them Mallia and Phaistos, soon showed that it was a civilisation which extended across the island. Who lived in the palaces is unknown. Evans claimed that they were seats of royalty, assuming that the Minoans had kings, as later legends suggested. However, it is only later that there is any record of any Minoan leaders (in the Linear B tablets) . . . and it has been argued that early Minoan society was not heavily centralised and even that the 'palaces' were, in fact, religious centres . . . The earliest burials suggest that society was organised around clans or extended families, and excavations in towns surrounding the palaces have shown that there were large independent households in control of their own stores.'

However, he says (on page 79) 'In about 1425 BC there was a . . . wave of destruction of the Cretan palaces. Only Knossos survived intact . . . When occupation was resumed a new culture had emerged. Its chamber tombs, those at Sellopoulo near Knossos, for instance, were similar to those of the mainland, and it was using a new script, Linear B, which borrows many signs from Linear A but is in a different language . . . The invaders were the Mycenaeans, the first known civilisation of mainland Greece.'

After the Mycenaeans came a dark age, which was part of a broader regional period known as the Bronze Age Collapse. From around 1100 BC to 800, Greece emerged from this ruled over by a type of aristocracy. Freeman continues to say (on page 85) 'In the eighth century there is a much more dramatic transformation. Mainland Greece goes through a period of rapid social, economic and cultural change. At one level the change is seen in a large rise in population. . . In the Geometric age, from around 900, and. . . initiated by Athens, rectilinear decoration becomes dominant. . . The painter becomes obsessed with the ordering of space to such an extent that by the middle of the ninth century many pots are covered with geometric designs, zigzags, swastikas, and borders in an endless variety of (on pages 86–7) motifs . . . One of the very earliest inscriptions in Greek, found on a vase at the Greek trading post at Pithekoussai on the Island of Ischia off the west coast of Italy, consists of three lines of verse describing the vase as belonging to Nestor . . . It dates from around 720.' This was the beginning of the period which led to Athenian democracy.

With its economic growth came a new type of society, one in which the rise of folk-culture and story-telling led eventually to philosophy and proper science. As this began, the work of Homer shows how a new dynamic had appeared. A. Thornton says, in 'People and Themes in Homer's Odyssey'[2], that we can look at the Epics of Poetry which evolved with the development of the Athenian period both in terms of what is happening at each point in time (Synchronic) and how events are evolving over time (Diachronic), adding that by cross-referencing these two methods we can see, by the nature of the characters and their interaction, that Greece was heading towards a more rational state of affairs which did not previously exist.

Freeman says of Homer, 'It is now generally accepted that the Illiad and Odyssey evolved over many centuries, originally as songs. Wandering around the homesteads and halls of the Greek world were the singers, men of prodigious memories who had mastered the art of communication through verse. Research in the Balkans, notably in the early part of this century by the American scholar Milman Parry, has shown how formidable the skills of such singers could be and how sophisticated their techniques. One Bosnian Muslim was found to have held in his mind twice as many lines as the Odyssey and Illiad combined. The singers did not simply rely on memory. Serial recordings of the survivors of this tradition show they have an extraordinary ability to improvise, never repeating stories the same way, and continually developing their themes.' This is how great epics came to tell the histories of Greece and, as its civilisation absorbed the traditions which flowed into it, the role of the singers and storytellers grew into the poets and philosophers of Athenian society.

The Dark Ages is traditionally said to have ended with the first Olympic Games in 776 BC and democracy began in 508 BC, as Cleisthenes reduced the power of the nobility over the People's Assembly. At first, he tried to abolish the Boule, the oligarchy of aristocrats who ruled Athens and occupied various administrative roles, but was subsequently exiled by them. However, they then recalled him to solve the problem of reforming the constitution in a way which enabled them to cope with the rise of the new society. It is thought that it was he who established the Law of Ostracism, whereby an Athenian citizen could be exiled for tyranny (attempting to set themselves up with power over others).

Greek Culture

The Greek gods represented the various aspects of life and also had roles as the protective deities of various cities. Zeus was the king of the gods, the god of law, order and fate. Aphrodite was the goddess of love, Dionysus of feasting and celebrating. Ares was the god of war, Demeter of the harvest, Poseidon of the sea. The most complete work of Greek Mythology, the Theogeny (literally, the genealogy of the gods), was written by Hesiod around the 8th Century BC. Exact interpretations differ, but in general it tells the story of the different ages before the birth of present society. Like the myths we have seen before, it is a story which can be told verbally and is possible to remember and reflect upon without any formal education or literacy. This is why myths in the ancient world became incredibly popular amongst people, while religion was more concerned with the state.

First there was just a void, then Gaia (the Earth) and Eros (Love) appeared. Chaos gave birth to Erebus, god of the underworld, and Nyx (night). Gaia gave birth to Uranus (the heavens) and Okeanos (the ocean). These gods then mated: Nyx and Erebus produced Hemere (day) and Aether (the pure, upper air breathed by gods, as opposed to the lower air breathed by mortals). Later, on her own, Nyx gave birth to Moros (destiny), Ker (destruction), Thanatos (death), Hypnos (sleep), the Oneiroi (dreams), Momus (blame), Oizys (pain), the Moirai (fates), Nemesis (retribution), Apate (deceit), Philotes (friendship), Geras (old age), and Eris (strife).

Uranus and Gaia became the first gods to rule, and produced a race of twelve giant Cyclops (Titans). However, Uranus was jealous of his children and condemned them to stay in the womb of Gaia. Gaia, with the help of Cronus (a Titan), then punished Uranus by attacking him. Some of his body parts and blood fell to the Earth, creating another set of gods (Aphrodite, Erinyes, Nymphs and Giants).

Uranus and Gaia told Cronus a prophecy that one of his sons would overpower him. Due to this, Cronus then swallowed their children. Gaia, however, was able to save the baby Zeus and they hid on the island of Crete. With the help of another Titan, Metis, they made Cronus regurgitate the children. Led by Zeus, his six brothers and sisters (Demeter, Hera, Hestia, Hades and Poseidon) then rebelled against their father and threw him into the underworld. They divided the universe amongst themselves and Zeus became the supreme god who lived on the peak of Mount Olympus.

Three of the other Titans, Epimetheus, Okeanos and Prometheus (who later joined Zeus), had not supported Cronus. However, they were all sent into Tartarus (the underworld), with the exception of Prometheus and Epimetheus. Prometheus then created man and enabled him to stand upright, something only the gods had previously done, and stole fire for him from the workshop of Hephaistos. However, in retaliation, Zeus took fire away from man and punished them both. Prometheus was chained to a rock on the Caucasus Mountain, where every night an eagle would appear and eat his liver. During the day the liver was replenished, and every night the eagle would return.

However, Prometheus was rescued by a Centaur (Chiron), and the half-god Hercules. Zeus then created Pandora (the first woman), to whom he gave a box which she was not allowed to open. Eventually she could not resist it, but it contained all sorts of diseases, natural disasters and other misfortunes. At the bottom lay hope. Because of this box, all manner of problems would affect man: toil, war, death; things that would separate human nature from the gods.

It is a creation myth which tells the story of how the elements of Greek society came to form. The fact that the young Zeus hid on Crete before rescuing his brothers and sisters obviously takes us back there, while the general theme of the structure of society emerging before humanity indicates the forces within the psyche are somewhat fixed or predetermined by society. As the Athenian period developed, the Pre-Socratic philosophers then discussed ideas like mathematics, logic and the gods, introducing the idea that people could think for themselves. Hence, the development of the Athenian period is generally regarded as being one of social progress, which led to more advanced thinking and democratic government.

Through the spread of its culture, the religious practices of the Greeks extended beyond the mainland, to the islands of Ionia, Sicily and southern Italy, and Greek colonies in the Western Mediterranean, such as Massalia (present-day Marseille). Early Italian religions, such as the Etruscan, were influenced by Greek religion and subsequently influenced much of ancient Roman religion.

Athenian Democracy

Freeman says (on page 94) that the progress Athenian society initially made in terms of being able to support a large population was possible because the livestock kept by the aristocracy was 'the ideal form of wealth in a time of instability.' However, as they achieved enough growth to become stable they moved on to more intensive farming techniques. Grain was more efficient than cattle, as much of the calories are lost in feeding the animals. He says that, despite this undermining 'the traditional aristocratic way of life . . . The transition may have been easier because the aristocracy had no secure control over the local peasantries. There was, in fact, a deep rooted prejudice against providing any form of regular labour for others. In Homer the landless labourer hiring himself out to others is presented as the lowest possible form of life, only marginally better than death. As a result the mass of the Greek population was never restricted in its mobility, and as population grew this made it possible for larger settlements, towns and cities, to emerge without hindrance, often through the merging of neighbouring villages.' He adds that towns had walls by the sixth century and a comparison with other European languages reveals the term Politics emerged from the type of debate which emerged in these early walled cities (or Polis).

He also says 'The emergence of politics follows naturally from life in the ideal polis. . . The polis is necessarily preoccupied with its identity. It finds a protecting god, Athena for Athens and Sparta, Hera in Samos, Apollo in Eretria (on Euboea) and Corinth.' He adds (on page 95) that social life in this period was characterised by the 'formation of a coherent Greek culture alongside the growth of individual loyalties to the polis'. The priesthood functioned like a network of sects which assisted in the life of and relationships between city states. Religious analogies were often used in politics, and at certain times there was no division between the priesthood and the magistracy.

Part 2: The Greek Philosophers

As the Athenian period developed, the polis required more logical, analytical methods for its political debates, as they could become very claustrophobic and intense. They feared the 'Tyrant', a typically ambitious, aristocratic figure who felt excluded from power, and were willing to use extreme methods to achieve their own ends. The rise of democracy obviously helped to encourage the idea that philosophy was beneficial, as it enabled people to solve problems through conscious reasoning.

Bryan Magee says, in 'The Great Philosophers', [3]'Our view of the philosophy of the ancient world is dominated by the writings of two figures, Plato and Aristotle. Plato is the first philosopher whose works have come down to us in the form which he wrote them, and Aristotle was his star pupil. There is an extraordinary line of personal succession here, for just as Aristotle was a pupil of Plato, so Plato had been a pupil of Socrates. It is doubtful whether there has been to this day a philosopher whose influence has exceeded any one of these three.'

The build-up to the great philosophers starts in the period known as the 'pre-Socratics', which goes all the way back into the 600s BC. They started by covering all the different areas of human life, exploring ideas like logic, mathematics, religion and humanistic issues. Rather obviously, this made Greece the complete opposite of the religious empires of the East. They even discussed the gods, questioning whether they were not merely anthropomorphised images of a shared reality. One Greek philosopher, Xenophanes, claimed that we personify gods, that is, make them in our own image. He said that 'The Ethiops say that their gods are flat-nosed and black, while the Thracians say that theirs have blue eyes and red hair. Yet if cattle or horses or lions had hands and could draw, and could sculpt like men, then the horses would draw their gods like horses, and cattle like cattle; and each would shape bodies of gods in the likeness, each kind, of their own!'

As the philosophers appeared out of folk-culture, initially they lived like the wandering sages of China but, with the rise of democracy, they became important figures in society. This culminated in the founding of the famous 'Academy' in Athens, where Plato taught. Through them we can see how the Greek philosophers' work ran parallel with the development of Athenian society and its values.

Socrates (470 – 399 BC)

Forstater says, in 'The Living Wisdom of Socrates', that [4]"Socrates was the first philosopher to be concerned with human values, who wanted to discover the essence of what it meant to be human. His aim was to illuminate the principles by which one could live a life which was fulfilling, that led to happiness and not suffering or pain.

In doing so he was the first person to reveal that what made us human was our souls, and the way we treat our souls makes the difference between suffering and happiness. He was on a similar path to the Buddha, a near contemporary, who also wanted to find a method to eliminate pain and suffering. Socrates lived his life not only in intellectual pursuit of these principles, but also embodied them in the way he related to himself and others.'

In Plato's 'Metaphysics', he describes Socrates as being concerned with becoming the first to find a universal definition of moral virtues, which we can see evolved into the rational exploration of society we see in Plato's work. However, he left no writings and is only known through the school of thought he founded, through the work of his pupils, especially Plato and Xenophon, and is thus posthumously credited as one of the founders of Western philosophy. Through them, we can see he discussed morals, virtues and the things people believe in. In this way, he contributed to Greek society by starting the enquiry into human nature which led to the founding of the Academy in Athens by Plato, in 387 BC, where Aristotle studied for twenty years before founding his own school, the Lyceum. However, despite functioning in his later life as a member of the Boule, and military service, he was put to death by drinking hemlock for his perceived criticism of democracy and defence of Spartan morals at a time when Athens was at war with Sparta.

Plato

Plato took the issues Socrates discussed and raised them to the level of society as a whole. He talked about how philosophy benefitted people and suggested all the problems of the world were caused by a lack of it. His famous 'Allegory of The Cave' describes the people who live without philosophy. In this, Cross and Woozley say, [5]'He asks us to picture an underground Cave with a long steep passage opening eventually into the daylight, though because of the length and steepness of the passage, no daylight enters the Cave itself. At the lower end of the Cave are men who have been there from childhood, chained in such a way that they face the end wall of the Cave and can see only what is in front of them, because their chains will not let them turn their heads. Higher up the Cave a fire is burning, and between the prisoners and the fire there is a track with a parapet built along it, like the screen at a puppet show. Behind this parapet and screened by it are men passing along the track, some of them talking to one another and carrying all sorts of manufactured objects — statues of men and animals which overtop the parapet and cast their shadows on the end wall of the Cave which the prisoners face. This, Glaucon interjects . . . is a strange picture and these are strange prisoners, and Plato answers, in a very important phrase, that the prisoners are like ourselves. Chained as they are, they can only see the shadows of themselves and of the objects carried past by the men behind the parapet thrown by the fire on the wall of the Cave. Again, if they could talk to one another, their talk would be about the passing shadows, and if any of the people behind the parapet spoke, the prisoners would suppose the sound, reflected from the wall of the Cave, to come from the shadows before them. The prisoners would then recognise nothing as reality but the shadows.' Clearly, this is an analogy for the way people see events, as people who are uneducated can only see the world from the position they are in.

They continue to say (on page 207) 'Plato now . . . describes the release of a prisoner and the curing of his lack of wisdom. First he is freed from his chains and forced to turn around and see the objects (the statues, etc.) whose shadows he had formerly seen on the wall, and the fire itself. This is a painful process: he is dazzled and cannot see clearly, and he believes the objects he now sees to be less real than their shadows with which he was familiar before. Next he is dragged up to the entrance to the Cave to the sunlight. This again is a painful process, again he is dazzled, and at first finds it easier to look at shadows and reflections in the outside world.'

What he is talking about here is the state many people exist in, having never been able to comprehend the way events occur in the outside world, he is immediately drawn to the shadows as a way of understanding them. The reason the analogy is still famous today is that it is still a valid criticism of society. Plato largely blamed ignorance for the public attitudes which led to the death of Socrates, and went on to develop the Platonic method of teaching — without putting direct questions to the student, it starts off by asking the student what they think, then encourages them to develop their reasoning, while having patience with stubborn or irrational personalities.

He is also famous for his theory of 'Forms', which stated that what most people believe is determined by their position in society, but this is not objective reality. Hence, 'ideal' achievements such as high positions, the ideal partner or great wealth are simply illusions created by the way society behaves. The solution, found through philosophy, is that we can learn to understand that 'forms' exist only in the mind, and are relative to each society. What would be better for us is to perceive the truth found in nature, and enjoy a human condition free from social conditioning.

Aristotle

A pupil of Plato, he was an empiricist, who believed all the knowledge we have has come to us through our senses, and thought there was no need for belief in innate ability, which was the worldview promoted by the aristocracy, as they wished to perpetuate the idea of a class-based society and inherited wealth. He thus argued that the theory of 'Forms' was outdated, since people could obviously see the ideas of each society were relative, as the mind could grasp that ideas belong to a particular culture, and learns to understand different types of 'forms' in terms of both origins and usage. He applied his ideas directly to practical issues, such as 'purpose'. For example, 'If I drop a hammer on my foot, is its purpose still the same?' His worldview developed towards the idea of an interactive reality, which we create for ourselves, and our state of knowledge determines our level of achievement.

He also invented 'Dialectics', the art of formulating a proper argument based on evidence and research, in order to win debates in politics and the law courts. Woodfin and Groves say that [6]'Two people take different positions, and, as in chess, attack and defend. Questions are pursued to expose contradictions, until the opponents view is reduced to agreement'. He says this works by enabling them to explore each other's logic, which brings the two mutually exclusive arguments closer together and enables them to interact.

He also promoted the idea of 'The Middle Way', the idea that people must seek to achieve a balance amongst extremes and learn to rationalise issues. Woodfin & Groves say he rejected the idea that we could not have an explanation of the world, but found Plato's dualistic theory of 'forms' unsatisfactory. He believed that, even though it works on an abstract level, it does not explain how events come into being. He solved the problem with a new theory on the universe which added the element of creation, and was thus able to extend the limits of philosophy to the idea of discussing an objective reality which exists independently of ourselves. Hence, he is known as the first real scientist.

Part 3: The Decline of Athens

Freeman suggests that it was the nature of Greek democracy, combined with the problem of Persia, which eventually brought the Athenian period to an end as, under a more united leadership, it may have been possible to accept limited Persian occupation of the Ionian states. What also contributed to the problem is that the whole direction of the country pointed geographically eastwards. He says (on page 97) 'Greek trade and settlement went hand in hand although the emphasis was different in different periods. In the ninth and eighth centuries, as Greece emerged from the Dark Age, the focus was on trade with the east ... The Levantine coast, Syria, Egypt and Mesopotamia were homes to well-developed and opulent civilisations supported by a range of craft skills unknown to the Greeks. For the Greeks, whose lives were always frugal and where a surplus had to be painfully won from the land, the east offered a glittering lure ... Contact with the east was supported by Greece's position. The country is naturally focused towards the east. The mountain ranges run from west to east and the mountains continue as the Aegean islands, stepping stones for eastern traders. All the best harbours are on the east coast. In contrast, Italy is protected from the east by the Apennines, and this was one reason why cultural contact with the east was delayed.'

Conflict with Persia began when they invaded Ionia in the 540s BC. Freeman says that (on pages 150–1), by 495, they had become locked in a series of battles which started to go back and forth, drawing both sides deeper into the conflict. In 498, he says, a group of twenty ships from Athens and five from Eretria had crossed the Aegean to join the Ionian fleet, and another expedition was sent to Sardis. By 495 the Persians had counter-attacked, but not regained control. When they did, according to Greek historian Herodotus, governments were allowed to grow stronger until the situation began to undermine democracy. When the Persians attacked Athens, according to Freeman, they were trying to establish a 'controllable ruler.' He says they landed on mainland Greece at the beach at Marathon, where they fought the famous battle and, according to the Greeks, a massive 6,400 Persians and only 192 Greeks died (it was a Greek runner who went to fetch troops which inspired the 26 mile race, the distance from there to Athens). However, he adds, many famous commanders fought classic battles and the situation changed, but a final breakthrough never emerged.

Various elite groups also still existed within Greek society from the Dark Ages and, while this aristocracy was still trying to compete for powerful roles, criticism of the dialectic-style argument was that it only really worked for the people who were relatively high up in society and could afford a good education, while the progress society was making as a whole was being limited by the war with Persia. Criticism of Greek society became that it was caught up in its own debates, while the situation called for action. The aristocracy were still the ruling power in Macedonia and, as the rest of Greece could not decide what to do about Persia, they were envisaging the possibility of leading a Greek Empire which could invade Persia.

As the conflict persisted, it led to a resurgence of the aristocracy within Greece, and calls for the creation of an empire of their own. They argued that it could be run more efficiently by a smaller number of people, and this suited the position of Greece better at the time. Freeman says that many people in Greece saw the situation involving Persia called for a simpler social system, which was more effective at co-ordinating resources. He adds that the general feeling in Athens was that an empire would be more effective as a war-economy, while democratic society tended to produce excess.

However, many people within Greece did not want this to happen. He says (on page 175) '. . . (as recorded by the historian Xenophon), Cleocritus led an attack on the oligarchs in the city who wish to destroy democracy:

'Fellow citizens, why are you driving us out of the city? Why do you want to kill us? We have never done you any harm. We have shared with you in the most holy religious services, in sacrifices and in splendid festivals; we have joined in dances with you, gone to school with you and fought in the army with you, braving together with you the dangers of land and sea in defence of our common safety and freedom.'

The eventual decline of the Athenian period is generally attributed to a sustained inability to create progress using the methods of democracy, which is then directly related to the problem of Persia.

Subsequently, a number of crises emerged which culminated in the creation of the Macedonian-Greek empire.

The Amphictyonic League, an ancient association of Greek tribes which had existed since the rise of the polis, was involved in a series of Sacred Wars which had sporadically occurred since the 600s. The first (595– 585 BC) was a fairly localised conflict between the League, led by the city of Delphi, and the city of Kirra. The second (449–448 BC) was an indirect confrontation between Athens and Sparta during the First Peloponnesian War, during which Athens detached the city of Delphi and handed it over to the Phocians. Sparta took it back, but Athens then recaptured it when the Spartans left.

However, the third (356–346 BC) was much more serious. It was caused by a huge fine imposed upon the Phocians by the League (at this point led by Thebes) for cultivating sacred land. Refusing to pay, the Phocians seized the Temple of Apollo at Delphi and stole its treasure to pay for armies of mercenaries. The war was exhaustive and continued for many years. Meanwhile, the rising power of Macedonia, enabled by both strategic manoeuvring and reforms to their army, allowed them to intervene and force the Greeks to make a peaceful settlement. Then, having a foothold in Greek society, there was not enough stability to prevent a Macedonian takeover.

Part 4: The Alexandrian Period

Freeman says (on page 253) that it was during 'the accession of Phillip II in either 360 or 359 BC that ruler and resources became combined in a formidable expansionist force which was to transform the Greek world in less than fifty years.' While Greek society had been engaged in the wars involving Sparta, Corinth and Thebes (on pages 240–56), Phillip II of Macedon was able to round up 'scattered and weak states' to build up their empire. Between 359 and 336 he created a new order in Greece based around the idea of Macedonian hegemony.

Freeman adds (on page 252) that Jason of Thessaly described Macedonia in the fourth century BC, as being 'a fertile area with good rainfall and potentially strong if its resources were mobilised.' Also, while the Greeks tried to persevere with the idea of democracy, Macedonia used Greece as a shield to protect themselves from the Persians, as they steadily became more powerful. Phillip carefully created marriage alliances, manoeuvred well politically and took advantage of the weakness of Athenian democracy, which was being fuelled by continuing problems with Persia. He hid behind Athens in his relations with foreign powers and internally created a situation where a Greek empire (led by Macedonia) would have a future in invading Persia. In 346 the Macedonian army was poised to invade Greece, but a meeting with the Athenians created a settlement treaty known as The Peace of Philocrates.

However, when this broke down into hostilities, it resulted in a war between Macedonia and a Greek coalition led by Athens and Thebes. When this was defeated by Phillip at the battle of Chaeronea in 338 BC, the League of Corinth was formed, which forced all Greek states into an alliance with Macedonia. The League then voted Phillip as the *strategos* (general) in what would become a planned war against Persia. However, when Phillip was assassinated by one of his royal bodyguards, his son, Alexander, quickly took control.

Freeman says (on page 258) that Alexander's bloodlines went back on his mother's side to Achilles and on his father's to Heracles, so he was just about the most powerful mix of physical and mental abilities Greek society could produce at the time. In his childhood he read Homer and, for his tutor he had Aristotle.

As his father's death inspired widespread revolts across Greece, he invaded immediately to suppress them. Freeman continues to say (on pages 259–62) that Alexander marched an army southwards on the Greek cities of Athens and Thebes, defeating the Thracians and Illyrians in brilliant campaigns in which six thousand Thebans died, thirty thousand were enslaved and Thebes temporarily ceased to exist. Also, that this took no more than a few weeks and left the Greek world stunned.

Then, he says, Alexander embarked upon an invasion of Persia, with 37,000 troops, accompanied by surveyors, engineers, architects, scientists and a historian. He adds that paying for this mission cost Greece virtually all its money, but the oracle at Delphi had pronounced him invincible. He also adds that 10,000 of his father's troops had been stranded in Persia, by events which had occurred during his reign, who Alexander rescued on the way. Maybe he saw this as a way of gaining popularity within his army to compensate for the way he had brutally invaded Greece.

Freeman further adds that their first battle against the Persians was on the far side of the river Granicus in the spring of 334, their weapons and discipline being so much better than that of their opponents that they left nine tenths of the infantry dead. However, he continues, their major battle was against Darius on the plain of Gaugamela. He adds (on page 266) that 'The new army raised by Darius was almost exclusively made up of cavalry drawn from the centre and east of the empire. (What infantry there was, was of poor quality.) Arrian reported an unbelievable total of 400,000 horsemen: a more sober estimate is 37,000, still probably five times as many as Alexander could muster. Darius took his men north into Assyria, and positioned his army where the cavalry could be used most effectively on the plain of Gaugamela, in the foothills of the Zagros mountains.

Here, Alexander followed him to arrive in September 331. It was the most frightening situation which he had yet faced. After resting his men, he drew up his army as before, the infantry in the centre, the Macedonian cavalry on the right, and the Thessalians on the left. Battle was joined on 1 October when Alexander began moving his cavalry around the flank of the Persians. They counter-attacked and Alexander had to feed in more and more troops to contain them. As the Persians responded by sending yet more troops, Alexander finally saw what he had been waiting for, a gap opening between the Persian left and its centre. Rushing his Companions forward with infantry supporting them on each side, Alexander forced his way through the gap. Within a few moments the state of the battle was transformed as the Persian army was broken into two.'

He says Darius fled and Alexander followed for about 30 kilometres before giving up the chase. From there, he adds, 'Alexander could rightly claim the title Lord of Asia...' and was seen by many as its great liberator from Persian rule. Its second city, Susa, welcomed him with camels and elephants as gifts. Also, he says, they found 40,000 talents of gold and silver stolen from Greece over 150 years before and stripped Persepolis of 8,000 talents from Darius' bedchamber, so effectively that archaeologists did not find anything there.

This map shows how the massive territories he conquered, in such a short space of time, completely replaced the Persian Empire at the world-centre.

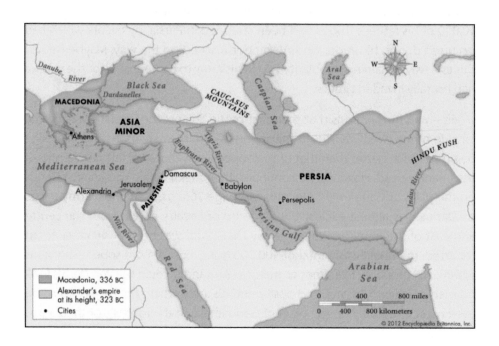

Part 5: The End of Alexander

However, as Freeman says (on page 267), the nature of his campaign then changed, as his army had achieved much more than they hoped to when they set out and felt they had done enough. Alexander had one of his cavalry commanders, Philotas, tortured and executed for conspiring against him, along with his father who had campaigned against his recklessness. This started to fuel his increasing unpopularity. Then, he says, Alexander began to rely increasingly on mercenaries rather than have troops sent from Greece. Following this, he marched his men through the Hindu Kush, in April 329 BC, where they suffered frostbite and breathlessness. After that, soldiers died of over-drinking from marching across 75 kilometres of desert.

The Persians, by this time, had found a new king, Bessus, but even though he was captured and executed (on page 268), it seems that Alexander was still not satisfied. Freeman adds that his final campaign in Bactria was 'marked by scenes of terror as entire male populations of captured cities were massacred and their women and children enslaved.' Clearly, the whole situation was affecting everyone concerned and the relationships between the people in his army were being pushed beyond their limits. Many of them were asking to go home.

Freeman then says, 'The combined effects of the stresses of the campaigns and Alexander's own personality were now causing serious problems within his own court. When his army was resting at Macaranda . . . in the autumn of 328, a row broke out at a drunken banquet between Alexander, and the cavalry commander Cleitus, who had saved Alexander's life at Granicus. It was said that Cleitus taunted Alexander. Alexander in response seized a weapon and struck Cleitus down. The row concealed more deep-rooted problems. The Macedonian kingship was one in which personal loyalty to the king persisted alongside a rough camaraderie. The king was not removed from his commanders — he ate and drank, often heavily, alongside them. The tradition of the Persian monarchy was very different. Here the king lived in unbelievable splendour and even the most senior of his courtiers were treated as subjects. The whole approach was symbolised by the act of proskynesis, a traditional obeisance of a subject before his king. Alexander had now begun to insist on this for himself. The Macedonian commanders, already resentful of the way that Alexander had appropriated all credit for military success to himself, deeply resented submission to what was for them a humiliating ritual.'

It appears that Alexander was hoping to carry the Greek leadership back on his shoulders triumphantly, like the Golden Fleece of Greek legend. Having won their respect in battle, he could then return and establish a permanent monarchy. However, he seems to have remained in Asia for too long, when he should have returned home to organise his empire politically. It seems at this point he began to push against the tide of events which he had previously worked with so ingeniously.

Despite this, he marched on into India. Freeman says (on page 269) that there were legends in Greece that Heracles and Dionysus originated there and Alexander may have been spurred on to equal their exploits. Additionally, in 327, Alexander's army passed through the Hindu Kush and down the Cophen valley, storming and conquering cities, slaughtering their inhabitants. Only one city, Nysa, apparently survived by successfully claiming to be the origin of Dionysus. He adds that, as he passed into India over the Indus river in 326, he was met by the king of Taxila whose plan was to use his army to defeat their own enemies to the east.

However, Freeman says, by the time his army reached the river Beas, his troops had faced 70 days of monsoon and were close to mutiny. He adds, 'For the first time in his life, Alexander accepted defeat. He claimed that a sacrifice had shown that the gods did not want him to continue further and ordered the retreat. There was a jubilation in the ranks which he was neither to forgive nor forget.' However, Freeman adds, on their way home they did not march back, as would be expected, through the conquered territories. Instead, they took a flotilla down the Indus river to the Southern Ocean, which Alexander still wanted to explore. He says (on page 270) that they departed in November 326. The journey was dangerous and he was hit in the chest by an arrow from one of the tribes who lived on the river whose cities were stormed, from which he never fully recovered. Then, he adds, Alexander marched them for 60 days across the Makram desert and losses were heavy. Finally, a thoroughly demoralised force reached the conquered satrapy of Carmenia, from where they walked back to Greece.

Freeman says that, as a consequence of what had happened during his campaign, his behaviour had become erratic, dressing up regularly as the god Zeus and had coins minted depicting him with a thunderbolt in his hand. Then, in 323, while he was in Babylon planning an invasion of Arabia and engaged in a heavy drinking session, he died at the palace of Nebuchadnezzar II. Freeman says (on page 272) that by some accounts he was poisoned, others say he drank a bowl of beer worth twelve pints. Other sources claim the 'The Prophesy of Calanus' raises an issue over the way he died. Calanus was a Hindu Sage who Alexander had brought back from the Punjab earlier that year. He was 73 years of age and, weakened by travel fatigue, requested that he should be allowed to die rather than live on as an invalid. According to the story, he burned himself alive and, whilst doing so without flinching, eerily said to Alexander, 'We shall meet in Babylon'. How did he know the location of his death? Perhaps Calanus knew something of a plot to kill him. It has been a mystery for 2300 years. Recent scientific studies have shown the way he died correlates with Varatrum poisoning.

It appears that Alexander came from an educated, aristocratic background and was naive about the way the world worked, not expecting there to be any consequences if he were victorious. From the very beginning of his reign, he was thrust onto the front line of his empire, and commanded it in a dictatorial manner, which led to deep divisions within his ranks. It was through his campaign that he acquired many of his life experiences, and the more time he spent there, the more dangerous a place it seems to have become. Even though he had brought progress on a world-scale, he had also committed terrible deeds and, finally, it seems he had paid the price. Despite his ambition to create a permanent empire, it collapsed quickly after his death. Leaving no heir, it was divided amongst his commanders. They were appointed as leaders of the territories they occupied at the time. The only legitimate heir was his half-brother, who was retarded, and this caused a power struggle which lasted twenty years. During this time the empire broke down. Perdiccas, the governor of Phrygia, eventually managed to take over until he was killed in 301. In Asia, Seleucus declared himself divine ruler of the eastern side, which became the Seleucid Empire. Shortly after, the Mauryan Empire conquered most of the Indian subcontinent from 322 BC. Freeman adds, the Seleucid Empire was full of Asian factions and his Greek-style government faltered in 64 BC. The Parthian Empire then re-emerged out of the underlying Persian culture in 247 and had re-conquered Mesopotamia by 129. In the West, the complete collapse of the Greek Empire left one tiny state, with little ambition outside of itself at the time, with the opportunity to become a new superpower... Rome.

CHAPTER 6

Rome — Republic to Empire

Rome acquired massive wealth as it found itself at the new geographical centre of trade in the West. This led to its expansion, but also caused wars with Carthage, the large empire in North Africa, and the Celts. After this, further expansion over-extended its social system and led to a series of civil wars which eventually led to it becoming an empire to stabilise itself. Thus it grew, from a small state around 500 BC, into the next great empire...

Part 1: The Early Expansion of Rome

After the Greek invasion of Persia and the subsequent collapse of Alexander the Great's empire, separate empires emerged in East and West. In the East, China and India co-existed while the Parthian Empire eventually took back the territory captured by the Greeks. In the West, the rise of Rome created a more permanent empire which lasted until the AD 400s, and continued as the Byzantine Empire until the end of the Middle Ages.

With their mythological origins heavily influenced by Greek religion, Rome had a similar type of polis-based society, and it seems their empire lasted for a much longer period of time owing to lessons learned from the Greek collapse. They built themselves up slowly, their social system produced leaders who were ambitious, and they produced a type of government in which senior members could be replaced, unlike the autocratic style of Alexander. For this reason, the management styles of both the Roman Republic and the Empire are very logical and systematic.

S. P. Kershaw says, in 'The Roman Empire', [1]'The history of the Romans stretches well in excess of a millennium on even the shortest calculation, and their mythology extends the time frame even further. They traced their origins back to Troy via the mythical Trojan prince Aeneas, who escaped from the carnage inflicted by Greeks after they had used the trick of the Wooden Horse. He and a small band of survivors made their way to Italy, where they fought, and then united with, the inhabitants to form the future Roman race. Legend has it that the city of Rome was founded by Romulus in 753 BCE, and was then ruled by seven kings until 510 BCE, when the populist but tyrannical King Tarquinius Superbus was expelled by Brutus the Liberator. Rome became a Republic the year after, and the Romans always remained acutely sensitive to the difference between a kingdom (Regnum) and a Republic (Res Publica, literally 'the Public Thing'). During the Republican period (509–27 BCE), when the government was (theoretically) controlled by elected magistrates, Rome gradually became the dominant power in Italy, and then in the Mediterranean.'

Its gods are similar to the Greeks', with a king and queen in the form of Jupiter and Juno. Neptune is the god of the sea, Venus of Love, Bacchus of feasting and wine, Ares of war, Pluto of death. Rome reinterpreted the myths of the Greek gods using ones of their own. Once again, religious cults arose around the polis but, due to the success of their empire, Roman politics grew far more powerful than its religion.

Charles Freeman says, [2]'Rome becomes a Mediterranean power', following a period in 265 BC when its influence only reached as far as northern Italy. She had the Italian peninsula, yet the Celts blocked any further expansion to the north and, with no navy, treaties with Carthage guaranteeing them naval supremacy in the south meant no foreign expansion looked likely. However, he adds, increasing wealth was getting her into a position from which expansion was possible and, when a group of Italian Mercenaries calling themselves the Mamerines took over the city of Messina (in northeast Sicily), they were able to take the opportunity.

Freeman adds, 'In 265 the ruler of Syracuse, Hiero, had tried to dislodge them. While some looked to Carthage for help, others appealed to Rome. The Senate was reluctant to intervene, as it had already condemned one group of Roman citizens who had seized a Greek city and felt it inconsistent to now uphold the Mamerines' seizure. On the other hand it was clear that a Carthaginian takeover in Messina would threaten Roman control of the straits. The debate was taken to the popular assembly, and after speeches by the consuls stressing the threat to Rome and the hope of plunder it was the assembly who committed the state to action, the only example known when the citizen body, rather than the senate, set in hand a war.'

However, Syracuse (another city in Sicily), seeing the possibility of the whole island being annexed by Rome, subsequently made an alliance with Carthage in an attempt to stop them. He says that, while the Romans occupied Messina, Carthage and Syracuse then besieged the city together, causing the first of the Punic Wars (264–241 BC, *Punicus* is Latin for Carthaginian). Carthage had originally developed as a ninth century colony of the Phoenicians, whose power had declined in the 600s following defeats to Assyria, Egypt and Persia, which then emerged as an independent city, at the centre of all the former Phoenician coastal cities. It was then able to expand into North Africa, Spain, Sardinia, Sicily and other islands of the western Mediterranean, becoming the largest empire in the area at the time.

The Romans constructed a naval fleet with the sole purpose of strategically destroying the Carthaginian fleet around Sicily. Despite having massive assets (on page 321), Carthage would then no longer be able to protect Sicily in practical terms and be forced to concede it to Rome. He says that additionally, in the following years, a mutiny among Carthaginian mercenaries gave Sardinia and Corsica to Rome, each of which had members elected to the Senate from 227 BC. Freeman adds that Carthage did not seem to regard its losses too seriously, but it put them in a situation where they were not favourable towards the Romans.

Then, he says that (on page 322), in 225 BC, central Italy was faced with a Celtic invasion which they crushed and took the Po Valley. Rome now needed support against the Celts and made a new agreement with the Carthaginians, which Carthage then broke and sided with the Celts. He continues to say that this resulted in the second, and considerably more serious, Punic War (218–202 BC). Freeman describes the Carthaginian leader, Hannibal, (on pages 322–324) as being a great general who had reformed Carthage's institutions and had been taught by a Spartan tutor in the methods used by Alexander the Great. He then famously carried the equipment for his army on elephants over the Alps into the Po Valley, and the Celts there regarded him as their great liberator.

He says, 'In the first encounter with the Romans at Trebia, west of the new Roman colony at Placentia, over half the Roman army was lost and with it the north of Italy. The next year, 217, Hannibal, now in central Italy, lured a large Roman army into the narrow plain between Lake Trasimene and the mountains and slaughtered it. A consul, Gaius Flaminius and perhaps 15,000 men died in the disaster. Luckily for Italy, Latium, Umbria and Etruria stood firm, and their support enabled Rome to survive. The constitution granted emergency powers under the dire circumstances and a dictator, Quintus Fabius Maximus was appointed, who declared that it was necessary to avoid any head-on confrontations with Hannibal, and wear him down gradually (in what became known as 'Fabian tactics'). Fabius, however, won little support and when, in 216, he was replaced by two new consuls, they raised an army of 80,000 men who marched down to Apulia where they met Hannibal's army again. . . Hannibal drew the Roman armies onto an open plain at Cannae, where he knew he could use his cavalry effectively. The Romans hoped that the sheer weight of their numbers would be enough and they drew their infantry together in a close formation so it could overwhelm the Celts and Spaniards who were holding Hannibal's centre. However, although the Carthaginian centre retreated it did not break, and the Romans found themselves enveloped by African infantry stationed on the two wings and the Carthaginian cavalry who had routed their Roman counterparts. In a devastating defeat all but 14,500 of the Roman army was wiped out.

His victory at Cannae now allowed Hannibal to consolidate his position in southern Italy. His greatest prize was Capua, the second city of Italy, and a number of other cities of Campania either came over to him or were captured in the aftermath of the battle. Hannibal was now in a position to march on Rome but he never made the move. He must have realised that the subjection of the city would be a very different matter from defeating its forces in the open field and there is no evidence he wished to destroy Rome. He appears to have stuck to his original aim of humiliating her and destroying her allies, probably in the hope that she would be forced to surrender Sicily and Sardinia and be reduced to her original territory in Latium.'

However, as Freeman says, the historian Polybius commented that this was the moment in Roman history when its resolution was at its strongest. He adds that, following this defeat, four new legions were raised from the city's youth, 8,000 slaves were freed to serve the empire, the centre of Italy remained loyal and its armies rebuilt. What happened then was an amazing turn-around of events. He says Fabius captured Tarentum in 212. In response, Hannibal marched on Rome, but when he saw how well it was defended, he retreated. Capua, on the other hand, fell to the Romans and, from there, Rome pushed Hannibal down into southern Italy. His brother, Hasdrubal, marched from Spain, but was intercepted in the north of Italy by the Roman consuls and defeated at the Battle of the River Metaurus, in 207. By this point Hannibal was trapped in southern Italy and unable to get his army out. In the meantime the Romans took the fight to Spain. They nearly lost a grip, until Publius Cornelius Scipio, a young, energetic commander, took New Carthage by launching a surprise attack across a lagoon at low water. After his victory (on pages 324–5) he claimed that Neptune, the sea god, had helped him. Victories at Ilipa and Gades saw the end of Carthaginian dominance in Spain, and the beginning of a new period where Rome could exploit its silver mines and other resources.

Freeman adds (on page 325) that, in 204, he then set off to take Africa and, at the Battle of Zama in 202, Hannibal's army was defeated as the Roman cavalry managed to drive their opposite numbers off the field before getting back to attack Hannibal's centre from behind. Carthage was thereby defeated and, reduced to her territory in Africa, forced to pay 10,000 talents over a period of fifty years.

Part 2: Rome Becomes the Largest Civilisation in the West

After the Second Punic War, there were no more major conflicts in the south, even though there were various uprisings. Carthage was destabilised and eventually destroyed in the Third Punic War (149–146 BC), which was more like an extended siege, and became the Roman province of Africa. With the new wealth it had gained from victory, Freeman adds, Rome then looked to the north and the Celts. He says, 'From 201 to 190 the senate assigned one or both consuls to the north, and the two main Celtic tribes, the Boii and the Insubres, were dealt with ruthlessly'. He adds that there is very little archaeological evidence of Celts in northern Italy after that point. Spain was divided into two parts, 'Nearer Spain' (on the east coast) and 'Further Spain' (stretching from the south coast inland). England became their main target to the north.

However, he adds that, in 205, Hannibal made a new alliance with Philip V of Macedon. Rome had sent a small fleet to Greece but primarily used the Aetolian League '. . . , traditionally hostile to Macedon, to contain him. Peace had been made in 205, but many senators felt that Philip had not been sufficiently punished and they responded when in 201 the king of Pergamum, Attalus, supported by Rhodes, came to Rome to appeal for help against the intrusions of Philip. There may also have been some who saw an attack on Macedonia as a chance for plunder to refill Rome's treasury, and the senate persuaded the assembly that despite the exhaustion of the state war was justified'.

He adds, 'The official pretext for war was that Rome was protecting the liberty of the Greeks against Macedonian expansionism'. He adds that the Romans defeated the army of Philip, in 197, and were praised by the Greek city-states who they kept independent. As the Macedonians tried to retake Greece, the Roman army defeated them again, in 172 and 168, dividing Macedonia into four parts. Additionally, in the same year, they forced the Seleucid king Atiochus IV, who had invaded Egypt without Roman approval, to make peace with Rome and, in 150, Greece effectively became a Roman province.

Rome thus became the major power in the Mediterranean. Freeman says (on pages 331–2) 'Not only did vast amounts of plunder including hundreds of thousands of slaves, pour into Italy, but the city was open now to the rich cultures of the east. The fall of Syracuse saw the first major influx of Greek art into Rome.' He adds that, 'Prior to this, Rome neither had nor even knew of these exquisite and refined things. . . rather it was full of barbaric weapons and bloody spoils', wrote Plutarch. The eastern wars brought the first booty from mainland Greece, engraved plate and inlaid furniture, music girls, and the conception that cooking was an art.'

This picture shows the approximate size of Rome at this point. Over time, the city itself grew to over 1.2 million people. There was not another city in Europe to exceed 1 million for over a thousand years.

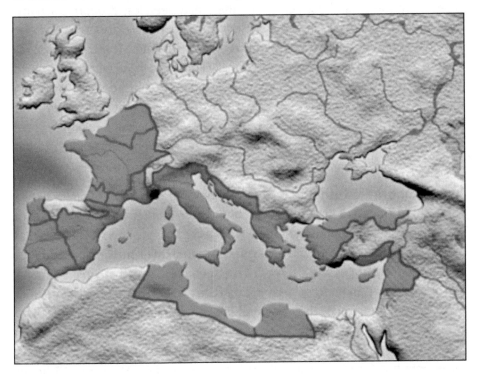

Part 3: The Problem of Reform and the Social War

The impact of these events on its society was that Rome had become a fine place, with a rich and successful establishment. However, this expansion changed its governmental system, making reforms difficult. Freeman says (on page 337) that its new wealth had caused the economy to expand internally, and problems with the existing social structure began in the second century when there was a 'land hunger'. When there had been less economic activity, there had been enough land for people to expand into. He also says (on page 339) that a new social class had been created, the Equites. The Equestrians, as they were formerly known, were traditionally known as those who were able to provide a horse for the cavalry in times of war, but had been redefined according to a new 'wealth qualification'. People were complaining that their society was becoming corrupt. Freeman adds, then came the reformers and their resistance who fought a battle which lasted nearly a century, eventually leading to the Social War.

According to Freeman, it all began with the Gracchi, a noble family with five consulships. Tiberius Sempronius Gracchus (whose mother was the daughter of the Scipio who had conquered Africa) was elected tribune in 134. He adds that his powers included being able to pass laws through the concilium plebis, block acts of the magistrates and decrees of the senate. He says that Tiberius set his aim on achieving land reform, claiming that the position of the small landowner had been undermined by the growth of the large estates. There had previously been an allowance of 120 hectares of land which had been confiscated from defeated Italian cities, which had been made available for distribution among the people, but some had acquired much more than others. He says that Tiberius proposed they give up their excess and it should be re-distributed amongst the poor. The poorer land-owners would also be guaranteed the right not to be bought out by their richer neighbours.

However, when he suggested (on page 338) that the wealth of Pergamum, bequeathed to Rome by its king, be used for monetary assistance to poor farmers, he had apparently interfered with the workings of the senate and, while standing for a second tribunate (which was another breach of convention), was killed in the riot which ensued. Freeman remarks that the land commission survived, however, with his brother Gaius as one of its members.

He adds that the land reform bill caused some opposition from the larger landowners, particularly ones from allied cities, who did not see why they should surrender their land to Rome. This produced a proposition, in 125, by the consul Fulvius Flaccus, that Roman citizenship should be offered to allied cities. He adds that (on page 342) 'The hopes of the upper classes of the allied cities now rested on Roman citizenship. Citizenship would give them a chance to participate in the government of the empire and also the rights enjoyed by any citizen against the power of the magistrates.' He then adds that one of the tribunes, Livius Drusus, proposed in 91 that citizenship be extended, but only to the upper classes of allied cities, to create more rich citizens to balance out the 'multitudes of poor'. In October he was assassinated and, Freeman says, the great dynamic had appeared within the Roman Republic which led to the Social War (he says 'social' comes from *socii*, allies).

He continues to say that (on pages 342–4) 'This new dashing of allied hopes was a catalyst for revolt. During the winter of 90–91, twelve major peoples broke away from the Roman Empire and formed the state of Italia. . . They copied the Roman government, in having two consuls, twelve praetors and a senate, and raised an army of 100,000. Rome raised an army of 150,000, but, for the first year they were outmanoeuvred. As a response, in 90 BC, Roman citizenship was extended to all the allies who had remained loyal, or who were prepared to put down their arms. With her opposition now split, Rome defeated the rest'. He adds, 'Italian unification had been achieved, but the price, in terms of disruption and lingering bitterness, was high'.

Freeman says, 'It had lasted longest in the south. The Rebels had looked for help from outside, and had made contact with a new enemy of Rome, Mithridates. . . , in 89 he invaded Bithynia. . . in Athens, there was a democratic coup in his support.

A consul was needed to restore control and one of those elected for 88, Lucius Cornelius Sulla, was granted the command. Sulla was of an old but not particularly distinguished patrician family and his main claim to fame was his success as a commander in the south of Italy during the social war.'

He says (on pages 345–6) that the big question in Rome had become how to incorporate the new citizens from allied territories and this resulted in a battle for the leadership. One of Sulla's rivals, Sulpicius, was attempting to place them in groups alongside Roman citizens for the purpose of voting, the only other option was to place them in their own group. This meant they would only be able to vote after the other groups had decided all the major issues, but it was the one favoured by the conservatives.

To win support for his plan, Sulpicius promised Marius the command which Sulla had been appointed for, which humiliated Sulla and he marched an army through Rome to force the senate to declare Sulpicius and his supporters outlaws. Sulpicius was betrayed and killed by a slave, while Marius fled to Africa. Then, Freeman says, Sulla dealt ruthlessly with the rest of his opposition before departing to take his command in Asia.

However, in Rome, unrest broke out again as Cinna, a consul for 87, tried to revive Sulpicius' proposal to assign foreign citizens to groups within the Roman Republic, but was blocked by the other consul, a nominee of Sulla's. Freeman says, 'Cinna had to flee the city, but now sought out Marius and the two returned to besiege Rome. They captured the city and, in 86, Cinna and Marius held the consulships, Marius' seventh. Marius died shortly afterwards but Cinna managed to hold four successive consulships and, although the details are obscure, seems to have maintained stability. Sulla was declared an outlaw.

In Asia, despite having been 'officially' deprived of his command, Sulla was rebuilding his position. Athens was retaken and the supporters of Mithridates slaughtered. The Pireaus was burnt down and treasures, including one of the great libraries and columns from the temple of Olympian Zeus, carried off from the city. In Asia, the reconquered cities were crushed with enormous indemnities. Mithridates, whose popularity among the Greeks collapsed as soon as the scale of the Roman retribution became clear, surrendered all his conquests and retreated to his kingdom. Sulla now had the glory of victory to back his return to Rome for revenge. As soon as he landed in Italy in 83 he initiated a civil war in which communities and peoples who had supported Marius, which included the Samnites, were crushed.' He says that Sulla then went on a systematic elimination of all his opponents, drawing up a list of between 2,000 and 9,000 equestrians and senators who could all be freely killed for a reward.

Freeman says that, in 82, he entered Rome with an army and declared himself dictator. He then appointed three hundred extra senators, to go with the existing three hundred. Additionally, he reformed the system of government, forbidding anyone to become a praetor before the age of 39, or a consul before 42, nor could anyone hold the same magistracies twice within ten years, or anyone who was a tribune hold any other magistracy. Additionally, Tribunes could no longer pass any legislation in the concilium without the prior approval of the senate. He thereby snuffed out the internal power struggle and, as Freeman says, prevented offices from being used as stepping-stones to the top.

He says that, however, when Sulla retired and died at the age of 78, the system collapsed into almost total corruption, as the tribunes started agitating for their powers back and massive bribery was used to secure verdicts in the senatorial courts. The system once again became the target of personal ambition and the sense of right and wrong was replaced by what everyone could get for themselves.

Part 4: The First Triumvirate —
Pompey, Caesar and Crassus

Freeman says that (on pages 347–9) 'They looked to Pompey, a young commander who had earned himself a triumph under Sulla, to restore order. He was used to mop up various civil disturbances, the senate gave him a special command to deal with Lepidus, and an uprising of 70,000 Thracian slaves led by Spartacus which ended with a row of 6,000 crucified slaves lining the road from Rome to Capua, where the uprising had begun. However, an older man of a more noble background, Marcus Licinius Crassus, claimed to have done most of the fighting against Spartacus, while Pompey took the credit. Pompey agreed that they should both stand for the consulships of the year 70. He and Crassus then began to undo Sulla's reforms by giving powers back to the tribunes, and opening the juries again to the equestrians, giving non-senators a majority there. After this, he retired into a private life, but, was later appointed around 67 to a force of 500 ships, 120,000 infantry and 5,000 cavalry to drive pirates out of the Mediterranean. He drove them away from important corn-supplying provinces in Sardinia, Sicily and Africa and then a further appointment to deal with the Mithridates threat in the east led to him securing Armenia, Jerusalem and Syria. News came back that Mithridates had committed suicide. He conquered all the way to Parthis in the east, took Cyprus in 58 . . .' He says the Roman Senate then allowed Pompey to make any settlement, treaty, peace or war, as long as it was ratified by the senate upon his return to Rome. Whereas, during the Punic Wars, they had been fighting for their own survival, now Rome had a general with a free hand to create and destroy kingdoms at will.

He says (on pages 350–4) 'It was an extraordinary achievement, Pompey had created a stable eastern empire which now provided a vast income from taxes and tribute for Rome.' However, he adds, 'There is little wonder that back in Rome, the senators and many others were apprehensive about his return. If he kept his armies intact he was unchallengeable. This was how vulnerable the Republic had become.' Freeman adds that Cicero, a lawyer who had successfully exiled plunderers and other villains through destroying their reputations in the law courts, tried to calm the situation down. Having shown that things could be achieved with words instead of violence, he was elected praetor in 66 and consul in 63, and hailed as 'the new founder of Rome'. However, the military power of the generals remained at large and his was limited to politics.

Freeman adds, 'As Pompey had shown in Asia, once abroad a commander operated largely beyond the control of the senate. It was only when he returned that the senate could refuse to ratify any decisions he had made overseas or hinder the settlement of his troops.' Cicero then looked to another consul, Julius Caesar, who had become a consul through his own 'naked ambition', consistently using the cause of the Populares (the democratic people's movement, as opposed to the aristocratic element in Roman politics). Born in 100 BC, he was noted for his magnanimity towards those he defeated. In 63 he was elected pontifex maximus, praetor in 62 and consul in 59.

As Caesar had been in debt, Crassus helped him in return for political support and, when he returned to Rome, Crassus, Caesar and Pompey formed an alliance which became known as the First Triumvirate (government of three). Freeman says many people were afraid that Pompey and Caesar could push Rome towards a dictatorship. Shortly after, Pompey married Caesar's only daughter, Julia, bringing them even closer together. Caesar then awarded himself a five-year command in Gaul and Illyricum. Freeman says Cicero complained to the courts in 59, but was politically outmanoeuvred by Caesar, who engineered the appointment of Publius Clodius as tribune. Clodius was a former enemy of Cicero, who had testified against him when he was on trial for sacrilege, and turned on him immediately. Caesar then offered Cicero protection, but (on page 356) he eventually fled to Macedonia when his house was ransacked by a gang of 'roughs' hired by Clodius.

He says that, in 58, Caesar took up his command in Gaul, seeking more territory, and forced the Helvetii back into Switzerland. The Suebi (a German tribe) were pushed back across the Rhine and, in 57, he brought the whole of Gaul under Roman control. Freeman says, 'In the senate the vote of thanks to Caesar was proposed by none other than Cicero. Cicero had returned from exile in September 57 thanks to the unremitting hard work of Pompey. As Clodius' confidence had grown he had set upon humiliating Pompey, and the restoration of Cicero was one way Pompey could reassert his authority.' However, he says, Clodius was not pleased about this and, as Cicero was rebuilding his house in November 57, a gang of thugs sacked it and his brother's.

He adds that Cicero wrote a letter to his friend saying (on page 357), 'On 3rd November, an armed gang drove the workmen from my site . . . smashed up my brother's house by throwing stones from my site, and then set it on fire. This was by Clodius' orders . . . Clodius was running riot even before, but after this frenzy he thinks of nothing but massacring his enemies, and goes from street to street openly offering slaves their freedom. . . A rival gang organised by one of the tribunes for 57, Milo, offered some resistance, and the effect was simply to escalate the use of violence in a city where the senate had no effective means of keeping order.' Freeman says Pompey was then given the task of restoring order by reducing the price of corn but, when this failed, he became increasingly dependent on Caesar for power. Caesar subsequently called a meeting of himself, Crassus and Pompey in Gaul, where they drew up the 'Luca' treaty.

The agreement said that Pompey and Crassus should become the consuls for 55, which would enable them to secure commands to follow their year of office. In return they would provide Caesar with an extension of his five-year command in Gaul. Freeman adds, 'The Luca agreement shows how far the senate had lost the initiative and was at the mercy of those with the commands.'

'What could be more degrading than our present life, especially mine,' Cicero wrote in 55. 'I am regarded as a madman if I say what I ought to on public affairs, as a slave if I say what I have to, as a prisoner of war if I say nothing . . . I am as miserable as you'd expect.' '

However, Freeman says (on page 363) that Caesar and Pompey then became caught up in a personal rivalry. This occurred as they both intended to use their consulships of 55 to secure further commands. Pompey managed to achieve one in Spain for five years, and grew armies for Spain, but kept them in Italy. In 54, Pompey's wife, Julia, died and this became seen as part of an increasing divide which had appeared between the two. Meanwhile, he says, Crassus had been determined to lead an army into Parthia, but was nearly 60 and had little experience of holding such a command. Foolishly, he allowed his army to be surrounded and was subsequently killed.

Additionally, he says, news of it reached Rome at a time of maximum public disorder, as Clodius and Milo's gangs fought with each other in the streets and Clodius was killed. They set fire to the body and it raged out of control, burning down the senate building and an adjoining basilica. Crowds started calling for Pompey's appointment as dictator. The senate conceded to allow Pompey to be the only consul until another one was elected in August, and Milo was put on trial in 52 for the murder of Clodius, before being forced into exile.

Caesar, meanwhile, was in trouble. In 52, the Celtic leader (on pages 363–364) Vercingetorix had united all the surrounding tribes and sought to starve the

Romans by cutting off their supply lines, isolating them in Gaul. However, Caesar had managed to corner them at the Battle of Alesia and forced their surrender. Vercingetorix graced a triumph of Caesar's, in 46, and was then executed. Freeman adds that, by this point, the Senate believed both Caesar and Pompey had grown too powerful and voted for them to surrender their commands. Pompey was asked, in December 50, if he would defend the Republic against Caesar if he were to attack, the move which effectively brought the end of the Roman Republic.

Still following the agreement he had with Pompey, Caesar intended to return with his army to celebrate his victory in Gaul. He adds, 'On the 7th the senate passed a senatus consultum ultimum, the emergency decree calling all magistrates to defend the city. If he was to preserve his dignity Caesar was left with little choice but to take the initiative. On 10 January 49, he crossed a small river, the Rubicon, which marked the boundary of Cisalpine Gaul within which he could exercise imperium and the rest of Italy which he could not. He had, in effect, declared war on the Republic.'

He continues to say that (on pages 365–7) there was no uprising in Pompey's favour to defend the city and Caesar subsequently defeated him in a series of battles fought across Italy, Spain, Africa and the Mediterranean. Pompey fled to Egypt, where he was killed upon his arrival by the Egyptians, who handed his embalmed head over to Caesar. He says this put Egypt instantly in a favourable position with Rome. It is likely they saw this as an opportunity to bring their power back into the Mediterranean as an ally of the Romans, or at least consolidate their long-term position in world affairs. Additionally, he adds, Egypt at this time was divided by a conflict between 15 year old Ptolemy XII and his 21 year old sister, Cleopatra. As they had fallen out, she had fled to Syria to gather support. He says (on page 368) that she smuggled herself into Caesar's apartment while he was staying in Egypt and managed to become his mistress. Together they ousted Ptolemy, as Caesar had found an ally who could rule Egypt for him in a way that would enable them to combine forces. In 47, following one of his victories at Zela in Pontus, came his famous phrase, "I came, I saw, I conquered."

Then, he says, the showdown between the old and the new orders occurred and, Quintus Metellus Scipio, the last survivor of the old noble family, and Cato of Utica both committed suicide after the battle which they lost. He continues to say that the old order finally fell when Caesar defeated Gnaeus, the son of Pompey, at the battle of Munda in Spain, March 45. In 49 Caesar had himself appointed as dictator, then (on page 368) consul for 48. Subsequently, he had the dictatorship given to him for ten years in 46, and for life in 44.

However, Freeman adds (on page 369) that the post was clearly designed to be held for only short periods in an emergency and was not suitable for an administrative term in government. He comments that Caesar had cleverly celebrated victories in the civil war by declaring them against foreigners: the Gauls, Egyptians, Pharnaces and Numidians, but questions now arose as to whether he could sustain this role on a permanent basis.

After establishing a system of fair debt settlement in 48, he banned the collegia to curb unrest in Rome and addressed the problem of the poor by reducing the number of families eligible for free corn. Overseas colonies were set up for 80,000 emigrants and citizenship was granted to these new Roman centres. The Roman calendar of 355 days (with 22 or 23 days added every four years) was replaced by the Alexandrian 365 days (with one day added every four years), and measures were taken to prevent the bribery of juries. However, Freeman says, now the situation was starting to look more like an empire, as he had a centralised body with absolute power to intervene on behalf of the people.

It was not long, though, before Caesar's position within the state became a problem. Freeman says, to get anything done he had to reward people, and the Senate in particular had become full of his own army officers and provincials. He adds that Cicero noted that opposition to him was growing, for the reason that he could neither appoint people who were against him, nor could he simply stop running the state. He says (on page 371) that opposition towards him then just seemed to grow until the situation became ridiculous, 'At one festivity a crown was placed on Caesar's knees. Caesar's fellow consul for the year, Marcus Antonius (Mark Anthony) attempted to place it on his head but Caesar threw it into the crowd.' It became a famous symbolic gesture which seemed to suggest that he had so much power that he no longer cared for it.

Freeman says that, as Rome did not yet have an empire officially, many people believed they could prevent one if they could stall the process of its creation long enough. There subsequently arose a plot to kill Caesar on the Ides of March, 44 BC. He says (on page 371) 'One of the conspirators was delegated to throw himself at Caesar's feet with a petition, then pull Caesar's toga downwards so he could not defend himself. The others were then to stab him. On 15 March 44, three days before Caesar was due to leave on campaign, the murder took place as planned. Caesar fell bleeding to death at the foot of a statue of Pompey.'

Part 5: The Second Triumvirate — Octavian, Mark Anthony and Lepidus

Freeman says, retaliation came swiftly from Caesar's side. Octavian, his great-nephew (on pages 372–81), whom Caesar had been in the process of adopting as a son, marched on Rome with eight legions to demand a consulship from the senate, aged just 19. He then marched north to meet Anthony and Lepidus. Between them they could muster forty five legions and, in November 43, they formed the Second Triumvirate.

He adds, 'The west of the empire was divided between them and they took on the responsibility of making laws and appointing magistrates. They drew up a death-list of 30 senators and 2,000 equestrians, and hunted down Cassius and Brutus, traitors and ringleaders of the Caesar plot. They finally defeated them at Phillipi in Greece, in autumn of the year 42.' Mark Antony was subsequently assigned to the eastern provinces, which included Egypt. It was ruled over by Cleopatra, and they subsequently had a love affair. He was also given the command in the war against Parthia.

However, disagreement set in between Anthony and Octavian, in 40 BC, when Antony married Octavian's sister, Octavia, while carrying on his relationship with Cleopatra, with whom he had three children. Lepidus was expelled in 36 BC and, in 31 BC, disagreements between Anthony and Octavian finally boiled over into another civil war when Octavian ordered the Roman Senate to declare war on Cleopatra. Later that year, Antony was defeated by Octavian at the Battle of Actium. He and Cleopatra fled to Egypt where they both committed suicide.

This left Octavian solely in charge of Rome and, in 29 BC, he adopted the title of emperor. Freeman continues to say that, 'In the years that followed he was to forge a permanent relationship with the senators which transformed the collapsed Roman Republic into an empire while still maintaining the pretence that republican ideals and institutions persisted.' He adds, though, (on pages 382–3) that 'Octavian's immediate aim in 29 BC, when he arrived back in Rome, was to play down any fears. . . that he might be a military dictator. He had soon disbanded over 100,000 men and discharged them with land bought out of his own wealth, notably from the treasury of Egypt, which he had appropriated for himself. It was a shrewd move as it bound the veterans directly to him, and at the same time avoided the need for new taxes or confiscations of land.' From the way he did this, we can see how his intentions were to create a smooth transition to the empire, as he made sweeping changes to its administrative structure.

The government of the old Republic had two Consuls and Praetor on top of the Senate, which had formerly regulated the power of the Consuls. This whole structure was theoretically balanced with the interests of the people by the Tribute of the Plebs. However, due to economic and military expansion, the roles of the Consuls had become too powerful and they had dominated the senate, making the Tribune of the Plebs largely irrelevant. The whole top tier was, therefore, replaced with a much wider and flatter system. Directly under the emperor there were more administrative titles at the top and a more even spread of positions of power between top and bottom, much more like in a modern government.

Under the empire, Rome would expand even further, invade Britain and reach its largest size in 117 AD under Trajan. In the meantime, a small religion had appeared in Judah. In the centuries to come, it would replace the national religion of Rome, combine with the Roman Empire to create the Roman Catholic Church, cause the rebirth of European culture, and become the largest world religion... Christianity.

CHAPTER 7

The Birth of Christianity

While Judah had a large degree of self-rule as part of the Persian Empire, it revolted under the Greeks and, as rebellion was starting again under the Romans, an alternative appeared in the form of a new religion. Under the Roman occupation the Jewish had considerable problems conducting their traditional way of life, as the Romans replaced many of the Jewish governors with their own. In traditional Jewish society, a 'Christ' was someone who had been anointed for a particular religious task, hence Christ-ianity offered a solution to the problem by encouraging people to think and act for themselves...

Part 1: The World at the Time of Christ

By the time of Christ, Rome was the largest power in Europe, Han China, with the Xiongnu Khanate to the north, had established an equally large territory in the Far East, and between them lay the Parthian and Kushan Empires. Geoffrey Parker writes, in The Times Illustrated History of the World, '"Two Thousand Years ago, about the time of Christ, a continuous web of complex, advanced societies stretched across the southern half of the continents of Europe and Asia. In the west, Rome had imposed its rule and imprint on the whole Mediterranean world from Asia Minor, through North Africa and southern Europe, to the Straits of Gibraltar, and was in the process of further extending its dominion beyond the Alps and Pyrenees to the Rhine, the Danube and Britain. . . The whole structure was integrated by an imposing network of roads, and communications by sea and river. Meanwhile, in China, the Han ruled a state that equalled the Roman Empire in population and territorial extent. Just as Julius Caesar and Augustus had carried Roman power far to the north, so the Chinese Emperor Wu-ti and the first century BC had carried the power of the Han dynasty to the Tarim Basin of central Asia, far to the west. Separating these two superpowers were two other important states: the Kushan Empire, straddling the mountain passes of Afghanistan and extending south into the Punjab and northern India; and the Parthian empire, dominating Persia and Mesopotamia. The existence — or rather the co-existence — of these great empires meant that vast areas. . . enjoyed internal peace and efficient government, conditions which made possible the growth of trade on a scale never seen before. For the most part it was internal trade, between one province and another. In the west, for example, Italy supplied wine, pottery, oil and metalware to Spain, Gaul, Britain and the western Balkans. But, there was also long-distance trade by land and sea. China was famous for its export of silk, India produced large quantities of textiles (calico, muslin, linen and cotton) for both domestic and foreign markets; other exports included pepper, spices, ivory and precious stones. In return, gold and silver, mostly in coins, moved eastwards from the Roman Empire; also clothing, wine, glass, coral and metals. In between, on the land routes, the Kushan and Parthian empires both fostered this interchange — maintaining and garrisoning the roads, protecting the caravans, and thriving on the tolls.'

The Silk Road, as it became known, was a huge network of trade routes which made connections between Asia, Europe and the Horn of Africa. Beginning during the Han dynasty (207 BC– 220 AD), its Asian section was expanded around 114 BC through the explorations of their imperial envoy, Zhang Qian. Such was its importance that they even extended the Great Wall of China to protect it. During this time, eastern empires traded with western governments and this new balance of power between East and West was a real step forwards from the breakdown they had experienced during the Greek-Persian wars.

Part 2: The Circumstances Which Produced Christianity

Nicholas de Lange says, in ²'Atlas of the Jewish World', (on pages 22–26) that when Cyrus the Persian allowed 'the Jews to return to Jerusalem and rebuild the temple, many chose to stay where they were. Neither the Babylonians nor the Persians interfered with the inner religious and social life of the Jewish communities. They lived on a level of equality with the majority of the king's subjects, and some of them achieved prominence at court.' He adds that when life under Greek rule came (as they conquered Persia in 331 BC) the status of the Jewish way of life was not fundamentally altered; they were allowed to continue with a limited amount of self-rule and encouraged to settle in the newly founded cities. This meant an expansive exodus, known as the Diaspora occurred throughout the Greek world and, he says, the Jews continued to develop as loyal citizens in various regions who enjoyed their presence.

He adds that (on page 23) the Jews comprised a majority of the population in Jerusalem and were largely allowed self-rule, as they had under the Persians. Also that, 'The leadership in Jerusalem was entrusted to the hereditary high priests and to a Greek-style council. They were permitted to administer the territory under their "ancestral laws," and to apply them even to the non-Jewish inhabitants. Although Judea formed part of the Ptolemaic, and later (from 200 BCE) the Seleucid kingdom, there was little interference in the autonomy of the Jewish government until the reign of Antiochus IV (175–164 BCE). The course of events is not entirely clear, but it appears that at the beginning of his reign Antiochus deposed the high priest, Onias, and sold the office to Onias' brother Jason, who abolished the traditional "theocracy" and established the Greek polis, under the name of Antioch-at-Jerusalem. A complicated civil war broke out, in the course of which, Antiochus captured Jerusalem (169), settled it with Syrian soldiers and sanctioned the introduction of pagan worship in the temple (167).

Resistance, however, continued, and under the leadership of Judah Maccabee (died 160) achieved remarkable military and diplomatic success. The eventual outcome was the establishment of Judah's family, the Hasmoneans, as the ruling dynasty in an independent Judea.' Maccabee arose as the collapse of the Greek empire caused various revolutions and uprisings. At this time, the large empires seemed to care less for control of the smaller states than at a time when there was more stability, like when Assyria and Babylonia were the major empires in the region . Known as 'The Hammerer', his guerilla style of fighting was to attack the enemy with a series of lightning fast strikes, known as 'hammer blows'.

He continues to say that Judah itself was then able to extend to a size comparable to that of even king David. He adds, 'Jews were settled in the conquered territories, their populations were forcibly Judaized and some cities which resisted were destroyed. The name Judea was extended to the whole enlarged territory, and its rulers from Aristoboulos onwards used the royal title like other Hellenized rulers of the region.' After the death of Alexander Yannai, his widow Salome Alexander ruled as Queen from 76—67 BC, with their eldest son, Hyrkanos, as high priest. However, the dynasty Judas established was then to be blamed for them losing their kingdom again as, upon the queen's death, a civil war broke out between Hyrkanos and Aristoboulos, during which the Roman commander, Pompey, intervened and captured Jerusalem.

De Lange adds, 'The image of the Roman general and his staff entering the inner sanctuary of the temple — a place reserved exclusively for the high priest — left a lasting impression on Jewish minds. But the consequences were more far-reaching. Josephus puts it succinctly: "We lost our freedom and became subject to the Romans. We were forced to return to the Syrians the territory which we had captured from them. In addition the Romans extracted from us in a short time more than a thousand talents, and the kingship, which was previously given to the hereditary high priests, devolved on laymen." '

In a section entitled, 'Judaea under Roman Rule', de Lange then carries on to say that, 'For the next 700 years, the land was, with only a few brief interruptions, ruled by the Romans. On the whole they were content, like former rulers of the region, to allow Jews to administer their own affairs, but it was they who made or ratified official appointments, and in times of stress they did not hesitate to intervene with force to maintain the Roman peace. Under Pompey's arrangements the area of Judea was much reduced, and it was placed under the supervision of the governor of Syria. Hykanos was ratified as high priest, but he lost his royal title. Later, Julius Caesar made him ethnarch (47 BCE), but by now the real power was in the hands of Antipater, Hykanos' able general. The period was marked by frequently renewed fighting, much of it led by Aristoboulos and his sons, who had not given up hope of regaining the throne. For a few years (40–37) one of the sons, Antigonos, actually reigned as king in Jerusalem by favour of the Parthians, who had overrun the region, but in the meantime Herod, Antipater's son, had been recognised as king of Judaea by the Roman senate (40 BCE), and with Roman help he reconquered the land and ruled it until his death in 4 BCE. . . Under Herod the high priesthood was reduced to little more than a ceremonial function under the king's dispensation. The Jewish sanhedrin (supreme council) was deprived of political power, and replaced by a new royal council. Although a Jew himself, Herod ruled over an extensive territory with a large non-Jewish population and he attempted to combine the roles of Jewish king and Hellenistic ruler. His reign was successful and prosperous, although marked by an appalling contempt for the lives of those around him (including members of his own family). His many grandiose building schemes included the rebuilding of the Jerusalem temple in a Hellenistic style, as well as several palaces and an important harbor at Caesarea. He was the last of the great Jewish kings, and many aspects of his reign recall king David. But he was always aware that his power depended on the favour of the Romans, and that his real role was to execute their policy under his rule. On his death his kingdom was divided up among three of his sons, none of whom was granted the royal title. But, the arrangement proved neither satisfactory nor permanent. Judaea was administrated by a series of Roman governors of equestrian rank, apart from a brief interlude (41–44) when Herod's grandson Agrippa ruled it as king. One of the governors married a daughter of Agrippa, another was of Alexandrian Jewish birth, but none of them had any real connection with Judaism and most were resented by the Jewish population. Roman rule was felt to be military domination and fiscal exploitation. The high priests and their council in Jerusalem had no real power, relations between Jews and Greeks were not good, and various revolutionary movements sprang up.'

Hence, the Roman occupation, while being economically successful, was like no other, as it replaced many of the Jewish governors with their own. This caused significant problems for the Jews in terms of being able to conduct their traditional way of life as, from the start, religion and state had been as one. The social structure of Judah had appeared in its early years organised around tribes. According to Biblical tradition there were thirteen tribes, twelve of which had a distinct geographical territory. The thirteenth, the tribe of Levi, was a priestly group which lived in territories in the other tribes' territories. The worship of a single God, Yahweh, gave them a centralised religious and administrative structure.

As rebellious groups started to grow under the Romans, beckoning people to join, Christianity emerged as an alternative, encouraging people to think and act for themselves. In traditional Jewish society, a 'Christ' was one who had been anointed for a particular religious task. So, the new idea in Christ-ianity was that people could step outside of Judaism and act as a 'Christ' in their own right. It was a progressive step which began to attract followers, as the existing social structure was having difficulty coping with the Roman occupation. It offered people an alternative to the nationalist revolution, as this threatened to bring destruction upon the nation if the Romans were to invade to put down an uprising. Thus, while the orthodox, conservative elements of Jewish society were having a problem speaking out about their issues, being dependent on the Romans for their social status, Christianity addressed the situation in a contemporary manner.

It used the idea that the problems the empires of the Ancient world had caused were because they themselves were a product of an imperfect world created by humans. Therefore, it needed replacing with the kingdom of God. This involved creating a whole new concept of society rather than continually re-creating more of the same type of problems with another new empire. As revolt against the Romans would only take them back to the situation they had in Ancient Judah, what they really needed to do was break the cycle of empires and create a new idea of how to live.

The proof of this was evident in the chain of events which had led through the creation of the four great empires, which became known in Christian history as the Four Monarchies, each of which had surrounded and oppressed Judah in turn. The Four Monarchies theory was a major part of European history until the Middle Ages, and was even used as late as the 18th Century. First Assyria–Babylonia, which had been conquered by Persia, which in turn had triggered the Greek and the collapse of Greece led to the rise of Rome. The direct chain of events moving forward through time only ever led to one empire replacing another. Additionally, while the previous empires had collapsed, Rome was considerably more permanent, larger and more powerful, so an attempt at rebellion was impossible in practical terms.

Part 3: How Did Christianity Appear?

From the start, the way it intended to save people was through the creation of a new type of kingdom, using ideas from religion, politics and social evolution. N.T. Wright says in [3]'Jesus and the Victory of God' (in a section entitled 'Revolution, Politics, Community and Theology') 'The picture of the Communities that Jesus intended to call into being, and the way of life that he enjoined upon them, enables us to hold together various strands that are normally kept apart. The split between politics and theology is familiar enough to us; it has dominated much western thought for the last two hundred years; but Jesus' world remained innocent of it. Less familiar is the difference between social and political action. . . Jesus was propagating local social revolution rather than nationalist (or anti-nationalist) politics... Jesus was implicitly in favour of the liberation of Palestine from the Romans, but the moves he actually made were towards revolution at the local, social level rather than the national or political.'

The rise of Jesus occurred as people at large were being encouraged to become part of the revolution by the nationalists, while everyone else simply had to accept the state of affairs. In other words, as there were people who were happy with neither of these two options, it offered them a new approach. Rather than revolt against Rome, instead, they could 'love thy neighbour'. They prayed for their enemies and lived a peaceful, existence, regardless of the greed, corruption and violence which had characterised the empires of the Ancient world. They used prophecies, like the impending disaster which would befall Judah (presumably, if everyone joined the revolution), and offered them salvation in the belief that people could create a better life for themselves.

The revolutionaries, on the other hand, were more concerned with the position the Jewish nation had already established and did not see why they should give up the society they already had. In other words, the Roman occupation was divisive, and most people continued to be complicit. But, as the situation continued, the barbarity of Rome generated its own criticism and both groups were able to attract more followers. In the case of Christianity, it was the broader idea of the need to create a more global vision of society which seems to have become responsible for its success.

This next map shows Judah at the time of Christ. Bethlehem is near Jerusalem, to the northwest of the Dead Sea, while Bethlehem and Mount Tabor are near Lake Galilee in the north.

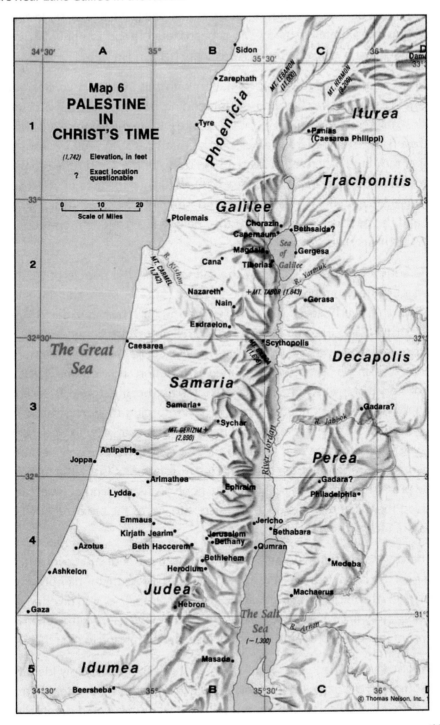

He says (on page 321) that, 'If Jesus was telling a story anything like that which we have outlined so far, he must have had some idea of where it was going to end. No one tells a new version of a story without a sense of what the new ending might be. The retellings of Jewish stories which we find in, for instance, the Psalms, the Qumran texts, the Maccabean literature and Josephus all have a sense that the story is going somewhere; there is an end in view.

When we examine Jesus' proclamation with this in mind, two clear lines emerge. First there are warnings of impending national disaster: a coming political, military and social nightmare, as a result of which Jerusalem will be destroyed. Secondly, there is an assurance that those who follow Jesus will escape; they are challenged to be ready to do so at the opportune moment.' Thus, even though its implications reach much further, the idea of Christianity as a social movement arises out of the proposition of a new covenant between God and the people of Judah, which they believe is a genuine proposition for them which has arisen through history.

He adds (on pages 274–5) that the call to live as the people of the new covenant comes from his proclamation that he is the Messiah, and those who come with him will be saved. The disciples, who function heavily in the founding of Christianity, also become involved in the religion which continues after his death, so presumably these two plots are interlinked. He then says, 'The story of kingdom, which we have seen, functioned as invitation and welcome. It was the kind of story that invites its hearers to make it their own: the story of Israel finally being released from bondage, and of YHWH returning to Zion, included the emphasis that the gates were being thrown wide open to all who would come and give loyalty to Jesus. But the story did not stop there. Precisely because it concerned the renewal of the covenant, the restoration of Israel, the fulfilment of the promises, and the realization of the hope, Jesus' retelling of Israel's story included the call and challenge to his hearers to live as the renewed Israel, the people of the new covenant.'

The covenant, stemming all the way back to the Ark of the Covenant, has long been an issue with the Jewish people and the fact that it had previously been renewed indicated that it could be changed again. They also diverted their followers away from the revolutionary perspective by changing the enemy to Satan, not Rome, as part of the new global perspective arising in their theology.

Wright says (on page 451) in a section entitled 'The Real Enemy Identified: not Rome, but the Satan', that 'Israel's story had sometimes been told in terms of four great empires that had oppressed her. The last one would eventually be destroyed when her god finally acted to bring in his kingdom . . . In first-century Jewish retellings of this story, the fourth kingdom was bound to be Rome. But Rome, from Jesus' point of view, could be at most the penultimate enemy. The pagan hordes surrounding Israel were not the actual foe of the people of YHWH. Standing behind the problem of Israel's exile was the dark power known in some Old Testament traditions as the satan, the accuser . . . The struggle that was coming to a head was therefore cosmic, not merely martial (just as the Temple was the focal point not merely of Israel but of the cosmos; one constantly has to remind oneself of the multi-dimensional way in which first century Jews understood their world).'

The theory of the Four Monarchies hence became an intrinsic part of Christianity. Each of them represented a step forward in the way societies had evolved through the Ancient period, yet each had its own problems and had oppressed Judah in turn. What this suggested was that there was a problem with the way the empires of the Ancient world had evolved; in themselves they were self-centred entities, each justifying their own existence through their own pantheon of gods. The fact that people realised this towards the end of the Ancient world is a large part of the reason why the rise of monotheism occurred and continued into the Middle Ages, as people were looking for a unifying factor which would bring societies together, rather than compete.

Commentary on the Bible prophecies states that, in Daniel 7, Daniel has a vision of four beasts arising out of the sea and is told that they represent four kingdoms. A beast like a lion with eagle's wings represents Babylon under Nebuchadnezzar; a beast like a bear, raised up on one side, with three ribs between its teeth represents Medo–Persia under Cyrus and Darius; a beast like a leopard with four wings and four heads represents Greece under Alexander the Great; a fourth beast with iron teeth and ten horns represents the Roman Empire. So if Rome was the last, what was to be the future from there?

Considering the separate empires which had come to exist on both sides of East and West, it was evident that there needed to be some kind of resolving factor if competition between the two was seen as a problem with global society. The thing they all had in common was the way humans had evolved out of Africa. Judah had emerged directly from Africa, so it was in their interests to resolve the issue. At the same time, we can see the unresolvable element which was created by the world order in the form of Rome — imposed upon Judah, triggering this reaction.

Judah had a monotheistic religion, which put a single, all-powerful God above everything else, but it was only for the Jews. What they needed to create was a more universal form of monotheism, one which allowed a new type of society to exist. Christianity thus offered a solution as a social movement which could grow and attract new members. This is why many Christians attach great importance to this early period, because understanding its whole reason for existence goes back to this time.

The way it functions on a personal level is by offering people forgiveness for their sins which are connected to the past, and allowing them to start a new way of life. It uses the idea that we can accept the 'fallen state' of humanity, which is result of how the human world was created imperfectly.

Leon Morris here describes St. Paul, summing up the significance of Christ:

⁴'4B. Justification, 3:12–5:21

Having made it devastatingly clear that all mankind is caught up in sinfulness, Paul turns his attention to the way sinfulness is overcome. It is central to his understanding of the Christian way that no human merit can ever avail before God, but that the death of Christ on the cross changes all that . . . One of his ways of viewing it is as a process of justification. This is not confined to Paul, but in Paul's hands it takes on an importance that makes it central. It is a way of saying that man has no merit at all; his sin has disqualified him in the heavenly court. But, because of what Christ has done, he can now face that court with assurance. The verdict that will be rendered on the believer is "Not Guilty" . . .

But now a righteousness from God, apart from law, has been made known, to which the law and the prophets testify. This righteousness from God comes through faith in Jesus Christ to all those who believe. There is no difference, for all have sinned and all fall short of the glory of God, and are justified freely by his grace through the redemption that came by Jesus Christ.

In what is possibly the most important single paragraph ever written, Paul brings out something of the grandeur of Christ's saving work. He speaks of the righteousness of God, the sin of man, and the salvation of Christ.'

How Christianity functions as a social system after the Crucifixion is to use that as a point which epitomises the problem with the empires of the Ancient world in general. Their greed, corruption and inevitable guilt is used to show, in comparison to one who gave his life so freely, that people should be able to embody a more universal meaning of life. It encourages people to believe that redemption is possible, not only on an individual level, but for society as a whole. This was appealing, not only to people in Judah, but members of other societies all over the world who were trapped in a life which had been created for them. The missions of the Twelve Disciples included Georgia, Rome, India and Greece. They were preachers who established churches and eventually converted the Roman Empire.

Part 4: Christianity Separates from Judaism

The problem with a new religion emerging in Judah became inevitable as there was no room for an alternative in its theological framework. Thus, Christianity had to break free from Judaism and become a new religion in its own right. Unfortunately, this separated Jesus from the society which created him, and this appears to have led to a divide between Jesus as a historical figure and the spiritual leader which he became as founder of the Church.

In an event known as 'The Transfiguration' Jesus of Nazareth became Jesus Christ in a ceremony held with his closest companions on Mount Tabor. Through it the elements of the situation combined to create the leader of this new religion. By all accounts, he went up onto the mountain and was transformed in a moment of divine inspiration, during which he allegedly spoke with God. This simultaneously changed both his identity and the way other people perceived him. From this point onwards, he was no longer Jesus of Nazareth, but now 'Jesus Christ', the founding member of Christianity.

Many books have been written on his life, but Pope Benedict XVI's book, [5]'Jesus of Nazareth', specifically addresses the issue of the divide between the 'historical Jesus' and the 'Christ of faith'. It is a life-story of Jesus told through various detailed accounts of personal events, including conversations with people who were close to him and the way Christianity formed through the relationships within society at the time. In it, he says, he is attempting to address the relationship between the 'real' person that we find in history books and the 'ideal' figure we find in the Church.

He says, 'When I was growing up — in the 1930s and 1940s — there was a series of inspiring books about Jesus: Karl Adam, Romano Guardini, Franz Michel William, Giovanni Papini, and Henri Daniel-Rops were just some of the authors one could name. All these books based their portrayal of Jesus Christ on the Gospels. They presented him as a man living on Earth who, fully human though he was, at the same time brought God to men, the God with whom a son he was one. Through the man Jesus, then, God was made visible, and hence our eyes were able to behold the perfect man. But the situation started to change in the 1950s. The gap between the "historical Jesus" and the "Christ of faith" grew wider and the two visibly fell apart. But what can faith in Jesus as the Christ possibly mean, as Jesus as the son of the living God, if the man Jesus was so completely different from the picture that the Evangelists painted of him and that the Church, on the evidence of the Gospels, takes as the evidence of her preaching?' In saying this, he is stating that the mortal man, Jesus, must not only have a figurative or symbolic, but a 'real' relationship with the 'Christ of faith', being that they are the same person.

Therefore, if we consider the Transfiguration within the broader context of history, then we can see how the two have become separated due to the way events themselves have occurred. If we can understand why this happened, then we can see the two in the same context. Christianity breaking free from Judaism took it out of the context from which Jesus evolved (in Judah) and gave it a life of its own, on a global scale. However, as it combined with the Roman Empire three centuries later to create the Roman Catholic Church, this generated periods of history of its own, which built on top of what was there before.

In the next chapter we shall see how it converted the Roman Empire through a determined effort to create a better life for the people there. At a time when the nation was in crisis and the national religion went into decline, it created a suitable alternative which would affect the course of human civilisation.

CHAPTER 8

The Byzantine Empire

Meanwhile, the Roman Empire expanded further, producing two centuries of peace while Christianity began to spread its influence. However, during the Crisis of the Third Century, the Roman Empire split into East and West and moved its capital city to Byzantium (modern day Istanbul). Gradually, Christianity superseded the national religion which had arisen from its city-state culture, creating the Roman Catholic Church. Despite being briefly reunited, the western side fell to the Germanic tribes in the AD 400s, while the eastern side continued as the Byzantine Empire...

Part 1: The Principate

When Octavian created the Roman Empire, his aim was to bring stability. However, as this created the possibility of even further expansion, a new type of power struggle arose. Its new system of government became known as the Principate, as the concept of emperor, or 'Princeps', was equated with the idea of 'First Citizen'. Hence, there was no longer a power struggle between the Consuls and the Senate, but the title of emperor became more desirable than ever before and, many times, this resulted in the assassination of an emperor by their successor. At times, power changed hands on multiple occasions during the same year.

Historian David Potter says, in his book 'Emperors of Rome' (on page 6), "One murdered his brother. Another fought as a gladiator. Two were philosophers, while yet another is revered as a saint in the Eastern Orthodox Church. What all these diverse personalities had in common was that they were emperors of Rome. Given the extreme behaviour exhibited by many of the holders of this office, it is little wonder that much of the political comment that has come down to us from Ancient Rome focuses on individual personalities. In polemical tones all too familiar to modern ears, Romans lambasted their leaders as lunatics, murderers or imbeciles or lionized them as heroes or geniuses.'

Most of its history is so closely tied to its leaders that its story can be told through them and the dynasties they founded correlate with the periods in its history. Thus I have continued the story of Rome in this way. Some were educated and coped well with their role, but those who did not often became victims of their own incompetence, arrogance or eccentricity. They all had to cope with wars on two sides: against Germanic tribes in the West and resurgent Persian empires in the East, which eventually contributed to the divide of the empire. The first dynasty was established by Julius Caesar, who created the empire which appeared under Octavian.

The Julio–Claudian Dynasty (27 BC–AD 68)

When Octavian (Augustus Caesar) reformed the Roman system of government into the empire, issues of the old Republic still remained. It was thus of great importance that they did not return to the days of the civil war. Potter adds (on page 56) that, 'Augustus put the imperial system on such a firm footing that even the dysfunctional behaviour of his four successors would not overturn his achievement. The pillars of the new regime were the army's loyalty to the princeps, concern for the welfare of the population of Rome and the emperor's patronage of loyal members of the ruling class. The overarching ideological principle that informed all the regime's policies was domestic propriety. Romans recalled that the years before Actium were haunted by violence and uncertainty, and the ideals of the Republic became inextricably linked with civil war.' Historians were not allowed to portray the protagonists of the old Rome, such as Brutus and Cassius, in a good light. He adds that people were still afraid the system would break down into anarchy, despite the fact that Tiberius who came after him held a firm grip on power.

Tiberius was a relatively straightforward emperor, who inherited a solid position from Augustus and left both the empire and its treasury in good condition. However, Caligula came next, and had previously only held one junior position. For this reason he was unfit for a position of absolute power and, during his terrible performance, he became most famous for a failed invasion of Britain, during which his army were told to take home seashells from the beach and declare it a victory over the god Neptune. Upon announcing that his horse was to be made a high-ranking member of Roman society he was assassinated by the Praetorian guard.

When Claudius took over from him, it was his aim to reinstate confidence in the government. He used techniques in his arguments which demonstrated intelligence and versatility. Price and Thonemann give an example of this: [2]'In AD 48 a small delegation arrived at Rome from the distant plains of Gaul. The leading nobles of the north Gallic provinces were seeking the right to hold office in Rome itself, in particular the right to apply for membership of the Senate. The Senate was, unsurprisingly, not especially keen on the idea. The issue was decided by a lengthy speech of the emperor Claudius to the Senate in support of the Gauls' petition:

Do not shudder at the thought of some dangerous novelty being introduced. Reflect, instead, on how many innovations our state has seen; think how many different changes our constitution has undergone, starting right from the very foundation of our city itself. Once, the city was ruled by kings, yet, they failed to pass it on to native heirs. Instead, it was other men, foreigners, who took their place. Romulus was succeeded by Numa, a native of the Sabine country — a neighbour, for sure, but a foreigner nonetheless. . . it was a wholly novel policy, too, when my great-uncle the deified Augustus and my uncle Tiberius Caesar wished to bring into this Senate house the flower of the colonies and the municipalities, wherever it was to be found, so long as they were sound and wealthy men.'

The question of how to include foreigners into the expanding Roman state had been around since the Social War. Thus, for some time, it had been a sensitive issue and one which required political skill to navigate. This speech showed a proper politician was back in charge of the empire once again and lessons had been learned from the past. Potter also states that Claudius proved his competence through both his invasion of Britain and the appointment of effective administrators who ran the empire smoothly. Potter also states that he has been portrayed as a character who learned to play on his own weaknesses, appearing to be quite simple-minded, while using the company of practical men to guide him, and hiding behind the scholarly image of one who would prefer to spend time in the library, away from other politicians. It is suspected that he played a part in Caligula's death, but this not confirmed. However, in the late 40s, his extramarital affairs and those of his wife became public, and this led to his downfall. In AD 48, while he was away, she engaged in a mock marriage ceremony with one of her lovers and his reaction was to have her executed, along with several others. The next move he made appears to have been a political marriage in an attempt to restore his public image, but it led to his death and that of his son, Britannicus.

David Potter says (on page 66), [3]'Heeding the advice of his Freedmen, Claudius took a new bride straight away, and his choice fell on his niece Agrippina. The relationship was plainly incestuous, but Claudius had the law changed to accommodate his wishes. Agrippina moved into the palace with her son Nero (AD 37 – 68), who was three years older than Britannicus. A highly ambitious woman from impeccable stock (her grandfather by adoption was Augustus and her father Germanicus), Agrippina made sure that Nero was introduced to public life, and soon amassed enormous power for himself within Claudius' domus. She realised that Britannicus could not legally succeed Claudius until he reached manhood at the age of 14 in February AD 55. In late AD 54 she arranged for Claudius to be fed poisonous mushrooms at a banquet. Nero was proclaimed emperor at the tender age of 16, and Britannicus was poisoned a few months later. The people and especially the senate, many of whose members had been unable to penetrate the charmed circle of freedmen who enjoyed Claudius' confidence, greeted the news of Nero's accession with delight.'

Potter adds that it took some time to emerge, but Nero's appointment as emperor was a disaster. Initially, he had little interest in governing and left the state in the hands of competent people picked for the task by his mother. This enabled him to devote himself to poetry and acting. The reins of power were thus held by the famous Spanish–Roman philosopher Seneca the Younger (4 BC–AD 65, Nero's former tutor) and the Praetorian prefect, Sextus Afranius Burrus. He adds 'Nero fiercely resisted any attempts by others to regulate his private life. As part of his mother's succession project, he had been persuaded to marry Claudius' daughter Octavia, whom he found deeply uncongenial. As emperor he began to take concubines and play the field of senatorial women. Agrippina, who was well aware that such conduct had precipitated her brother Caligula's fall from grace with the Roman people, signalled her disapproval. Nero soon tired of his mother's interference, and communication between them broke down almost totally. It was at this point that Nero first met Poppaea Sabina, the daughter of one of Tiberius' generals, and a woman of powerful personality. He planned to divorce Octavia and make Poppaea his wife. Agrippina and the senior advisers counselled against this; Octavia was a valuable symbol of stability and continuity. Nero's response was to seek other counsel and hatch a plot to kill his mother.

In AD 59 Nero arranged for Agrippina to take a trip across the Bay of Naples on a boat that had been sabotaged so that its stern, where she would be seated, would break off during the voyage and sink. Yet Nero had failed to take into account that his mother was a strong swimmer. Having made it safely back to shore, the empress was an object of pity to the crowd that assembled as she dragged herself on to the beach. Her son showed no mercy. Learning of her escape, he planted a dagger on her freedman and, concocting a story that she had planned to kill him, sent a detachment of guards to detain Agrippina and put her to death.

The murder of Agrippina changed everything. Seneca's and Burrus' influence instantly began to wane, as Nero's megalomania took a firm hold. Seneca was fired in AD 60, while Burrus died a year later. Octavia was falsely accused of adultery, divorced and executed around the same time. Poppaea was installed as empress, and a man named Tigellinus (d. 69), previously a supplier of chariot horses for the circus, joined Nero's inner circle. Tigellinus would prove a loyal confederate in encouraging the worst of Nero's vices, and was rewarded in AD 62 by being made prefect of the Praetorian Guard.

Meanwhile, the foundations of the empire began to totter. In AD 60, a violent revolt broke out in Britain, led by Boudicca (d. AD 60/61), the queen of the Iceni tribe. Four years later disaster struck closer to home, when a fire destroyed most of Rome. The Roman version of disaster planning was sketchy, and relief efforts were not coordinated by Nero, who allegedly reacted very badly to news of the conflagration: it is said that he recited a poem on the fall of Troy even though his 'press office' claimed that he was instrumental in fighting the fire. Nero found a convenient scapegoat for the fire in the form of a minor religious sect — the Christians. Followers of this faith were subjected to hideous tortures for their alleged guilt, including being covered in animal skins and having dogs set upon them, crucifixion, and being burned alive.

Nero's regime lurched from crisis to crisis. A year after the fire, in a fit of rage, Nero kicked his wife Poppaea Sabina in the stomach while she was pregnant, causing her death. That same year, a conspiracy was uncovered among members of the senate and the guard to kill the emperor and install a new ruler. A round of executions followed, and Tigellinus and his confederates took advantage of the situation to settle old scores. Seneca was forced to commit suicide, and within the year other enemies were arraigned on trumped-up charges. In this orgy of bloodletting, Nero's advisers blundered by charging Corbulo, the all-conquering hero of the Parthian war, with treason and executing him. Yet Corbulo had many influential friends and admirers in Rome. In AD 67, when Nero left for Greece to demonstrate his skill as a charioteer in the Olympic Games (which were rescheduled to fit round his visit), a serious conspiracy arose among various generals and governors.

Nero's Greek trip was a great success, and he was crowned victor in all the events he entered. However, he was immediately summoned back to Rome by a letter from his freedmen warning of the conspiracy. Nero arrived too late to change the course of events. In March, AD 68, the governor of one of the Gallic provinces proclaimed his loyalty to the Roman government rather than to Nero; the governor of Judaea, who commanded a powerful army assembled to suppress the revolt that had broken out there in AD 66, suddenly suspended military operations, and Galba, the governor of a Spanish province, had himself proclaimed emperor. The commander of the major army in Germany switched sides to support Galba. Within Rome itself a fifth column was at work, which enjoyed the support of the Praetorian Guard. Its commanders may have grown weary of Nero and taken the pragmatic view that their troops were no match for a seasoned provincial army. On 9 June, AD 68, the guard declared for Galba and the senate deposed Nero, declaring him an enemy of the state. Nero fled the palace, making for the house of a freedman named Phaon, not knowing that Phaon had already betrayed him. As he heard his captors approach, Nero stabbed himself to death. Vain and deluded to the last, the emperor's reported last words were 'How great an artist dies with me!' '

The Year of the Four Emperors and Flavian Dynasty (AD 68–96)

Thus began a period of instability, as the dynasty which had founded the Roman Empire had lost power and several short reigns followed. Galba had loyally served Claudius, earning his reputation in the military, then became a Praetor in 20 and Consul in 33. In early 68 he had learned of Nero's plan to execute him, and put himself in a position whereby he could take power following Nero's death. As an emperor he put heavy taxes on provinces which failed to recognise his authority, and rarely accepted citizen requests. It appeared that he had little vision or ambition and saw himself as having to rule out of necessity, but succeeded by managing the state's finances while in office.

On January 1st, AD 69, unpaid soldiers in Germania Superior rebelled and destroyed his statues, followed by another group in Germania Inferior who proclaimed that Vitellius should become emperor instead. When Galba named Lucius Calpurnius Piso as his successor, he was assassinated by Marcus Salvius Otho, who had expected to be chosen for the role. He took power through the Praetorian guard, who declared him emperor. Galba initially sought to put the rebellion down, but was killed by a unit of Otho's cavalry, along with Piso. Otho committed suicide after losing the Battle of Bedriacum to Vitellius' troops.

However, Vitellius was only Roman Emperor for eight months, making insignificant adjustments to the empire and was accused of being an unambitious glutton. Subsequently, rival legions in the east declared their leader, Vespasian, to be emperor and killed Vitellius at the second Battle of Bedriacum in December, AD 69, founding the Flavian dynasty. His son, Titus, reigned from AD 79–81, the first ever to be the biological son of the previous emperor. He was a military commander who conquered Jerusalem during the First Roman–Jewish War (which ended with the destruction of the Second Temple, a million dead and 97,000 captured). For this, he was awarded an official Triumph, and the Arch of Titus stands to this day. Two crises occurred during this reign: Mount Vesuvius erupted on August 24th, AD 79, covering Pompeii and Herculaneum in ash, and a year later a three day fire in Rome destroyed a number of important buildings which he launched projects to rebuild. However, he died of a fever after just two years.

Domitian, his brother, inherited the position and held it from 81 to 96, the longest since Tiberius. He was an authoritarian, which brought him into conflict with the senate, and was eventually assassinated by a conspiracy by the Praetorian Guard and his own freedmen. However, he was an efficient autocrat and his cultural, economic and political programs created stability which lasted into the next century. He revalued the coinage, improved the empire's border defences and launched a huge repair operation to restore Rome.

The Nerva–Antonine Dynasty (AD 96–192)

Nerva, known as the first of the 'Five Good Emperors', ruled from AD 96 to 98. At 65 years old, he had served the empire since Nero, and played a part in exposing the Piso conspiracy of AD 65. Under the Flavians he attained consulships in 71 and 90, during the reigns of Vespasian and Domitian.

When Domitian was assassinated, Nerva was declared emperor by the Senate, the first time it had elected an emperor. He immediately promised to return the liberties which had been taken away during the rule of Domitian and set about restoring order. However, his brief reign suffered from bad finances and he was unable to control his army. A revolt by the Praetorian Guard in 97 forced him to adopt an heir, Trajan, who was a young and popular general, before he died of natural causes in January 98.

Under Trajan, the Roman Empire reached its greatest size. He embarked upon massive building and social welfare programs which reshaped Rome, leaving behind Trajan's Forum, Market and Column. His conquest of Dacia captured several large gold mines, he annexed the Nabataean kingdom, and created the province of Arabia Petraea. War against the Parthian Empire led to the sack of Ctesiphon (its capital), and the annexation of Armenia and Mesopotamia. However, while sailing back to Rome in AD 117, he died of a stroke.

He was succeeded by his adopted son of Spanish origins, Hadrian, from 117 to 138. He rebuilt the Pantheon, built the Temple of Venus and Roma, and Hadrian's Wall on the Anglo-Scottish border. He spent much of his time travelling throughout the empire and, a great admirer of Ancient Greece, sought to make Athens the cultural capital of Europe by building a number of temples there. He had no children, a male Greek lover called Antinous, and his wife, Sabina, is believed to have had an affair with his secretary. In his later years, he adopted Antoninus Pius as his successor.

Antoninus Pius reigned from AD 138 to 161. There were no major revolts or other military problems in this period, and he never left Italy. His military campaigns in southern Scotland led to the construction of the Antonine Wall. An effective administrator, he left a large surplus in the treasury, expanded free access to drinking water across the empire, encouraged legal conformity and the enfranchisement of freed slaves, and adopted Marcus Aurelius as his heir.

Marcus ruled jointly with Lucius Verus from AD 161, refusing to accept the role from the senate unless Verus was granted equal powers. When Verus died in 169, Marcus ruled with his son Commodus from 177. He defeated the Parthian Empire, sacking the capital Ctesiphon (for a second time) in 164. They were also victorious against the Marcomanni, Quadi and Sarmatians in the Marcomannic Wars. However, the threat of the Germanic tribes was increasing, as was the persecution of Christians.

Commodus ruled alone after Aurelius' death in 180 and this is said to mark the end of the 'Pax Romana', the long period of relative peace following the end of the Roman Republic. It is also said to mark the beginning of the decline of the Roman Empire, due to several economic, social and political factors. When Commodus devalued the Roman currency, the biggest since Nero, it was said by Dio Cassius (a Roman historian) that the empire moved from a period of gold, to one of iron and rust.

He had little interest in administrating and left many affairs of the state to Saoterus, a freedman from Nicomedia who had become his chamberlain. This prompted anger from the Senate and a number of conspiracies arose. After an attempt on Commodus' life in 182, Saoterus was implicated by the praetorian prefect Tigidius Perennis, and then murdered by the freedman Cleander, who succeeded him as chamberlain. Commodus subsequently attempted to take charge of the situation eventually but, did not have the political ability to cope with running the empire alone. After a series of unrests and executions, he became a megalomaniac, declaring himself the son of Jupiter and ritually 're-founding' Rome with himself as the new Romulus. Subsequently, he changed the months of the year to match his own twelve names and, in December 192, a plan to replace him with Pertinax emerged which resulted in him being poisoned, then strangled in his private chambers by his own wrestling partner.

Year of the Five Emperors and Severan Dynasty
(AD 193–235)

Pertinax began the Year of the Five Emperors, which was chaotic even by Roman standards. He was the son of a freed slave who worked as a teacher before becoming an army officer. Following the Parthian war in the 160s, he achieved a higher rank in the military before moving into politics, became a provincial governor, then urban prefect, then a member of the senate.

However, he tried to immediately implement a number of measures which caused a massive reaction, the most significant of which was the restoration of discipline among the Praetorian Guards, which led to him being assassinated by them. To make things worse, the Praetorians auctioned off the imperial title, which was taken by the wealthy senator Didius Julianus, whose appointment was met by public disorder and lasted only sixty-six days. Hearing of the outcry, Septimius Severus, commander of the legions of Pannonia, marched on Rome gathering support along the way and deposed him. Yet, he still had to fight against two rival generals who also had claims to the throne. Pescennius Niger was defeated at the Battle of Issus in 194, and Clodius Albinus three years later at the Battle of Lugdunum in Gaul.

Severus also waged a short campaign in the east to annexe the Kingdom of Osroene and another against the Parthians, sacking their capital Ctesiphon (for the third time) in 197 and extending the eastern frontier of the empire to the Tigris river. In 202, he campaigned in Africa and Mauretania, capturing the capital city of Garama. In 208 he invaded Scotland, but fell ill and died in early 211. He was then succeeded by his sons Caracalla and Geta, founding the Severan Dynasty.

The rule of Caracalla was most famous for his edict of 212, which granted citizenship to almost all the freemen of the empire. At the time of Augustus, only 4–7% of the empire had citizenship, but it strengthened voting rights. However, he was more of a soldier than an emperor, and killed Geta when they could not agree on how to rule. He then embarked on a campaign to destroy all evidence of Geta's existence and made it a crime to even speak of his name. Thus, he is known as one of the most tyrannical emperors. However, he also built the second largest baths in Rome and increased army pay by up to a third. He was assassinated in 217 in Edessa by a disaffected soldier, Martianis, under the influence of Praetorian Guard Prefect Macrinus, following a military campaign against the Parthians.

Macrinus was a Berber from Mauretania, and ruled with his son Diadumenian as co-emperor. However, he never had the chance to return to Rome. As Caracalla had set the empire at war with several kingdoms (including Parthia, Armenia and Dacia), Macrinus' attempt to bring diplomatic stability brought additional financial costs which led to unrest in the military. Caracalla's aunt then started a rebellion in Legio III Gallica, proclaiming that her eldest grandson (Caracalla's cousin), the 14 year old Elagabalus, should be emperor, and Macrinus was defeated in June, 218, at the battle of Antioch.

Elagabalus was clearly too young to hold such a position, and entirely departed from Roman traditions and culture. Historians have suggested that he showed a total disregard for religious traditions and social taboos. He replaced the traditional head of the Roman pantheon, Jupiter, with the deity 'Elagabalus', of whom he was the high priest, and made leading members of Rome's government participate in the religious rites of this 'deity'. He was married as many as five times to male courtiers thought to have been his lovers, and is even believed to have prostituted himself in the imperial palace. This eventually offended the Praetorian Guard and senate so much that he was assassinated, aged 18, and replaced by his cousin Severus Alexander in March AD 222.

Severus was only 13 and spent much of his time under his mother's supervision, but his reign was peaceful and prosperous. However, Rome at this time was challenged militarily by the rising Sasanian Empire and the tribes of Germania. When he attempted to bribe the Germanic tribes, he was assassinated by his own troops, aged 26, following the nomination of Maximinus to replace him, leading to the Crisis of the Third Century.

The Crisis of the Third Century and Gordian Dynasty (AD 235–84)

During this period the Roman Empire broke down into three main parts: the central Roman area, the western Gallic Empire (Britain, France and, temporarily, Hispania) and the eastern Palmyrene Empire (which included the provinces of Eagyptus, Palaestina and Syria). It is also known as the Military Anarchy, or Imperial Crisis.

Maximinus was competent, mainly as he had worked his way up the ranks of the Roman army. As emperor he successfully fought the Germanic tribes, then the Dacians and Sarmatians in the winter of 235–6. However, following a full-scale revolt in the province of Africa, Gordian I and II were declared co-emperors, supported by the senate, which Maximinus opposed with military force.

Gordian I and II were both killed by the governor of Numidia, a supporter of Maximinus, but the senate then appointed a further two emperors of their own, Pupienus and Balbinus. When this proved unpopular with the people of Rome, they made Gordian III the heir. In 238, the resulting siege of Rome by Maximinus ended with him being killed by his own soldiers. However, Pupienus and Balbinus were greeted with popular riots, military discontent and a fire which ravaged Rome. They were then killed by the Praetorian guard, making Gordian III the sole emperor.

Gordian was only 13 at the time, the youngest ever, thus control of the government was given to his family. In 241, he was married to Furia Sabinia Tranquillina, the daughter of the praetorian prefect, Timesitheus, who then became the real ruler of the empire. While Gordian joined the army, Rome was attacked by the Persians and Timesitheus died. Marcus Julius Philippus (Philip the Arab), the new Praetorian Prefect, made sure Gordian was sent on a retaliatory expedition from which he never returned.

Philip was born in the Roman province of Arabia, and was emperor from 244–9. His brother prompted him to take the role in the Praetorian Guard when Timesitheus died, and it has been alleged that he conspired in Gordian's death. He spent much of Rome's money on a settlement with the Persians (following a Roman defeat), consisting of 500,000 denarii. He then raised taxes, but failed to pay off the Germanic tribes. When war with Persia broke out again, in 245, he was in Rome for the AD 248 celebration of Rome's 1000th anniversary. Then, the legions in Pannonia rebelled, declaring Tiberius Claudius Pacatianus emperor. At the same time, incursions by the Germanic tribes (including the Quati and the Goths) raided Pannonia. Other uprisings emerged and Philip offered to resign but, after receiving the backing of the Senate, he appointed Decius with an army to restore order. The Danubian armies then proclaimed Decius emperor instead and he marched on Rome. Philip was killed after meeting him with his own army near Verona, in September 249.

Decius ruled from 249 to 251. He was a senator who had served as Suffect Consul in 232, governor of Moesia and Germania Inferior, governor of Hispania Tarraconensis (235–238), and urban prefect of Rome under Philip the Arab. He improved the position of the state, including a national program to restore state religion. However, a number of Christian Bishops refused to sacrifice on behalf of the emperor, including Pope Fabian in 250, which led to them being tortured and executed. Meanwhile the plague broke out, reaching its height between 251–66 (claiming 500 lives a day in Rome). Decius' reign was ended when the Goths crossed the Danube to raid Moesia and Thrace, as both he and his son were killed in the battle which ensued.

Trebonianus Gallus then reigned in 251 with Hostilian and, from 251–3, with Volusianus. When the Roman troops heard of Decius' defeat, they proclaimed him emperor despite the fact that Hostilian was Decius' son and heir, and they co-ruled. Shortly after, though, Hostilian disappeared from the historical record. During this time, an Antiochene nobleman, Mariades, rampaged in Syria and Cappadocia then defected to the Persians. Gallus deployed his troops, but the Persians invaded Armenia and defeated a large Roman army in 253. The Persians then attacked Syria and the Scythians invaded Asia Minor by sea. However, when Lower Moesia was attacked in early 253, Aemillanus, governor of Moesia Superior and Pannonia, successfully defended it. The army then declared that Aemillanus should be emperor instead and he marched on Rome. Hence, both Gallus and Volsianus were killed in 253.

Aemillanus was only emperor for three months when another general, Valerian, marched on him and declared himself emperor (253–260). It is said by some that Valerian's army was actually mobilised earlier in support of Gallus, but others say it was raised in support of Valerian's bid for the emperorship. However, Valerian was then captured by the Sasanian-Persian king, Shapur I, following the Battle of Edessa.

Gallienus, who had been co-emperor (253–260), had taken the western provinces while Valerian fought against the Persians in the east. At this point, the Romans were once again fighting the Germanic tribes instead of appeasing them. He ruled with Saloninus in 260, then alone. Following the capture of Valerian, he issued a decree of tolerance towards Christians and created cavalry units which could be deployed quickly throughout the empire. However, both east and western sides of the empire (Gallic and Palmyrene territories) ceded from the empire and became autonomously administrated units.

After this Claudius Gothicus took power after Gallienus was struck down by conspirators, in 268. He was emperor from 268–270, and defeated the Goths to the extent that they were pushed back for a whole century. Under his reign, Rome also recaptured Hispania from the Gallic Empire. However, while travelling to the east, he contracted the plague and died in 270.

His successor, Quintillus, lasted only a few months, being killed in an internal dispute, and was succeeded by Aurelian (270–275). He defeated the Alamanni, the Goths, the Vandals, the Juthungi, the Sarmatians and the Carpi. Additionally, he restored the eastern provinces after his conquest of the Palmyrene Empire in 273 and conquered the Gallic Empire in the west. In 275, though, as he was marching eastwards towards another campaign against the Sasanians, he was murdered by the Praetorian Guard while waiting in Thrace to cross over into Asia Minor.

Tacitus then became emperor (275–76) and fought with the Goths, Heruli and barbarian mercenaries who had been assembled to assist with a campaign in the east which was cancelled, and subsequently plundered towns in the east Roman provinces. Chosen by the Senate and ratified by the army, he died the next year of a fever.

Florianus was allegedly Tacitus' maternal half-brother, who he had appointed as Praetorian Prefect during his campaign against the Goths. He was chosen by the army in the west without the approval of the Senate and, while he was fighting the Heruli in the west, Probus was declared emperor by troops in the east. Florianus had the support of Gaul, Britain, Hispania, Italia, Africa and Mauretania, and the battle was fought in Cilicia. It is believed that Probus was the more experienced general and Florianus was assassinated by his own troops as they lost confidence in him.

Probus was then emperor from 276 to 282. He strengthened the position of the empire in the Rhine and Danube area, after abandoning much of Germanicus Superior. He fought wars against Germanic invaders who attacked over the Rhine in 278, the Vandals in 279–80, and put down three revolts in 280–1. He had a policy of keeping his troops busy while not at war, planting vineyards in the devastated province of Gaul and Panonnia, which was integrated with the policy of re-settling of conquered Germanic tribes in order to revive their economies. However, he was killed by his own soldiers who, it is said, rebelled over being used for civic and other non-military purposes. Carus was then declared the new emperor by them, apparently unwillingly.

The 60 year old Carus was then emperor from 282–3. He successfully fought the Germanic tribes along the Danube frontier, but died shortly after his forces sacked Ctesiphon (for the fourth time). It is generally believed that he died from natural causes, due to the fact that he was succeeded by his sons, Carinus and Numerian.

Carinus (283–5) successfully fought the Quadi but, when he returned to Rome, accounts claim he abandoned himself to all kinds of excess. Meanwhile, the army in the east was returning with Numerian, who was found dead at

Chalcedon on the way. Diocletian, commander of his bodyguards, claimed he was assassinated, and was then himself proclaimed emperor by the soldiers there. When Carinus found out and opposed this, he lost the Battle of the Margus River and Diocletian succeeded him from 284–305.

Part 2: The Dominate

Under Diocletian the entire governmental system changed. In an effort to bring stability to the office of emperor itself, it was designed to ensure a legitimate line of succession existed. Hence, we see another change in its administrative structure from the Principate system which had been established under Augustus. The Dominate ('Dominus' meaning 'Lord') divided the empire into eastern and western sides, each of which was then sub-divided into two regions, one with their own emperor and a region with a co-emperor acting as deputy and heir. The emperors were referred to as the 'Augustus', and each nominated their own deputy, who was referred to as the 'Caesar'. Thus, the emperorship was shared between a set of individuals who were known as the 'Consortium imperii'. Diocletian created this system, and it became known as the Tetrarchy (government of four).

The Constantinian Dynasty (284–364 AD)

Under Diocletian, Maximian was appointed as fellow emperor in 286, while Constantius I and Galerius became junior emperors in 293. Each ruled over one quarter of the empire, which was divided into four districts. The position of the empire did not change much internationally, though, and they soon found themselves facing the same threats. The Sarmations and Carpi were defeated (AD 285–99), the Alamanni (288), along with uprisings in Egypt (297–8), and the Persian capital, Ctesiphon, was sacked again (299). At home, they added new regional centres in Nicomedia, Mediolanum, Antioch and Trier — closer to the empire's borders, producing the most bureaucratic system the empire ever had.

This map shows the four territories of the empire which existed at this time. Constantius was the Caesar in France and Britain, while Maximian ruled as Augustus in Italy, Africa, Spain and the western Mediterranean. On the eastern side, the eastern Mediterranean was divided between Galerius, who was the Caesar in Greece and Illyria, and Diocletian, who was the Augustus of Turkey, Syria, Palestine, Arabia and Egypt.

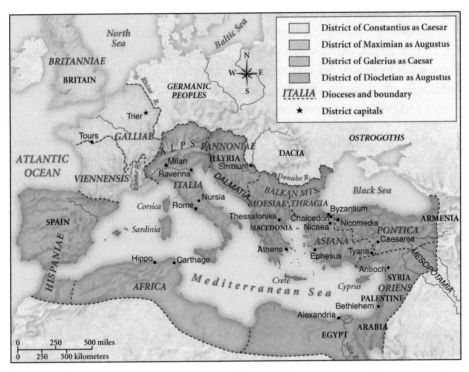

Economic growth further expanded the size of the state itself, meaning that both military and civil expenditure increased, leading to higher taxation. From 297 the tax system was standardised, creating greater efficiency, but Diocletian's 301 Edict of Maximum Prices (designed to halt inflation) failed to recognise the law of supply and demand, and was thus considered counter-productive. His 303–311 persecution of the Christians shows his reign to have been somewhat autocratic and, although it appears to have brought stability, his administrative reforms created a new level of centralisation. Thus, it shifted from a republican style to one of authoritarianism. In May 305, both he and Maximian retired from office (at Diocletian's request), the first to retire as senior emperors.

However, the stability established by the Tetrarchy would not last. In 304, the Dacians threatened to take power for themselves as Galerius managed to engineer a meeting with Maximian to usurp the succession. Up until that point, Constantius's son (Constantine) and Maximian's son (Maxentius) were to be promoted to Caesar when Diocletian and Maximian had retired. However, Galerius had convinced Diocletian (who, in turn, convinced Maximian) to adopt Galerius's nominees, Severus and Maximinus Daia. Both of these new Caesars were connected to Galerius and, through them, he hoped to rule with absolute power.

In Milan, Maximian proclaimed Constantius the new Augustus and Severus the new Caesar. Diocletian, considered the senior emperor, performed the same act in Nicomedia, with Galerius as Augustus and Maximinus Daia as Caesar. Constantius took over the western side of the empire and Galerius took the east. Constantius then launched a campaign against the Picts, but died the next year in York and declared his son, Constantine, as his successor.

Galerius, on the other hand, declared that Severus should become emperor. At the same time, Maxentius, son of the former emperor Maximian, decided to rebel against the taxation of Italy in Rome, declaring himself emperor. Previously, Italy had not been subject to taxation, and Galerius had caused outrage by subjecting its citizens to torture in order to carry out extensive wealth-assessments. When Galerius sent Severus to deal with the matter, Maxentius offered his father the role of co-emperor, which he controversially accepted. Severus moved towards Rome to besiege it with an army (previously commanded by Maximian) which changed sides. He then fled to Ravenna, but was forced to surrender and died a captive in 307. Galerius then invaded Italy on his own, but made little progress. He offered them a meeting, but when this failed he was forced to withdraw, allowing his troops to riot in northern Italy. In 308, Galerius arranged a meeting (at Carnuntum, on the Danube) with Diocletian and Maximian, through which he organised a plan by which Licinius, a companion of Galerius, would become Augustus of the west, with Constantine as his Caesar. In the east, Galerius would remain Augustus and Maximinus his Caesar. Maximinus, however, then demanded the position of Augustus (on hearing of Licinius' promotion). The empire now had six emperors and was divided between East and West.

As the situation continued like this for a while, Galerius undertook civil projects and ended the Diocletian-era Christian persecutions (which he had apparently initiated himself), but died later that year of an illness. According to the early Christian author, Lactantius, who was advisor to Constantine I and guided his religious policies, Galerius was a Dacian who wanted to ruthlessly rule over the Roman Empire, as the Romans had ruled Dacia 200 years earlier under Trajan.

Upon the death of Galerius, Maximinus divided the Eastern Empire between himself and Licinius. However, when Licinius and Constantine began to work together, he entered into a secret alliance with Maxentius, who still controlled Italy. The situation came to a head in a battle with Licinius, in 313 at Tzirallum, which he lost. He fled to Nicomedia, then later Tarsus, and died in August 314. The early Christian writer Eusebius described that he was pagan, and had urged his followers to revel in debauchery and the abuse of power, which had a profound effect on the culture of the empire and influenced Constantine's conversion to Christianity. Although he had been a Dacian like Galerius, and chosen by him to represent the same cause, Eusebius said he was consumed by avarice after the death of Galerius and encouraged both governors and generals alike to abuse their subjects, such that the women there would rather have surrendered their lives than their bodies to the impurity.

Licinius (who had been a close childhood friend to Galerius) continued as emperor until 324. In the meantime, Constantine had defeated Maxentius in 312, then Constantine and Licinius divided the empire between themselves. Licinius became the Augustus of the east, while Constantine took the west. However, they then came to be at war with each other, in 314, with Constantine winning the battle at Cibalae in Pannonia, then again in 315 after Licinius appointed co-emperor Valerius Valens (who was killed shortly afterwards). For about ten years, they managed to co-exist, but Lucinius accused Constantine of breaking the truce, as he pursued the Sarmatians and Goths over their border, following attacks on the western side of the empire. Constantine won the battle at sea in 323, then on land in 324. Licinius was imprisoned in Thessalonica and executed a year later.

This is the point when Christianity is generally seen to be adopted by the Roman Empire, as Constantine put the Christian symbol on his armies. The general theme he propagated was that the evil Dacians had risen to power through a conspiracy which undermined the governmental system, causing a series of civil wars, before the empire was rescued by the virtuous Constantine.

Part 3: The Byzantine Empire

Hence, what appeared was no longer the Roman Republic or the Empire, but a new political and economic entity, as Constantine established a dynastic monarchy. Additionally, it was not just a simple case of Christianity 'taking over' the national religion. We must see it in terms of the way Constantine needed to move the situation forward. Reforms to the system had been ineffective at keeping it stable, and the only other option was to change its culture. In other words, after the reforms of Diocletian had only resulted in a more complex form of chaos, it was ultimately realised that there was a need for a completely new sense of direction. One of the major cultural reasons we can see the Roman Empire already leaning towards Christianity by this time is that it offered people a more universal and less imperialistic type of society, which combined with the fragmentation of the city-state culture which had emerged out of its Graeco-Roman origins. Its democracy was built upon this, but with the empire came a new type of power and Constantine saw that was what needed reform. At the same time, Christianity had grown consistently on a local, social level, driven by the missions of the Apostles, developing into a form which could support a larger following.

Historian Edward Bispham describes Roman religion at the time, in his book 'Roman Europe' (on page 203), "Both gods of the Graeco-Roman Pantheon and deified Roman emperors were venerated across the empire. They were not alone, however, in receiving the devotion of its inhabitants. Local deities survived in urban and rural, public and private, contexts. Moreover, some of these transcended their original confines, moving with administrators, soldiers, merchants, and slaves, to take root in new soils very far from home: thus, the Graeco-Roman cultic melange of Mithraism flourished within the forts of Hadrian's Wall, thousands of miles from its Persian roots. In this situation we cannot hope to define one single entity which is 'Roman religion', or even single coherent phenomena, such as the 'imperial cult'."

He continues to say (on page 225), 'The middle of this century was a time of crisis in politics. . . but the third century was also one in which new religions like Christianity finally came of age, and in which others, notably the so-called

Oriental religions, were in their pomp. The tide of their popularity began in the Severan period, during which they swept across the empire. It is worth examining the religious 'prosperity' of this period. A new religiosity is often connected with the empire's troubles, as men sought to find a more satisfying account of their position in the cosmos, and a better earnest of salvation, in an age of gloom.

The rise of the 'new' cults is also explained by the rebarbative austerity of the 'state religion': this account is as unsatisfactory when evoked for AD 200 as it is for 100 BC. Rather, we should realize that the world had moved on, and that Rome had become a global idea and a universal identity... And their rise cannot be understood independently of a religious 'turn' in the leading philosophical schools, especially the contemplative spirituality of the Neoplatonists, who sought mystical identification with the divine...'

Even though the Graeco-Roman culture continued to spread under the empire, it was undermined at home by the global position Rome had acquired. Also the reason why Christianity was preferred to the eastern religions was because they tended to lean away from the greater tendency in public affairs towards centrality and one-ness. By the fourth century, Christianity had become part of the state. Bispham says (on page 199–200), [5]'We have already seen that the political turmoil of the third century was accompanied by coinage debasement and inflation. The state's resources were increasingly absorbed by wars, the cost of the army, and additions to the annona at Rome to keep the populace loyal (the state went from handing out grain to distributing bread; Aurelian further increased these distributions and added free pork and subsidized wine). The wider effects on the economy may be judged from several other indicators. The evidence from building inscriptions shows a general cessation in large building projects after Alexander Severus, for both privately funded euergetism and for imperial projects. Apart from defensive walls, which were constructed at many cities — including Rome — across Europe from Carcassone in Gaul to Tomis on the Black Sea during the middle and later third century, large building projects resume only with the Diocletianic recovery. Municipal elites, crippled by the cost of public building programmes, became increasingly unwilling to shoulder the duties and burdens of public office, and may have engaged less in town life. The rise of the church during the fourth century provided a new institution that helped to fill the gap in local government... In some regions also the balance of power between town and country may have shifted; in Britain, the richest villas are those of the fourth century.

Social inequality intensified after the third century, and while the general standard of urban living falls below its second-century peak, and overall numbers of villa sites in occupation drop, we find more lavishly ornate residences in the very top band. The position of elite landowners was strengthened by Diocletian's reforms to simplify tax-collection, which tied the rural population to places they were registered, making it impossible for tenants to move. Landowners were successful in getting the government to enforce this against their tenants, although any relationship between this tied 'colonate' and the feudal system of the Middle Ages remains unclear. The late Roman state extended its control over individuals in other ways too, to ensure the supply of goods or services which it could not otherwise guarantee.'

Thus we can understand the conversion to Christianity as being part of the progression in the life of the empire as a whole, as economic decline combined with increasing social inequality created a new type of political environment. Constantine became the sole leader until 337, and built himself a new imperial capital at Byzantium, which he renamed after himself, Constantinople. Then he embarked upon a series of reforms to the military, society, economy and administration. A new gold coin was minted to counter inflation (the Solidus), which was used in the Byzantine Empire and widely across Europe for 1000 years, and he replaced the Tetrarchy with a dynastic monarchy. Also, he had the Church of the Holy Sepulchre built around Jesus' burial site in Jerusalem, the Church of the Holy Apostles on a site previously occupied by a temple of Aphrodite in Constantinople, and had figures of old gods either replaced or made into a new framework of Christian symbolism. His Christian activities led to him being venerated as a Saint by both the Eastern Orthodox and Byzantine Catholic Church.

His reign was thus hugely significant in terms of the development and position of Christianity worldwide, and influential upon it as he oversaw its early debates. Most notably was the Ecumenical First Council of Nicaea, which decided upon the issue of its first heresy, Arianism. Arius (256–336) was a Christian presbyter (senior priest, but not yet of the rank of Bishop) in Alexandria, Egypt. He suggested the concept of the Christ the Son had not always existed, but had been begotten by (God) the Father and, therefore, the two should be regarded as being separate. The opposing view of the Homoousian Christians was that the unity of the Holy Trinity (that is, God the Father, Christ the Son and the Holy Spirit) was inseparable within the context of the formulation of Christian doctrine and, this was the view which was upheld by the first two ecumenical councils. The Ecumenical First Council of Nicaea in 325 thus declared Arianism a heresy.

Yet, the debate continued and, at the regional First Synod of Tyre in 335, Arius was exonerated and Constantine was baptised by the Arian bishop, Eusebius of Nicomedia. However, after the later death of both Constantine and Eusebius, Arius was re-declared a heretic by the Ecumenical First Council of Constantinople in 381. Both Constantius II (337–61) and Valens (364–78), who ruled after him, were regarded as Arian or semi-Arian.

As the capital of the Roman Empire moved permanently to Constantinople, the importance of Rome declined. Following the illness and death of Constantine (337), his sons (Constantine II, Constantius II and Constans) ruled together until a disagreement between Constans and Constantine II (340). It was then Constantius II on his own, after the assassination of Constans by one of his generals, Magnentius (350). After defeating Magnentius, he also fought the Alamanni (354) and both the Quadi and Sarmatians (357). In 351 he made his cousin (Constantius Gallus) Caesar, but had him executed three years later after reports of misconduct. In 355 he promoted Gallus' half brother, Julian, to the rank of Caesar, but civil war threatened again as Julian claimed the title of Augustus. Before they could go to war with each other, though, Constantius II died, allowing Julian to become his successor.

Having previously fought the Alamanni and the Franks with success, Julian engaged in a revival of paganism and campaigned against the Sasanians, but died of battle wounds in 363. He was succeeded by Jovian who re-persecuted the Pagans and re-instated Christianity as the official state religion. Jovian created a peace treaty with Persia which saw Rome's withdrawal from several territories in the east, but was poisoned in 364.

The Valentinian Dynasty (364–92 AD)

A meeting of senior military and civil officials declared Valentinian as the best qualified to be the next emperor in 364. He appointed his brother, Valens, co-emperor in the east, and took the west for himself. He fought the Quadi, Alamanni and Sarmations, and defeated both a revolt in Africa and The Great Conspiracy (an assault on Britain by the Scots, Picts and Saxons). He is known as the last of the great western emperors, having fought campaigns across the Rhine and Danube rivers, but the empire went into steep decline after him.

Founder of the Valentinian dynasty, his rule over the western half of the empire was succeeded by his sons Gratian and Valentinian II.

Gratian was his elder son and had accompanied him on earlier campaigns, sharing power since 367. He was emperor until 383 and Valentinian II from 375–92. The empire was relatively stable, although the Gothic Wars (376–82) meant fighting for territory continued to the north and east in Europe. However, taking a group of Alans (an Iranian tribe) into his personal service created distrust within the army and a general in Britain, Magnus Maximus, started a revolt which led to the invasion of Gaul. Gratian fled to Lyon and was killed in 383. Magnus Maximus attempted to invade Italy, but the eastern Roman emperor, Theodosius, stepped in on behalf of the twelve year old Valentinian II.

The Theodosian Dynasty (379–457)

Theodosius I (379–95), also known as Theodosius the Great, was the last emperor to rule both eastern and western sides. After fighting another civil war against Eugenius (the last emperor to support Roman religious Polytheism), he made Orthodox Nicene Christianity the official state religion. His reign saw the destruction of ancient Hellenistic temples, including the Temple of Apollo in Delphi and the Serapeum in Alexandria.

Together with Gratian and Valentinian II, Theodosius issued the Edict of Thessalonica, which declared Nicene Trinitarian Christianity to be the only legitimate imperial religion, and the only one entitled to call itself Catholic (from the Greek 'katholikos' or 'universal'). After his death, Theodosius' young sons Arcadius and Honorius inherited the eastern and western halves respectively.

However, at the start of the 400s, the Germanic tribes finally managed to unite, and sacked Rome shortly after. For a long time they had identified the weakness of the empire to be the loyalty of its generals, as it was Roman foreign policy to incorporate whole territories they conquered, then appointing rulers whom they felt would maintain order. Alaric of the Visigoths followed in this tradition, biding his time and waiting for his moment, and in the early 400s managed to take advantage of two young emperors who were largely under the guidance of their parental guardians at the time.

Arcadius was Byzantine Emperor (395–408), although he was influenced by Rufinus, the Gallic Praetorian Prefect who had served his father. Rufinus wanted to control both emperors and tried to assassinate Stilicho, the guardian of Honorius. He also prevented Rome from defeating Alaric when it had the chance as, in 395, Stilicho trapped Alaric and the Visigoths in Greece, but his Eastern troops were recalled by Arcadius. The same Gothic mercenaries he recalled then killed Rufinus, in November 395. In the west, Honorius is described as another one of the worst Roman emperors. He reigned from 393–423 and, during this time, Rome was sacked for the first time in 800 years. His main supporter was Stilicho, his general, who had been his childhood guardian and whose daughter he had married.

In 397, the province of Mauretania (known as 'the granary of Rome'), and its leader, Gildo, was thinking about joining the eastern side. Rome feared food shortages if they lost this province and Stilicho declared Gildo an enemy of the state before invading. Fortunately, it was almost bloodless and Gildo was imprisoned before he died. Honorius' capital city was Milan, but when Alaric's Visigoths attacked Italy in 401, he moved it to Ravenna as it was easier to defend. However, it was not best placed to defend central Italy from the barbarian incursions which ensued. Then, in the early 400s, everything changed. The Germanic tribes in Europe became powerful enough to invade Rome and establish Ostrogoth and Visigoth empires in Italy and Spain respectively.

Originally in the Goth army, Alaric then joined the Romans. He was the leader of a mixed band of Goths and their allies who invaded Thrace in 391, but were defeated by Stilicho. In 394 he led an army of 20,000 troops who helped the Eastern Roman Emperor, Theodosius, defeat the Frankish usurper Arbogast at Frigidus, but lost around 10,000 men. He then left the army, became Reiks of the Visigoths in 395, and marched on Constantinople until he was diverted by the Romans. He then moved southwards upon Greece, ransacking Athens, Corinth, Megara, Argos, and Sparta. To appease him, the eastern Roman emperor Flavius Arcadius appointed him master of the soldiers in Illyricum.

In 401 he invaded Italy, but was defeated by Stilicho at Pollentia (present-day Pollenza) and in the Battle of Verona in 402. However, the Roman Senate was then forced to pay a large amount to the Visigoths. Radagaisus then invaded Italy in 406, while Alaric remained in Illyria. But, in 408, Honorius had Stilicho and his family killed, along with all their supporters. Then he encouraged all Romans to kill the families of Goths who served in the Roman army and 30,000 Gothic soldiers subsequently defected to Alaric, who attacked Rome. They sacked the cities of Aquileia and Cremona before besieging it. The result was a massive payment from the Senate and the release of 40,000 Gothic slaves. In 409, they besieged Rome again, declaring that Attalus should be the western emperor. After a power struggle between Alaric and Attalus in 410, they besieged Rome yet again and plundered the city. However, after the destruction of his fleet in a storm, Alaric died.

Acadius died in 408, and his son became Theodosius II of the eastern side from 408–450. Adopted by the Sasanian King, Yazdegerd I, he is most famous for the Theodosian Law Code. Meanwhile, Constantine III rose to power on the western side. As his troops in Britain declared him emperor, he moved to Gaul and took all of his forces to confront the Germanic invaders there. Honorius recognised him as a co-emperor in 409 and appointed his son, Constans II, to assist him. However, there were Saxon raids on Britain, the desertion of top commanders, and Honorius sent Constantius III (who was a general at the time) to recover much of the western side of the empire for himself. He was captured in 411, while Constans II was killed in the fighting. In the same year, the Suebi established the first independent Christian kingdom, in Northwestern Portugal.

During this time, we begin to see the fall of the Western Roman Empire. In 423, when Honorius died, the announcement of his death was delayed, leading to Joannes volunteering himself as emperor in Rome. This prompted Theodosius II to nominate the 5 year old Valentinian III as his Caesar before a brief war ended with Joannes death. Valentinian's reign took place until 437 under the regency of his mother, supported by Theodosius. Its main theme was strong imperial policy and the stabilisation of the west. During this time, there was a significant restructuring of the Danubian defences, victories against the Visigoths in Gaul (426/7) and the Franks (428 and 432). However, there was a major fall-out between three senior army leaders in the west and the Vandals in Hispania invaded Morocco (429). By 439, they had conquered the province of Carthage.

Both eastern and western Emperors sent forces to Sicily, intending to launch a joint invasion force, but both the Huns and Sasanian Persians attacked and the force had to be redeployed elsewhere. During 443 two Roman armies were defeated by the Huns. Anatolius negotiated a peace agreement and the Huns withdrew in exchange for an annual tribute of 687 kg of gold. In 447 the Huns destroyed, amongst others, the city of Serdica (Sofia) and reached Athyra (Büyükçekmece) on the outskirts of Constantinople.

Attila the Hun was the leader of a group of tribes spread across Eurasia which included Huns, Ostrogoths and Alans. After a failed attack on Persia, they invaded the eastern side of the Roman Empire (441) but, after attempting to cross the Rhine and conquer Gaul in 451, they were defeated at the Battle of the Catalaunian Plains. After this, Ardaric of the Gepids led a Germanic revolt against Hunnic rule which led to the collapse of the Hunnic Empire. The eastern and western sides of the Roman Empire then joined forces again and tried to recapture Carthage, but failed again.

Marcian then came to power (450) and reversed many of the actions of his predecessor, Theodosius II, in religious matters and the Eastern Roman Empire's relationship with the Huns. He revoked all treaties, ending all subsidy payments and, in 452, while Attila was raiding Italy, sent an army across the Danube into the Hungarian plain, defeating the Huns in their own homeland. Following this, Attila retreated from Italy.

The Last Emperors of the Western Empire (455–76)

After Marcian came the Leonid Dynasty. Founded by Leo I, he led the eastern side for nearly 20 years. He was competent, and helped the Western Roman Empire reclaim lost territory. Majorian was his co-emperor in the west (457–61), along with Libius Severus (461–65), Anthemius (467–72), Olybrius (472) and Glycerius (473–4).

However, while the Balkans were ravaged by Ostrogoths, there were raids by the Huns and he attempted an expedition against the Vandals in North Africa which failed at great cost. Zeno took over in 474, and saw the end of the western side of the empire, following the deposition of Romulus Augustus and the death of Julius Nepos. However, he largely stabilised the eastern side, which carried on as the Byzantine Empire (although the term Byzantine only emerged later; at the time they were simply known as the Roman Empire). He was an Orthodox Christian from Isauria, in Anatolia, whose family had made a contribution to defending Constantinople against Attila in 447. He then moved to Constantinople and became emperor through his relationship to Leo I, which developed in 464 when he found letters proving Ardabur, Aspar's son, had offered to support a Sasanian invasion of Roman territory. Through this, Leo dismissed Ardabur and it reduced Aspar's ambitions. In 465, while Leo and Aspar argued over the appointment of consuls, Zeno's position was strengthened as he married Leo's eldest daughter, Ariadne. In 467, his first born son became heir to the throne, whom he also named Leo.

In 468, he was appointed as a member of the protectores domestici, and Consul the following year. During this time he was also appointed magister militum per Thracias and led a military expedition into Thrace, but became the target of a conspiracy to kidnap him (Aspar had bribed some soldiers sent by Leo to protect him). When Zeno found out he fled to Serdica as Aspar and Ardabur still had considerable power. After moving from there to Chalcedon, he was appointed magister militum per Orientum. Taking a monk, Peter the Fuller, he then moved to Antioch for two years to carry out this role, putting down the rebellion of Indacus.

After a couple of military achievements and incidents involving the Church, Leo passed a law in 471 that monks should not leave their monasteries or incite rebellion, then had Aspar and Arbadur killed. He made Zeno's son his Caesar, Leo II, before dying in January 474. As Leo II was only seven years old at the time, Zeno was crowned emperor in February. He immediately stopped the Vandals from raiding coastal cities and persecuting Orthodox Christians, which he did with the help of Severus. Despite this, though, he was unpopular with the people and the Senate due to his barbarian origins. For this reason, he relied on the loyalty of two Isaurian brothers, who were also his generals, for support: Illus and Trocundes.

Meanwhile, the widow of Leo I, Verina, sought to overthrow Zeno and put her lover, Patricius, on the throne with the help of her brother, Basiliscus. They caused riots in the capital, and even persuaded Illus, Trocundes and the Ostrogoth general, Strabo, to join their side. By 475, Zeno was forced to flee to Isauria with his wife, mother, and the imperial treasure, where he took refuge in a fortress. Illus and Trocundes were sent after him, and besieged the fortress, capturing Zeno's brother, Longinus. However, back in Constantinople, Basiliscus had killed Patricius and declared himself emperor, and was encouraging people to kill all Isaurians in the city. He also appointed his nephew, Armatus, as magister militum, alienating Strabo. However, with no money in the treasury, this position was difficult to maintain. With the support of the Senate and bribed by Zeno, Illus changed sides and united his army with Zeno to march on Constantinople. Armatus was sent with an army to stop him, but was also persuaded to change sides. Basiliscus then fled to the church of Hagia Sophia. In 476 Zeno was allowed to return to power and executed Basiliscus. In 477 he went back upon the deal he made with Armatus, denying him the title of magister militum, and the title of Caesar he had promised to Armatus' son (also called Basiliscus). Armatus was executed and his son ordained as a priest.

Meanwhile, as the western emperor, Olybrius, had died in 472, Gundobad (the western magister militum) declared Glycerius, the commander of the Imperial Guard, emperor in Ravenna. Leo I refused to accept this and, in 473, appointed Julius Nepos, his nephew. Supported by Zeno, Nepos took his post in 474, deposing Glycerius. Then, in 475, Orestes revolted, causing Nepos to flee to Dalmatia. Orestes then declared that his son, Romulus Augustus, was the new emperor in the west. However, the year after, when Zeno returned to Constantinople, Romulus and Orestes were deposed by the Arian Christian and Barbarian chieftain, Odoacer. He referred to himself as King of Italy, while accepting Zeno as the overall ruler of the empire. At this point the Western Roman Empire fell, marking the point when the Middle Ages began.

CHAPTER 9

The Early Middle Ages

With the fall of Rome, the Germanic tribes migrated across Europe, creating their own kingdoms out of the lands which had formerly been the Western Roman Empire. However, the Byzantine Empire remained a powerful influence and maintained Europe's eastern borders with Asia. Meanwhile, as Christianity spread further into Europe, the Middle East created its own type of monotheism, Islam. Starting on the Arabian Peninsula with the prophet Muhammad, a series of empires appeared which surrounded Europe, preventing any further European expansion. The Papacy subsequently consolidated Europe by converting the Germanic tribes, creating the Holy Roman Empire in AD 800...

Part 1: The Migration of the Germanic Tribes

Odoacer continued to rule Italy with the acceptance of the senate, advised by Zeno and the exiled Nepos in Dalmatia, while the Germanic tribes continued to migrate westwards across Europe. However, Marcian led a revolt in 479 in Constantinople, in which Zeno was captured, but he was then rescued by Illus and his Isaurian guard. Subsequently, there was a more serious uprising by Illus himself, as the widow of Leo I, Verina, attempted to assassinate him, which led to her being banished to the fort of Papurius. Her daughter, Ariadne, attempted to secure her escape, firstly approaching Zeno, who referred her to Illus, who then refused. Then Ariadne tried to assassinate Illus, who responded by retiring from court. He then went along with his brother, Trocundes, and two other associates, Leontius and Pamprepius, to Nicea where he was made magister militum, but then started a revolt in which Leontius was declared emperor in 484. Zeno sent an army to stop them, but was defeated and Illus captured the fort of Papurius, then forced Verina to crown Leontius emperor at Tarsus. However, in 485, Zeno sent another army which drove them back into the fort. Trocundes died a few months later, and a four year siege resulted in Leontius and Illus being executed in 488.

Zeno continued until 491, and events moved to a more organised footing through Anastasius (491–518), due to budget surpluses created by his minimisation of government corruption. He was chosen by Ariadne, Zeno's wife, whom he married. Unfortunately, this upset Zeno's brother Longinus, whose supporters rioted and this led to the Isaurian War (492–7), which finished with the deportation of many Isaurians to Thrace. Anastasius then let the Ostrogoth King, Theoderic, rule Italy as his deputy. As they practiced different versions of Christianity (the Ostrogoths were Arians), the Papacy began to become important in resolving differences between the two.

In the Anastasian War (502–5) against the Sasanid Persians, the cities of Theodosiopolis and Amida were captured (although Amida was bought back). After peace was made in 506, Anastasius built the fortress of Daras, which was named Anastasiopolis. However, the Balkans were weakened and this led to invasions of Slavs and Bulgars. He then built the Anastasian Wall from the

Propontis to the Black Sea and fortified his home city of Dyrrachium. He then left the throne to a member of his own staff, Justin, founding the Justinian Dynasty. A peasant by birth, he was a loyal soldier, and possessed strongly Orthodox Christian views, passing edicts against non-orthodox sects. His reign saw the end of the Acacian Schism, between the churches of Rome and Constantinople. A career soldier with little education or knowledge of politics, he consolidated his position by assassinating political opponents and surrounded himself with trusted advisors. Of these was his nephew, who became Justinian I after him. Warfare during this period mainly involved minor conflicts with Persia, and the most significant crises he faced involved two major earthquakes in Antioch (in 526 and 528) which killed 250,000 and destroyed the city twice.

Justinian I took over in 527 and reigned until 565. During this time, he attempted to retake the western side of the empire. He recaptured Carthage from the Vandals, then Italy, Sicily, Dalmatia, Rome and southern Spain. He also unified Roman law, in the Corpus Juris Civilis, which became the basis of civil law in many modern states. However, in the 530s, there was a famine followed by an outbreak of the Bubonic Plague (542) which killed tens of millions. Justinian caught it himself, but survived.

His nephew, Justin II, succeeded him (565–574). He discontinued several alliances and stopped payments to the Avars. However, when they joined forces with the Lombards (a Germanic tribe of Scandinavian origins) to defeat the Gepids, pressure from the Avars caused the Lombards to migrate further south into northern Italy, which they then ruled from 568–774. From 572 he is reported to have suffered fits of insanity, and was succeeded by Tiberius II (574–82) when the Empress Sophia asked if he could manage the empire. They immediately negotiated a one-year truce with the Persians and another with the Avars, allowing them to transfer troops to the Persian conflict. In 574 Justin made him Caesar. In contrast to Justin's austere economic policies, he gave 7,200,000 solidi to the poor and removed taxes on bread and wine.

In 575 he sent troops to Italy and made an alliance with the King of the Franks, thereby saving Rome from them. On the eastern side, when the Sasanians attacked Armenia, they were pushed back across the Euphrates, leading to a counter-attack on Atropatene. However, Rome was forced to withdraw following a defeat in 577. At this time, the general in charge was replaced by the future emperor, Maurice. When the Persians attacked again, he was able to push them back across Mesopotamia. During his reign as Augustus (578–82) events went back and forth militarily in both east and west, a plot to marry him by Sophia ended with a failed attempt to remove him from power and, in 582, Maurice succeeded him as emperor.

Maurice brought the Persian war to a successful conclusion. He expanded the borders of the Eastern Caucasus, pushed the Avars back across the Danube (by 599), and created the Exarchate of Italy (584) to halt the Lombards. However, he was plagued by constant warfare and, in 602, faced a rebellion from Phocas who declared himself emperor. Deeply mistrusted by the elite, he appointed his own family in high places and purged the opposition. However, it proved insufficient to run the country and, due to the amount of time spent dealing with internal opposition, he could not cope with attacks by the Slavs, Avars and a new Sasanian invasion from the east. The Exarch of Carthage, Heraclius the Elder, subsequently rebelled against him and, in 610, captured Constantinople.

Heraclius, his son, reigned until 641, and oversaw the period during which the Islamic Empire emerged. He took control of the Sasanian-Byzantine War (602–28), during which the Persians reached the Strait of Istanbul, but Constantinople was defended by large walls and a strong navy. Following this he drove them out of Asia Minor and defeated them at the battle of Nineveh. The Persian King, Khosrow II, was overthrown and executed by his own son, Kavadh II, who then sued for a peace treaty. However, the appearance of Islam meant that new empires were competing for land with the Romans in Africa and Persia to the east. Over the next few hundred years, this changed the geopolitical landscape and the Middle Ages began to emerge.

Part 2: The Emergence of Islam

Muhammad (from the Arabic verb *hamada*, meaning to praise or glorify) was the prophet who wrote the Koran, the sacred text of Islam. He was born in AD 570 in the town of Mecca, a mountain town on the high desert plateau of western Arabia. The only son of Abd Allah bin Al-Muttalib and Amina bint Wahb, his father died before his birth and he was raised by his mother, assisted by a nurse called Halima. When he was around five years old, his mother took him to Yathrib, an oasis town a few hundred miles north, to stay with relatives and visit his father's grave. On the journey home, she grew ill and died. Halima subsequently returned him to Mecca and placed him in the care of his paternal grandfather, Abdul Al-Muttalib. It was there that he was exposed to the workings of statecraft and politics, as Mecca was Arabia's most important pilgrimage centre and Al-Muttalib one of its most senior leaders. He controlled pilgrimage concessions and frequently presided over Mecca's Council of Elders.

Upon his grandfather's death in 578, aged about eight, he passed into the care of a paternal uncle, a merchant named Abu Talib. He remained under Talib's protection for many years, working as a shepherd to pay for his keep. In his teens they traveled together in caravans to various trade centres. The other merchants called him El–Amin, 'the one you can trust'. In his early twenties, he began working for a widow named Khadija bint Khawalayd, a wealthy Meccan merchant. He traded her goods to the north and, impressed by the profits he made, she proposed to him. They married around 595. He was only around 25 at the time and she was nearly 40, but they still managed to have six children, two sons who died in infancy, and four daughters.

During this time, Mecca was an important commercial centre for many tribes. Christians and Jews also lived there and there was a large Ḥanīf movement (which lay somewhere between Judaism and Christianity). Hanifs were people who rejected the worship of gods represented by idols in favour of the religion of Abraham, which involved submission to a single God. At this point, tribal affiliations played a major role in the culture of the region, which was polytheistic. Each tribe had a protective god or goddess associated with sacred trees, stones, springs and wells. As well as being the site of an annual pilgrimage, the Kaaba shrine in Mecca housed 360 idols of tribal deities.

In the second half of the sixth century, there was a period of political disorder, in which religious divisions between tribes had been an important factor. As Judaism became the dominant religion in Yemen and Christianity extended into the Persian Gulf, many people were showing an interest in a more spiritual form of religion and, while reluctant to convert to a foreign faith, Islam provided the Arabs with their own version of monotheism, uniting their world like Christianity had united the Roman.

Around 610, Mecca's materialist mentality and traditional idolatry appears to have led to Muhammad to search for a new way of living. At this point he began making long retreats to a mountain cave outside of town, where he fasted, meditated and claims to have been visited by the Archangel Gabriel. After a number of visionary experiences, it is believed by Muslims that he was guided to recite the words of the Koran. It was several years, though, before he spoke about it outside his family.

Around 613, Muhammad finally began to reveal his revelations to his tribe. These were gathered verse by verse and gradually became the Koran. It proposes that God is a singular, spiritual entity whose realm lies over and above everything, surrounding the physical world. He is all-powerful, yet merciful to those who accept this and believe in the truth. Its teachings focus on a universal moral code designed to help humanity in everyday terms, giving examples of practical issues and tells stories of the reasoning behind the outcome of past situations. In a historical sense it is like the Bible, but includes Jewish and Christian history in its own. It mentions Adam, Abraham, Moses, Jacob, Ishmael and Isaac, retelling various stories from the Bible, but adding new perspectives which have arisen since the Bible was written. Both Jews and Arabs are traditionally regarded as descendants of Abraham, and this meant that the eastern side now had its own version of monotheism.

The first section of the Koran, The Opener, is short and gives praise to Allah. The second is the longest and is called The Cow (as it mentions a cow sacrificed by the Jews). It is this section which I have chosen to quote, as it gives clear examples of what Muslims believe in a general sense, before the book goes on to give accounts of particular types of situation. In total there are over 6000 verses, divided into 114 Suras (chapters). They mostly cover the topics of promising success to the believers, tales of what happens to the wrongdoers, commands to the people from God, recollecting stories from the history of Islam, warnings and examples of guidance, instructions on how to rule, invocations and the glorification of God.

'Sura 2 — The Cow
In the name of God, the Gracious, the Merciful.
1. Alif, Lam, Meem.
2. This is the Book in which there is no doubt, a guide for the righteous.
3. Those who believe in the unseen, and perform the prayers, and give from what We have provided for them.
4. And those who believe in what was revealed to you, and in what was revealed before you, and are certain of the Hereafter.
5. These are upon guidance from their Lord. These are the successful.
6. As for those who disbelieve — it is the same for them, whether you have warned them, or have not warned them — they do not believe. . .
14. And when they come across those who believe, they say, "We believe"; but when they are alone with their devils, they say, "We are with you; we were only mocking."
15. It is God who ridicules them, and leaves them bewildered in their transgression.
16. Those are they who have bartered error for guidance; but their trade does not profit them, and they are not guided.
17. Their likeness is that of a person who kindled a fire; when it illuminated all around him, God took away their light, and left them in darkness, unable to see.'

In the first set of verses, it makes clear the difference between the believers and the unbelievers. In general terms, the believers take seriously what has come to them through the prophets of Abraham, Moses, Jesus and Muhammad, and will be rightly guided, the latter will not. A few verses later, it continues by retelling stories from Jewish/Islamic history, portraying Allah as having been present before the time of Moses (being pre-existent in the universe), and even having given him the knowledge of the Ten Commandments:

'47. O Children of Israel! Remember My favour which I bestowed upon you, and that I favoured you over all nations.
48. And beware of a Day when no soul will avail another in the least, nor will any intercession be accepted on its behalf, nor will any ransom be taken from it, nor will they be helped.
49. And recall that We delivered you from the people of Pharaoh. They inflicted on you terrible persecution, killing your sons and sparing your women. Therein was a tremendous trial from your Lord.

50. And recall that We parted the sea for you, so We saved you, and We drowned the people of Pharaoh as you looked on.
51. And recall that We appointed for Moses forty nights. Then you took to worshipping the calf after him, and you turned wicked.
52. Then We pardoned you after that, so that you might be grateful.
53. And recall that We gave Moses the Scripture and the Criterion, so that you may be guided.
54. And recall that Moses said to his people, "O my people, you have done wrong to yourselves by worshipping the calf. So repent to your Maker, and kill your egos. That would be better for you with your Maker." So He turned to you in repentance. He is the Accepter of Repentance, the Merciful.'

It retells the story of Israel in such a way as to incorporate its history. In this way, we can see it becoming a valid successor to the Jewish faith from the point of view of the Arabs. However, some of the Jews responded to this by suggesting that Muhammad had declared himself a prophet, without performing any miracle or showing any personal requirement required by the Hebrew Bible. They gave him the derogatory nickname, 'ha-Meshuggah' (Hebrew: הַמְשֻׁגָּע, 'the Madman' or 'the Possessed'). The claim that Jewish history was part of Arab history was thought by some to interfere with the independence of Jewish thought and their ability to fulfil the Bible's prophecies, which they regard as also being a product of the 'divine will'.

'62. Those who believe, and those who are Jewish, and the Christians, and the Sabeans—any who believe in God and the Last Day, and act righteously—will have their reward with their Lord; they have nothing to fear, nor will they grieve.'

But, it also criticises the Jews and Christians who do not accept the existence of this new faith, and warns its believers not to turn themselves over to them.

'120. The Jews and the Christians will not approve of you, unless you follow their creed. Say, "God's guidance is the guidance." Should you follow their desires, after the knowledge that has come to you, you will have in God neither guardian nor helper.
121. Those to whom We have given the Scripture follow it, as it ought to be followed—these believe in it. But as for those who reject it—these are the losers.
122. O Children of Israel! Remember My blessing which I bestowed upon you, and that I have favoured you over all people.

123. And beware of a Day when no soul will avail another soul in any way, and no ransom will be accepted from it, and no intercession will benefit it, and they will not be helped.

124. And when his Lord tested Abraham with certain words, and he fulfilled them. He said, "I am making you a leader of humanity." He said, "And my descendants?" He said, "My pledge does not include the wrongdoers." '

Here we see that the Jewish and Islamic religions have a recognisable shared history, which also includes the origins of Christianity, making Abraham a true 'leader of humanity'. A few verses later, it then advises them of how to protect themselves from groups who are hostile towards them.

'190. And fight in the cause of God those who fight you, but do not commit aggression; God does not love the aggressors.

191. And kill them wherever you overtake them, and expel them from where they had expelled you. Oppression is more serious than murder. But do not fight them at the Sacred Mosque, unless they fight you there. If they fight you, then kill them. Such is the retribution of the disbelievers.

192. But if they cease, then God is Forgiving and Merciful.'

If we compare this to the introduction of other new ideas, we can see overtures of earlier religions, like the Jewish and Christian. Islamic culture also has its own unique features, for example, in Islamic law interest rates (usury) are banned on all monetary loans. If an Islamic bank organises a mortgage deal, they will get directly involved and buy the house outright, then add an amount onto the price rather than loan the money to the buyer with interest.

'275. Those who swallow usury will not rise, except as someone driven mad by Satan's touch. That is because they say, "Commerce is like usury." But God has permitted commerce, and has forbidden usury. Whoever, on receiving advice from his Lord, refrains, may keep his past earnings, and his case rests with God. But whoever resumes — these are the dwellers of the Fire, wherein they will abide forever.

276. God condemns usury, and He blesses charities. God does not love any sinful ingrate.'

There are also rules for marriage, divorce, inheritance and such like civil matters. A strong theme is that God looks after the believers, and those who consciously do things properly will prosper. Thus it offers a new, single set of rules which are clearer and more unified than the myriad of tribal traditions which existed in Arabia at the time, and many other places in Africa and the East as it spread. Its basic philosophy is that,

'286. God does not burden any soul beyond its capacity. To its credit is what it earns, and against it is what it commits. "Our Lord, do not condemn us if we forget or make a mistake. Our Lord, do not burden us as You have burdened those before us. Our Lord, do not burden us with more than we have strength to bear; and pardon us, and forgive us, and have mercy on us. You are our Lord and Master, so help us against the disbelieving people." '

Islamic jurisprudence: the Quran, Hadith, Ijma (scholarly consensus) and Qiyas (analogy) layout the guidelines for the stance that Islam takes on different matters. From the way that it evolved out of the earlier, tribal period of belief systems we can see that it promotes the idea of moving forward into a new cultural period, where people are encouraged to be honourable in both public and private dealings, linking the two together with a recognition of God's purpose for humanity.

However, despite being designed to promote good relations between people, over the next decade, Muhammad and his followers were persecuted and even physically attacked for departing from traditional Meccan culture. For several years, they faced a trade ban by the Quraysh, which subjected them to near famine conditions. Toward the end of this decade, Muhammad's wife and uncle died. Finally, the leaders of Mecca attempted to assassinate him and, in 622, he and a few hundred followers left Mecca for Yathrib, the town where his father was buried. This migration event, the Hijra, marks the beginning of the Islamic calendar. When they arrived there, its leaders were suffering from civil war and Muhammad united their tribes, creating the Constitution of Medina. Hence, Yathrib became known as 'Medina, the City of the Prophet'. He remained there for six years, building the first Muslim community and gradually gathering more followers.

AD 625–8 is known as The Military Period. During this time skirmishes with the Meccans led to three major battles. The Muslims won the first (the Battle of Badr, March 624), lost the second (the Battle of Uhud, March 625), and survived the third (The Battle of the Trench and Siege of Medina, April 627). In March, 628, a treaty was signed between the two sides, which officially recognised Muslims and gave them freedom to travel throughout Arabia. However, the Meccans then breached the treaty a year later, leading to the retaliatory Conquest of Mecca by Muhammad. In December 629, after eight years of intermittent fighting with Meccan tribes, he gathered an army of 10,000 followers and marched on the city. The conquest went largely uncontested and Muhammad seized it with little bloodshed. However, 630–2 were Muhammad's last years, and he returned to live in Medina. During this time he named Ali ibn Abi Talib as his successor in a sermon given at Ghadir Khumm. Attended by over one hundred thousand people, the final verse of the Quran was revealed there, proclaiming the perfection of the religion of Islam. Over the next three years, he converted most of the Arabian Peninsula and, in March 632, returned to Mecca to perform a final pilgrimage, where tens of thousands of Muslims joined him. After the pilgrimage he returned, but died three months later, on June 8th, after a brief illness and is buried in the mosque at Medina.

The Rashidun Caliphate (632–61)

However, shortly after, a group of Muslims gathered at Saqifa for a Shoura (a traditional-style council designed to discuss courses of action with those affected by them). It was here, on this fateful day, that Umar ibn Al Khattab and various Bedouin tribesmen pledged allegiance to Abu Bakr, electing him the first caliph. He subsequently ruled over the Rashidun Caliphate, causing the divide to first appear between the two largest factions in Islam: he and his followers take the name Sunni Muslims from 'Sunnah' or 'examples of Muhammad's teaching', while the Shi'a Muslims take their name from 'Shī'atu 'Alī', or 'followers of Ali', the successor nominated by Muhammad. The reason for this appears to be that they considered Ali too young for such an important role, yet he was immediately regarded as one of their most senior leaders and later became Caliph himself.

During this time, Abu Bakr seized land from Muhammad's daughter, Fatima, and was victorious in the Ridda Wars against the Hanifs, which were primarily aimed at spreading the new religion outside of Medina, but were also directed at those who would not accept his rule. He also launched wars against Syria and Persia, but died in 634 of an illness before their conclusion. Henceforth, the Islamic Caliphate was born, a system of government unique to Islam. It is similar to a divine kingship, except that the caliph's role is to ensure that only God rules over the people. He is not required to receive any 'revelations' from God, nor is the Qu'ran to be updated, as it is already deemed to be perfect. However, its teachings can be reinterpreted to suit the needs of different societies over time. During this period it is said that healthcare and education were provided to the highest level, assistance was given to the poor and the aim was to create a virtuous environment in which people could prosper. Thus it was a step forward from previous empires, as it actively involved the state in assisting people to live together and help each other.

During this period, Islam achieved the majority of its expansion. The first of the four major caliphates, its name in Sunni Islam means 'rightly guided'. Shi'a

Muslims, however, do not use this term as they do not recognise the legitimacy of the first three caliphates (until Ali ruled as the fourth caliph).

The second Rashidun caliph was Umar Ibn Al-Khattab, who reigned from August 634. He was the appointed successor of Abu Bkr and was from the Banu Adi clan. Under Umar, the caliphate expanded massively, conquering the Sasanian Empire in less than two years (642–644), leading to its fall in 651. This was the last of the Persian Empires before the conquest of Islam and was regarded as a cultural high point. Much of what later became known as Islamic art, architecture, music and other ideas were transferred from the Sasanians into the Muslim world. He also conquered more than two-thirds of the Byzantine Empire, but was killed by the Persian, Piruz Nahavand, in November 644.

Umar was succeeded by Uthman, as had been declared by Abu Bkr before he died. There was an election involving Ali, but Uthman was able to equal him both in terms of cultural standing and his direct relation to Muhammad. Married to two of Muhammad's elder daughters and a long-term companion of the prophet himself, he was from a prominent Meccan clan, Banu Umayya (of the Quraysh tribe). He had also played a major role in early Islam, having ordered the creation of a standard version of the Koran.

Under him, the empire both expanded and consolidated, into Fars (modern-day Iran) in 650, and Khorasan (modern-day Afghanistan) in 651. The conquest of Armenia began in the 640s. He delegated military authority to Abdullah ibn Aamir, Mu'awiyah I and Abdullāh ibn Sa'ad, enabling the conquest of the Sind (in modern-day Pakistan). He also enabled people to borrow funds from the public treasury, and allowed conquered land to be divided amongst conquerers and sold, a practice which had been forbidden under Umar. Mu'awiyah I was appointed the governor of Syria in 639 to stop Byzantine sea attacks during the Arab–Byzantine Wars and, in 649, was allowed to set up a navy. It was manned by Monophysitic Christians, Copts, Jacobite Syrian Christian sailors and Muslim troops, who defeated the Byzantine navy at the Battle of the Masts in 655, opening up the gateway to the Mediterranean. This led to the later conquests of Cyprus and Rhodes.

However, in 656, Egyptian rebels killed Uthman in his house. The cause of this is said to be a multitude of grievances against his appointment of wealthy Meccan family members as governors, over whom he believed he could exercise more influence, and would be more effective in establishing the Capitalist economy he had envisaged. However, when this policy became unpopular, they had started imposing an authoritarian rule upon their provinces. The third caliph was thus declared a martyr, making way for the reign of Ali.

Ali was Muhammad's cousin, the husband of his daughter, Fatimah, and of his granddaughter, Umamah bint Zainab. All the modern descendants of Muhammad come from him. Sources agree that he was a pious Muslim, devoted to the cause of Islam, and a just ruler, in accordance with both the Koran and Sunnah. As a warrior he distinguished himself at the Battle of Badr in 624 and had a special role in protecting Muhammad when most of the Muslim army fled from the battle of Uhud, in 625. Muhammad subsequently made him commander of the army at the Battle of the Trench in 627, where he defeated the legendary Arab warrior Amr ibn Abd al-Wud. He had also been appointed as a scribe who wrote down the verses of the Koran and, as Islam had spread throughout Arabia, he had helped to establish the new order. He was instructed to write down the Treaty of Hudaybiyyah, the peace treaty between Muhammad and the Quraysh, in 628, and ensured the conquest of Mecca was bloodless in 630.

During the 24 years since the death of Muhammad, though, he had taken no part in any battle or conquest. Instead, he had retired from public life and worked mostly as a farmer. Various sources describe an incident at his house, where he was coerced into pledging allegiance to Abu Bkr, presumably due to the dispute over the leadership. Some say he complied willingly, and also pledged allegiance to the second caliph, Umar, before helping him as a trusted advisor. It is said that Umar relied on him as the chief judge of Medina and that he also advised Umar to set the Hijra as the beginning of the Islamic calendar. He was on the electoral committee and one of the two main candidates for the election of the third caliph, and accepted the election of Uthman, perhaps under an agreement that his time would come.

Following the rebellion against Uthman, he was first offered the caliphate by the rebels, whom he turned down, primarily because this would have made them his main supporters. However, when the rebels threatened to take drastic action if a new caliph was not elected within 24 hours, he then accepted it from his own people. The majority of Medina's population, as well as many of the rebels, gave their pledge of allegiance. However, some important figures and tribes did not. The Umayyads, related to Uthman, fled to the Levant. Some remained quietly, but later refused his legitimacy. Sa'ad ibn Abi Waqqas was absent and Abdullah ibn Umar abstained, but both assured Ali they would not act against him.

As Uthman's appointment of his family members had caused the public dissatisfaction which led to the rebellion against him, Ali embarked on a new radical course of action, replacing them with his own trusted companions. However, he was advised this may not be a good political move, even though they had become known for their corruption and plundering, as it would disrupt the stability of the empire. Ali then moved his capital from Medina to Kufa (in present-day Iraq). While some officials did not complain about being replaced, others, such as Mu'awiyah I (a relative of Uthman and the governor of the Levant), refused his commands.

This led to the civil war known as the First Fitna (656–661). It was primarily between the supporters of Mu'awiyah and those of Ali. As demands to take revenge for the assassination of Uthman arose, a large army of rebels led by Zubayr, Talha and Aisha (the widow of Muhammad), captured Basra and put 4,000 suspects to death. Subsequently, Ali's army met the rebel army at the Battle of the Camel. Ali emerged victorious and the dispute was settled. Talha and Zubayr were killed in the fighting.

However, there then arose another demand for revenge, this time from Mu'awiya. Ali's army fought Mu'awiya's forces to a standstill at the Battle of Siffin, but lost the arbitration. Ali subsequently fought the Battle of Nahrawan against the rebel Kharijites, who, as a result of the arbitration, opposed both Ali and Mu'awiya. Weakened by internal rebellion and lack of popular support, Ali's forces lost control of much of the empire as, in the chaos, Sicily, North Africa, coastal areas of Spain and forts in Anatolia fell to other empires.

In 661, Ali was assassinated by a Kharijite plot to neutralise the different Islamic leaders and end the civil war, but they failed to eliminate Mu'awiya. At this point Ali's son, Hasan ibn Ali (grandson of Muhammad), briefly became caliph and came to a peace agreement with Mu'awiya. The treaty stated that Mu'awiya could not nominate a successor during his reign, and would let the Islamic world vote on the next caliph. However, Hasan was assassinated and Mu'awiya broke the treaty, founding the Umayyad Caliphate, thus consolidating the divide between Sunni and Shi'a Muslims.

The Umayyad Caliphate (661–750)

Under Mu'awiya, they extended Islamic territory further, across North Africa into Morocco, Spain, and also Transoxiana, the Sind, and the Maghreb. At its greatest extent, the Umayyad Caliphate covered 11,100,000 square km and had a population of 33 million, making it one of the largest empires in history. Christians, who made up the majority of its people, and Jews were allowed to keep their own religions, but had to pay a form of tax from which Muslims were exempt.

Mu'awiya's wife, Maysum, was a Christian and relations between Muslim and Christian subjects were stable during this period. Despite the Umayyads being involved in frequent battles with the Christian Byzantines, prominent positions were held by Christians, some of whom were families that had served Byzantine governments. Generally speaking, the Islamic Empire spread militarily through its empire, then filled in with its own culture over time, during which increasing numbers of people became Muslim.

Mu'awiya used Syria as a somewhat secular power base with Damascus as its capital. His dynasty, the Sufyanids (descendants of Abu Sufyan), reigned from 661 to 684, until his grandson Mu'awiya II. One major rebellion occurred, as Hujr in Kufa supported the claims of the descendants of Ali to the caliphate. This was suppressed by the governor of Iraq and Hujr, who had been a companion of Muhammad, was sentenced to death by Mu'awiya. During his reign, he spent much of his 20 years expanding the state, seeing this as an investment for the future. He also gave a famous speech, saying people should be grateful for what came from him, because even though it may only seem like a little, it would be constant. The Syrian military became a major force under his rule and, in 670 they started raiding Sicily. In 674, his forces laid siege to Constantinople by land and sea. However, they were forced to retreat when the Byzantines introduced Greek Fire (an incendiary weapon which destroyed most of the Arab fleet), forced to sign a peace treaty and pay an annual tribute.

The succession of his son saw the Second Civil War, as the appointment of Yazid I, in 680, was opposed by Abd-Allah ibn al-Zubayr, son of a companion of Muhammad, and Husayn ibn Ali, the younger son of Ali. The people of Kufa invited Husayn to their city in order to initiate a revolt against the Ummayads. However, Yazid I prevented this alliance by having Kufa occupied. Husayn and his family were intercepted on their way, leading to the Battle of Karbala, in which they were killed. This incited other opposition movements, one in Medina and another involving the Kharijites in Basra. In 683, Yazid's army suppressed Medina and besieged the rebel leader in Mecca. During this time, Medina was pillaged for three days and this is said to be one of the worst crimes committed by the Umayyads.

Yazid died during the siege, and the Umayyad army returned to Damascus, leaving Ibn al-Zubayr in control of Mecca. Yazid's son, Mu'awiya II (683–684), initially succeeded him, but two factions then emerged within Syria: the Confederation of Qays (who supported Ibn al-Zubayr) and the Quda'a (who supported Marwan). Marwan subsequently won the battle which broke out between the two, in 684, and became caliph shortly after. His first task was to defend himself against the rival claim of Ibn al-Zubayr, who was recognised as caliph throughout most of the Islamic world. He recaptured Egypt, but died in 685 and was succeeded by his son, Abd al-Malik (685–705), who regained control of the caliphate.

His early reign saw the revolt of Al-Mukhtar, who was based in Kufa. He hoped to elevate Muhammad ibn al-Hanafiyyah, another son of Ali, to the caliphate and war erupted in 686. They were defeated at the river Khazir near Mosul, followed by Ibn al-Zubayr in 687. In 691, the Umayyads reconquered Iraq and, in 692, captured Mecca, killing Ibn al-Zubayr. He then attacked the Byzantine Empire, recovering control over Armenia and Caucasian Iberia, and is famous for introducing the Islamic coinage system which replaced the Byzantine.

Following his death, he was replaced by his son, Al-Walid I (705–715), who was known for his buildings, funding the construction of Al-Masjid al-Nabawi in Medina and the Great Mosque in Damascus. In 712, he conquered both the Sind and the Punjab regions along the Indus River before being succeeded by his brother, Sulayman (715–717), who launched a failed siege of Constantinople, ending the Arab dream of capturing the Byzantine Empire. When the final son of Abd al-Malik, Hisham, became caliph (724–43) expansionism largely declined.

He held court at Resafa (in northern Syria) and resumed attacks on the Byzantines, but did not make any significant gains. From North Africa, raids on coastal areas of the Visigothic Kingdom led to the occupation of large parts of Spain and south-eastern Gaul. However, expansion in the west ended following the defeat of the Arab army by the Franks at the Battle of Tours in 732. Then, in 739, the Berber Revolt in North Africa created some of the first independent Muslim states (including Morocco). Things did not go any better in the East, as he tried to subdue Tokharistan and Transoxiana. There was also the collapse of the caliphate in al-Andalus and, in India, the Arab armies were defeated by the southern Chalukya and northern Pratiharas Dynasties. During the 8th century the Arabs were driven out of India in general.

Hisham was succeeded by the son of Yazid II, Al-Walid II (743–44), who was noted for his indulgent nature and famous for the decoration of the desert palaces which have been attributed to him. However, he quickly generated opposition by executing a number of people who had opposed his accession, and by persecuting the Qadariyya (a philosophical school within Islam which propagated the idea of freewill). As a result of this, Yazid III (a son of al-Walid I) was proclaimed caliph in Damascus, in 744, and his army killed al-Walid II. When he died six months later his brother, Ibrahim, succeeded him. Marwan II (the grandson of Marwan I), subsequently led an army from the north and entered Damascus in December 744, where he was declared caliph. He immediately moved his capital to Harran (in present-day Turkey). A rebellion subsequently broke out in Syria and, in 746, Marwan attacked the walls of Homs and Damascus in retaliation. He also faced opposition from the Kharijites in Iraq and Iran, who volunteered their own rival caliph. In 747, Marwan took control of Iraq, but by this time a more serious threat had arisen.

The Hashimiyya (a sub-sect of the Kaysanites Shia), led by the Abbasid family, rebelled and overthrew the Umayyad Caliphate. They were members of the Hashim clan, rivals of the Umayyads, and Hashimiyya refers to Abu Hashim, a grandson of Ali. The term Abbasid refers directly to Muhammad's uncle, Abbas ibn Abdul-Muttalib (566–653). Around a year earlier, Abu Muslim had assumed their leadership in Khorasan. In 747, he started an open revolt against Umayyad rule, which was carried out under the sign of the Black Flag (subsequently used by various insurgent Islamic armies to proclaim their legitimacy). Firstly, they took Khorasan, expelling its governor. Kufa fell in 749, the last Umayyad stronghold in Iraq. Wasit was also placed under siege and, in November, Abul Abbas as-Saffah was proclaimed the new caliph at Kufa. At this point Marwan mobilised his army towards Iraq and, in January 750, fought the Battle of the Zab, where the Umayyads were defeated. Damascus fell in April and, in August, Marwan was killed in Egypt.

The Abbasid Caliphate (750–1258)

At first, its government was in Kufa but, in 762, the caliph Al-Mansur founded Baghdad near the Sasanian city of Ctesiphon. The empire was noted for its reliance on Persian bureaucrats and increasing its ability to incorporate non-Muslims. During this time, Persian customs were adopted by the ruling elite and endorsed by the artists and scholars whom they supported. As Baghdad became an important centre of culture, philosophy, technology and science, this became known as the Golden Age of Islam. However, despite creating an initial unity, the Abbasids of the late 8th century were forced to concede Spain to the Umayyads, who had withdrawn into Northwest Africa (756). Morocco went to the Idrisid dynasty (788), Ifriqiya to the Aghlabids (800), and Egypt to the Fatimids (969).

The actual power of the caliphs mostly ended with the capture of Baghdad by the Iranian Buyids (in 945) and the Seljuq Turks (in 1055). Over time, Abbasid leadership of the Islamic empire was gradually reduced to a ceremonial function. However, they kept control over Mesopotamia. In 1258, the sack of Baghdad by the Mongols caused them to relocate themselves in Cairo in 1261. Despite having no political power, they continued to claim a type of religious authority, even after the Ottoman conquest of Egypt in 1517.

Aside from what happened to the central succession of the prophet Muhammad, other caliphates have included the Fatimid (909–1171), the Almohad (1121–1269, in Southern Spain and Northwest Africa) and the Ottoman Turks (1362–1924, which became modern Turkey). Also, a large number of Emirates, Sultanates and Kingdoms, including the Seljuk Empire, the Mughals (Mongols who ruled India 1526–1857), present day Saudi Arabia, Iraq, Iran, Afghanistan, Pakistan, Egypt, Tunisia, Algeria, Libya and Morocco.

Today there are said to be 45 sects in Islam. As well as the Sunni and Shi'a, there are Sufis, Kharijites/Ibadis. the Druze, Dervishes, Ismaili Islam, Wahabiism, Moorish Science, Nation of Islam, and the Qur'anists. There is no word for denomination in Islam which correlates directly with Christianity. There are sects, and within these sects there are schools. On separate axes, Muslims self-divide along the lines of Religiosity (liberal to extremist), Affiliation (secularist to Islamist), and Orthodoxy (jurisprudential to mystical). Therefore, there may be any combination of these factors within any community, but this tends to vary from place to place.

Part 3: The Origins of The Holy Roman Empire

As the Islamic empires not only occupied the Middle East, but also stretched across North Africa, they had come to surround Europe, making any further eastward expansion impossible. Henceforth, the Papacy began the conversion of Central and Western Europe to consolidate the position of Christianity. In the late 5th and early 6th centuries, the Merovingians who, according to some sources were related to the family of Jesus, (under Clovis I and his successors) had made the Frankish kingdom the largest in Europe, taking control over northern Gaul and the mid-Rhine valley area. However, by the mid–700s they were only figureheads and the Carolingians, led by Charles Martel, had become the new power. By 768, Charlemagne had become the King of the Franks and began an expansion period which included France, Germany, northern Italy, and even pushed his borders up to the Papal states.

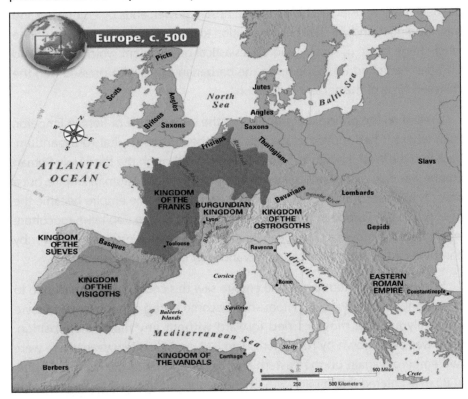

This map shows Europe in 500, with the largest of the western kingdoms being that of the Franks. Henceforth, the conversion of the Franks became of significant importance as the Papacy sought to align their kingdoms with the cause of Christianity. In 797, when the Eastern Roman Emperor, Constantine VI, was overthrown by his mother, Irene, she declared herself empress and the Latin Church at this time prohibited female leadership and property ownership. Hence, Pope Leo III sought a new emperor, and Charlemagne's good relations with the Church (particularly his defence of Papal interests against the Lombards) made him an ideal choice. On Dec 25th, 800, Pope Leo III crowned Charlemagne Roman Emperor.

Historian James Bryce said, of the empire's origins, ". . . one who seeks to explain out of what elements the imperial system was formed, might be required to scrutinize the antiquities of the Christian Church, to survey the constitution of Rome in the days when Rome was no more than the first of the Latin cities, nay, to travel back yet further to that Jewish theocratic polity whose influence on the minds of the mediaeval priesthood was necessarily so profound. Practically, however, it may suffice to begin by glancing at the condition of the Roman world in the third and fourth centuries of the Christian era. We shall then see the old Empire with its scheme of absolutism fully matured; we shall mark how the new religion, rising in the midst of a hostile power, ends by embracing and transforming it; and we shall be in a position to understand what impression the whole huge fabric of secular and ecclesiastical government which Roman and Christian had piled up made upon the barbarian tribes who pressed into the charmed circle of the ancient civilization.'

It relied on the principle of transferring the imperial title of Roman Emperor, from where it had moved eastwards with the Roman capital to Byzantium, back into the West, known as *Translatio Imperii*. Although the term Holy Roman Empire was only created much later, it was not the original Roman Empire, but a new Christianised Europe. Over the next few centuries the empire became the new hub of the European political economy, creating the Capitalist agriculture which became known as European Feudalism, with huge estates ruled over by barons in castles, bishops in cathedrals and knights in shining armour.

However, the eastern Byzantine empire saw this could bring a challenge to its authority, but the Papacy in Rome had become strong enough to manoeuvre politically and the move carried forward without any military opposition. Irene was overthrown by Nikephoros I, in 802, and for a few years there were two emperors again on the eastern and western sides of the Roman Empire. In 803, he entered into a pact with Charlemagne, but refused to acknowledge the new imperial title. Eventually this led to a war over Venice (806–810), where Nikephoros had put down a rebellion in 807, but then suffered heavy losses to the Franks. After Nikephoros' death in 811, Venice, Istria, the Dalmatian coast and Southern Italy were assigned to the east, while Rome, Ravenna and the Pentapolis went to the west.

Charlemagne died in 814 and was succeeded by his son, Louis the Pious. Upon Louis' death in 840, Lothair inherited the title, having co-ruled with him. But, by this point, the Frankish territories themselves had become divided and, during the late ninth century, the title was disputed by the Carolingian rulers of Western and Eastern Francia. First, Charles the Bald of West Francia (843–877) became king of Italy (875–877) and emperor of the Carolingian Empire (875–877). At home he was succeeded by his son, Louis the Stammerer, but he did not receive the imperial crown. In 878, he gave the counties of Barcelona, Girona, and Besalú to Wilfred the Hairy and his final act was to fight the invading Vikings, but he fell ill and died in April 879. Upon his death, the empire was divided between his two sons, Carloman II and Louis III of France.

Charles the Fat was crowned emperor in 881 by Pope John VIII and reunited the kingdom of East Francia. Following the death of his cousin, Carloman II, he inherited all of West Francia in 884, thus reuniting the whole empire, but then he died in 888. Around 900, several duchies: Franconia, Bavaria, Swabia, Saxony, and Lotharingia appeared in East Francia and, when the Carolingian king died in 911, these duchies did not return to the ruler of the west, instead going to Conrad of Franconia. He then gave the crown to Henry the Fowler of Saxony, who was elected king in 919. After this, the Carolingian Empire in the west broke apart and was never restored, while the eastern half of the Frankish Empire became part of the Germanic kingdoms. The title was thus passed to the German princes when it was revived in 962 with Otto I, starting a line of succession which would stay with the Germans for 900 years.

CHAPTER 10

The High Middle Ages

During this period a relatively stable balance of power emerged between Christianity and Islam. Within Christianity, though, a power struggle emerged between the Papacy and Holy Roman Emperor while the Byzantines remained stable in the east. However, after the Crusades were sent to defend the Byzantine Empire against migrating Turks, the appearance of the Mongols in the Far East altered the geo-political structure, as they created the largest contiguous land empire ever...

Part 1: The Holy Roman Empire

In 962, the Ottonian Dynasty started the new period of the empire. Now based in the German provinces, it would remain almost exclusively in the hands of the German princes until it was dissolved by Napoleon in 1806. Otto had been the Duke of Saxony since his father's death in 936 and was elected king within a few weeks. He then unified the Germanic tribes in the region into a single kingdom, extending the powers of the king at the expense of the aristocracy. Through strategic marriages and personal appointments, he was able to put family members in charge of important duchies and developed the power of the Roman Catholic Church on a secular level, as a method of managing the population.

He defeated the Magyars in 955, ending the Hungarian invasions of Western Europe and defeated the enemies of Adelaide, the widowed queen of Italy, whom he married in 951. By 961 he had become the King of Italy. His patronage of the arts and architecture became known as the Ottonian Renaissance and, in 962, he was crowned Holy Roman Emperor by Pope John XII in Rome. Due to this, some historians regard the start of the Holy Roman Empire to be with Charlemagne, others with Otto, as the earlier Frankish era can be seen as the move of the title back into the West. The empire, in fact, only later acquired the Latin title Sacrum Imperium Romanum (Holy Roman Empire), before 1157 it was still referred to as the Roman Empire.

His reign featured conflicts with nobles who wanted his title, and internal rebellions he faced while consolidating his position in Germany. Thus, from the late 940s, Otto began to see the Catholic Church as providing him with the 'divine right' to rule, and adopted it as an instrument of political power. He strengthened the authority of the clergy, especially bishops and abbots, at the expense of the aristocracy, investing them with the symbols of their office. He also sought to appease the Byzantine Emperor, who opposed his claim to the emperorship. As a peace offering, his son married the Byzantine princess, Theophanu, in 972, before Otto died in May 973.

Otto II succeeded him and reigned until 983. He had been co-ruler of Germany since 961 and his father had made him co-Emperor in 967 to secure his succession. He was aged only 18 when he started and continued the policy of strengthening the dynasty by extending its borders in southern Italy and expanding the amount of the Catholic Church under his control. Early in his reign he defeated a major revolt from within the Ottonian dynasty itself, which led him to excluding the Bavarians. From 980 onwards, he focused on annexing Italy, which brought him into conflict with both the Byzantine Empire and the Fatimid Caliphate. However, while he was able to unify the southern Lombard principalities and brought some Byzantine territory under his control, his campaigns in southern Italy ended with defeat to the Muslims in 982. While he was preparing to retaliate against the Emirate of Sicily he died, aged 28, and was succeeded by his three-year-old son, Otto III, resulting in a political crisis.

Otto III, who ruled 996–1002, was initially too young to take the throne. His cousin, Henry II Duke of Bavaria, became his regent, but then attempted to seize power for himself in 984. However, he failed to win support from the rest of the aristocracy. Otto's mother, Theophanu, then served as regent until her death in 991, then it was his grandmother, the Dowager Empress Adelaide of Italy until 994. In 996, he marched to Italy to claim the titles of King of Italy and Holy Roman Emperor. However, Rome had revolted and Crescentius II declared himself consul.

Otto III put down the rebellion and appointed his cousin as Pope Gregory V. Crescentius II then rebelled again, deposing Gregory and appointing the antipope, John XVI. Otto III returned in 998, reinstating Gregory V and executing both Crescentius II and John XVI. Otto III is thus regarded as further increasing the power of the Holy Roman Emperor over the Papacy, as he then appointed Sylvester II as Pope in 999. In the east he fought the Slavs who had revolted in 983, but managed to strengthen relations with Poland, Bohemia and Hungary. He supported missionary work in Poland and influenced the crowning of Stephen I as the first Christian King of Hungary. However, in 1001, he faced another rebellion in Rome and was forced to flee the city. While marching to reclaim it, he died of a sudden fever and left no heir, aged just 21, causing another succession crisis.

Henry II, who became the next Holy Roman Emperor (1014–24), had been the Duke of Bavaria since 995. He had been in the process of attempting to join his second cousin, Otto III, in suppressing the uprising in Rome when Otto died of the fever. He failed twice to persuade the German nobles to crown him before imprisoning the Archbishop of Cologne and declaring himself king in 1002 through Willigis, Archbishop of Mainz. His father had been involved in rebellions against the previous two emperors and, as a Bavarian, he had spent a long time in exile. Rival candidates, Ezzo of Lotharingia, Margrave Eckard I of Meissen and Duke Herman II of Swabia strongly contested his right to the throne, but he subsequently won the support of Bernard I, Duke of Saxony. Unlike a traditional election, he travelled around the kingdom, winning the individual approval of its various provinces, despite violent opposition from Herman II (who was defeated in a battle near Strasbourg). He also launched an invasion into Italy to support the bishops there, acquiring the title King of Italy in 1004, and fought the Polish in three wars over sixteen years.

He was finally made emperor by Pope Benedict VIII in 1014, in exchange for intervention in a crisis which involved the Patrician of Rome, who had installed the antipope Gregory VI. Escaping across the Alps to Germany, Benedict VIII appealed to Henry II for protection and Henry restored Benedict as the head of the Catholic Church. His reign was characterised by the further consolidation of centralised power, as he increased his control over various duchies which had largely fallen into the possession of their own ruling elites. It was already common practice for the emperor to use the clergy to supplant the authority of the nobles in each area with churchmen, as they were likely to be less self-interested. In return he made donations to the Church, created new dioceses and promoted celibacy within the Church, for which Pope Eugene III canonised him in 1146, the only German monarch ever to be made a saint. However, after his death he left no heir and his widow, Cunigunde of Luxembourg, became regent. She was assisted by her brothers (Bishop Dietrich I of Metz and Duke Henry V of Bavaria), the Archbishop Aribo of Mainz and the Primate of Germany. Subsequently, the German nobles elected the Franconian, Conrad II, great-great-grandson of Otto I.

Conrad ruled 1027–39, the first of the Salian dynasty which lasted over a century. He was King of Germany (from 1024), King of Italy (from 1026) and King of Burgundy (from 1033). The first major problem he had was the Italian nobles attempting to separate the Kingdom of Italy from the Holy Roman Empire and there had been riots in Pavia, which destroyed an imperial palace. Italian representatives went north to meet Conrad, arguing that Italy was never designed to be part of the German Empire and the rioters should be excused. But, Conrad replied calmly that, 'just as a ship remains after the death of its captain, an empire remains after the death of its emperor', implying it was his responsibility to punish those concerned. In 1026, he brought an army into Italy and besieged the city while receiving the Iron Crown of the Lombards from Archbishop

Aribert of Milan. From there he traveled to Vercelli, where he celebrated Easter with Bishop Leo, who had been a chief advisor to Otto III. Leo died a few days later, Archbishop Aribert became the main supporter of the Salian dynasty in Italy and Pavia agreed to a treaty in 1027.

His coronation as emperor took place in Old Saint Peter's Basilica in Rome and was attended by King Cnut the Great (of England, Denmark and Norway), Rudolph III of Burgundy, and the Archbishops of Mainz, Cologne, Trier, Magdeburg, Salzburg, Ravenna and Milan. Following this he brought the Church in Venice under imperial control and appointed his 10 year old son, Henry, as Duke of Bavaria. However, he then made the mistake of requesting a complete audit of the crown's assets in Bavaria, and asked the Dowager Empress Cunigunde of Luxembourg for the money and property left to her by her husband. As a result of this, the Bavarian nobles felt he had overstepped his authority. Various incidents in Swabia led to the appointment of his son as Duke there in 1038, and relations with Eastern Europe carried on with minor clashes, but no major change of territorial control. Poland offered to assist the uprising in Swabia, but it was put down before they could mobilise their forces, and battles were fought with Hungary. In 1039, he fell ill and died of gout in Utrecht.

He was succeeded by his son, Henry III. At the age of 11 in 1028, when Conrad became Holy Roman Emperor, Henry was elected King of Germany and, in 1036, married Gunhilda of Denmark, the daughter of Cnut the Great. He then became of Duke of Swabia, and his father also made him King of Burgundy. Upon the death of his father in 1039, Henry became the sole ruler of the kingdom, succeeding his father as the Duke of Carinthia and King of Italy. His first campaign was in Bohemia, which he lost and had to exchange hostages to secure the peace. Upon his return he appointed Suidger the Bishop of Bamberg, who would later become Pope Clement II. After an initial victory against Hungary (1041–2) he was remarried at Ingelheim in 1043 to Agnes, daughter of Duke William V of Aquitaine, before returning to defeat the Hungarians and incorporate them into his empire. He was then crowned Emperor (1046) by Pope Clement II in Rome and given the Golden Chain of the Patriciate. The situation was peaceful on a national level during his reign, with only minor campaigns including victory in 1049 against Dirk of Holland and, in the early 1050s, defeat to Hungary, unrest in Lorraine, war in Italy against the Normans, a Slav uprising and skirmishes with Poland.

However, drama then arose during the reign of his son, Henry IV (1084–1105), as the young King of Germany was kidnapped in the Coup of Kaiserswerth (1062) while under the regency of his mother, Agnes of Poitou. According to historical sources, it was caused by personal ambition on the part of the kidnappers, but they claimed it was provoked by the arrogant manner in which she and her sub-regent, Bishop Henry of Augsburg, conducted themselves with regard to his training and upbringing. The result of this was that power fell into the hands of Anno, the Archbishop of Cologne, who became his magister, and the Archbishop of Bremen who became his patronus. However, they paid good attention to him and he proved himself worthy when he came of age. With the power of the kingship being transferred back to him, he led expeditions against the Lutici and the Margrave of East Saxony in the late 1060s. He also suppressed rebellions by Rudolf of Swabia and Berthold of Carinthia. However, his major battle was against Otto of Nordheim, Duke of Bavaria. Having earlier been involved in his kidnapping, he had been accused in 1070 of being part of a plot to kill him. Trial by combat was prescribed to take place in Goslar but, when he failed to attend, he was removed from his post in Bavaria and his estates plundered. After this he sought support for a campaign against Henry, which lasted until 1071.

The Investiture Controversy

Meanwhile, reforms to the Church were being initiated by Cardinal Bishop Humbert of Moyenmoutier, who was calling for the right for the Papacy to elect the Pope from within. When the Tuscan monk, Hildebrand, inherited his position and became Pope Gregory II (1073), the issue became known as the Investiture Controversy. It had a huge effect on the power which was shared between the Pope and the Holy Roman Emperor, in a way which weakened centralised authority, as it subsequently extended to involve the right to invest all Church officials in their respective positions.

It all began when Henry needed support for his endeavours in Saxony and Thuringia, as Gregory saw the opportunity to push his agenda through into law. An ecclesiastical council of 1074–5 rejected the right for secular rulers to appoint the clergy into any office they chose, and also denied the Crown half its land, which weakened the power of the King. However, Henry continued to appoint Bishops as he pleased, refusing to recognise the legitimacy of the council.

In 1075, Pope Gregory excommunicated various members of the imperial court and threatened to do the same thing to Henry. In February, Gregory held a synod to affirm the supreme power of the Church over the Empire. Henry responded by holding a synod of his own. Subsequently, Pope Gregory was kidnapped and imprisoned by the Roman noble, Cencio I Frangipane. Later freed by the people of Rome, he accused Henry of being behind the plot.

In retaliation, at Worms (1076), a synod of princes and bishops subsequently declared Pope Gregory deposed. Gregory responded by excommunicating Henry and a number of bishops. However, by October, the German princes had decided they wanted a solution before the situation got any worse and suggested that Henry repented. For three days, he stood outside the Castle of Canossa performing the repentance, for which the Pope forgave him, although under certain conditions which Henry then broke.

At the same time, the power of the king was being weakened at home, as what followed shortly afterwards became known as the Great Saxon Revolt. Rudolf of Rheinfelden, Henry's brother-in-law, declared himself king through a council of Saxon, Bavarian and Carinthian princes in March, 1077. However, the population revolted against them, sending him into hiding. After battles in 1078 and 1080, Pope Gregory then supported the uprising and issued a further excommunication against Henry. But, this only caused Germany to rally around the king and he won the Battle of Elster (near Leipzig). The usurper Rudolf was mortally injured and died the next day.

Shortly after, another uprising occurred, whereby Hermann of Salm was fought back by Frederich of Swabia. Henry declared Pope Gregory deposed through a synod in June and replaced him with Guibert, the Primate of Ravenna (who became the anti-Pope Clement III). He then went to Italy and was crowned King of Italy with the Iron Crown of the Lombards, marched against Matilda of Tuscany and looted her possessions, then unsuccessfully besieged Rome in 1081 while taking up residence in Tuscany. He also received 360,000 gold pieces from the Byzantine Emperor, Alexios I Komnenos, who needed an alliance against the Normans.

After another failed assault on Rome, he faced a war of devastation from the followers of Matilda, but in 1082 captured the Leonine City (the area of Rome around the Vatican). Pope Gregory fled to Castel Sant'Angelo and a treaty was made with the Romans which led to them agreeing that the Pope should either crown him Holy Roman Emperor or another Pope should be elected. Henry upheld his treaty with the Byzantines by marching against the Normans, but was recalled in 1084 and crowned Emperor by the recently elected Clement III.

Henry then attacked the fortresses still loyal to Gregory, but was thwarted by Robert Guiscard, Duke of Apulia, who left the siege of Durazzo to march on Rome, causing Henry to leave the city and Gregory to be freed. Gregory died shortly after in Salerno in 1085 but, in a final letter, he appealed to the whole of Christianity to crusade against the emperor. Hence, a full-blown power struggle emerged between the Empire and the Papacy.

In 1088 Hermann of Salm died and Egbert II, the Margrave of Meissen, became the successor to the anti-king. Henry sanctioned him on both local and national levels, but was defeated when an army came to Egbert's rescue during the siege of Gleichen. When Egbert died, two years later, Henry launched a third expedition into Italy. After initial success against Canossa, defeat in 1092 caused the Lombard communes to revolt. To make matters worse, Matilda turned his eldest son, Conrad, against him, who was subsequently crowned King of Italy at Monza in 1093, and Henry was unable to return to Germany until 1097. Henry responded by declaring Conrad deposed at the diet of Mainz, in April 1098, before naming his younger son Henry (who became Henry V) as his successor.

The emperor subsequently continued to build up his power base in Germany, issuing the Landfrieden act in 1101. It was the basis of a new public order act, whereby breaches of the public peace were subject to severe punishments. This included protection for buildings such as churches, houses, bridges, roads, and also the right for imperial subjects to work and conduct themselves unhindered. It was, however, criticised for creating a new type of martial law and, in 1104, his son Henry revolted, having been encouraged by followers of the Pope to declare that he owed no allegiance to his excommunicated father.

Henry IV was then captured at an alleged reconciliation meeting at Koblenz and forced to resign, then imprisoned at Böckelheim castle. There he was also forced to say that he had illegally installed Clement III as anti-pope. However, in 1106 a large army was assembled to fight Henry V and Pope Paschal. Henry IV escaped to Cologne from jail, entering into negotiations with England, France, and Denmark, and was able to defeat his son's army in Lorraine, on 2 March 1106. However, he became ill and died shortly after, aged 56. Buried by the bishop of Liège, the controversy continued after his death.

Henry V was King of Germany from 1099 to 1125, and Holy Roman Emperor from 1111 to 1125. His reign oversaw the second half of the Investiture Controversy, during which he agreed to the demands of the second wave of reformers. The Papacy obviously hoped the new king would comply with its decrees, which it re-asserted at a synod in 1106, but he continued to invest the bishops and hoped the Pope would agree to a meeting in Germany. The Pope eventually agreed to the Council of Troyes, held in the more neutral France, but renewed his demands for the end of lay-investiture. In 1110, when negotiations broke down, Henry invaded Italy. Archbishop Grossolano intended to crown him with the Iron Crown of the Lombards and, at Sutri, he finally made an agreement with Paschal to renounce the rite of investiture in exchange for a coronation which restored to him the Empire of All Christendom, which referred to rights which had been bestowed on the state in the time of Charlemagne. He swore the oaths at St. Peter's Basilica in 1111, to cries of opposition at the new rules, upon which the Pope refused to crown him, and he refused to give up the right of investiture.

Subsequently, Pope Paschal and 16 Cardinals were seized by Henry's guards during a struggle in which Henry was wounded. A Church council later declared the Pope's earlier reversal on the matter to be invalid, as it was extracted from him by force, and a Norman army was sent to rescue the Pope, but was repelled by the Count of Tusculum. Henry then left Rome with the Pope who, evidently under duress, agreed to crown Henry with the right of investiture. In 1114, Henry married Matilda, daughter of Henry I of England, while a further uprising in Cologne was joined by Saxons and others, but Henry cut them off by fortifying the town of Deutz which lay across the Rhine. Rebel forces gathered an army and pushed Henry's troops south, but they sacked Bonn and Julich. Upon returning to Deutz, several leading noblemen were taken prisoner and one killed. Frederick, Count of Westphalia, then brought a substantial army which enabled Henry to withdraw his and, in October, these two armies clashed in Andernach, Henry's side failed to take Cologne and the government forces lost the Battle of Welfesholz in February 1115. Henry then left for Italy, leaving Germany in the care of the Duke of Swabia and his brother Conrad (who became Conrad III).

Since he had last been there, an 1111 council had declared the statement made by the captured Paschal invalid and Guido, Archbishop of Vienne, had excommunicated him. Crossing the Alps in 1116, he took control of Matilda's lands and was received in Rome. But, by this point, Paschal formally withdrew his consent to lay investiture once again, and the excommunication was published in Rome. Subsequently, the Pope was required to flee from the city and Henry was crowned for a second time by Maurice Bourdin, Archbishop of Braga, who became Antipope Gregory VIII. Meanwhile, as news of excommunication had reached Henry's enemies, and was published in Cologne, Paschal began to make war against him with the help of the Normans. In January 1118, Paschal died and was succeeded by Gelasius II but, as the new Pope also fled the city, Henry secured the election of the Antipope Gregory VIII. Returning to Germany, the opposition against him was finally defeated and peace was declared.

The issue of the Investiture Controversy was only eventually resolved at the Concordat of Worms in September 1122, where Henry renounced the right. He recognised the freedom of election for the clergy, and agreed to restore all Church property. In return, the Pope agreed to allow elections to take place in the presence of imperial envoys, and the investiture with the sceptre was to be granted by the emperor as a symbol that the estates of the Church were held under the Crown. Henry was then received back into the communion of the Church, and Antipope Gregory sent into exile.

Part 2: The Crusades

Being able to elect its own officials created a new sense of stability within the Church, and its political power grew. This stability also applied to the nobility, owing to the resolution of the issue they had with the Pope, and various quasi-religious military orders were established, such as the Knights Templar, who received money and land as rich and influential people joined and donated their wealth. They also received support from various kings and the Pope himself, creating a powerful force which exerted influence over European culture as a whole. The result of this was that the Pope could issue Crusades, both to defend Christendom against foreign enemies and keep order between Catholic factions.

Crusades were sporadic rather than constant, and spanned several centuries, acquiring historical importance because of the geopolitical shift they caused. However, all did not go as planned. Apart from the six Crusades to the Holy Land, they brought the north-east Baltic and the tribes of Mecklenburg and Lusatia under Catholic control in the late 12th century, the Teutonic Order created a state in Prussia in the early 13th century, and the French monarchy used the Albigensian Crusade to extend their kingdom to the Mediterranean Sea.

Between 1095 and the 1200s, the Turkish migration into Anatolia led to the famous six Crusades which recaptured territory in the Holy Land, a relatively small event which took on global significance if we consider the consequences for the Byzantine Empire. Initially in defence of the Byzantines' eastern flank against Seljuk Turks who had been migrating into Anatolia after the fall of the Great Seljuk Empire, they created four Crusader States and lasted almost two hundred years. However, the term 'Crusade' was only used from the 1700s, originally they were known as 'negotium crucis' or 'affairs of the cross'.

The First Crusade (1095–9)

The idea of defending the Holy Land arose in Christian Europe, following the consolidation of Christian power in the west, due to the need to defend Byzantium from the rising Turkish threat in the east. Captured by the expansion of Islam in the 630s, Jews, Christians and Muslims all regarded it as sacred, but in different ways. Firstly, Jerusalem was the holiest city in Ancient Judah. Secondly, it was where the ministry of Jesus took place. Thirdly, Muslims regard it as holy because of the Isra and Mi'raj event which occurred around 621, when Muhammad took a journey to the farthest mosque in Jerusalem and is said to have ascended to heaven with the Archangel Gabriel and met the seven prophets. Hence, an agreement providing access to Christian pilgrims was long established with the Muslims due to their shared history.

However, fighting between Turks and Fatimids was causing problems. Before the Crusaders' arrival, the Byzantines had fought the Seljuks and other Turkish dynasties for control of Anatolia and Syria. Egypt and much of Palestine were controlled by the Shi'a Fatimid Caliphate, which had also been reduced by the Seljuks. The initiative for the First Crusade began in 1095 when the Byzantine Emperor, Alexios I, requested military support from the Council of Piacenza. Pope Urban agreed and called for an armed pilgrimage to Jerusalem, provoking massive support across many social classes in Europe.

The first group to go was led by a French priest, Peter the Hermit, and was a group of thousands of Christian peasants (known as the People's Crusade). However, they attacked Jews as they passed through Germany before being massacred by a Turkish ambush at the Battle of Civetot (1096), upon leaving Byzantine-controlled territory in Anatolia. A better organised expedition (known as the Princes' Crusade) involved members of the high aristocracy from Normandy, Boulogne, Toulouse, Flanders and Lorraine, and their followers (estimated at around 100,000). This set off mid-summer 1096 and arrived at Constantinople between November and April, before marching through Anatolia. A Frankish siege, assisted by a Byzantine naval attack, captured Nicea in June 1097. The first Crusader state, the County of Edessa, was established and Antioch was captured after a siege in June 1098. However, while the Seljuks were distracted by the Crusaders, the Fatimid caliphate in Egypt had taken control of Jerusalem in February. The Fatimids, who were Shi'a, offered the Crusaders an alliance against their common enemy, the Seljuks, who were Sunni. They offered the Crusaders control of Syria while they retained Jerusalem, but the Crusaders would not compromise their original mission to take Jerusalem, leading to conflict with the Muslims.

Jerusalem was reached in June 1099 and taken on 7 July. A counter attack was launched, but defeated at the Battle of Ascalon. After this most of the crusaders went home. The Kingdom of Jerusalem was established by Godfrey of Bouillon and lasted until 1291. In total, four Crusader States were created: the County of Edessa, the Principality of Antioch, the Kingdom of Jerusalem and the County of Tripoli.

The Second Crusade (1147–49)

A Turkish ruler on his path to leadership, Zengi, conquered various territories, including the County of Edessa in 1144. The disastrous Second Crusade was proclaimed by Pope Eugene III and led by the European kings Conrad of Germany and Louis VII of France. A number of nobles joined their armies which marched separately across Europe and Anatolia, but both were defeated by Turkish forces.

Odo of Dueil, a French historian who went on the mission, and Syriac Christian sources (Syriac was one of the three most important Christian languages in the early centuries, along with Latin and Greek) accused the Byzantine Emperor of secretly hindering the crusaders and deliberately ordering the Turks to attack them. However, Conrad of Germany claimed that the Byzantine Emperor treat him 'like a brother', and had not seen any evidence of this.

Following this the remains of their armies reached Jerusalem and, in 1148, engaged in a poorly executed attack on Damascus which ended in their retreat. This victory for the Muslims was followed by the fall of Jerusalem to the Ayyubid Sultan, Saladin (1187), leading to the Third Crusade. The Muslims also took Ascalon, Acre, Nablus, Jaffa, Toron, Sidon and Bierut, and thousands of Muslim slaves were freed. The only surviving Christian stronghold, Tyre, took in the survivors.

The Third Crusade (1189–92)

This venture was led by the French King Philip Augustus, the English King Richard the Lionheart and the Holy Roman Emperor Frederick Barbarossa. Their armies included tens of thousands of troops and thousands of knights. However, the German King drowned in a river along the way and most of his army returned home. The rest reached Constantinople in the autumn of 1189, only to discover a secret alliance between the Emperor of Constantinople and Saladin. The Christians managed to reverse many of Saladin's gains, and captured the cities of Acre and Jaffa, but not Jerusalem.

The Fourth Crusade (1202–4)

Called for by Pope Innocent III, it was inspired by the failure of the Third Crusade to recapture Jerusalem, and this was their initial aim. However, in 1202, financial issues led to them sacking Zara, which was subsequently brought under Venetian control. Then, in 1203, on the way to Jerusalem, they entered into an agreement with the Byzantine Prince, Alexios Angelos, who wanted his father restored as ruler in Constantinople. Financial and military aid were then promised for the conquest of Jerusalem, should they succeed. Most went to Constantinople while some continued on to Acre. Meanwhile, the Pope excommunicated the entire Crusader army following the attack on Zara.

In August, Alexios was crowned co-emperor but, by January 1204, he had already been deposed by a popular uprising. The Crusaders no longer received his support and, following his death in February, they decided to sack Constantinople instead and plunder it for the money they were owed. In April they captured it and took its enormous wealth. This weakened it considerably and is seen as a major factor in its later fall to the Turks, which closed land trade routes into Asia and forced the Europeans to explore the sea routes by which they rediscovered the Americas.

The Fifth Crusade

This was an attempt to recapture Jerusalem by first conquering the Ayyubid state in Egypt. Pope Innocent III and his successor, Honorius III, organised armies which were led by the Hungarian King Andrew II and Leopold VI, Duke of Austria, but they failed to capture the city. However, in 1218, two new armies joined. These were a German army and one comprising Dutch, Flemish and Frisian soldiers, led by William I Count of Holland. They attacked Egypt, after making an alliance with the Seljuk Sultanate of Rum, who attacked the Ayyubids to free one of the Crusaders' flanks. After occupying Danietta, the Crusaders marched South towards Cairo in July 1221, but low supplies forced them to turn back. A night attack by Al-kamil led to heavy losses and forced them to surrender, but the Muslims subsequently agreed to an eight year truce with Europe.

The Sixth Crusade

This involved the Holy Roman Emperor, Frederick II, successor of Frederick Barbarossa, and finally achieved victory in terms of re-establishing Christian influence in Jerusalem. In 1227, Frederick had been excommunicated by Pope Gregory IX in a dispute over the cancellation of a Crusade. However, it seems this was more related to him consolidating imperial power in Italy at the expense of the Pope.

Due to this, support for his Crusade was split, with the Teutonic Knights and his own army supporting him unconditionally, plus the Knights Templar and Hospitaller after he removed his name from the official documents. Public support had been reduced due to the Papacy, meaning that his force was much smaller than anticipated, and he realised that his only hope of success was to negotiate. Fortunately, the Egyptian sultan was preoccupied with the suppression of a rebellion in Syria and conceded Jerusalem to the Franks, along with a narrow corridor of land to the coast, plus Nazareth, Sidon, Jaffa, and Bethlehem.

The Muslims retained control over the Temple Mount area of Jerusalem, the al-Aqsa Mosque and the Dome of the Rock, in a treaty formalised on 18 February 1229 which also invoked a 10-year truce. From 1229 the Pope lifted the excommunication order on Frederick, who had shown that a crusade could succeed without violence. When the treaty expired, Pope Gregory IX called for a new venture, leading to the Barons' Crusade, which then had support from both Frederick and the Pope, and regained even more land.

Subsequent crusades were launched by individual kings, such as Louis IX of France (Seventh and Eighth Crusades), and Edward I of England (Ninth Crusade), largely due to a decline in papal authority. This map shows how territories had changed since the establishment of the new Europe.

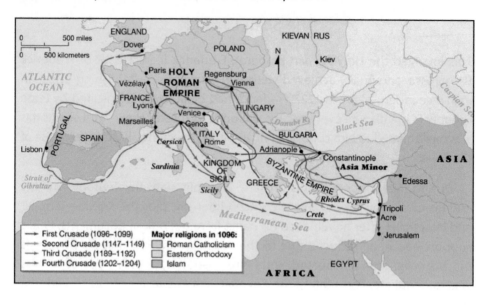

Part 3: The Mongol Empire

Genghis Khan, the most famous warlord of all time, founded the Mongol Dynasty which conquered more continuous territory than any other empire, and subsequent dynasties such as the Timurid and Mughal empires which both became a major part of Asian history. The story starts on the Central Asian plateau north of China, which was divided among several tribes, including Naimans, Merkits, Tatars, Khamag Mongols and Keraites. They all had evolving sets of alliances, but would periodically engage in raiding each other, revenge attacks and plundering.

Genghis Khan was born Temüjin (meaning Iron Worker or Blacksmith) in 1162 in Delun-Boldog, Mongolia. His father, Yesügei, was the chief of a minor clan, the Borjigin. His mother, Hoelun, was born to the Olkhunut tribe and was engaged to Chiledu of the Merkit confederation, but was kidnapped by Yesügei on her way back to the Merkit camp after her wedding around 1159. They were nomadic and survived by hunting rather than herding or farming. Temujin began his path to power by swearing allegiance to his father's 'Anda' (sworn blood brother), Toghrul. At around 9 years of age, his father arranged his marriage to Börte, of the Olkhonud of Khongirad, a tribe friendly to the Borjigin. The daughter of Dei-Sechen and Chotan, she is described as being a year older than him with a fair complexion, light in her face and fire in her eyes, indicating intelligence and beauty.

He stayed a while with her family but, shortly after this a rival tribe, the Tatars, poisoned his father and his tribe abandoned them, leaving them to survive on fruit, fish, rodents and any other animals they could find, a period which led to his later belief that people will only follow a strong leader. During this time, he had to return to his mother to help the family. They lived for a while in desperate circumstances and his half-brother Begter began to exercise power as the eldest male. When it transpired he would eventually have the right to claim Hoelun (who was not his mother) as his wife, he was killed in an argument with his younger brothers during a hunt.

Temüjin was subsequently captured and held prisoner during a raid by his father's former allies, the Tayichi'ud, around 1177. But, he escaped owing to a sympathetic guard, earning him a reputation among his compatriots. Jelme and Bo'orchu, who joined forces with him, and the guard's son, Chilaun, eventually became his generals. After his escape, in 1178, Temüjin traveled downstream along the Kelüren River to honour his relationship with Börte, and took her and her mother to live in his family's yurt (a portable tent covered in animal fur), which was camped along the Senggür river. Her dowry was a fine black sable fur.

However, soon after they married, the Merkit clan attacked their camp, in retaliation for the abduction of Hoelun. This time, while Temüjin and others were able to escape on horseback, Börte was captured. Assisted by his childhood friend and blood-brother, Jamukha (who had become the Khan of his own tribe, the Jadaran), he used his alliance with Toghrul, who offered the assistance of his soldiers to recapture her. As he achieved this, by around the age of 20, he had destroyed one of Mongolia's main tribes.

For the next few years Temüjin's small group lived with Jamukha's tribe and they shared the leadership. However, they both used different methods, and this led to their relationship developing into a personal rivalry. They were both aristocrats, sons of tribal leaders. Yet, Temüjin's experience of true hardship meant he had more empathy for the problems of those lower down in society and wanted to enable reforms. His experiences led him to believe that a warrior did not win battles by his birthright, but with the strength of his heart. He used a merit system which rewarded ability, loyalty and good behaviour. One of his most promising warriors, Subutai, was the son of a herdsman.

Jamukha, on the other hand, saw himself as being first among equals and was concerned that Temüjin was departing from their traditional culture, one in which social status was strictly determined by family ties. He saw Temujin as attempting to build up his own power-base, surrounding himself with people of much lower rank than himself, breaking the social code. While Temüjin believed his new methods were innovative, Jamukha saw two different tribes appearing and attempted to assert his authority. However, the tribal shaman then proclaimed that the supreme God had told him in a trance that he would give the entire surface of the earth to Temüjin and his sons, thus initiating his rise to power.

Jamukha divided the tribes and left the camp, along with his followers and livestock. In 1186, Temüjin was elected khan of the Mongols and, threatened by this, Jamukha attacked Temüjin in 1187 with 30,000 troops, defeating him at the Battle of Dalan Balzhut. Following this, though, Jamukha then horrified his followers by boiling 70 young male captives alive in cauldrons. Toghrul, Temüjin's patron, was exiled to the Qara Khitai. However, around 1197, the Jurchen Jin dynasty launched an attack against the Tatars, with help from the Keraites and Mongols, and awarded Temüjin a command. After victory, he and Toghrul were restored by the Jin to positions of power; Toghrul received the title of Ong Khan, while Temüjin was given the lesser title, j'aut quri.

Following this, a rift with Toghrul occurred, over Toghrul's refusal to give his daughter in marriage to Jochi, Temüjin's first son. This led to a war in which Toghrul allied himself with Jamukha, but a dispute between them, combined with a number of their allies deserting to Temüjin, led to victory for Temüjin's side. Jamukha escaped during the conflict, but this defeat led to the fall and eventual dissolution of the Keraite tribe. After additionally conquering the Alchi Tatars and Uhaz Merkits, acquiring at least one wife each time, Temüjin turned his attention to the Turkic Naimans, with whom Jamukha had sought refuge. The Naimans did not surrender, although some sided with Temüjin. In 1201, a khuruldai elected Jamukha as Gür Khan (Supreme Ruler), and he formed a coalition to oppose Temüjin. However, several generals abandoned Jamukha and, after several battles, Jamukha was handed over to Temüjin by his own army in 1206.

According to the Secret History of the Mongols, Temüjin once again offered his friendship to Jamukha, and even executed the men who had betrayed him, saying he did not want disloyal men in his army. But, Jamukha refused, saying 'there can only be one sun in the sky', meaning that he would rather die than accept the changes Temüjin was making to Mongol society, and asked for a noble death.

After this, Temüjin was elected leader of all the tribes and given the title Genghis Khan (Universal Ruler), before initiating the Mongol invasions of Eurasia. His campaigns included Khwarezmia, the Western Xia, the Jin, and raids on Georgia, the Kievan Rus, and Bulgaria. They were often accompanied by large-scale massacres of civilians, especially in the Khwarazmian and the Western Xia regions, which killed millions. Thus he is often considered one of the most brutal and dictatorial leaders in history, but he claimed to justify his actions with a set of law codes which forced populations to either assimilate or die.

The Yassa law codes were a forty millenary oral law code declared in public, in Bokhara, by Genghis Khan, even though the way they ruled was kept secret from the public. Absolute obedience was expected, in exchange for the profits of future wars. When rivals were defeated, he took the conquered tribe under his protection and integrated its members into his own tribe, even having his mother adopt orphans and making them part of the family. Subsequently, the law codes were codified and used to create reinterpretations of cultural conventions for conquered territories, as well as being for the ruling Mongols themselves. Overseen by Genghis Khan and his stepbrother, Shikhikhutug, the high judge of the empire, they were its political system. He appointed his second son, Chagatai, to supervise their execution.

The army was turned into a war machine, which would become the main source of their success in spreading their power. Already a tough nomadic people who were good with horses, archery and survival in the wilderness, it was built around strong leadership, good supply lines, flexible tactics and a pragmatic ideology which allowed them to manage public relations with conquered territories. Strong on all levels, they used whatever means necessary to defeat their enemies, including open battles, guerrilla tactics, misinformation, spies, and could deploy multiple armies at a time to achieve different objectives. During an attack their commanders operated like the modern special forces, each with a broad outline of the campaign strategy and the freedom to achieve their objective as they saw fit.

One of their tactics was to tire their opponents' horses by charging into battle, then feigning retreat, and enticing their opponents into the open. Then they would ride to an appointed location, switch horses, and return to defeat the enemy. Their re-curve bows were the best in the world at the time and could penetrate plate armour. Also, they employed Chinese engineering units in the event of siege warfare. Preferring their opponents to surrender, most areas fell under their control in this way, as their reputation grew and people knew what to expect if they did not. However, they treat their own populations favourably and economic growth was encouraged. Their economic policies appealed to merchants and poor farmers far more than the ruling elites, whom they deposed, making people well disposed towards them as it lowered taxes. It also made people like merchants more keen to supply them with information. They dealt harshly with people who fought back, massacring whole populations and making an example of them to deter others. They encouraged trade by establishing safe routes across Asia, allowing exchange to take place between China, East Asia, Persia, the Muslim world and Europe and, through this, they built an economy-of-scale which both lowered taxes and generated a huge income, allowing for a strong support network.

Within five years, Genghis Khan had control of much of Siberia and the Chinese province of Xinjiang. In 1214 he conquered the Jurchen Dynasty in northern China and their 50 million citizens with an army of just 100,000. Tribesmen in Kazakhstan and Kyrgyzstan overthrew their Buddhist rulers and joined this growing empire and, by 1219, it stretched from northern China to the Afghan border and from Siberia to the border of Tibet. He then sought a trade alliance with Sultan Muhammad II of the Khwarizm Empire in Central Asia (from Afghanistan to the Black Sea), but they murdered his first trade convoy and stole their goods. By the end of the year, Genghis Khan had conquered all their cities.

Ögedei Khan

In 1222, the 61-year-old Khan called his family to discuss who would become the next leader, and his four sons disagreed. As Jochi, the eldest, was born soon after Borje's kidnapping, he might not have been Temujin's son. Hence, his second son, Chagatai, challenged his right to the title. However, Ogodei had always been the favourite to succeed. He was intelligent, pragmatic like his father and, even though he was under no illusion that he was as good a commander, he used the capable generals which Genghis Khan left behind. All of his sons had been trained as warriors from a young age, and were part of the plan to establish a world empire. Tolui held the regency for two years, following the death of Genghis in 1227, before Ögedei was elected by a kurultai council in 1229.

Using the methods Genghis had created, Ögedei continued to expand the empire, which reached its furthest expansion west under his rule. He also revitalised the Silk Road, making trade and communication routes between different civilisations stable and, in 1235, finished the construction of Karakorum, the capital of Mongol Empire. At the same time, the Mongols completed their conquest of the Jurchen Jin empire (1234), before encountering the Southern Song. Henceforth, in 1235, a new war began which lasted for 45 years, resulting in the complete annexation of China. In the East, Korea and Persia were added to their territory while, in the West, almost all of Russia, Hungary, and Poland were conquered.

Ögedei Khan granted permission for the complete invasion of Europe, and there is evidence that suggests it was only his death which prevented this.

When he died (in 1241), Mongol forces were attacking Vienna, as part of a brutal campaign against Austria and Germany. His widow, Töregene, took over as regent, and arranged the succession of her son Güyük.

Güyük Khan

Güyük's reign was short (1246–8). He was trained in the military and became an officer, marrying Oghul Qaimish of the Merkit clan. His coronation, held near Karakorum on the 24th August, was widely recognised, and was attended by a large number of foreign ambassadors. These included an envoy of Pope Innocent IV, Grand Duke Yaroslav II of Vladimir; representatives of the throne of Georgia, the brother of the king of Armenia, the future Seljuk Sultan of Rum, ambassadors from the Abbasid Caliph, and Ala ud din Masud of the Delhi Sultanate. Around 3,000 to 4,000 visitors from all parts of Asia and Europe brought tributes.

However, when one of the envoys, John of Plano Carpini (of the Papacy) protested about Mongol attacks on Catholic kingdoms, Güyük said that it was retaliation for Mongol envoys slain in the time of Genghis and Ögedei, and subsequently stated that 'from the rising of the sun to its setting, all the lands have been made subject to the Great Khan'[1]. He wrote a letter to Pope Innocent IV saying, 'You must say with a sincere heart: 'We will be your subjects; we will give you our strength'. You must in person come with your kings, all together, without exception, to render us service and pay us homage. Only then will we acknowledge your submission. And if you do not follow the order of God, and go against our orders, we will know you as our enemy.'

At home, his relationship with Toregene had deteriorated and he ordered that her favourite, Fatima, be arrested, tortured and executed for bewitching his brother, Khuden. Abd-ur-Rahman was also beheaded for corruption. The problems he faced were no longer just those of expansion, it was a case of managing the centralised power within the empire with massive resources to control and political relationships to adjudicate. In 1248, he recalled one of his generals, Batu, to Mongolia but, fearing it was another purge, Batu brought a large army with him. However, the confrontation never happened, as Güyük died on the way to meet him. Some historians believe he may have been poisoned, or killed in a brawl with Shiban (the fifth son of Jochi and brother of Batu), but he also had acquired a drinking habit which caused his health to deteriorate. His widow, Oghul Qaimish, took over as regent, and Möngke succeeded him in 1251.

Möngke Khan

Born in 1209, Möngke was a son of Tolui and had taken part in many earlier campaigns. He made significant reforms to the system of administration and, by this time, the empire had a religious policy which caused them to turn many of the Taoist monasteries over to the Buddhists. As the situation started moving away from the initial phase of conquering, the personal power was taken away from the merchants they sponsored and a standard taxation system introduced. However, Möngke still expanded, conquering Iraq, Syria and the kingdom of Dali.

His legitimacy was considered genuine and supported by Batu, who called a kurultai at Ala Qamaq for his election. The leader of the families of Genghis Khan's brothers, and several important generals were there. It was confirmed by a second kurultai in 1251. However, when Oghul's son, Khoja, and Ögedei's grandson, Shiremun, came to pay homage to him, they intended to bring an army with them. When this was discovered, trials took place all over the empire. Oghul was accused of using black magic against Möngke, sewn up in a sack and drowned. Up to 300 commanders were killed, while the descendants of Genghis Khan who took part were driven into exile.

After this purge, he ordered a general amnesty for prisoners and captives. Then he gave his brothers, Kublai and Hulagu, supervisory powers in North China and Iran. After a brief dispute with Kublai over tax regulations, he then drew up plans for reform. These included restricting the excessive costs of the Borjigin nobles and limiting gifts to the princes, which he converted into regular salaries. He also made all merchants subject to taxation. Teams of inspectors were appointed to supervise the businesses of merchants they sponsored, and the use of tablets which had previously enabled them to demand goods and services from local populations were forbidden. To ensure his reforms were successful, he compensated them by paying off loans which had been issued by Güyük.

In 1253, he established a Department of Monetary affairs to control the issuing of paper money, which prevented an overextension of the currency. His rule also established a standard measure based on the silver ingot, while allowing subject nations to mint coins according to the denominations and weights they already used. In diplomatic affairs, he built a secure position and held court to foreign kings.

Historian Jack Weatherford[2] describes how not only the size of their empire, but also their pragmatic geo-political thinking had an effect on the creation of the modern world. Up until now, Christianity and Islam had represented the new balance of power as the world came out of the Ancient period. Yet, the size of the Mongol Empire forced people to consider a new balance of power, which had come to exist between the Mongols and the rest of the world. Weatherford says that, though they were accused of simply returning to tribalism following the reforms which monotheism had made to the empires of the Ancient world, what they did made an important contribution to later periods. Asserting that they were not afraid of the West, he says, Mongke sent this message to Louis IX,

'We Mongols believe in one God, by Whom we live and die. . . Just as God gave different fingers to the hand so has He given different ways to men. To you God has given the Scriptures and you Christians do not observe them. . . If, when you hear and understand the decree of the eternal God, you are unwilling to pay attention and believe it. . . and in this confidence you bring an army against us — we know what we can do'.

Under the commander Kublai Khan, they outflanked the Chinese in the south and captured both the Thai kingdom and Vietnam. In 1257 Möngke took personal charge of the full-scale invasion of China, but disease struck his armies and he died in the field, leading to a succession crisis between two of his brothers.

Kublai Khan

By the time of the grandchildren of Genghis Khan, multiple claims to the throne existed, and civil war ensued. Several historians have claimed that the whole problem of the empire stemmed from the initial doubt over Jochi's claim to the throne as, without this, it could have functioned as a dynastic monarchy. As the families of various brothers had held power in positions throughout the empire, all claimed to be equally related to Temujin through their kinship ties. In 1258, Mongke had put Kublai in charge of his eastern army and, when he died, Ariq Böke (his brother) was elected Khan at a kurultai at the capital, Karakorum, supported by most of Genghis Khan's other descendants.

However, Kublai and the fourth brother, the IlKhan Hulagu, opposed this, and Kublai's Chinese staff encouraged him to take the throne, supported by most of the senior princes in North China and Manchuria. Upon returning to his own territories, Kublai summoned his own kurultai, which proclaimed him the

Great Khan, on 15 April 1260. This led to warfare between the two sides (1260–4) which caused the destruction of Karakorum. Kublai attempted a diplomatic solution, but his envoys were arrested. He then sent Abishqa to become the new leader of the Chagatai Khanate, but he was captured by Ariq Böke, who then appointed his own, Alghu. In the first real battle between them, Ariq Böke lost and his commander Alamdar was killed. As revenge Ariq had Abishqa executed. Kublai then cut off food supplies to Karakorum, which subsequently fell to his army, but was then recaptured following his departure in 1261.

However, the Chagatayid Khan, who had been appointed by Ariq Böke, then defected to Kublai and defeated an army sent by Ariq Böke to depose him in 1262. With the Ilkhan Hulagu also on the side of Kublai, Ariq Böke surrendered at Xanadu on 21 August 1264. Kublai pardoned him, although he executed his major supporters.

In 1271, Kublai established the Yuan dynasty, which ruled over present-day Mongolia, China, Korea, and some adjacent areas, and assumed the role of Emperor of China himself. By 1279, the Mongol conquest of the Song dynasty was complete and Kublai became the first non-Han emperor to rule all of China. Kublai reigned until 1294, but another civil war broke out as he tried to gain control over the whole empire through the Chagatayid and Ögedaid dynasties and, by time of his death, the empire had fragmented into four parts: the Golden Horde Khanate in the NW, the Chagatai Khanate in Central Asia, the Ilkhanate in the SW and the Yuan Dynasty which ruled China from Beijing. In 1304 the three western khanates accepted the suzerainty of the Yuan dynasty, but by 1368 the Han Chinese Ming dynasty had taken back their capital, and the Mongolian court retreated to their homeland where they ruled until 1634 as the Northern Yuan Dynasty. It appears the end of their unity meant a breakdown in their system, and subsequently the end of their expansion, as it relied on an increasing state of organisation and a strong sense of legal hegemony.

Subsequent spin-off empires included a revival by Timur, who converted the empire to Islam, and the Mughals, descendants of Genghis Khan who ruled India (1526–1540 and 1555–1857). One in twenty people today claim to have Mongol heritage.

CHAPTER 11

The Late Middle Ages

As the Mongol Empire receded back into Asia and fragmented, the European Renaissance began. The late 1200s brought economic prosperity in Europe, however, the 1300s saw the Bubonic Plague, popular revolts and wars, and the Hussite Rebellion became the predecessor of the Protestant Reformation. In Asia, the Timurid Mongol revival converted them to Islam, while the Ottomans capturing Constantinople in 1453 closed the land trade routes into Asia, forcing the Europeans to explore the sea routes which led to the rediscovery of the Americas...

Part 1: The European Renaissance

While the Mongols had a massive impact on global affairs, they largely retreated to Asia after failing to capture Europe. Meanwhile, the system which emerged under the Papacy led to social progress, and the absolute power of kings started to reduce. For example, the English Barons made King John I sign the Magna Carta (1215), guaranteeing the right to justice, freedom for all citizens and a fair trial. It also meant the King became subject to the law. In the early 1200s, Universities began to appear, creating systematic progress in terms of detailed scientific, religious, language and social studies. This addition to the system meant not only an improvement in methods, but also a greater retention of knowledge, as records of the way new discoveries were made could became more accessible to future students.

Thomas Aquinas (1225–74) is widely seen as the first major pioneer of the Renaissance. He established a new basis for natural law, Christian philosophy and speculative theology, based on finding reason in the worship of God and religion. He reinterpreted Aristotle and Plato in a contemporary sense, through a range of political and socio-economic doctrines. Appointed at the University of Paris, he preached in Naples and served the Church in Rome. Even in modern times, his works are still used as core studies for those seeking ordination as priests or deacons, and he is known as one of the 12 most important philosophers of the West. In economics he argued that a 'just price' should cover the costs of production, but it was immoral to raise prices just because buyers were in desperate need. In politics, he believed monarchs should be regarded as God's representatives, but the Church was above them in matters of doctrine. Therefore, rulers should adapt their policies to the doctrines of the Catholic Church.

Following the previous stages of the Carolingian and Ottonian Renaissance, Europe began a full-scale cultural renaissance (French for 'rebirth'), which occurred from the 1200s to the late 1500s. It featured groundbreaking artisans such as Leonardo da Vinci (artist and designer), Lorenzo De Medici (patron of the arts), Petrarch (the humanist philosopher who coined the phrase 'the Dark Ages' as a reference to the previous 900 years), William Shakespeare (playwright),

Brunelleschi (engineer and designer), Galileo Galilei (astronomer), Michelangelo (sculpture and art), and was later assisted by an influx of Greek scholars which came flooding into Europe due to the Turkish conquest of Byzantium in 1453. With even the Vikings now largely converted to Christianity, a whole new continent began to appear.

A rural exodus to more urbanised, industrialised areas occurred, along with the beginnings of organised Capitalism, and investment in rapidly industrialising areas became more profitable. This also caused the rising power of the banks (such as those run by the Medici family), governmental politics, the decline of the feudal estates (as the most important provider of labour), and Europe became full of towns and cathedral cities with busy markets filling the streets.

The European Crisis of the 1300s

However, disaster hit Europe in the 1300s, as the Great Famine (1315–17) and Bubonic Plague (1347–1351) resulted in the deaths of 75 to 200 million people across Eurasia. It is thought to have originated on the plains of Central Asia, then transported to Europe via the Silk Road, reaching Crimea around 1343, carried by fleas living on the rats on merchant ships. It is estimated to have killed 30% to 60% of Europe's population and, in total, reduced the world population from an estimated 475 million to 350–375 million. It took 200 years for it to recover, although it has grown ever since, and the plague has returned periodically in various outbreaks over time.

The result of this was a demoralised population, with peasant uprisings in France and England. In Scotland the death of Alexander III (1286) threw the country into a succession crisis, and the English king, Edward I, was put in charge, leading to the Wars of Scottish Independence. When the Scots won they established a state under the Stuarts, who later became kings of England under James I.

In the 1300s, England and France fought the 100 years war, as the 1066 invasion of England by the Plantagenet dynasty led to the kings of England believing they had a claim over the throne of France. Following the death of Charles IV of France, this led to a claim by Edward III of England. Henry V's victory at the Battle of Agincourt, in 1415, led to a brief unification, but his son Henry VI faltered. The emergence of Joan of Arc turned the overall course of war towards the French, before this was taken further by King Louis XI. Soon after the end of the war, in 1453, the Plantagenet civil war broke out in the English Wars of the

Roses (1455–1485), involving the rival Houses of Lancaster and York. This ended with the reign of Henry VII of York, and the Tudor dynasty created a powerful, centralised monarchy. Europe's centre remained strong, with the title of Holy Roman Emperor passing to the Habsburgs (where it largely remained until 1806).

The Hussite Rebellion

The Papacy, realising that neither England or France would partake in a Crusade to the Holy Land while fighting their 100 year war, attempted to end it with a series of measures, including a declaration of authority over the French Crown, and objected to using taxation of the clergy to fuel the war. He issued a decree, threatening anyone who took money from the Church with excommunication. Philip IV of France responded by stopping money going from France to Rome, which the Church needed to operate, and banned papal envoys from France who were raising money for a Crusade. The whole issue of the Papacy's secular power was raised as the situation escalated, culminating in the death of Pope Boniface VIII, following his arrest and mistreatment by Philip. Furthermore, after the natural death of Pope Benedict XI, Philip forced the Papacy to elect the French Clement V as Pope in 1305. Clement subsequently refused to move to Rome and, in 1309, held court in the papal enclave at Avignon, where the Papacy then resided for 67 years. This is sometimes referred to as the 'Babylonian captivity of the Papacy', and a total of seven French Popes reigned during this period.

During this time, the culture and traditions of the clergy became increasingly similar to those of the monarchy, including the methods used to extract payment for various services provided by the Church. Tithes (taxes on income), offerings or donations, and payments to the Church from its members were seen by most people as legitimate. However, the Church also received money for crusades which never took place, people could pay to enter office without the basic qualification of literacy, and converted Jews would have to pay to be allowed to visit their unconverted parents. Popes spent fortunes on diplomatic attempts to appease the royals with their wealth, such as expensive clothes, carriages, artwork, and gold plates at banquets.

Over time, the lives of leading church figures began to look more like princes than holy men, and this corruption began to work its way down into the lower ranks in various ways. For example, when a bishop had to pay up to a year's income for gaining a new office he sought ways of passing this charge on. This led to all kinds of practices, such as payments for the forgiveness of sins. The clergymen who did this were commonly regarded as being divergent from the Church's teachings and subsequently despised, while people were calling for a return to the traditional life of poverty, relinquishment of personal possessions, and preaching as Jesus and his disciples had done.

On top of this, upon the return of the Papacy to Rome, no less than three men claimed to be the true Pope during the time of the Western Schism (1378–1417), causing further damage to its reputation and criticism of the Church became widespread. Around 1402 Jan Hus, who was both a priest and a scholar, denounced the Catholic Church for its corruption, promoting the ideas of reformist theologian John Wycliffe (1320s –84).

Wycliffe was an English philosopher, biblical translator, priest, and professor at the University of Oxford. He became a dissident figure within the Roman Catholic Church and the movement he started, the Lollards, became regarded as an important predecessor of the English Reformation. He disapproved of the privileges of the clergy and their luxurious lifestyle, which they took as personal wealth, using the powerful position they had created in England. Both he and his followers advocated the concept of predestination, iconoclasm, and the idea that the Papacy was not founded through a partnership of Christianity and Rome, but arose as a compromise. They translated the Bible from Vulgate into Middle English in 1382, and attempted to refute the veneration of saints, sacraments, requiem masses, and monasticism.

However, Hus was subsequently suppressed by the Church, as it had previously declared Wycliffe heretical. Following this, in 1411, Antipope John XXIII proclaimed a crusade against the King of Naples, who was protecting rival Pope Gregory XII and, to raise money he offered indulgences to Bohemia. Hus then denounced this and further quoted Wycliffe, provoking more accusations of heresy, but it gained him support in Bohemia. In 1414, Sigismund of Hungary (head of the Holy Roman Empire, but not yet Emperor) used the Council of Constance to solve the problem and Hus was sent to the Council under a guarantee of safe-conduct from Sigismund. However, he was imprisoned, tried, and executed on 6 July 1415. Later that year the nobility of Bohemia and Moravia, who were in favour of church reform, strongly condemned the execution of Hus. Sigismund replied to this by saying that he would drown all the Wycliffites and Hussites.

What further contributed to this situation was that commercial activities had created new urban centres, to which people gravitated, and the amount of poor and homeless tended to concentrate in those areas. Mendicant orders, such as those founded by Francis of Assisi (1181–1226) and Dominic Guzman (1170–1221), went back to the methods of Jesus by preaching in the street and relying on charity to fund their Churches (mendicant being derived from the Latin mendicare, meaning literally 'to beg'). Having seen the wealth which the Church had acquired, they wanted to return to the original values of Christianity and prove the value of their teachings at grass-roots level.

However, as the mendicant movement grew in France and Italy, it became more popular in the poorer regions, while the wealthy wanted to create a system which paid more tax and, hence, receive more indulgences and approval from the Popes. The Mendicant method meant they could not pay tax, which was seen as threatening to stability within the Church as it was planning, amongst other things, a crusade financed by tithes and indulgences. For this reason, some of the Mendicant orders were officially suppressed by Pope Gregory X at the Second Council of Lyon (1274) and others were reformed, so as to be capable of contributing to the mission of the Church.

Hence, there were both internal and external pressures on the Church to reform and, after the death of Jan Hus, civil unrest broke out in Bohemia, forcing Catholic priests in various parts of the country out of their parishes. When the King of Bohemia, King Wenceslaus IV, tried to suppress the movement, (under the guidance of Sigismund), a number of Hussites led by Mikuláš of Hus (no relation to Jan Hus) left Prague. Meetings were held in various parts of Bohemia and they prepared the country for war. The Hussites were divided into two factions, the more moderate Utraquists (from Latin, meaning 'in both kinds') maintained that a communion of bread and wine (as opposed to bread alone) should be administered during the celebration of the Eucharist. The Taborites were the more radical faction who, led by Petr Hromádka, seized the town of Sezimovo Ústí and the nearby Hradiště Castle in the spring of 1420.

They turned it into a model Hussite town, Hradiste Mount Tabor (abbreviated to Tabor as it was named after Mount Tabor in Galilee). Hussites from all over the country then joined them there. Social and economic equality were their main priorities, and they addressed each other as brothers and sisters. Using local gold mines as a source of finance, they created a communal society, announcing the Millennium of Christ, and declaring there would be no more servants and masters, all property would be held in common, and there would be no taxation. The ultimate aim of this was that people should be returned to a state of pristine innocence. Historians have found parallels with modern revolutionary movements, and it appears to be a type of proto-Communism which was seen as a solution to the problem with European Feudal Capitalism.

The Hussites laid out their policy demands in a statement known as the "Four Articles of Prague", recorded by Laurence of Brezova:

1. The word of God shall be preached and made known in the kingdom of Bohemia freely and in an orderly manner by the priests of the Lord.

2. The sacrament of the most Holy Eucharist shall be freely administered in the two kinds, that is bread and wine, to all the faithful in Christ who are not precluded by mortal sin — according to the word and disposition of Our Saviour.

3. The secular power over riches and worldly goods which the clergy possesses in contradiction to Christ's precept, to the prejudice of its office and to the detriment of the secular arm, shall be taken and withdrawn from it, and the clergy itself shall be brought back to the evangelical rule and an apostolic life such as that which Christ and his apostles led.

4. All mortal sins, and in particular all public and other disorders, which are contrary to God's law shall in every rank of life be duly and judiciously prohibited and destroyed by those whose office it is.

When Sigismund became emperor, he obtained permission from the Pope to launch a Crusade against them, and Crusaders came from all over Europe to fight five Crusades, all of which ended in defeat. Initially, Prague was taken and abandoned by the Hussites. However, when they counter-attacked, besieging the garrison of the Crusaders, they took back nearly all the land they had lost. The reason for their success was the Hussites used a unique style of warfare which was devastating to the feudal style of knights and foot soldiers typically employed by European armies at the time. Based on a solid defence then counter-attack, it consisted of a circle of wagons chained together, with handgunners and crossbow men behind the barricade. Sometimes they would dig a trench in front of it for extra defence. Then they would fire artillery at the enemy encampment, forcing them to attack, shooting the enemy knights' horses and flanking them from the sides with artillery and handguns, often leaving knights stranded in heavy armour on the battlefield.

A second crusade under the Germans was defeated by the Hussites, under the command of the priest, Jan Žižka, at the Battle of Deutschbrod. Then, after a third attempt by the papacy also ended in defeat, the Germans were forced to seek peace. It was only after 1434, when the Hussites had fought amongst themselves, and the Utraquists defeated the radical Taborites, that this created a unity which enabled the Hussites to eventually accept the authority of the King of Bohemia and the Roman Catholic Church, while subsequently being allowed to carry on practicing their alternative rite.

Part 2: The Timurid Mongol Revival

Meanwhile, in the East, the revival of the Mongol Empire occurred under Timur (meaning 'Iron' in the Chagatai language). Born in Transaxonia, he was the product of an Islamicised, Persianised branch of the Mongols, not a steppe nomad like the early Mongols. He styled himself as a warrior and, through his descendants, the Mongol Empire continued until the British Raj took control of India, thus making the empire in relation to Islam like the Holy Roman Empire was to Christianity in the West.

Born around 1330 into the Barlas confederation (present day Uzbekistan), Timur envisioned the restoration of the Mongol Empire of Genghis Khan. Though not directly related, he claimed to share a male-line ancestor with Genghis Khan through his father. In his younger days, he and a small band of followers raided travellers, especially taking domesticated livestock such as horses, cattle and sheep. Around 1363, it is believed he was shot by two arrows, in both the leg and hand, while serving as a mercenary to the Khan of Sistan in Khorasan, others say it was while trying to steal a sheep from a shepherd. Both injuries were crippling and earned him the name Timur the Lame (Tamerlane to Europeans).

However, by around 1360, he had gained importance as a military leader, in campaigns for the Chagatai Khanate. Using his family connections, he allied himself with Qazaghan (the Chagatai leader and conquerer of Volga Bulgaria) and held the position of leading 1000 men on horseback into Khorasan, then subjugated Khwarezm and Urgench. However, Qazaghan was then murdered and there was a dispute over who had the claim to power. At this point, the Khan of the Eastern Chagatai Khanate invaded and Timur was sent to negotiate, but changed sides and was awarded Transoxania. The Eastern Chagatai Khan later attempted to put his son in charge of the region, but Timur then defeated him with his own army.

He subsequently reduced the Chagatai Khans to the role of figureheads and used the title of Amir ('Khan' could only be used by a direct descendent of Genghis Khan). He was known as a good ruler, unlike his brother-in-law,

Amir Husayn, who imposed heavy taxes and spent the money on expensive buildings. Initially they were rivals but, by around 1370, Husayn surrendered to Timur and was then assassinated, allowing Timur to marry his wife, Saray Mulk Khanum, a descendant of Genghis Khan. He was then able to declare himself official ruler of the Chagatai.

After this, he led military campaigns across Western, South and Central Asia, the Caucasus and Southern Russia, and emerged as the most powerful ruler in the Muslim world. From the conquest of the Mamluks of Egypt and Syria, the fledgling Ottoman Empire and the Delhi Sultanate of India, he founded the Timurid Empire, the third largest empire established by a single ruler. Culturally speaking, it became a Persianate Turco-Mongol Islamic empire, which included present-day Uzbekistan, Iran, the southern Caucasus, Mesopotamia, Afghanistan, most of Central Asia, and parts of India, Pakistan, Syria and Turkey.

He adopted both Islamic symbolism and language, calling himself the "Sword of Islam", and promoted Islamic educational and religious programmes. During his lifetime he converted nearly all the Borjigin leaders to Islam and eventually gained control over the remnants of the Mongol Empire: the Chagatai Khanate, the Golden Horde and the Ilkhanate, and even attempted to restore the Yuan dynasty in China.

However, when he died in 1405 his son and first choice successor had died of an illness in 1376. His grandson, Muhammad Sultan, had been fatally injured in battle in 1403. On his death-bed he appointed Muhammad Sultan's younger brother, Pir Muhammad, who was subsequently unable to gain sufficient support to run the empire. Civil war then broke out between Timur's descendants, as multiple candidates vied for the title. It was not until 1409 that Timur's youngest son, Shah Rukh, was able to take the throne and rule until 1447.

Yet, he only ruled over the eastern side of the empire, most of Persia and Transoxiana, the western side having been lost to the Qara Qoyunlu (Black Sheep Turkoman) who had taken advantage of the war of the succession. Despite this, though, it remained the largest power in Asia. controlling the main trade routes between Asia and Europe, including the Silk Road, which generated wealth that lasted his successors. Moving his capital from Samarkand to Herat, he ruled not like his father, as a Turco-Mongol warlord-conqueror, but as an Islamic sultan. Diplomacy and economic stability increased during his rule, and he was a patron of the arts, sciences and learning.

However, when he died (in March 1447), another succession struggle emerged. As the dowager-empress Gawhar Shad and his grandson, Abdal-Latif, were taking his body on the journey eastwards for burial, Abdal-Latif took both her and the deceased Shah Rukh hostage. Ala al-Dawla, another grandson, rescued them and had Shah Rukh buried in Herat. However, Abdal-Latif's father, Ulugh Beg, captured the city the following year and ordered his father's body to be exhumed before reburying it with Timur's in Samarkand.

Ulugh Beg was more of an astronomer and mathematician than a ruler, but emerged victorious in a conflict with Ala al-Dawla. However, his lack of control over the empire led to his betrayal and assassination by Abdal-Latif in 1449, who was angry that the rule of Samarkand had not been given to him. He also killed his brother just a few days later, and became ruler of Transoxiana, but within six months had been killed in a conspiracy by the Amirs. Succeeded by his cousin Abdullah Mirza, the empire was taken over again two years later due to an uprising by Abu Sa'id Mirza, who was based in Bukhara.

Ruling Samarkand (1451–69) and Herat (1459–69), he reunited much of the Timurid Empire but, by this point, there were too many other factions competing for land in the region and his ambition to restore it completely ended after he died during an invasion of Iran. Thus, by the later part of the 1400s, the Timurid dynasty suffered the same problem as the Khans in keeping the Mongol Empire together, only worse, as competing descendants of Timur taking the throne in their own regions ultimately turned them all into warlords.

Most of Persia was lost to the Aq Qoyunlu confederation in 1467, and the reduced empire broke down into smaller states, known as the Timurid Emirates, in Central Asia and parts of India. By 1500, they were pushed back on all fronts: Persia, the Caucasus, Mesopotamia, and Eastern Anatolia fell to the Shi'a Safavid dynasty (which created a newly independent Persian state, later Iran). Central Asia was taken by the Uzbeks of Muhammad Shaybani, who conquered Samarkand and Herat in 1505 and 1507, and founded the Khanate of Bukhara.

However, the Mughal Empire emerged from Timurid dynasty, established by Babur, great-great-grandson of Timur, in 1526 from Kabul. By the 17th century, the Mughals ruled most of India, before competition between Great Britain and France led to it being taken over by the British Raj.

Part 3: The Ottoman Conquest of Byzantium

As the Timurid Empire spread eastwards into Asia, the Turks began a recovery. The Seljuq Turks had survived the attacks by the Crusaders, but were eventually defeated by the Mongol invasion of 1243 (at the Battle of Köse Dağ), thus becoming vassals of the Ilkhanate until the end of the century. When the last of their sultans, Mesud II, was killed in 1308 their state fell apart, resulting in the fragmentation of the Great Seljuk Empire. From small principalities known as Beyliks, on the frontier of the Byzantine Empire, in the town of Söğüt, the new Ottoman dynasty was founded by the Oghuz Turkish tribal leader, Osman I. He eventually conquered and reunited Anatolia into the Ottoman Empire (Ottoman is derived from Osman).

They were then able to take territory in Europe due to the crisis of the 1300s, as the Bulgarian Empire had suffered decline and defeat by Serbia in the Battle of Velbazhd (1330) and in 1346 the Serbian king, Stefan Dušan, was proclaimed emperor. However, they were then defeated by the Ottomans at the Battle of Kosovo, in 1389, whereby most of the Serbian nobility were killed and the south came under Turkish control. Southern Bulgaria had been taken by the Ottomans in 1371 and the north was captured in 1396. Serbia fell completely to the Turks in 1459, Bosnia in 1463 and Albania in 1479.

Around 1450, they made a direct attack on Constantinople. It had withstood earlier attacks, in the 7th and 8th centuries by Arabs, in the 9th and 10th centuries by Bulgar Khans, in the 9th, 10th and 11th centuries by the Rus and, also in the 9th century, by Thomas the Slav. It had huge defensive walls, 6.5 kilometers long, which had been built by the 5th century Emperor Theodosius II. Furthermore, it was on a peninsula of land surrounded by the sea on three sides, and ships could be kept out of the harbour by stretching a massive chain across it.

However, half the Byzantine population had died from the plague in the 1440s, and the Turkish force was strong. The city's troop garrison was relatively small, at only around 5,000, as was its navy. The Ottomans, under Mehmet II, had between 60,000 and 200,000 troops, and the largest siege cannons ever built: 9 metres long, with a muzzle a metre across. They could fire a cannon ball of 500 kilograms over 1.5 kilometers. The defenders subsequently had to repel attackers which came through enormous holes in the walls, which they had to repair at night. They also used a massive chain across the harbour, but the Ottomans custom-built a railroad to get 70 of their ships in. Constantinople only lasted around six weeks.

The geopolitical consequences of this were hugely significant in the long term, as the Byzantine Empire had for a long time influenced the culture and economy of the eastern Mediterranean region. As it became a tributary state of the Ottoman Empire its empire dissolved. Thus, it no longer provided a defence against the empires of the East or protection for trade routes into the West.

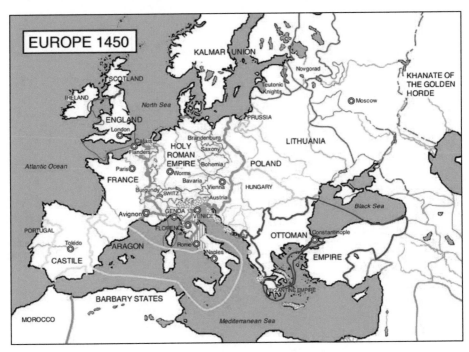

Additionally, the Golden Horde occupied present-day Russia and the Islamic Empires stretched across North Africa, so the Europeans were blocked in on all sides by land. Thus they had to seek another method of creating trade routes, and the only other way was by sea. Hence, by the 1490s, expeditions were sent to explore Africa, India and, through this, discovered the Americas. Christopher Columbus' voyage to the Americas (1492) and Vasco da Gama's discovery of Africa and India (1498) mark the beginning of the Age of Discovery, as the Europeans sought to develop global sea trade opportunities with the assistance of large fleets which protected their merchant vessels, thereby creating seafaring empires. These European colonial empires signalled the start of the Early Modern period.

CHAPTER 12

The Early Modern Period

The main feature of this period became the globalising effect of the European sea-empires, as they embarked on a period of maritime expansion known as the 'Age of Discovery'. Starting with the Spanish and Portuguese Empires, followed by the French, Dutch and British, they created a network of trading posts and colonies linking the Americas, Africa, India and the Far East. However, within Europe itself, the Protestant Reformation led to the Papacy losing control of Europe's centre and a series of wars over the balance of power, before new political ideas arose...

Part 1: The Age of Discovery

Starting with the Spanish and Portuguese, the Europeans established a series of colonial empires which recolonised the Americas, linking them to Africa, India and the Far East. For this reason, the Early Modern Period is noted for its globalising influence. Protected by large naval fleets, their expeditions created trading posts which later evolved into colonies, with the purpose of acquiring commodities such as raw materials, sugar, spices and textiles for both resale and use in manufacturing industries at home. This led to a new period in East-West relations known as the Great Divergence, as Europe became the world's industrial superpower.

Immanuel Wallerstein says, in his book 'The Modern World System', ¹'In the late fifteenth and early sixteenth century, there came into existence what we may call a European world-economy. It was not an empire yet it was as spacious as a grand empire and shared some features with it. But it was different, and new. It was a kind of social system the world has not really known before and which is the distinctive feature of the modern world-system. It is an economic but not political entity, unlike empires, city-states and nation-states. In fact, it precisely encompasses within its bounds (it is hard to speak of boundaries) empires, city-states and the emerging "nation-states". It is a "world" system, not because it encompasses the whole world, but because it is larger than any juridically-defined political unit. And it is a "world-economy" because the basic linkage between the parts of the system is economic, although this was reinforced to some extent by cultural links and eventually, as we shall see, by political arrangements and even confederal structures.'

In terms of its total effect, which included the conquest of the Americas by Spain, and the British occupation of India, it appeared through two main stages, the first of which is known as Mercantilism (from the concept of a 'Merchant-based' economy, in which government policy was designed to keep taxes low and create investment in trade), before the free-market Capitalism we know today emerged during the industrial revolution. The first period produced the first mega-corporations like the British and Dutch East India companies, which had their own ships and military resources granted to them by governments.

However, they had learned from previous empires that it was no longer necessary to completely invade and conquer nations, but instead to make use of their people under a limited 'colonial' occupation which would produce economic growth.

The Spanish and Portuguese Empires

The first European countries to create colonial empires were Spain and Portugal, who embarked on voyages to the Americas and India in the late 1400s. They created colonial outposts along the way around Africa and divided most of the Americas between themselves. The Spanish Empire had its roots in the Reconquista, which emerged as the Umayyad Caliphate had allowed several small Christian kingdoms to continue to exist in the north: León, Castile, Aragon, Portugal and Navarre. Their gradual southwards expansion culminated in the seizure of the last Muslim stronghold, the Nasrid Kingdom of Granada, in 1492. Meanwhile, the dynastic union of Castile and Aragon under the Catholic Monarchs, Ferdinand and Isabella, saw the emergence of Spain as a unified country.

Following Columbus landing in the Caribbean and Vasco Da Gama's discovery of India, expeditions were sent out to pursue trade and establish colonies which could act as permanent points of contact, acquire resources and harbour naval fleets. Columbus' initial voyage, in August 1492, consisted of only 87 men on three ships. The first island they found in October was named San Salvador. Despite being in the Caribbean, they actually believed themselves to be in Asia and referred to the native people as Indians, suggesting they had no prior knowledge of the Americas even existing! Columbus even thought the island of Cuba was part of China. Subsequent islands they found were named after his ship, king, and queen: La Isla de Santa María de Concepción, Fernandina, and Isabella.

In January, 1493, Columbus sailed back to Europe to report what he found. However, rough seas forced him to land in Portugal, where King John II was not pleased to hear about his Spanish-backed voyages. John sent a letter to the Spanish monarchy invoking the earlier Treaty of Alcáçovas (1479), stating all the land south of the Canary Islands belonged to Portugal. Therefore, he argued, all of the lands Columbus had discovered should belong to him. When the Portuguese King stated that he was preparing a fleet to take possession of the new lands, Spain realised they could not compete with him militarily and pursued a diplomatic solution by involving the Papacy. In May 1493, Pope

Alexander VI (Rodrigo Borgia) decreed in a Papal Bull that all lands west of the north-south line 100 leagues west of the Azores should belong to Spain. The Bull did not mention Portugal, which prevented them from making their claim. Accepting this, Portugal then entered direct negotiations with Spain, which moved the line 270 leagues west, granting the Portuguese their route down the coast of Africa and giving them eastern Brazil. This was a diplomatic success for both sides as, by this point, Portugal had discovered the route to India around the Cape of Good Hope, and the conquest of Indian territory was their ultimate aim.

In 1493 Columbus sailed once again, this time taking a large fleet to conquer native territories and establish colonies. The native Americans retaliated by attacking Fort Navidad, killing settlers there. However, the colonists managed to enslave many of the natives, sending some to back Europe while they used others to mine gold. The third trip was to further explore the islands and the mainland. Columbus was then appointed governor of Hispaniola, but sent home at the request of the colonists and replaced by Francisco de Bobadilla. On his fourth and final voyage in 1502, the year when the first slaves from Africa arrived in the Americas, his mission was to find India, but storms at sea left them stranded on Jamaica for two years until help arrived and he returned to Spain in 1504.

In the following decades Portugal explored the islands of East Africa, establishing forts and factories, and creating a series of naval outposts from Lisbon to Nagasaki. Spain began building their American empire from the Caribbean, based on the islands of Cuba, Puerto Rico and Hispaniola. Florida fell in 1513 and Hernán Cortés conquered the Aztec Empire (1519–21), which had been ruled by Moctezuma II. This was achieved by expanding into northern Central America and up into the present day United States. From Mexico they also sailed over the Pacific Ocean to the Philippines. The Conquistadors took over the Incan Empire after crossing the Isthmus of Panama and sailing around the Pacific to northern Peru. Francisco Pizarro then led the conquest of the Incan Empire, and Peru was used as a base for the conquest of Ecuador and Chile. In Colombia, Bolivia, and Argentina, conquistadors from Peru linked up with others coming directly from the Caribbean and Paraguay.

Henceforth, the Spanish Empire, known as the Hispanic Monarchy (and also the Catholic Monarchy) became one of the largest in history, and is described as the first global empire because of the spread of its territory around the world. Castile became the dominant region in Spain, because of its jurisdiction over the territory in the Americas and the Philippines, and they became more powerful than the Holy Roman Empire under Philip II (1556–98). Under Philip the empire expanded to rule over Portugal, the Netherlands, Sicily, Naples, Franche-Comté, the Rhineland and large parts of the Americas (from the border of present-day Canada all the way down to Argentina), trading ports in India and South Asia, the Spanish East Indies, and parts of Guinea and North Africa.

Its major industries were spices, sugar plantations (which used slave labour taken from Africa, a highly profitable system which was copied by the British and others) and later textile trade with India. However, social change was coming in Europe, as new discoveries stimulated politics, the rise of its empires raised questions over the direction of progress, and scientific ideas started challenging the doctrines of the Church.

Part 2: The Protestant Reformation

Christian Europe split in half when opposition to corruption, and reforms to make the Church more functional, were proposed by Martin Luther, and supported by German lawmakers who regarded them as being consistent with other legal and societal developments. This led to direct contradiction with the Ecumenical Council of the Catholic Church and, when challenged by the Holy Roman Emperor, Charles V, revolts and civil war within Germany broke out before the Reformation spread uncontrollably throughout Europe.

For centuries the Church had been deeply involved in the creation of the new Christian Europe, which had emerged from the fall of the Western Roman Empire. The political requirements of this, combined with the church's increasing power and wealth, led to scholars identifying this as the cause of corruption of Christianity by the Church, and in particular they began to point to specific practices. Problems with the system itself came to the attention of scholars who could see that the Church's internal reform procedures could only address issues so far, and did not take into account broader changes in society. These included, law, civil rights, and the rise of scientific ideas which had been growing since the Universities began in the 1200s. The invention of the Printing Press meant the ability to read and write became something everyone could possess, meaning a rise in the ability to propose and discuss ideas which had previously been the exclusive property of the higher levels of society.

Secondly, abuses of power by the Church were highlighting social inequality, such as the selling of 'indulgences' (paid forgiveness from sins). Also, the ascension of each Holy Roman Emperor caused a power struggle, first as he established himself in Germany, then internationally, meaning allies and family members were appointed in high positions and the practice of holding more than one office simultaneously (simony) led to rulers exercising virtually absolute power over various regions. Social reformers began to accuse the Church of not being the 'real' Christianity, as it was born out of a compromise between early western Christian missionaries and the Roman Empire.

In other words, during the establishment of feudalism, the Church saved Europe from the Dark Ages, as the German migrations which sacked Rome lacked unity. The Christians enabled people to live in a more organised type of kingdom with a better financial system and technology. However, this brought its own problems as most people could not even discuss the new ideas, most of whom were illiterate peasants who were tied to the land (serfdom). By the 1500s, though, the beginnings of Modern Capitalism was creating a fast rise in social awareness and urbanisation, so it could be said that the centralisation of power in Christian Europe was being destabilised by this. Hence, the type of power the Catholic Church was creating and endorsed fundamentally became seen as a problem, which the Church was not able to accept, as St. Peter was sent by Jesus himself to found the Church in Rome.

Martin Luther

The first churches to demand amendments to the Catholic doctrine were not Lutheran. Utraquist Hussitism was acknowledged by the Council of Basel (1436) and officially tolerated by the Crown of Bohemia, although other movements were still subject to persecution, like the Lollards (led by John Wycliffe) in England and the Waldensians in France and Italy (founded by Peter Waldo, who rejected the ideas of purgatory and transubstantiation). The reform movement within the Church, Conciliarism (during the 14th, 15th and 16th centuries), believed that supreme authority resided with the Ecumenical council, not the Pope. However, Martin Luther became most popular, as he not only discussed theological issues, but also suggested practical reforms to the Church and proposed new methods by which it could become more successful.

It all began with his publication of the 95 Theses (or 'Disputation on the Power and Efficacy of Indulgences'), a list of propositions written in 1517 when Martin Luther was professor of moral theology at the University of Wittenberg, Germany. According to his later work, they were only intended as philosophical propositions for debate, rather than his own opinions, but by this point they had caused a massive effect on society.

Primarily, the theses were against the practice of the clergy selling 'plenary indulgences' (certificates believed to reduce temporal punishment in purgatory, the place in the afterlife Christians believed they could go to repent their sins if they were not sent directly to Heaven or Hell). Luther claimed that, in reality, actual repentance involved inner spiritual experience rather than simply an external confession. He argued that it enabled people to avoid true repentance, and discouraged them from giving to the poor and other acts of mercy, believing that indulgence certificates were merely enough to justify redemption. He also refuted a 14th-century Papal Bull which had stated that the Pope could use the 'Treasury of Merit' (a term used to describe the 'total goodness' of the Church, accumulated by previous Saints and Popes) to decide what should be done with regard to the forgiveness of sins.

Initially, he had gone to college to become a lawyer, but became a priest, and found evidence of wrongdoing by the Church in St. Paul's writings. His training enabled him to formulate arguments which would not normally have been possible for a priest, such as challenging the idea that the Pope could have authority over purgatory, and pointing out that the Treasury of Merit had no foundation in the Bible. Furthermore, if the Church were to derive its idea of centralised authority from the mission of St. Peter (who was sent by Jesus to found the Church in Rome), it should lead by example in terms of its own conduct. He also claimed that Christians were saved by their faith in Christ, not by the Church, and hence the Church was not able to pardon their sins, only God was able to do that.

The Theses were sent with a letter to Albert of Brandenburg, the Archbishop of Mainz, on 31 October 1517, the date which is now commemorated annually as Reformation Day. It was also posted on the door of various churches in Wittenberg, in accordance with University customs, between the end of October and mid-November. They were quickly reprinted, translated, and distributed around Germany and Europe. This started a personal dispute with Johann Tetzel, a Dominican preacher who was commissioned by Cardinal Giovanni de' Medici (later Pope Leo X) in 1502, to preach the Jubilee Indulgence. A direct conflict of interests appeared as, in 1517, Tetzel was made the commissioner of indulgences for Archbishop Albert of Brandenburg, who intended to use half the money recovered to pay off his own debts.

In 1515, Pope Leo X had granted the sale of plenary indulgences to finance the building of St. Peter's Basilica in Rome, which could even be purchased on behalf of the dead who were suffering in purgatory, and applied to almost any sin. All other indulgences were cancelled for the eight years it was offered. Indulgence Preachers had been given instructions on how the indulgence was to be sold to the public, and Johann Tetzel's campaign covered cities near Wittenberg, in Luther's electoral Saxony, where their sale was prohibited by Duke George. Wittenbergers were thus being prompted to travel to purchase the indulgences from cities where they were legal, to the objection of Luther, and others who were against their sale.

The popular advertising slogan, 'As soon as the coin in the coffer rings, the soul from purgatory springs' was criticised by Theologians at the University of Paris in the late 15th century, and others including John Wycliffe, who also argued that the Pope had no jurisdiction over Purgatory. Jan Hus had advocated a system of penance which prohibited indulgences and invited individuals to genuinely question their own actions. The 95 Theses prompted moral criticism of the type of logic the sale of indulgences purported and, following this, Tetzel died in Leipzig in 1519, having both fallen into disrepute and completely withdrawn from public life.

While Archbishop Albrecht of Mainz had not replied to Luther's original letter containing the 95 Theses, he had them checked for heresy and forwarded them to Rome. Subsequently a series of papal theologians and envoys were sent to investigate Luther and the Dominican theologian Sylvester Mazzolini drew up a heresy case which led to him being summoned before Pope Leo X. Fortunately for Luther the Elector of Saxony, Frederick III, had a strong belief in a fair trial for all citizens (which was guaranteed by statutory imperial law) and persuaded the Pope to hold the hearing at Augsburg.

He also had an interest in Luther's work, as he had to pay money to the Church for his collection of religious artefacts, such as a twig from Moses' burning bush and hay from Jesus' manger, the veneration of which could land him in purgatory. By removing Church authority over purgatory, he would be free to keep his exclusive collection at no cost. Over a three day period in October 1518, Luther was formally questioned by the papal legate Cardinal Cajetan. The prosecution made the Pope's right to issue indulgences the centre of the dispute, which descended into a heated argument. Cajetan's instructions were to arrest Luther if he failed to withdraw his work, but with help from a Carmelite monk, Christoph Langenmantel, Luther escaped from the city at night.

Papal nuncio Karl von Miltitz, a relative of Frederick, adopted a more strategic approach in January 1519, resulting in Luther agreeing to remain silent if his opponents did. However, theologian Johann Eck was determined to expose Luther's work publicly and, in June and July 1519, held a disputation with Luther's colleague, Andreas Karlstadt, at which he invited Luther to speak. After his work reached France, Italy and England, students flocked to Wittenberg to hear Luther. He lectured on the Psalms, the books of Hebrews, Romans, and Galatians, using terms such as penance and righteousness in ways which implied the church had lost sight of important truths within Christianity. He also published (in 1520) 'To the Christian Nobility of the German Nation', 'On the

Babylonian Captivity of the Church', and 'On the Freedom of a Christian' (a copy of which he sent to the Pope).

On 15 June 1520, the Pope warned Luther through a Papal Bull that he risked excommunication unless he recanted 41 sentences from his writings within 60 days. Johann Eck subsequently proclaimed the Bull in Meissen and other towns, but Luther publicly set fire to it at Wittenberg on 10 December 1520, and defended his actions by writing 'Why the Pope and his Recent Book are Burned and Assertions Concerning All Articles'.

He was subsequently excommunicated on 3 January 1521. The enforcement of this then fell to the secular authorities and, on 18 April, Luther appeared before the Diet of Worms, a general assembly of the estates of the Holy Roman Empire, presided over by Emperor Charles V (head of the Austrian House of Habsburg, Archduke of Austria, King of Spain and Lord of the Netherlands). Frederick III managed to obtain safe conduct for Luther to and from the trial, which resulted in the Edict of Worms. This declared Luther an outlaw, banned people in Germany from supporting or propagating his work, and required his arrest.

Intervention by the German Princes

However, while returning to Wittenberg Luther was kidnapped by three masked men impersonating highway robbers, sent by Frederick III as part of a plan to rescue him from prosecution by the Church, and they took him to safety in Wartburg Castle at Eisenach. While there he translated the New Testament from Greek into German and published more writings. These included the idea that it was wrong to attempt to attract God's favour through good deeds, as sinfulness was a natural part of human life, but people's faith in Christ should be stronger than their sins in order for them to succeed. He criticised the idea that Confession could be demanded by the Pope, asserting that it was a private matter for people to consider for themselves, and condemned the idea that Mass should be seen as a sacrifice. Instead, he asserted, it should be seen as a gift to be received with thanks from the whole congregation. He also encouraged monks and nuns to break their vows without believing this to be sinful, as vows were an illegitimate attempt to achieve salvation.

Meanwhile, his companion Andreas Karlstadt (supported by the ex-Augustinian Gabriel Zwilling), was carrying out radical reforms to the Church in Wittenberg, which Luther had secretly visited in December. As this provoked demands for revolutionary reform, including a revolt by the Augustinian friars, Luther subsequently wrote 'A Sincere Admonition by Martin Luther to All Christians to Guard Against Insurrection and Rebellion.'

After a group of visionary zealots known as the 'Zwickau Prophets' arrived in Wittenberg, in early 1522, the town council asked Luther to formally return. For eight days in March he preached eight sermons (known as the Invocavit Sermons) which were focused on traditional Christian values such as love, patience, charity, freedom, and the renunciation of violence, which were well received by the local population. He then addressed the issue of new church practices, worked with the authorities to restore public order, and argued for reinvention to be used as a conservative force within the reform movement.

However, despite banishing the Zwickau Prophets, Luther was unable to stop radicalism spreading under preachers like Thomas Müntzer and the Zwickau Prophet, Nicholas Storch. They gained support from the urban poor and peasantry between then and 1525. Luther's pamphlets had, by this point, led many to believe he wished to initiate an attack on both the Upper Classes and the Church, and revolts broke out in Swabia, Franconia and Thuringia in 1524. These were then supported by dissatisfied nobles, many of whom were in debt under the current regime. Under the leadership of Müntzer, Hipler and Lotzer, these revolts then turned into war, resulting in the widespread burning of convents, monasteries, bishops' palaces and libraries.

Luther wrote 'Against the Murderous, Thieving Hordes of Peasants' upon his return to Wittenberg, continuing to argue rationally in the tradition of Thomas Aquinas, that Baptism does not make people free in terms of body or wealth, but in their soul. Therefore, he argued, rebels were the worst type of people, ones who embody the opposite of Christian values. Without his direct support, much of the rebellion calmed down. Defeat by the Swabian League at the Battle of Frankenhausen on 15 May 1525, and Müntzer's execution, ended the revolutionary stage of the Reformation. Thereafter, radicalism was limited to the Anabaptists and other fringe movements, while Luther's Reformation grew with the assistance of secular power.

In June he was married to Katharina von Bora, one of 12 nuns he helped to escape from the Nimbschen Cistercian Convent in April 1523. She was 26 years old at the time and he was 41. They moved into a former monastery, 'The Black Cloister', which was a wedding present from the new Elector, John the Steadfast. They had six children between 1526 and 1534, and appear to have been happy together, making money by farming and taking in lodgers.

After a period of theological argument with Erasmus, a Dutch Catholic scholar, through works published on both sides, he then addressed the issue of how to reform the Church. He did not want to simply replace one form of authority with another, but instead created a new form of the religion, which could better serve the contemporary needs of society. Identifying problems to the existing system, he set about improving it through a number of practical measures.

In 1527 he reviewed the level of pastoral care across various territories and amended the Church service to be more inclusive: people were allowed to partake in the wine along with the bread during Mass, hymns and psalms were also sung in German, and religious instruction was added into weekday services in the form of the Catechism. In 1529, he wrote the Large Catechism, a guide for pastors, and the Small Catechism, to be read by members of the public. They provided instructions on how to understand the basic principles of Christianity such as the Ten Commandments, the Apostles' Creed, The Lord's Prayer and Baptism. There were also questions and answers to stimulate intellectual thought, having seen many pastors to be quite unskilled in the art of teaching. It particularly helped parents to teach their children, and encouraged a discussion of the type of society people lived in. Additionally, his translation of the Bible used a variant of German which could be understood by people all over the country, making it a widespread and easily accessible publication.

It was Luther's belief that the unredeemed human is dominated by his animal nature, but through Baptism their souls could be liberated and thus able to serve God. He saw that people could not achieve salvation through their own willpower alone, but needed a society which encouraged them to do so. Nor do they fundamentally choose between good or evil, because everyone has different circumstances into which they are born, and it is much easier for a person born into wealth to commit good deeds. Therefore, the aim of the Church should be to help people to build the type of society which encourages people to turn towards God, encourage moral equality across social class divides, and ultimately move the whole situation forward as the previous age which had created the Church had moved people forward.

The Augsburg Confession

However, in 1530, Holy Roman Emperor Charles V called on the Princes and Free Territories in Germany to explain their religious reforms. This resulted in the 'Augsburg Confession', which was written in both German and Latin, and presented by a number of German rulers to the Diet of Augsburg on 24 June. It makes several clear amendments to the Catholic religion, not only in terms of its practical duty to serve the community, but also in terms of general theology and personal morality. These include:

'II. Original Sin: Lutherans believe that the nature of man is sinful, described as being without fear of God, without trust of God and with concupiscence. Sin is redeemed through Baptism and the Holy Spirit.

VI. Of The New Obedience: Lutherans believe that good deeds of Christians are the fruits of faith and salvation, not a price paid for them.

VII. Of The Church: Lutherans believe that there is one holy Christian church, and it is found wherever the gospel is preached in its truth and purity and the sacraments are administered according to the gospel.

XXIII. Of the Marriage of Priests: Lutherans permit their clergy to enter the institution of marriage, for the reasons that the early Church bishops were married, that God blesses marriage as an order of creation, because marriage and procreation is a natural thing.

XXVII. Of Monastic Vows: Man cannot achieve purity in community or isolation from the rest of the world, and perfection cannot be attained by any vow taken or actions of man alone.

XXVIII. Of Ecclesiastical Power: The only power given to priests or bishops is the power offered through Scripture to preach, teach and administer the sacraments. The powers given to the clergy in issues of government or the military are granted and respected only through civil means; they are not civil rulers of governments and the military by divine right.'

In two main sections, one on matters of faith and the other on corrections of abuse of religious power, it clearly outlined changes to Church doctrine, modernising it according to the rules of contemporary law. It moved away from the idea that the mission of St. Peter was to be considered the only true Church, yet they claimed that nothing had actually been written against the Catholic Church or its political position.

However, the main concern of Charles V was to restore religious and political unity within the Holy Roman Empire and gather support against the Turkish invasion. From a Catholic point of view, the Protestants were the problem as they could not see the implications of the Pope losing control over Europe, as it would not have the organisation it needed to defend itself. What followed is known as the consideration of the Augsburg Confession by the Church, and Charles V gave the Protestants until 15 April 1531 to respond to its findings. In response, Philipp Melancthon published a lengthy argument supporting the Augsburg Confession and refuting the arguments of the Confutation, which became known as the 'Apology of the Augsburg Confession'. While the Confutation was not published, or even read out loud in public, the Apology was translated into German and distributed across the country.

The Schmalkaldic Wars

The German princes who supported Luther formed an alliance known as the Schmalkaldic League, to guard against any potential military action by Charles V. By 1535, the League admitted any city or state to the alliance that supported the Confession of Augsburg or the Apology. Theological disputes prevented England from joining, yet Henry VIII converted to Protestantism and pursued an extensive campaign against the Catholics, which resulted in him being excommunicated by Pope Paul III in 1538. In 1536, the king of Denmark-Norway, Christian III, marched on Copenhagen and initiated the Reformation era there. Other reformist movements around Europe also appeared, such as the Calvinists, stoking fears among Catholics of a full-scale religious revolution.

This situation continued until the Ecumenical Council of Trent (1545–1563), which has been described as the embodiment of the Catholic Counter-Reformation. It issued condemnations of heresies committed by the Protestants, and clarified the position of the Roman Catholic Church on doctrines of the time. In response, the Schmalkaldic League met in July 1546 at Ichtershausen to decide how to deal with the anticipated conflict. John Frederick and Philip of Hesse agreed that the Emperor may have a larger army, but they could be quicker to mobilise their troops. Subsequently, they decided to launch a pre-emptive campaign against the Catholics, in an attempt to force a peace treaty. Martin Luther died in February, preventing his objection, as he had always been morally against war.

However, the small Protestant force was quickly defeated and the captured Elector, John Frederick I, signed the Capitulation of Wittenberg in May 1547. His cousin, Maurice, with whom Charles V had been forming an alliance since 1544, became the new Saxon Elector in June. In May 1548 Charles V declared the Augsburg Interim, which demanded the reintegration of Protestants into the Catholic Church. However, by this point the influence of Protestantism had spread across Europe and could not be contained within Germany, leading to the Second Schmalkaldic War. In 1552 the Protestant princes were led by Elector Maurice of Saxony, but this time backed by King Henry II of France, who was concerned about the new relationship between the Holy Roman Emperor and the Church. Charles V then had to escape a large Protestant army and sign the Peace of Passau, which freed John Frederick I of Saxony and Philip I of Hesse. An official document recognising Protestantism appeared three years later, known as the Peace of Augsburg. Charles V resigned the next year and was replaced by his brother, Ferdinand I.

Part 3: The New Balance of Power in Europe

As a result of the Reformation, a new order emerged in Europe, one in which the central authority of the Papacy had been fundamentally undermined and France emerged as a rival to the Holy Roman Empire. Yet, its empires continued to grow, producing a complex situation. Due to the success of the Spanish in the Americas others were seeing the possibility of creating overseas empires to improve their position within Europe. Subsequently, French, Dutch and British colonies began appearing in North America, Africa and Asia, leading to a series of wars over the balance of power.

Spain at the time was under the influence of an alliance with the Holy Roman Empire, since Queen Joanna of Castile (crowned in 1504) was married to Philip I, the Habsburg son of the Holy Roman Emperor, Maximilian I. While they were tied to the Papacy, the western Protestant nations such as Britain and Holland formed their own alliances. Thus the Peace of Augsburg only provided a temporary reprieve from the hostilities, and the underlying cause of the conflict was not resolved. The rulers of the 224 German states had been allowed to choose Lutheranism or Catholicism, but their subjects had to accept their decision or leave. Prince-bishoprics ruled by the Catholic clergy were excluded (thus remaining Catholic), and those who converted to Protestantism were required to resign, but the Protestants were allowed to keep the territory they had taken from the Catholic Church since the Peace of Passau in 1552. The situation became even more complex as Calvinism (a series of doctrines which also drew heavily on St. Augustine and early Church traditions) spread throughout Germany in the following years. Additionally, some of the converted bishops then refused to give up their bishoprics, and various Catholic rulers sought to restore order using the power of the Church.

This led to the Cologne War (1583–88), which occurred as the prince-archbishop of the city, Gebhard Truchsess von Waldburg, converted to Calvinism. As an imperial Elector, he threatened to create a Protestant majority in the College that elected the Holy Roman Emperor. As a result, Spanish troops expelled him and replaced him with Ernst of Bavaria. After this, the Catholics began to enforce the law more strictly, forcing Lutheran residents into conversion or exile. Then several lords, of the Palatinate (1560), Nassau (1578), Hesse-Kassel (1603), and Brandenburg (1613) also converted to the new Calvinist doctrine. Hence, at the beginning of the 1600s, the area from the Rhine to the Danube remained mostly Catholic, Lutherans dominated the north, Sweden and Denmark-Norway, while Calvinists had a majority in areas such as west-central Germany, Switzerland, and the Netherlands.

Religious tensions turned to violence in 1606, when the Lutheran majority in the German city of Donauwörth, Swabia, barred Catholics from holding their annual Markus procession, causing a riot known as the Battle of the Flags, before Duke Maximilian of Bavaria intervened on behalf of the Catholics. After this, the Calvinists in Germany formed the Protestant Union (1608) under the leadership of the Palatine Elector, Frederick IV. To counter this, the Catholic League formed (1609), under Duke Maximilian.

In 1610 the War of the Jülich Succession occurred as Rudolf II, Holy Roman Emperor, occupied Jülich-Cleves-Berg until the Aulic Council resolved the dispute between two rival Protestant claimants. However, several Protestant princes claimed that the emperor wanted to keep the territory for himself and Henry IV of France, assisted by the Dutch Republic, launched a counter-invasion. He was assassinated by a Catholic. In 1614 the three Duchies were separated, with Jülich and Berg given to the Catholic Count Wolfgang Wilhelm, while the Calvinist Elector of Brandenburg, John Sigismund, gained Cleves, Mark, and Ravensberg.

The 30 Years War (1618–48)

Initially this was a conflict between rival Catholic and Protestant factions within the Holy Roman Empire, but it became one of the deadliest wars in human history, in which over 8 million people died. This included 20% of the whole of Germany and 50% in the area between Pomerania and the Black Forest. When France intervened, it permanently altered the balance of power in Europe, as the French then fully emerged as a force to rival the Habsburgs.

By 1617, it became apparent that the Holy Roman Emperor (and King of Bohemia, Matthias), would die without an heir, and the title would pass to his cousin, Archduke Ferdinand II of Austria, who was the Crown Prince of Bohemia at the time. However, Ferdinand was a traditionalist Catholic who had been educated by Jesuits, and wanted to impose religious uniformity on the whole country. This made him hugely unpopular in Protestant Bohemia, which had a Hussite majority, and the Bohemian nobility rejected him. Ferdinand's representatives were subsequently thrown out of a window in Prague (known as the 'Defenestration of Prague'), which provoked an open revolt and drew in support from other Protestant-majority states.

While Protestants and Catholic Habsburgs started preparing for war, the Protestant Bohemians ousted their Habsburg ruler, and elected Frederick V, a Calvinist, as the new king of Bohemia. The southern states, led by Bavaria, then formed the Catholic League to expel Frederick in support of the Emperor and the Empire subsequently crushed the Protestant rebellion at the Battle of the White Mountain, then executed the leading Bohemian aristocrats. Subsequently, Protestant rulers across Europe condemned the Emperor's actions and Saxony joined the Protestant Union. Sweden then intervened in 1630 under king Gustavus Adolphus, turning the situation into a full-scale war. Habsburg Spain, whose motive was to defeat the Dutch Republic, then entered the war on the side of Habsburg Austria, and Catholic France subsequently entered on the side of the Protestants, due to their rivalry with the Habsburgs.

The war devastated entire regions, especially the German and Italian states, Bohemia, and the Southern Netherlands. Both mercenaries and soldiers looted and extorted tributes to fund themselves, thereby imposing severe hardship on local populations. The war also bankrupted most of the nations who took part, as there was no real gain from the victory. In 1648, it ended with the Peace of Westphalia, having altered the political order of the European powers. The emergence of Bourbon France was a challenge to Habsburg control of Central Europe, and Sweden emerged as a major military force.

The Dutch Republic benefited massively, as not only did it obtain independence from the Holy Roman Empire and its former masters, Spain, it ended the 80-year revolt against the Spanish and led to the Dutch Golden Age. In this period, it became one of the world's leading economic, colonial and naval powers, most notably through the merging of rival trading companies into The Dutch East India Company, the world's first mega-corporation. It created a trade-based system which encouraged merchant enterprise through control of international maritime shipping routes through strategically placed outposts, thus avoiding the costly invasion and control of large territories. Mostly, its empire was comprised of coastal forts, factories, and port settlements, and while some expanded (such as the Dutch Cape Colony into the Republic of South Africa) and the Dutch East Indies (into Indonesia) most remained smaller than their host-nations.

Britain had not taken part, as it was in the middle of the English Civil War at the time, which had the effect of ending the absolute power of the monarchy. Fought between the Parliamentarians (Roundheads, after the helmets their soldiers wore) and the Monarchists (Cavaliers), it ended in the execution of Charles I and established a Constitutional Monarchy. Since then, it has been the House of Commons' role to formulate and pass laws, which must then receive the approval of the House of Lords, before being officially signed by the monarch.

The Fronde Rebellion and French Absolute Monarchy

However, all this progress brought new internal problems and caused social upheaval within these nations. France, in attempting to move forwards, went backwards following the Fronde rebellion (1648 and 1653), leading to the Absolute Monarchy of Louis XIV, XV and XVI. This is said by historians to be one of the major cultural factors which led to the French Revolution. During this time, King Louis XIV faced multiple opponents, including the nobility, law courts and parlements (parliaments), eventually defeating them all and turning the Palace of Versaille into a cultural centre to control politics.

It began over fiscal edicts, six of which involved increasing taxation due to the recent war. The first period of this was known as the Parlementary Fronde (from the French 'Parle', meaning 'to speak'), as the parlements pushed back against new taxation measures by questioning the constitutional rights of the King. It was not a revolutionary movement, but a legal battle to defend the rights of chartered towns in terms of powers already awarded to them. While the nobility refused to pay, under previous laws guaranteeing this privilege, it fell to the bourgeoisie, middle-class elements of the government, and this not only caused a refusal to pay but also a condemnation of earlier financial policies by all the sovereign courts of Paris, who called for constitutional reform.

Cardinal Mazarin, chief minister to Louis XIV, arrested the leaders of the parlement, causing Paris to break down into civil disorder with barricades in the streets. The nobility called for an assembly of the Estates General (a meeting of all the social classes of France, last convened in 1615), believing that they could control the situation this way. This meant that France simply gave up the first stage of parliamentary reform which it had been entering and went back to the Feudal system to try and solve the problem.

However, with their army still away on duty because of the 30 year war, the royalty then had to release the parlement leaders and fled from Paris on 22 October. However, France's signing of the Peace of Westphalia allowed the army to return and, by January 1649, they had Paris under siege, leading to the Peace of Rueil in March. From then on the Fronde became a battle between two groups of princes for control of the state. This became known as the Fronde of the Princes, as there were prominent figures on both sides, fighting a civil war which saw France descend into anarchy before the King's side finally won. The result of this was the Palace of Versaille was turned into a political centre to spy on the rebellious aristocrats of France, paving the way for the French Absolute Monarchy which lasted all the way until the French Revolution of 1779.

The War of the Spanish Succession (1701–14)

This occurred as the Austrian Habsburgs challenged the ascendancy of a Spanish monarch who was so closely related to the French monarchy that it would have effectively handed the French control over the Spanish territories in the Americas. When King Charles II, the last Habsburg ruler of Spain, left the monarchy to Louis XIV's grandson, Philip (in 1700), the Holy Roman Emperor, Leopold I, proposed that his younger son, Archduke Charles, should be crowned 'Carlos' instead.

Disputes over territorial and commercial rights led to war in 1701, as it threatened to upset the balance of power in Europe on one side, or reverse progress on the other. On one side was the Grand Alliance led by Austria, Great Britain, the Dutch Republic, Portugal (from 1703), Habsburg Spain, Prussia, Saxony and Savoy; on the other was the Bourbon monarchy of France, Bourbon Spain, Morocco, Bavaria, Cologne, Liège, Portugal, Savoy and Hungary.

It was a large conflict, with both political and economic interests at stake. Battles were fought all over Europe and, by extension, in the colonies of North America and the West Indies. The Austrian-led coalition forces were on the offensive right from the start, and the 1703 Battle of Vigo Bay caused Portugal to change sides, opening a new front in Iberia. Savoy also changed sides, putting pressure on Spanish and French holdings in Italy, and during 1704–8 the Alliance also pushed forward in Central Europe, forcing Bavaria out of the war, while Savoy enabled the Allies to contain France. Temporary occupations of Madrid, Barcelona and Valencia occurred, but Philipe of Anjou remained on the throne due to popular support within Spain.

By the end of 1708, both sides were deadlocked, and costs had severely hit the French and Spanish treasuries. France was forced out of northern Italy and Spain out of southern Italy. Britain was the dominant naval force in the Mediterranean and captured Gibraltar and Minorca from Spain. However, in 1711, Archduke Charles, the man whom Austria proposed should rule Spain, became the Holy Roman Emperor and nobody wanted one man to have that much power, thus ending the war.

The French Philipe was formally recognised as King of Spain, but with certain concessions such as renouncing his right to inherit the French throne, both for himself and his descendants. Newfoundland, St. Kitts, Gibraltar, Minorca, Hudson Bay and Nova Scotia went to the British. Austria gained parts of the Netherlands and secured its rule over Hungary and Italy. Spain kept most of its territory outside Europe, but lost parts of Italy and the Netherlands to Austria and Savoy. The Dutch regained their Barrier and France acknowledged Protestant rule in Britain and ceased supporting the Jacobites.

Britain now had the biggest navy, hence the war improved Britain's position and caused the decline of the Dutch Golden Age as Britain was able to get ahead of them in terms of colonial trade in the Far East. It also caused the centralisation of the Spanish state, the weakening of Habsburg control over the Holy Roman Empire, and France was also weakened. Various other conflicts occurred around this time, which were interconnected, but significant for different reasons. The Nine Years' War (1688–1697) saw armies grow from an average of 25,000, in 1648, to over 100,000 by 1697, a level not possible before the onset of the industrial revolution. Also the Great Northern War (1700–21), in which Russia challenged the power of Sweden in northern, central and eastern Europe, accompanied by Denmark-Noway and Saxony-Poland-Lithuania. This marked the rise of Russia as a major power in the north and east of Europe, as they established the Russian Empire (the third largest in history).

The next map shows the world of the Early Modern period. Russia had been created by this point as Moscow, by the end of the 15th century, had united the NE and NW Russian principalities, and in 1480 they finally overthrew the Mongols. The Grand Duchy of Moscow became the Tsardom of Russia in 1547 and, by 1721, Tsar Peter the Great had renamed it the Russian Empire.

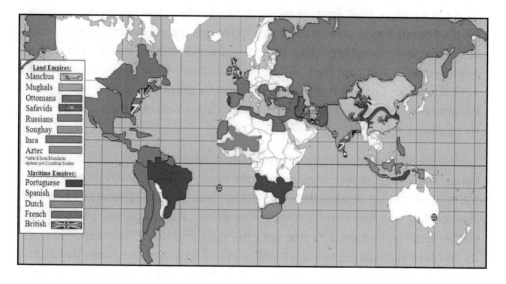

The War of the Austrian Succession (1740–48)

Each empire continued to advance its own interests once again, against a backdrop of European politics, until 1740, when events spilled over into another major war, caused by a dispute over the succession to the throne of the Holy Roman Empire itself. The Catholic Church at the time did not permit female royal inheritance but, in the 1703 Mutual Pact of Succession, Emperor Leopold I and his sons (Joseph and Charles) agreed that if the Habsburgs did not have a male heir, their possessions would go first to the female heirs of Joseph, then those of Charles. When Joseph died in 1711, he left two daughters, Maria Josepha and Maria Amalia, and Charles became the last male Habsburg. In April 1713, Charles issued the Pragmatic Sanction, permitting female inheritance, but then he placed his own daughters ahead of Joseph's. The birth of Maria Theresa, in 1717, thereby caused a challenge to her succession by France, Prussia and Bavaria. Maria Theresa was supported by Britain, the Dutch Republic, Sardinia and Saxony.

It progressed through three distinct stages: in the first, Prussia militarily took control of Silesia in less than a year. In the second, France aimed to weaken Austria in Germany, while Spain sought to recapture territories in Italy lost due to the War of the Spanish Succession. In the third, Britain took advantage of the situation to get ahead of France in the colonies, during which time, French conquest of the Austrian Netherlands gave them victory on land, while Britain gained the upper hand at sea.

The war ended with the Treaty of Aix-la-Chapelle in 1748, whereby Maria Theresa was confirmed as Archduchess of Austria and Queen of Hungary, but Prussia retained control of Silesia, much to the dismay of the Austrians.

The Seven Year War (1756–63)

Skirmishes between the French and British had not really stopped since the previous war and, as the two powers battled for global supremacy, trouble flared up in North America in 1754 (known as the French and Indian War). Meanwhile, Austria was preparing to recapture Silesia and signed a defensive alliance with Russia to secure their position to the east. Prussia subsequently signed a treaty with Great Britain, in the interests of maintaining the balance of power. This became known as the Diplomatic Revolution, as the previous sets of alliances had swapped partners. Prussia did not renew its treaty with France, assuming the French would remain neutral due to their antagonism with Austria, but France then signed a treaty with Austria and Russia, hoping to curtail the rising ambitions of Britain in exchange for assistance against Prussia, thus resolving the rivalry with Austria over central Europe.

War broke out as Austria prepared to retake Silesia and Prussia counter-attacked in Saxony. The British, under William Pitt, avoided mainland war with France, concentrating instead on capturing hundreds of French ships in the colonies and supporting the Prussian army financially, before opening up a new front in India and fighting a proxy war there, using various Indian factions to usurp the French and Mughal elements. This led to the British East India Company taking control of Bengal, then the whole subcontinent. Britain also captured Canada, which it then divided into the English speaking north and French speaking south, both under the control of Britain (which were later united into present-day Canada). France's position in the colonies was thus destroyed, weakening their empire overall.

Meanwhile, in Europe, Prussia was driven back by the Austrians and Russia occupied east Prussia by the end of 1758, while Sweden attacked in Pomerania. Prussia tried to envelop the invading forces to cut them off, but the Russians were well prepared and, by 1761, Prussia had lost Berlin. Britain subsequently withdrew its support for the Prussian army and Prussia went to the Ottomans for help, which was denied. In 1762 Spain attacked Portugal and a war between Spain and Britain broke out. However, the Prussians were saved when the new Russian Tsar, Peter III, changed sides and aligned himself with Prussia, in 1762, before King Frederick of Prussia was finally killed by his wife, ending the war.

A treaty was signed between France, Spain and Great Britain, and another one between Saxony, Austria and Prussia, in 1763. Britain benefitted greatly, as it gained most of New France in North America, Spanish Florida, Caribbean islands in the West Indies, Senegal in West Africa, and superiority over France in India. It is thus thought of by many historians as being the first true world war, almost 160 years before World War I, and caused another restructuring of the political order within Europe. Nothing could stop Britain's ambitions in North America after that, and it sent France into such decline as to lead to the French Revolution. It also paved the way for the British Empire of the 19th century, and the rise of Prussia as the leading state in Germany.

Part 4: The Enlightenment

At the centre of European Philosophy was an intellectual and scholarly movement generally known as 'Renaissance Humanism'. Yet, with the effective end of centralised power in Europe and the rise of the modern nations, people realised that ideas such as political economy, taxation, the morality of governments and personal ethics needed to be discussed. Hence, what we see here is something new and different, as the influence of scientific ideas upon government grew between AD 1600 and 1800. Subsequently, the separate strands of Catholic and Protestant thought sought to evolve in a way which makes a rational discussion of both sides possible.

The Catholic side developed from the earlier position of Thomas Aquinas, who wanted to find a sense of reason in the worship of God and religion. Meanwhile, Protestants developed the Empirical school of thinking, based on direct, sensory experience of the world. As new politics had taken over from the age of the Medieval Church, it meant new perspectives emerged and a new level of thought arose, which took us beyond the issues which had appeared during the Reformation.

In both political and economic terms, the rise of the Middle Class had a huge influence, as Modern Capitalism was evolving out of Mercantile economics, meaning the relationships between upper, middle and lower classes transformed Feudal society into a land-owning aristocracy, Middle Class business owner and lower class worker, each of whom had to be theoretically happy with the improvements to their condition. Right-wing, traditionalist and conservative thinkers like Thomas Hobbes and Adam Smith solved the new problems with society by enabling the system to function more efficiently, while Left-wing thinkers criticised systematic injustice, social inequality and suggested reforms that would improve people's quality of life, like Spinoza and Rousseau. In this period we can see much of the origins of modern political thought, before it became polarised between Capitalism and Communism during the 20th Century.

René Descartes (1596–1650)

A French philosopher, mathematician, and scientist, he is widely regarded as one of the founders of modern philosophy. Following from the earlier Catholic doctrines such as those of Thomas Aquinas, he attempted to resolve deeper issues within the new Western culture which had appeared since the Renaissance. He is most famous for his statement 'I think, therefore, I exist', as a solution to the problem of mind-body dualism which religious 'idealistic' thinking caused. After a long discourse of questioning what we can definitely know to be real, he concluded that, as he could think, therefore, he must exist. (from Discourse on the Method, 1637).

In Cartesian Dualism, he rejected the idea that there was a final end, or purpose to natural phenomena and proposes the absolute nature of God's power through creation. In so doing, he influenced Spinoza and Leibniz. He also developed analytical geometry and the Cartesian co-ordinate system.

Thomas Hobbes (1588–1679)

During this time the Protestant religion was being designed to serve a secular ruler, so Christianity could survive outside of Papal control. Hobbes theorised that human nature was fundamentally animalistic, which thus became evil if not regulated by society. His 1651 book, Leviathan, shows why a 'social contract' must exist between the individual and the state. The main conclusion he reaches is that society cannot be safe if the system is not regulated objectively, which is why an absolute sovereign is needed. For this reason, no individual can hold rights of property against the sovereign, and the sovereign may take from their subjects without consent. His work assisted in terms of the state establishing a legitimate sense of objective morality, even though it promoted the idea of absolute power. In addition to political philosophy, he also contributed to history, law, geometry, physics, theology and ethics. However, his political theory is criticised for being a 'quasi-geometrical system', in which the conclusions follow inevitably from the premises.

John Locke (1632–1704)

His theory of mind is referred to as the origin of the modern concept of identity and self, as it was defined in terms of the stream of consciousness each person possesses. He proposed that, at birth, each person's mind was like a 'blank slate' (*tabula rasa*). Contrary to the idea that we are born with a pre-programmed biological condition, he maintained that we are born without innate ideas, and everything we learn about our world is obtained through direct sensory experience.

This is now known as the basis for philosophical Empiricism. It demands that all observations be derived from direct experience and evidence must be used to prove an argument. Even proof must be capable of being tested to destruction, and no argument is exempt from being eventually disproven or superseded by a better one. His work influenced Hume, Rousseau, and Kant.

Baruch Spinoza (1632–1677)

A Dutch rational philosopher of Portuguese Sephardi origin, he became famous for his criticism of the Bible, including the concept of the self and the universe. Inspired by the ideas of René Descartes, he became one of the leading thinkers of the Dutch Golden Age. Born into the Portuguese-Jewish community in Amsterdam, his ideas were regarded as highly controversial, as they questioned the ultimate legitimacy of the Hebrew Bible. Jewish religious authorities and his family expelled him at the age of 23, and his books were added to the Catholic Church's 'Index of Forbidden Books'.

His most famous work, the Ethics, was published after the year of his death. A committed determinist, he stated that absolutely everything happens out of necessity. For example, in Ethics he wrote, 'the infant believes that it is by free will that it seeks the breast; the angry boy believes that by free will he wishes vengeance; the timid man thinks it is with free will he seeks flight... All believe that they speak by a free command of the mind, whilst, in truth, they have no power to restrain the impulse which they have to speak.'

He argues that the illusion of choice is only created by the attempt of philosophers and theology to separate mind and body when, in fact, no such distinction exists. People are created from their conditions and thus behave the way they do. If mind and body were truly separate, each would be free to pursue its own course of action, but people are bound by the human condition. Therefore, the ethics of society should be directed towards improving the subjective experience people have of life, and not towards prescribing an objective 'one size fits all' code of morality for everyone. In other words, it is not possible, nor ethical to consider people as one, as good and evil are relative concepts, yet by accepting this truth we can each find God through reason.

Isaac Newton (1642–1726)

Some historians say the whole of the Enlightenment began with Newton's Principia Mathematica, although his work continued directly from that of Copernicus and Gallileo in the 1500s. He embarked on a detailed study of calculating the precise mathematical measurements of force, distance, velocity, weight, energy and the way the planets orbit the Sun. His work is still used in practical terms, in engineering, navigation and construction.

By this point it was effectively proven that the Earth revolved around the Sun, and it thus became increasingly difficult for the Church to argue to the contrary. Until the 1500s, the idea that the Earth was at the centre of the universe and God had created man had remained unchallenged for centuries. Thus, scientific ideas provided a huge boost for rational thought, just as the Reformation had undermined centralised power in Europe, as they brought into public question important factors which were previously the exclusive property of the Church and aristocracy.

Gottfried Leibniz (1646–1716)

One of the most important logicians and mathematicians of the Enlightenment, Leibniz developed the ideas of differential and integral calculus independently of Newton's, and was an inventor of mechanical calculators, adding automatic multiplication and division. He also was the first to describe a pinwheel calculator in 1685, and this became the Leibniz wheel, used in the arithmometer, the first mass-produced mechanical calculator. He also refined the binary number system, which is the foundation of all digital computers. While a senior worker at the Wolfenbüttel library in Germany, he devised a catalogue system that would become adopted by many of Europe's leading libraries.

He also contributed to probability theory, biology, medicine, geology, psychology, linguistics, computer science, philosophy, politics, law, ethics, theology, history, and philology. He wrote in several languages, but primarily in Latin, French and German as well as English, Italian and Dutch.

Jean-Jacques Rousseau 1712–1778)

On the progressive Catholic side, Rousseau was a Genevan philosopher, writer and composer, whose political philosophy influenced the French Revolution and the development of modern political, economic and educational thought.

His work included Discourse on Inequality and The Social Contract, which argued for a renewal of the social contract based on the values of human rights and dignity. The New Heloise (1761) was also important to the development of Romanticism in fiction. He also wrote On Education (1762), an educational treatise on the place of the individual in society, and Confessions (published after his death, 1769), one of the first modern autobiographies. During the period of the French Revolution, Rousseau was among the more popular members of the Jacobin Club and interred as a national hero in the Panthéon in Paris, in 1794.

David Hume (1711 – 1776)

On the progressive side of Protestantism, Hume was a Scottish Enlightenment philosopher and British Empiricist, historian and economist. He is best known for his philosophical empiricism, scepticism and naturalism. A Treatise of Human Nature (1739–40) was part of his effort to create a naturalistic science of human psychological behaviour. In contrast with the philosophical rationalists, he believed that passion, not reason governs human behaviour.

Challenging the belief of classical thinking, and the traditions based thereon, he denied the existence of causality in the sense that one event necessarily leads to another, only that we learn to habitually associate connections between certain events. He also argued against the existence of God, on the grounds that we can have no direct experience of Him, nor is there any evidence which proves His existence. This is generally regarded as the most significant argument against the existence of God before Darwinism.

Hume influenced utilitarianism, logical positivism, Immanuel Kant, the philosophy of science, early analytic philosophy, cognitive science and theology. Kant himself accredited Hume with having awakened him from his 'dogmatic slumber'.

Adam Smith (1723–90)

A Scottish economist and philosopher who studied at the University of Glasgow, he was a key figure in the Scottish Enlightenment, to the extent that he is known as 'The Father of Economics' and even 'The Father of Capitalism'. His most famous work, An Inquiry into the Nature and Causes of the Wealth of Nations (1776), sought to explain the changing situation as free-market Capitalism evolved from the Mercantilist period. Hence, it was an explanation of the new principles involved, as industrial and technological progress brought a new division of labour and new rules for the relationship between employers and workers.

For example, Price Elasticity explains how prices rise due to increased demand, and fall due to increased supply. Market Segmentation divides markets into different types of goods, each with their own types of customer, thus the profitability of each sector should lead to the percentage of resources directed towards producing goods in that industry. The price of labour is also affected by the law of supply and demand as, when labourers bid against one another for limited opportunities of employment, the wages of labour collectively fall. When employers compete over a limited supply of labour, the wages of labour collectively rise.

This led to the rise of both Labour Unions and Employers Associations, who both sought to improve their own interests. He also outlined how these special interest groups, which also included the banks, attempt to influence governments according to their own needs. However, it is then for the government to meet with the leaders of all relevant factions and allow them to negotiate the best outcome for all.

As it shows how an understanding of rational self-interest and competition led to economic prosperity, it created a new theory of Capitalism for the modern period which profoundly influenced the management of the workforce and increased the importance of domestic markets over imports. He found diversification is greatest for the nations with more industrial development, while agriculture produces less wealth than manufacturing. This influenced the policies towards increasing industrialisation in many countries, including the U.S., Britain, and later Germany and Japan.

David Ricardo (1772 – 1823)

A British political economist, and one of the most influential of this period, he encouraged industrialisation, but also criticised the problems it brought, and saw Adam Smith's view of affairs as being somewhat mechanical. In his most famous work, 'Political Economy and Taxation', he argues that industrialisation increases the value of land, and increases productivity as mechanisation lowers production costs, thus also the real price of commodities. However, while the landowning classes and capitalists benefit from lower prices, the workers do not benefit as it is not in the interests of the capitalists, nor is it required of them, by law, to pass on their profits to the whole of society.

Also as less workers are required to do the same amount of work, wages are forced down as more workers are forced to compete for fewer jobs, causing 'technological unemployment', and reducing the overall well-being of the Working Class. He was also a slavery abolitionist, speaking at a meeting of the Court of the East India Company in March 1823, where he said slavery was a stain on the character of the nation.

Adam Weishaupt (1748 – 1830)

One of the most famous secret societies in the world emerged in this period, founded by Adam Weishaupt, the Order of the Illuminati. It started in 1776, the year of U.S. Independence, and appears to be an attempt to bring the influence of the new U.S. constitutional government into Europe, where both the Church and monarchy exercised high levels of political and social control, and discouraged radical ideas. In the U.S., religion was kept separate from state. He was a German philosopher, and professor of civil and cannon law, who was initiated into a Masonic lodge in Munich (Theodor zum guten Rath), in 1777. From this position he was able to expand his own membership, made up of different levels of intelligence-gathering spies who reported back into the centre with their own experiences of the world.

Its goal was to oppose superstition, religious influence over public life and abuses of state power. They wrote in their general statutes 'The order of the day is to put an end to the machinations of the purveyors of injustice, to control them without dominating them'. The benefits its members received were that it assisted each of them to improve their personal understanding of the world, reach a natural state of enlightenment (free from government and organised religion), and encouraged them to better the lives of others. Weishaupt and Adolph Freiherr Knigge organised the ritual structure, which was used as a communal basis for assessing the personal development of its members and assisted them in achieving a greater clarity of expression in their own ideas, thus helping them to extend their influence in terms of liberating society from political and social control.

However, his project of 'illumination, enlightening the understanding by the sun of reason' was seen as too radical by some who saw the Church and monarchy were still necessary for managing society and some writings were intercepted in 1784 which were interpreted as seditious. The Society was subsequently banned by the government of Karl Theodor, Elector of Bavaria. Weishaupt lost his position at the University of Ingolstadt and fled. While in exile he received the assistance of Duke Ernest II of Saxe-Gotha-Altenburg (1745–1804) and, while living in Gotha, wrote a series of works on illuminism, including 'A Complete History of the Persecutions of the Illuminati in Bavaria' (1785), 'A Picture of Illuminism' (1786), 'An Apology for the Illuminati' (1786), and 'An Improved System of Illuminism' (1787). He died there on 18 November 1830.

As it is the generally established view that his project was naive and utopian, it is thus ironic that such an attempt should result in him becoming one of the most famous conspirators of all time. Many versions of the order have since existed, both real and fake.

Voltaire (1694 – 1778)

François-Marie Arouet, better known by his pen-name Voltaire, was a French Enlightenment writer, philosopher and historian famous for his wit, advocacy of freedom of speech, freedom of religion, separation of church and state, and criticism of Christianity — especially the Roman Catholic Church. He was a lawyer and minor treasury official, whose wife's family was part of the lower levels of French nobility, and it is thought he may have been the illegitimate son of a French nobleman. His most famous quote, which describes the Holy Roman Empire as neither holy, Roman, nor an empire, can be taken to epitomise the style of his writing.

Other famous quotes from him include,

'If you want to know who controls you, look at who you are not allowed to criticise.'

'God gave us the gift of life; it is up to us to give ourselves the gift of living well.'

'Love truth, but pardon error.'

'Beware of the words "internal security," for they are the eternal cry of the oppressor.'

'Cherish those who seek the truth but beware of those who find it.'

'It is dangerous to be right in matters on which the established authorities are wrong.'

'If God did not exist, it would be necessary to invent him.'

'The more often a stupidity is repeated, the more it gets the appearance of wisdom.'

'The most important decision you make is to be in a good mood.'

In general, the Enlightenment period is regarded to have arisen out of the Renaissance period, as its ideas ceased to be relevant to contemporary society, and the rise of both literacy and the Middle Classes fuelled democratic movements. Meanwhile, as European expansionism was enabling the industrial revolution to start earlier there than anywhere else, this paved the way for the Late Modern period, during which these ideas manifested as political realities.

CHAPTER 13

The Late Modern Period

*As various European nations continued to expand their empires, creating indus-
trialisation and social change, calls for more representative forms of government
led to U.S. independence and the French Revolution. However, after this turned
into the Napoleonic Wars, Europe was run by a strict Congress System which
restored the monarchies. During this time Communism appeared, before Europe
broke down into WWI, the Russian Revolution empowered the communists, the
League of Nations was established to encourage international co-operation,
and the rise of Fascism led to WWII...*

Part 1: The Age of Revolutions

Due to the onset of the industrial revolution, major changes occurred to society and everyday life in Europe, such as the widespread use of powered machinery, the expansion of cities, continuous developments in science and medicine, wealth increase, and the global population grew rapidly, reaching 1 billion around 1800. New mechanised manufacturing processes also appeared, especially in Europe and the U.S., using both water and steam power.

This created a new social landscape, especially the rise of the Middle Classes, who grew in importance due to the creation of new offices, an increase in paperwork, more regulations, and the need to administrate a more complex government. However, it also resulted in a rise in tension between social classes and demands for increased equality. While Labour Unions formed to represent workers rights, the aristocracy struggled to manage their position, under pressure from the Middle Classes to give up traditional privileges which had been established under the Feudal System.

U.S. Independence (1775–83)

Even though the British gained the upper hand over France in terms of their overseas empires during the Seven Years War, and spread the idea of constitutional government into their colonies, it was not all plain sailing for them, as their political position in Europe led to the period of 'Splendid Isolation', and various colonies rebelled as their attention shifted to their overseas empire. Despite taking control of the whole of Canada, political control over the Thirteen Colonies of North America broke down during the American Revolutionary War (1775–1783), resulting in the overthrow of British rule and the establishment of the United States. From 1765, opposition to the Townsend Acts grew, a series of laws passed by the British for the colonies, leading to protests against 'taxation without representation', as the Americans did not get to vote on British laws. The problem was seen as their political motive, as revenue from them was not only used to pay the wages of governors and judges in the colonies, but also to ensure they would remain loyal to the British Crown, create better compliance with trade regulations and punish the Province of New York for disobeying the Quartering Act (1765).

This was followed by the Stamp Act (1765), issued by the parliament of George III, which imposed a direct tax by demanding certain documents were to be printed on stamped paper made in England. These included legal documents, magazines, playing cards and newspapers, and had to be paid in British currency. However, enforcing it was a problem and caused tensions between the British and Americans, so much so that when the American ship, Liberty, was arrested for smuggling in 1768, there was a riot. British troops seized Boston and the British Parliament threatened to extradite the colonists.

Tension turned to violence when an 11 year old colonist, Christopher Seider, was shot by a Loyalist customs officer in Boston, in February 1770. His funeral became a major political event, as it led to the harassment of British troops, who then fired on civilians in the Boston Massacre in March. In 1772, Americans from Rhode Island boarded and burned a customs boat. Parliament then repealed all taxes except the one on tea, passing the Tea Act in 1773, attempting to make the colonists buy East India Company tea, on which Townsend duties were paid. The tea was boycotted by all the colonies and, when the governor of Massachusetts allowed the British tea ships to dock in Boston Harbour, the Sons of Liberty (a secret revolutionary group founded by Samuel Adams) destroyed the tea chests in what became known as the Boston Tea Party. Britain responded by closing Boston Harbour and passed a series of measures against the Massachusetts Bay Colony. These included the removal of self-government, hoping to make an example of them to others.

The leaders of Suffolk County, Massachusetts, then responded with the Suffolk Resolves (1774), which declared a complete boycott on all British Goods unless the measures (known as the Coercive Acts in Britain and the Intolerable Acts in the Americas) were revoked. Twelve colonies formed the Continental Congress, which functioned as a provisional government. British attempts to disarm their militia led to open warfare, and a shock defeat for the British in April 1775. Militia forces then besieged Boston, forcing a British evacuation in March 1776. The Americans then failed to invade Quebec and cause an uprising there against the British, and the Second Continental Congress succeeded in passing the vote for independence, which it declared on July 4.

The British counter-offensive captured New York City, but this was offset by victories for the Americans at Trenton and Princeton. In 1777, the British launched an invasion from Quebec which was defeated at Saratoga in October before France joined the war on the side of the Americans in 1778 (in the hope of revenge for the Seven Years' War). Spain joined in 1779 as an ally of France and, by the end of September, Spanish troops had cleared the entire region along the Mississippi. The British counter-offensive (known as the Southern Strategy) relied heavily on an anticipated Loyalist uprising which did not occur and they suffered subsequent defeats at King's Mountain and Cowpens. The British then retreated to Yorktown, Virginia, intending to evacuate, but a Franco-American army surrounded them and they surrendered in October 1781.

The Articles of Confederation and Perpetual Union were published in March 1781, as the Second Continental Congress became the official Congress of the Confederation. This held eight sessions, until 1789, when the 1st United States Congress took over under the new constitution. Meanwhile, in Britain, the Whig Party (later the Liberal Party), who had been against the war, were empowered by the surrender and urged Parliament to vote for the end of hostilities in early 1782. Despite the war against France continuing overseas, the Treaty of Paris was signed in September 1783, in which Britain formally recognised the sovereignty of the United States.

The long term implications of U.S. independence were felt globally. The fact that a new nation, as big as Europe itself, had broken free of British control was an inspiration for independence movements all over the world. It had a big impact on promoting free trade, human rights, and equality under the law. It also showed the Europeans that modern government could be used to create administrative, legislative and judicial bodies without a monarchy and with Church separated from state. Shortly after, the politics of revolution spread throughout the Americas and back into Europe, starting with France.

The French Revolution (1789–99)

Involvement in the Seven Year War and assisting the U.S. in their struggle for independence bankrupted the French treasury, and King Louis XVI was forced to impose high taxes to pay off various debts. However, when this was compounded by two years of bad harvests, it led to labour strikes, rioting and looting. In 1786 the Controller General proposed a reform package which would make the aristocracy pay tax, from which they had been exempt under Feudal laws. But, when the aristocracy began talking about their own revolt, the King called a meeting of the Estates General (a massive, national assembly of the Clergy, Nobility and the Middle Classes) to avert conflict.

However, it had not been called for 200 years and, while the nobility previously made up the majority, now the Middle Classes had 98%, yet the nobility and clergy still managed to overturn them with only 2% of the vote. The Middle Classes majority immediately began calling for a more representative system but, while everyone agreed there was a need for systematic reform, when asked to give up their privileges the aristocracy argued that they were necessary to keep order, and hostile arguments nearly turned to violence. Consequently, the representatives of the Middle Classes decided to hold a meeting of their own, calling it the National Assembly.

It was held in a tennis court, leading to the Tennis Court Oath being sworn by all, which proclaimed that none of them would stand down until constitutional reform was achieved. Having seen what happened in the English Civil War and U.S. War of Independence, 47 nobles and most of the clergy aligned themselves with this new parliament and King Louis dissolved the meeting of the Estates General, hoping to incorporate its members into the new assembly.

However, most of the nobles were against this, and the King moved several army regiments into and around Paris, anticipating trouble. People became afraid their new parliament would be crushed and, when the King dismissed his only non-noble minister, who was popular due to his support for reforms, they rioted and took 32,000 muskets and cannons from a military hospital armoury, then stormed the Bastille to raid its gunpowder store. Completely outnumbered, the governor of the Bastille allowed delegates from the revolutionary horde inside to negotiate but, as time wore on, the people outside feared that their members had been captured and climbed an outer wall, then lowered a drawbridge to let the mob into the courtyard. However, when they tried to lower a second drawbridge, the army opened fire upon the orders of the governor, killing 100 civilians. Later, soldiers loyal to the people besieged the fort with heavy cannons and forced the governor to surrender. He was then marched down to the city hall and executed.

After this victory in Paris, peasants across France joined in an open revolt, burning the houses of tax collectors, landlords and the elite, triggering an exodus of nobles known as the Great Fear. On August 4, 1789, the National Assembly passed an act known as 'Declaration of the Rights of Man and of the Citizen'. It founded a new society, based primarily on free speech, popular sovereignty and representative government. They proceeded to adopt a Constitutional Monarchy, like Britain, as it gave them the ability to take control of the aristocracy and discourage a counter-revolution, but it also gave the King the right to veto laws and appoint ministers. The most influential of the revolutionary leaders did not like this at all, as they wanted France to have a constitution like the U.S., and demanded the King was put on trial for crimes against the people.

The Revolutionary Wars

In April 1792 the newly elected Legislative Assembly declared war on Austria and Prussia, for harbouring members of the exiled French monarchy, who they believed were part of a counter-revolutionary plot. This started the War of the First Coalition, as the Holy Roman Empire, the Habsburg Monarchy, Prussia and Great Britain sided against France, Spain, the Dutch Republic, Portugal, Sardinia and Naples. Prussia and Austria launched the first invasion, which was turned back at the Battle of Valmy. This victory incited the National Convention to abolish the monarchy, giving rise to Maximilien Robespierre, a French lawyer and statesman who was a member of the Constituent Assembly and the famous Jacobin Club. On 10 August, 1792, King Louis was arrested and tried for crimes against the state, including being part of the counter-revolutionary plot, and sent to the guillotine.

However, a string of French victories ended with a series of defeats, starting at Neerwinden in the spring of 1793, and continued throughout the year. This led to popular unrest and forced the government to impose martial law, which became known as the Reign of Terror, during which thousands of counter-revolutionaries were persecuted by Robespierre's Committee for Public Safety, leading to another Revolution (known as the Thermidorian Reaction), during which Robespierre himself was tried and executed, and a five-person council known as the Directory assumed control of France in 1795. In 1794 the situation had improved militarily, with victories against the Austrians and Spanish and, by 1795, the French had captured the Austrian Netherlands. They took Spain and Prussia out of the war with the Peace of Basel and General Napoleon Bonaparte began his first campaign in Italy, in April 1796. In less than a year he drove out the Austrians, winning almost every battle, capturing 150,000 prisoners, then marched on Vienna and forced the Austrians to sign the Treaty of Campo Formio.

However, in 1798, the monarchies of Europe came back to fight France again, in the War of the Second Coalition. This involved the Holy Roman Empire, the Habsburg Monarchy of Austria, Britain, Russia, Portugal, Naples, the Grand Duchy of Tuscany, the Sovereign Military Order of Malta, the Order of Saint John, the Ottoman Empire, the French Royalists and the United States, who sided against France, Spain, the Polish Legions, Denmark–Norway, the Batavian Republic, the

Helvetic Republic, the Kingdom of Italy (Napoleonic), the Cisalpine Republic, the Roman Republic and the Parthenopaean Republic.

It began as Napoleon invaded Egypt, which the Allies had taken to reclaim territories lost in the first war. They pushed the French out of Italy and invaded Switzerland, before French victory at Zurich in September 1799 forced Russia out of the war. Napoleon also defeated the Egyptians and Ottomans at the Pyramids, Mount Tabor and Abukir. This enhanced Napoleon's popularity in France and, when he returned in the autumn, he led a coup against the unpopular Directory, appointing himself Consul of the First French Empire. He then reorganised the army and resumed hostilities against Austria in Italy during the spring of 1800, leading to victory and an Austrian withdrawal. Victory in Bavaria forced the Austrians to sign the Treaty of Lunéville in 1801 and, with both Austria and Russia out of the war, the UK was isolated and signed the Treaty of Amiens in 1802, ending the Revolutionary Wars.

The Napoleonic Wars

With Napoleon in command of France, Britain broke the Peace of Amiens in May 1803, leading to the War of the Third Coalition. By December 1804 an Anglo-Swedish alliance had started and, in 1805, Britain signed an alliance with Russia and Austria. The French army at this point numbered about 200,000, organised into seven independent units with 36–40 cannons each, giving his tacticians multiple options during each campaign. They also had 22,000 cavalry, supported by 24 artillery pieces. By 1805, Napoleon's 'Grande Armée' had grown to 350,000 well-trained soldiers.

Napoleon planned to draw the Royal Navy away from the English Channel by attacking the West Indies, allowing a Franco-Spanish fleet to take control of the channel long enough to launch an invasion. However, British victory at the Battle of Cape Finisterre in July meant that his Admiral, Villeneuve, had to retreat to Cádiz. However, the 200,000 strong force he launched across the Rhine in August, to hunt isolated Austrian armies in Southern Germany before Russia could mobilise, met with great success.

The Austrians gathered mostly at the fortress of Ulm in Swabia, but Napoleon's troops performed a flanking manoeuvre to the southeast and completely surrounded them, leading to the Battle of Ulm. When the Austrians realised they could not break the French encirclement, 60,000 Austrian soldiers were captured with only 2,000 French casualties. The Royal Navy won the Battle of Trafalgar on 21 October, giving Britain control of the seas, but the French took Vienna from the Austrians in November, capturing 100,000 muskets and 500 cannons, followed by victory against Russia and Austria at the Battle of Austerlitz in Moravia on 2 December. The Third Coalition was thus defeated. France and Austria signed the Treaty of Pressburg on 26 December, taking Austria out of the war, giving France Austrian territory in Italy and Bavaria. Also, land in Germany went to Napoleon's German allies and the Austrians were forced to pay 40 million francs. The Russians were allowed free passage back home.

However, the War of the Fourth Coalition then broke out as France dissolved the Holy Roman Empire and reorganised the German territories in a way which gave Napoleon a strategic advantage, causing Prussia to lose its German allies. In February 1806, the Ottoman Emperor (Selim III) recognised Napoleon as the Emperor of France and they formed an alliance. A Franco-Persian alliance was also made, which ended when France made a pact with Russia in 1807.

The new German state was called the Confederation of the Rhine, creating a buffer zone between France and Central Europe. Berlin became steadily more opposed to France throughout the summer, and Frederick William III declared war. France began the invasion of Prussia in September, marching an army of 180,000 on the right bank of the River Saale. Once again, he aimed to destroy his first opponent quickly before reinforcements could arrive. After finding out where the Prussian army had gathered, the French crossed the Saale and overwhelmed them at the twin battles of Jena and Auerstedt on 14 October, killing several major commanders and leaving the Austrians incapable of leading their army. They captured 140,000 soldiers, over 2,000 cannons and hundreds of ammunition wagons.

Napoleon then began imposing the Continental System through the Berlin Decree (November 1806), preventing other European nations from trading with Britain, before marching against the advancing Russians through Poland, leading to indecisive battles at Eylau in February and Heilsberg in June 1807. On 14 June Napoleon achieved victory at Friedland, destroying most of the Russian army, leading to a peace treaty on the 19 June which recognised the Vistula River as the natural border between French and Russian influence. The Russians were given relatively lenient terms, which included imposing the Continental System, withdrawal from Wallachia and Moldavia, and losing the Ionian Islands to France. Prussia then lost half its territories, which created the new kingdom of Westphalia, with Napoleon's younger brother, Jérôme, as its monarch.

The next thing he did was to reorganise the Continental System in order to fully isolate the British, whom he could not invade, using treaties with other nations. However, certain countries decided to violate it, including Russia and Portugal. After the Franco-Spanish defeat at Trafalgar, Napoleon set up an army through a secret treaty with Charles IV of Spain to invade Portugal and, on 17 October 1807, 24,000 French troops under General Junot began heading across the Pyrenees to start the six-year Peninsular War. During the winter of 1808, French agents also incited chaos in the Spanish royal family and, on 16 February 1808, the French Marshal Murat 'intervened' with 120,000 troops, occupying Madrid from 24 March. However riots occurred within weeks, and Napoleon appointed his brother, Joseph Bonaparte, as the new King of Spain in the summer. Resistance soon spread throughout Spain, prompting Napoleon to personally intervene.

Prior to this, he ensured Russia stayed on his side with the Erfurt Convention, which called upon Britain to end its war against France, while recognising the Russian conquest of Finland from Sweden in return. He then prepared the Grande Armée, which crossed the Ebro River in November and won a series of victories against the Spanish before entering Madrid on 4 December with 80,000 troops and drove the British out of Spain at the Battle of Corunna in January 1809. However, a few months later, the British sent another army to Spain under the future Duke of Wellington and guerrilla fighting broke out throughout the Spanish countryside. France could not win, despite having around 300,000 troops in Iberia, due to the nature of the new conflict. Eventually, the invasion of Russia in 1812 caused France to withdraw so many troops that they were pushed out by 1814, but not before the situation had a huge impact on the Spanish Bourbon monarchy. In the Spanish territories in America local governors formed military juntas in support of Ferdinand VII of Spain, leading to the outbreak of the Spanish-American wars of independence across most of the empire as most of them sought to break with the mother country in order to avoid French rule.

These wars began as local conflicts, which later developed into a united effort to promote independence. The new national boundaries which appeared were based on the colonial provinces, and later formed the independent countries of Latin America. They abolished the Casta System (a formal system of racial classification) along with their social hierarchy, and the Inquisition (to combat heresy and religious dissent). Slavery was abolished within a quarter of a century. From then on, the conservatives and liberals have argued over whether to reverse or reinforce the political changes which resulted. The royal family of

Portugal additionally relocated to Brazil (1808–1821), meaning that Brazil had a separate monarchy from Portugal.

Meanwhile, back in Europe, the War of the Fifth Coalition was beginning against Napoleon, as Austria sought to reverse its previous defeats. Russia was at war with Britain, Sweden, and the Ottoman Empire in 1809 and Frederick William of Prussia promised help which never arrived. Despite warnings from the Austrian finance minister that the country would bankrupt itself if it kept its army mobilised, on 8 February 1809, the Imperial Government secretly voted for another war against France.

On 10 April the Austrian army crossed the Inn River and invaded Bavaria. The French army was surprised by the early Austrian attack as its two wings were separated by 120 km, joined only by a thin line of Bavarian troops. However, Napoleon realigned their axis and remobilised them, leading to victory at the Battle of Eckmühl, and caused the Austrians to retreat over the Danube into Bohemia. On 13 May, the French took Vienna for the second time in four years, although most of the Austrian army survived.

At the Battle of Aspern-Essling, on May 21, the Austrians had 110,000 soldiers against 70,000 French, but it resulted in a stalemate. Six weeks later, Napoleon made another attempt at crossing the Danube and, in early July, the French took 180,000 troops to face 150,000 Austrians at the Battle of Wagram. The largest battle of Napoleon's career so far, it lasted two days. The Austrians lost over 40,000 men and were forced to retreat. Shortly after, the French hunted down King Charles of Austria at Znaim and they signed a peace treaty on 12 July.

Despite the British launching the Walcheren Campaign against the French in Holland to take pressure off the Austrians, by the time they landed at Walcheren on 30 July, the Austrians had already been defeated. After little fighting the British withdrew in December, while the Treaty of Schönbrunn (October 1809) imposed harsh terms on Austria. While succeeding to preserve most of the Habsburg Empire, France received Carinthia, Carniola, and the Adriatic ports. Galicia was given to Poland and the Salzburg area of Tyrol went to Bavaria. As a result, Austria lost over three million subjects, about one-fifth of its population and there were no more wars for the next three years.

Shortly afterwards, Napoleon divorced Joséphine, who did not give him an heir, and married Marie Louise, the Duchess of Parma and daughter of Francis II (1811). She gave birth to a boy, who was made heir and given the title King of Rome. He never actually ruled the empire, but his cousin Louis-Napoléon's naming himself Napoléon III cause some historians to refer to him as Napoleon

II. By this time, Russia had been in violation of the Continental System, and the Tsar was under internal pressure to break his treaty with France. Napoleon threatened Alexander with what would happen if he formed an alliance with Britain but, by 1812, Alexander's advisors were demanding a war to recapture Poland. Despite repeated warnings against an invasion of Russia, Napoleon launched a campaign on 24 June, on the pretext of defending Poland. The Grande Armée was 685,000 at the time, the largest army ever assembled.

After a series of long marches into western Russia, the French won a number of minor engagements as it pursued the retreating Russian army, and one major battle at Smolensk, in August, before the Russians left it to burn. Luring the French forward, they employed scorched-earth tactics, destroying villages, towns and crops, which made the French supply lines grow increasingly thinner. On 7 September the French caught up with a Russian army dug into the hills by the town of Borodino, seventy miles west of Moscow, and the battle which ensued became one of the deadliest, resulting in 72,000 casualties and a narrow French victory. The Russian Army then withdrew again, drawing the French deeper into Russia.

Napoleon reached Moscow only to find it abandoned and the city set on fire. Despite obviously having walked into a trap, Napoleon stayed in Moscow for a month waiting for a peace offer which never arrived. On 19 October he marched his army forward again, this time southwest toward Kaluga, and met the Russian Army again. But, after the Battle of Maloyaroslavets, he then began to retreat towards Poland. Weeks later, most of the Grande Armée was stranded in the Russian Winter, suffering from starvation, hypothermia and guerilla warfare from Russian peasants and Cossack forces. The Battle of Vyazma and Krasnoi resulted in more losses for the French and, by the time the army crossed the Berezina River in late November, only 27,000 soldiers remained. The French had lost 380,000 dead and 100,000 captured, the Russians lost 150,000 soldiers and hundreds of thousands of civilians. Following this Napoleon returned to Paris in an attempt to save his empire.

It was the turning point in the Napoleonic Wars, as Napoleon's reputation suffered extensively, and French hegemony was irretrievably weakened in Europe. His army was reduced to the point where it could not even defend France, and a major shift subsequently occurred in European politics. Prussia, soon followed by Austria, broke their treaty and joined Russia, Britain, Spain and Portugal in the Sixth Coalition. The French army took to the field in Germany but, opposed by a force twice its size, it was finally defeated at the Battle of Leipzig.

The Allies' peace terms were outlined in November 1813, allowing Napoleon to remain Emperor of France, which would be reduced to its natural borders, meaning he could retain Belgium, Savoy and the Rhineland. But he would have to withdraw from Spain, the Netherlands, Italy and Germany. Napoleon refused these terms and, by December, the Coalition had withdrawn the offer. Napoleon tried to renegotiate in 1814, but the Allies drew up new terms, including the loss of Belgium. Napoleon could have still remained Emperor, but he rejected this.

With his army reduced to 70,000 soldiers and a few cavalry, British armies attacked from the south, while other Allied forces positioned themselves in the German states. Napoleon won a series of victories in the Six Days' Campaign but, it was not enough, and France surrendered in March 1814. The Allies then set about removing Napoleon from power. On 1 April Alexander proposed to the French that the Allies were fighting against Napoleon, not France, and they were prepared to offer good terms if Napoleon was deposed. The next day, the Sénat agreed and his senior officers mutinied. They confronted him on 4 April, and he abdicated in favour of his son, with Marie Louise as regent. When the Allies objected to this he was then forced to abdicate unconditionally on 6 April.

Hence, the French Revolution had a major impact on human history, especially in Europe, as it caused a complete reorganisation of its politics, even though the monarchies took Europe back under their control.

Part 2: The European Congress System

After the Napoleonic Wars, the four victorious powers established a new system to keep the peace and oversee progress in Europe. Also known as the 19th Century System, the Vienna System, and the Concert of Europe, it was designed to create stability and a lasting alliance between the major powers. France was re-admitted after the restoration of the French monarchy and other nations attended sporadically, to discuss issues they were involved in. Austria, Prussia, Russia and Britain signed the initial treaty which made them the Quadruple Alliance (1815), and they became the Quintuple Alliance (1818) when France rejoined. It bound them to support the terms of the Second Treaty of Paris for 20 years and additionally required them to meet at regular intervals to discuss their common interests, the prosperity of their nations, and the peace in Europe. Territories around France, such as Parma, Lombardy, the Netherlands and Belgium were strengthened militarily to secure French borders.

However, it was not exactly stated when or where the conferences should meet, and they tended to be announced whenever a crisis arose, rather than being held in regular sessions like a council. There was also a second treaty, the Holy Alliance (1815), initiated by Tsar Alexander I, which bound the monarchs together into a type of personal alliance, which promoted Christian social values and the monarchy. Britain did not sign this, as their constitutional monarchy was more liberal and progressive, and its government did not wish to get involved in the political issues of continental Europe. Lord Castlereagh, the British Foreign Secretary, called it 'a piece of sublime mysticism and nonsense'.

Generally speaking, the history of the Congress System breaks down into two main phases, the first being the relatively peaceful new order within Europe after the Napoleonic Wars, when Austrian conservatism was its main political influence. The second phase, which led to its collapse, followed after a freshly united Germany attempted to impose hegemony on Europe from the 1870s onwards. Soon after it was created, though, waves of revolutionary movements began to resume, starting in the 1820s, including both nationalist uprisings and political unrest, peaking in 1848.

The first congress was held in November 1814 in Vienna, Austria, and lasted until June 1815. The objective was to settle the territorial issues which had arisen during the revolutionary wars, and create a long-term peace plan, which was achieved by negotiating the redistribution of land in Europe, resizing the main powers so as to maintain the balance of power between them. France lost all its recent gains while Prussia gained small German states in the west, Swedish Pomerania and 60% of Saxony. Austria gained Venice and most of northern Italy, while Russia took parts of Poland.

In the last few weeks of the Congress, Napoleon attempted to re-assert himself as the French ruler in the relatively minor Hundred Day War. On 13 March, the Congress of Vienna declared him an outlaw and, on the 25th, Austria, Prussia, Russia and Britain formed the Seventh Coalition. Each contributed 150,000 soldiers and finally defeated Napoleon at the Battle of Waterloo, resulting in the second restoration of the French monarchy, and the permanent exile of Napoleon to the island of Saint Helena, where he died in 1821.

At the 1818 Congress of Aix-la-Chapelle, France was allowed back into the major European powers, ending the occupation of France. At the 1820 Congress of Troppau, held in Austria, they decided to suppress the Napoleonic Revolution in Naples, which had caused King Ferdinand I to agree to a constitutional monarchy. The subsequent Troppau Protocol proposed that, if any state which had a change of government through a revolution, then threatened other states, they would be banned from the European Alliance. Not only this, but the Alliance should then also be responsible for the recovery of the allegiance of that state by any means necessary. The 1821 Congress of Laibach, Slovenia, met to discuss the resulting invasion of Naples.

The 1822 Congress of Verona, held in Italy, then dealt with the question of the Spanish Revolution (1820). Russia, Prussia and Austria agreed to support France's intervention in Spain, while Britain opposed it. At the 1830–32 London Conference in Britain, Belgium and the Netherlands also attended to address the issue of the Belgian Revolution (1830), which saw it acquire independence from the Netherlands. Austria, Prussia and Russia tried to convince Belgium to return, while Britain and France supported Belgium and were able to achieve its recognition as a sovereign state. Generally speaking, this period began to see a split between the more progressive western side, of Britain and France, and the more conservative east, of Austria, Prussia and Russia.

However, despite old feudal ties re-emerging between the monarchies of Europe, the rise of the U.S. began to influence progress in terms of science and technology, as the Industrial Revolution accelerated. Throughout the 1820s and 30s the growth of railways and canal networks assisted economic growth, bringing people closer together, while the invention of the typewriter led to the founding of various newspapers, like the Pennsylvanian Enquirer and The Economist in London, increasing the transmission of information. The discovery of electro-magnetism led to the electric motor, while the first Atlantic crossing was made by a paddle steamer, taking approximately two weeks. The first ships with propellers then appeared, and huge suspension bridges made travel faster between previously unconnected areas. Photography meant eye-witness accounts of events could be spread publicly, biochemistry began as the first enzymes were discovered, liquid fuel was first produced from crude oil and Charles Darwin researched his Theory of Natural Selection. Hieroglyphs were also deciphered for the first time in the West, using the Rosetta Stone, making the understanding of ancient cultures more accessible.

Britain was able to develop its overseas empire, establishing colonies in Australia and New Zealand, and London became the most populated city in the world, with its first bus service. In the 1820s a mission by the East India Company to Siam (present-day Thailand) forced them to let more foreign trade in by reducing tax on it, and reduced state-held monopolies. The Crown Colony of the Straits Settlements established Malaysia and Singapore (1825) and Britain took Hong Kong from the Chinese following the first Opium War (1838–42). Additionally, victories in India against Burma gave them territory in Assam, Manipur and Arakan, and the British-led Bombay army defeated the Talpur Emirs at the Battle of Hyderabad (1843), leading to the annexation of the Sindh. The Anglo-Sikh War (1845–6) also gave Britain control of Kashmir.

Russia became the leading power on land, although its invasion of the Caucasus led to the ethnic cleansing of Cirassians, and the Muslim resistance there became known as the 'Jihad'. Russia took East Georgia (including Armenia and Azerbaijan), while West Georgia went to the Ottomans. Russia also took Varna in 1828 during the Russo-Turkish War, triggered by Russia's intervention in the Greek War of Independence against the Ottoman Empire. It took five years for the Congress System to decide what to do about the Greek uprising, but it was seen eventually as a victory for the Europeans against the Islamic empires.

Cultural advancements also occurred, with various universities being founded in Britain, Australia and the U.S. The Cairo University of Medicine also appeared, along with the first Polytechnic in New York and the first Medical School for Women in Boston. In England, the Oxford Union debating society, the Society for the Prevention of Cruelty to Animals, the YMCA and Rugby Football appeared, along with the first public parks, and the Penny Black became Britain's first postage stamp. Charles Dickens and the Bronte Sisters were active in literature, and a liberal, progressive British Parliament repealed repressive laws, like the Seditious Meetings Act and the Act banning Trade Unions. Also in Britain, the Death Penalty was revoked for over 100 crimes, flagellation went out of use and Catholic emancipation became widespread.

However, there were also resistance movements and uprisings, with varied outcomes. The Portuguese Liberal Wars (1828–34) established a new constitution, a Javan revolt against the Dutch ended with 200,000 dead and victory for the Dutch, who also made progress colonising areas of South Africa. Following the 1838 Anglo-Afghan war, fought to protect British interests in India from a potential Russian invasion, mobs attacked British people in the streets during 1842, forcing their withdrawal and the return to power of Dost Mohammad Khan. The First Carlist War (1833–1840) was a civil war in Spain as the monarchists sought to re-assert themselves against the liberal republicans, but ended with victory for the government with the support of Britain. The Decembrist revolt in Russia (1825) was suppressed, as was the Polish uprising against Russian rule (1831) and revolts in the Kingdom of the Two Sicilies against the Bourbons. In Modena, Parma and the Papal States, uprisings were put down by Austrian troops.

In the 1840s the nationalist uprisings intensified in terms of their achievements, establishing many new written constitutions. These included the Wallachian Revolution (1848), the Netherlands, and the Second French Revolution (1848), which deposed the Bourbon King and put Napoleon III (nephew of Boneparte I, cousin of II) back in charge, leading to the invasion of Rome, and the Republic of San Marco appeared in Venice (1848). The Second Carlist War (1846–1849) resulted in the suppression of the Carlist (monarchist) uprising. In Switzerland, Republican troops defeated the Catholics and created a federal republic, based on the U.S. Constitution, the first fully modern democracy in Europe.

Also known as the Spring of Nations, People's Spring, Springtime of the Peoples, or the Year of Revolution, 1848 was the most intense year of revolutionary waves in European history. Discontent at poor government in states which had experienced the rich getting richer through their colonial ambitions and alliances, leaving the industrial workforce in poverty with no political representation, led to widespread criticism of society. Once again, the focus was on social reform, freedom of speech and of the press, demands for better conditions, hours and wages for workers. Many were suppressed, and tens of thousands killed or forced into exile. However, significant reforms occurred, including the abolition of serfdom in Austria and Hungary, and the end of the absolute monarchy in Denmark.

The Appearance of Communism

In the midst of the 1848 turmoil, the Communist Party emerged as a political entity in Germany. Communism (from the Latin *communis*, meaning common, or universal) is a philosophical, social, political and economic movement whose goal is a socioeconomic order based upon the common ownership of the means of production, a system administrated to achieve the best life for all citizens, and the end of inherited social classes. In principle, the idea had existed since the Ancient world, for example, in the 5th-century BC Mazdak movement in Persia, which challenged the privileges of the Upper Classes, private property and strove to create a more equal society; the Essenes, a community in Ancient Judah who lived and worked together communally; in the Christian Church of the Middle Ages, where monastic communities shared land and property; and the Taborite branch of the Hussites, which proposed an end to private wealth and social hierarchy. The English writer Thomas More proposed, in Utopia (1516), a society based on the common ownership of property ruled by reason and, in the 1600s, the Puritan religious group known as the Diggers advocated the abolition of private land ownership.

Founded mainly on the ideas of Karl Marx, assisted by Frederick Engels, it appeared within Germany following developments in both philosophy and politics which had been occurring since Enlightenment times. Marx argued that if imperialism was causing the problems of society, then people must invent something which forced it to change, as it would not do so of its own accord. The proof of this lay in its inability to reform: as modern free-market Capitalism had evolved out of Feudal Capitalism through mercantile Colonialism, the system could only extend itself further in this way. Hence, the failed French Revolution was a warning that this social structure could not tolerate reforms, workers would forever be exploited, and an alternative must be created.

He agreed with Ricardo, who had said the law protected the capitalist business owner from sharing their profits, so the only solution was to create a new type of political system which put the rights of people above all minority interests. The Communist Revolution was, therefore, unlike the Middle Class revolution, which sought only to create reforms to the existing system. Instead, it proposed that the only solution was to replace the bourgeois, Middle Class revolution, with a full-scale workers' revolution, as whatever resulted from the Middle Class revolution under the present conditions would only result in a continuation of Capitalism. In this version, after the initial revolution liberated the nation from its existing power-structure, ownership of the 'means of production' (factories, farms, laboratories, etc.) would be transferred to the state and managed by people with the same technical knowledge, but in a way which gave workers an increased share of the profits from the goods they produced.

The reasoning behind this was not something which made sense to many people at first and, following the failed 1848 revolution, he had to escape Germany and set himself up as an English author in London. But, he then set about creating proof of his argument in a way which gathered support. After two decades of economic study and academic work, the first volume of Das Capital appeared, 'The Production Process of Capital' (1867). After his death (1883), his companion Engels published Volume II, 'The Circulation Process of Capital' (1885), then Volume III, 'The Overall Process of Capitalist Production' (1894). These three volumes are collectively known as Das Capital, and were the most widely cited book on the social sciences until the 1950s.

Engels, who had met Marx earlier in Paris, wrote 'On the Condition of the Working Class in England', in an attempt to describe the problems most people faced at the time. They agreed that the way free-market Capitalism had created the exploitation of the worker meant poor living conditions and a shorter life, thus creating the need for revolution, but the French Revolution had been inadequate in providing the new framework by which society could succeed. The Manifesto for the Communist Party (1848), co-written by Marx and Engels, henceforth proposed that only the creation of an entirely new social system could solve the problem, one which created equality and self-sufficiency. He claimed that the Capitalist system had never been the natural state of humanity, as people had always worked together to solve problems before the empires of history had corrupted global society.

This new system would allocate roles within society 'from each according to their abilities, to each according to their needs', rather than inherited upper, middle and lower class positions. He said the class-based system was only enforced by beliefs within society itself, as 'The ideas of the ruling class are in every epoch the ruling ideas, i.e. the class which is the ruling material force of society, is at the same time its ruling intellectual force. The class which has the means of material production at its disposal, has control at the same time over the means of mental production, so that thereby, generally speaking, the ideas of those who lack the means of mental production are subject to it. The ruling ideas are nothing more than the ideal expression of the dominant material relationships... grasped as ideas.'

Hence, what people needed was an ideology which enabled them to think in a new way, in order to produce a new system and, the only reason this had not happened before is because society had not evolved to the point where it was possible. Much of Das Capital was thus dedicated to proving points through detailed studies of economic history, the allocation and function of roles within the system, and the relationship between social classes.

Additionally, he suggested that the role of the Middle Class had been subverted by the establishment's response to the revolution. The Middle Class, he said, had gone from attempting to establish democracy to being appeased by the monarchy, in exchange for financial gain and direct political control of the workforce. 'The bourgeoisie, wherever it has got the upper hand, has put an end to all feudal, patriarchal, idyllic relations. It has pitilessly torn asunder the motley feudal ties that bound man to his natural superiors, and has left remaining no other nexus between man and man than naked self-interest, callous cash payment. It has drowned the most heavenly ecstasies of religious fervour, of chivalrous enthusiasm, of philistine sentimentalism, in the icy water of egotistical calculation. It has resolved personal worth into exchange value, and in place of the numberless indefeasible chartered freedoms, has set up that single, unconscionable freedom — Free Trade.'

The feeling of betrayal by their own representatives was a large reason why many socialists subsequently began to lean towards Communism after its arrival. He also criticised religion, as it was perpetually used by the ruling classes to enforce their idea of moral goodness. Marx claimed this was born out of the need to create illusory happiness, which should be secondary to a demand for real happiness. The foundation of this criticism, he asserts, is that humanity makes religion, religion does not make humanity, as 'Religion is, indeed, the self-consciousness and self-esteem of man who has either not yet won through to himself, or has already lost himself again. But man is no abstract being squatting outside the world. Man is the world of man — state, society. This state and this society produce religion, which is an inverted consciousness of the world, because they are an inverted world...'

The point of this is that it goes so far back into the way religion was designed to solve the problem of society, his philosophy is revolutionary to the point of questioning the very origins of the world order itself. However, as the age of mass industrialisation dawned, machines were doing all the work, making the reorganisation of society possible for the first time. He argued that, however, this was being unnecessarily prevented by a system which protected the interests of the ruling elite.

For this reason, it appealed to many people who were dissatisfied with the existing system, as it presented them with the idea of a possible alternative. His work was well-received by its critics, because he used empirical evidence, and Marx became known as one of the greatest philosophers. Buried in London, these words are inscribed upon his grave, 'Workers of all lands unite. The philosophers have only interpreted the world in various ways; the point is to change it.' After 1848, Europe continued to head in a direction which favoured the growth of Communism, as it became ever more apparent that there was no resolution to the inherent conflict between the social classes and, as the problems of Capitalism continued, the socialists were increasingly persuaded to accept where the cause of the problem lay.

However, the next major conflict was between the major powers, showing how much power they still had. In the 1850s the Crimean War (1853–6) was the largest between the Napoleonic Wars and WWI. It shook European politics, as people were afraid of a return to the age of wars. In retrospect, it was a pre-emptive war against Russia, which was stopped in its first phase through diplomatic efforts, leading to the 1856 Congress of Paris when Austria threatening to enter the war forced Russia into a peace treaty. It was fought in the Baltic, the Caucasus and Black Sea, but mainly on the Crimean Peninsula, with Russia on one side and the Ottoman Empire, Great Britain, France and Sardinia-Piedmont on the other. It was also the first to feature the first use of telegraph communication lines and railroads.

Additionally, failed rebellions also broke out in China against the Manchurian Qing dynasty, and revolt against British rule in India led to the creation of the British Raj in 1857, causing the dissolution of the Mughal Empire. The South African Republic was established by Dutch Afrikaaners, along with the Orange Free State by the British. In the U.S., the period known as Bleeding Kansas (1854–9) saw clashes between pro-slavery and anti-slavery settlers which preceded the U.S. Civil War.

The next map shows the 1800s starting to take the shape which ran through the next centuries, as the U.S. was forming, and we can see the current world order forming out of these nations.

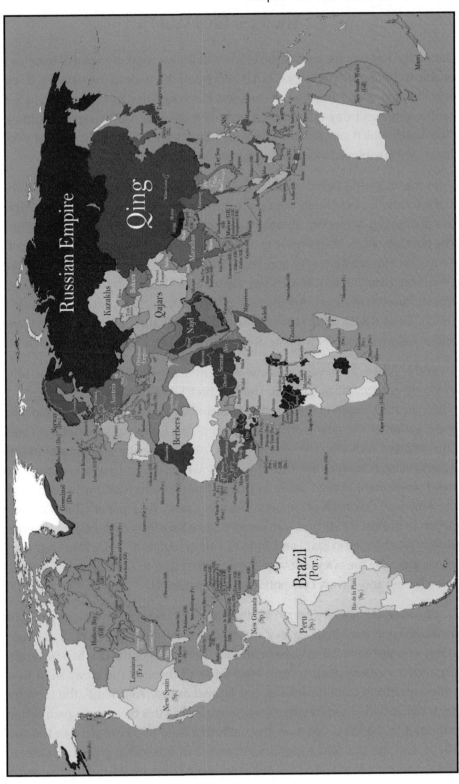

The U.S. Civil War

During the Napoleonic period, the U.S. was still quite weak on a global scale and unable to have much influence, but it addressed this issue in the early 1800s by acquiring more land, buying the Louisiana Purchase (the segment of land in the centre of present-day U.S. on the previous map). The southwestern territory, New Spain, which subsequently became Mexico, was won through a war over Texas, which achieved independence from Mexico in 1836.

In the 1820s the Democratic Party was founded, initially supporting slavery in the southern states, while seeking reforms in the electoral system, but shifted to a philosophy of modern liberalism and socio-economic equality in the 1830s. The number of U.S. states grew to around 30 from the original 13, as Vermont, Kentucky, Virginia Kentucky and Tennessee had been admitted in the 1790s; Ohio, Louisiana, Indiana, Mississippi, Illinois and Alabama by 1820; and Maine, Massachusetts, Missouri, Arkansas and Michigan by 1840. After that, Florida (1845), Texas (1845), Iowa (1846), Wisconsin (1848) and California (1850) were added following the war with Mexico, which lost over 50% of its territory.

In the Americas slavery was still widespread, with 32,000 Angolans sold in Rio de Janeiro, Brazil, in 1828. The U.S. had 1.5 million slaves, growing to 2 million in 1830, showing how far the problem of imperialism had extended into the creation of the new world. Treatment of the indigenous population was also criticised, including the relocation of 60,000 natives by the Office of Indian Affairs (1834), known as the Trail of Tears. However, things began to change, as freed slaves were able to settle in Liberia from around (1820) with help from the American Colonization Society. The anti-slavery newspaper 'The Liberator' began in Boston (1831), and Nat Turner's Slave Rebellion broke out in Virginia. Slavery was banned in Brazil and, in 1839, a slave mutiny on a U.S. ship was taken into custody by the navy, but won the right to return to Africa in court. In 1841, there was an anti-slavery convention in Massachusetts.

However, U.S. society began to head towards civil war, as the government in Washington abolished slavery and standardised this policy upon southern states who were unable to cope financially. As it formed, the U.S. had generally expanded southwestwards from New England through the creation of new states, gradually colonising what was known as the 'Wild West', the term for areas not yet colonised by white Europeans. During this time, many people had migrated to the West Coast, as the California Gold Rush occurred in the late 1840s, and the U.S. was experiencing an era of economic growth. However, while manufacturing and heavy industries were being established in the north, the southern economy was mostly based on large-scale farming and dependent on black slaves, especially in the growing of cotton and tobacco.

When the U.S. Congress passed the Kansas-Nebraska Act (1854), the Republican Party was formed by its opponents, who supported classical liberalism and social reform. It opened all new territories to slavery, and pro- and anti-slavery forces struggled violently in Kansas. After the Supreme Court's ruling in the Dred Scott case (1857) confirmed the legality of slavery, abolitionist John Brown's raid on Harper's Ferry (1859) led to southerners believing that the north was going to destroy their economy. Republican anti-slavery Abraham Lincoln's election in November 1860 then led to seven southern states breaking away and forming The Confederacy: South Carolina, Mississippi, Florida, Alabama, Georgia, Louisiana and Texas.

The Knights of the Golden Circle played a large part in the secession movement. They were a Catholic Secret Society in the south, which had emerged in 1858 when a secret society founded by a Cincinnati businessman merged with the pro-expansionist Order of the Lone Star, which already had 15,000 members. The following year, they established a headquarters in Washington, D.C., and began to publish their own newspaper. They proposed the alternative solution of invading Mexico and making it a slave state, thus acting in the interests of the U.S. as they perceived it. Members supported southern governors in the secession movement, helped to recruit the Confederate Army, assisted with the pro-Confederate Copperhead movement in the north and fought rearguard actions in the war.

1860 was their first attempt at creating the Golden Circle, as several thousand Knights assembled in southern Texas to invade northern Mexico. However, when this attempt was abandoned they turned to staging independence rallies and intimidating Unionists in the south.

They appointed regional military commanders and established an alliance with the pro-independence 'Fire-Eaters': Barnwell Rhett, Louis Wigfall, Henry Wise and William Yancey. Promoting pro-southern feeling on a national level, they hoped to oppose the government through creating a feeling of popular opinion around slavery, and planned the assassination of Abraham Lincoln as he passed through Baltimore on the way to his inauguration.

War broke out in April 1861 when secessionist forces attacked Fort Sumter in South Carolina. The Confederacy grew to control at least a majority of territory in 11 of the 34 states, and it claimed the additional states of Kentucky and Missouri. Two other 'slave states', Delaware and Maryland, were invited to join the Confederacy, but intervention by Unionist troops stopped them, and the Confederate states were never diplomatically recognised as a legitimate political entity by any country. Both sides quickly raised volunteer and conscription forces who fought the war, mostly in the south over four years, with 620,000 to 750,000 dead.

The war ended on 9 April, 1865, when General Lee surrendered to General Grant at the Battle of Appomattox Court House. Confederate generals followed his decision, the last being on 23 June. Much of the south had been destroyed, especially infrastructure such as transport systems. The Confederacy collapsed, slavery was abolished, and four million African-American slaves were freed. During the Reconstruction era which followed the war, national unity was restored, the national government expanded, and civil and political rights were granted to freed slaves through amendments to the Constitution. The country also embarked on a massive industrialisation programme which led to its rise as a major world power.

With the war a lost cause, various Knights supported one of their members, John Wilkes Booth, in his plot to assassinate President Lincoln. According to some theorists, the Knights of the Golden Circle went underground after the Civil War and changed their name, with the intention of causing a second southern uprising against the north. However, no such uprising ever occurred, and they gradually dispersed throughout the southern states. This paved the way for a new Protestant organisation, which subsequently became active in terms of supplanting Catholic power in the south, presumably in the hope of preventing a second civil war. It absorbed and managed much of the dissatis-faction in the South, and died out towards the end of the century, but was then reinvented by the white Working Class in the early 1900s under a new regime. Originally, it was founded by a former Freemason and Confederate general, Albert Pike, a controversial figure who allegedly predicted three world wars, but also ordered such atrocities against the North that the army stripped him of his rank. Starting off as a social club for ex-Confederate soldiers, its name was the Ku Klux Klan (Kucklos being Greek for 'circle').

The Second Phase of the European Congress System

The main event of the 1860s in Europe was the rise of Prussia. Following this, the Austro-Prussian War (1866) caused a shift in the European balance of power. The Prussian technology was far superior, obliterating the Austrian forces in only two weeks, making Prussia the most powerful state in Germany. Otto Von

Bismark, Prussia's leading statesman, was the grand architect behind it, and it ended without actually taking any territory, for fear of involvement by the other major powers. In 1867, the Austrians entered into a dual-monarchy with Hungary, having lost support from Russia, and the rise of Prussia continued as Bismark then launched into a war with France (in 1970–1), capturing Napoleon III and forcing them into the Treaty of Versailles.

This formally founded the German Empire, with Bismark as the head of government and diplomacy, while Wilhelm I became emperor. The unification of Germany (as the National German Federation) created the Second Reich and instantly made it the leading power in Europe, in terms of industry, population and the military. Germany proceeded to exert a major influence over continental Europe, pursuing the diplomatic agenda of isolating France, while announcing a peaceful foreign policy. However, this also had the effect of repressing revolutionary movements further and encouraging the rise of nationalism as the primary means of social change.

By the 1870s the revitalised Congress System included France, Britain, Austria, Russia, Italy and Germany. Germany made an alliance with Russia and Austria known as the League of the Three Emperors (1873–1880), to control Eastern Europe and isolate France. The Congress of Berlin and the Conference of Berlin then asserted the new power of Germany as it presided over the outcome of the Russo–Turkish War of Liberation (1877–8), which had been fought to free the Balkan states: Bulgaria, Romania, Serbia, and Montenegro from Ottoman control.

Romania achieved full independence, and was made to turn over part of Bessarabia to Russia, but gained Northern Dobruja. Serbia and Montenegro also gained independence, but with reduced territory, while Austria-Hungary took over the Sandžak region, Bosnia and Herzegovina. Additionally, Britain took over Cyprus. Although victorious, Russia felt somewhat humiliated, as Austria-Hungary had gained a large amount of territory, which also angered the South Slavs and led to the tension in Bosnia and Herzegovina which preceded World War One. The Congress also returned land to the Ottomans that a previous treaty had given to Bulgaria, including Macedonia.

Additionally, the French occupied Mexico (1863–7); Argentina, Brazil and Uruguay invaded Paraguay, killing 60% of its population; the British–Maori wars in New Zealand involved 14,000 troops; Italy unified under Victor Emmanuel II (1861–70); in China, the Fall of Nanjing ended the 14-year Taiping Rebellion (1864); the La Gloriosa revolution happened in Spain (1868); the Suez Canal was built in Egypt (connecting the Mediterranean Sea to the seas of South Asia, avoiding the trip around the horn of Africa); the British-Bhutan War (1864–5) led to more territorial gains for Britain; and Japan began to industrialise under the Meiji Restoration (1866–9).

In the 1870s, the Reconstruction Era in the U.S. caused racial segregation which lasted until the 1960s; the Third Carlist War (1872–6) occurred in Spain, leading to a final defeat for the monarchist faction, and the First Spanish Republic (1873–4); the Anglo-Zulu War (1879) ended Zulu dominance over their domestic region; and the Long Depression (1873–1896) put pressure on governments to promote home industries, leading to a widespread abandonment of free trade policies in Europe.

In science, the prototype telephone was invented, along with the electric lightbulb, phonograph, steam drill, the first submarine, the transatlantic telegraph cable, dynamite, antiseptic, iron-hulled warships and the machine gun. Expositions took place in Philadelphia and Paris. In literature, Jules Verne published 'Around the World in 80 Days', while Monet and Renoir became famous for their art.

New Imperialism (1881–1914)

While the Congress System had a strong Germany functioning as its new centre, its states still had the problem of revolutionary movements, and began building their empires as far out as they could, giving governments more leverage at home. This became known as New Imperialism, as it was different from the establishment of colonial empires, being more concerned with maintaining political power and stability. The social system was a problem too large for anyone to solve, and they still had the responsibility of maintaining the peace in Europe. With the Americas conquered, the world was running out of territory to colonise, and thus it came to be more about maintaining diplomacy in Europe, while exploiting the resources of developing countries, extracting raw materials and creating industrialisation to create jobs for the Working Classes at home. In the 1880s, Western powers came to control almost all of Africa and large parts of Asia.

They used the ethos of a civilising mission to bring modern government to areas which still had tribal conflict, and especially Christianity into Africa to counter Islam, leading to the Partition of Africa between the Christian south and Muslim north. However, while followers of these doctrines became exceptionally wealthy, people in the colonies had terrible working conditions, food, and lost the chance to develop economically. It took until the period following WWII for many of these colonies to gain independence. In 1870, only 10 percent of Africa was under European control but, by 1914 this had increased to almost 90 percent.

After the Scramble for Africa, which began with the Berlin Conference of 1884, which regulated European activity in Africa and divided it into regions of imperial influence, only Abyssinia (present day Ethiopia), the Dervish state (part of present-day Somalia) and Liberia remained independent. France had most of the northwest, while Britain was strong in the east. Spain, Belgium, Germany and Italy all had territories which they exploited for raw materials and used the local populations as a source of cheap labour. Previously, Europeans had suffered defeats in attempting to colonise Africa, but technological advances led to success this time: repeating rifles, the machine gun (which they refused to sell to African leaders), transportation in the form of steamships and railways, the telegraph, and medicines — especially a new treatment for malaria.

Compared to the policy of creating trade with Asia, however, investment in Africa was directed at the acquisition of resources. and was largely strategic. For example, Britain wanted ports in the east which were on the trade route to India. Colonies could also be used as bargaining chips in times of political crisis. This was reflected in the lives of the people who lived there, racial segregation was rife and, for example, in the Belgian Congo they lived under a curfew which was imposed on the Congolese between 9pm–4am. Blacks could not rise above the rank of non-commissioned officer in the military and city centre areas were reserved for whites. However, almost all of those countries have since gained independence, education systems, and equal memberships of the U.N.

Generally speaking, the situation worked well for the major European powers, but it also meant that all the world's land was effectively owned, and further pressure started building up on governments to create reforms. Having generated much of this progress through imperialism, though, this became difficult. Nor could the West look to the East for an example, or vice versa. The trend during this period was for the East to follow the methods of industriali-sation used by the West, starting with Japan, who achieved an empire perhaps half the size of the larger Europeans', by sending students to study at Western universities and learning Western Capitalist methods.

However, this period of progress was all set to collapse, due to two major wars which ended the modern era. In 1888, Wilhelm I of Germany died, leaving the throne to his son Frederick, who also died. In the Year of the Three Emperors, Wilhelm II, the eldest grandchild of Queen Victoria, succeeded the throne. His first cousins included the British George V and many princesses who became European consorts, and he was not well trained for the task. Additionally, a traumatic birth had given him Erb's palsy, which caused his left arm to be 15 centimetres shorter than his right. He tried to conceal this in many photographs showing him holding gloves or the hilt of a sword, and several historians have suggested that it affected his emotional development. In 1863, at the wedding of the future King Edward VII of England and Princess Alexandra of Denmark, he bit his eighteen year old uncle on the leg. Shaped by the hyper-masculine military culture of the Prussian monarchy, he was rarely seen out of uniform as an adult and, despite being mentally alert, he possessed an impatient disposition. Bismark attempted to separate him from his parents at an early age, and he became alienated from them, later accusing them of putting Britain's interests first. When he came to the throne, he dismissed Bismark and, in 1890, embarked upon a radical new course of military, foreign and domestic affairs, which ignored the diplomatic conventions of the European Congress System.

Alienating the British by congratulating their suppression by the Transvaal Republic, he propagated the idea that China and Japan would unite to attack Europe as the 'Yellow Peril', and publicly made friends with the Ottomans. Hoping to convey the image of Germany as a leading world power, he made frequent, tactless, and alarming public statements without his ministers' advice, and effectively created a military dictatorship. Tension built through his expansion of the armed forces, especially his desire to rival the British navy, as it upset the balance of power in Europe. This behaviour culminated in Germany's absolute guarantee of military support to Austria-Hungary during the Balkan Crisis which preceded World War I.

By the early 1900s, the technology of the 1880s and 90s had created substantial progress in terms of daily life: mass-scale electric lighting, the first automobiles, zinc powered batteries, the diesel engine, the kinetoscope (an early form of motion picture), a widespread use of aluminium, the voltmeter, electric fan, electric arc-welder, electrocardiogram and automatic telephone exchanges. In 1904 New York had a subway. By 1900 there were 8,000 cars and almost ten miles of road and, by 1908, there were 200,000 cars, half of them made by Ford. Radioactivity was discovered, along with X–Rays, helium, Argon, Krypton and Xenon. In literature, William James published his Principles of Psychology and the James–Lange Theory of Emotion helped to establish the social sciences.

The U.S. had its own type of economic development, pursuing pure Capitalism, and skyscrapers began to fill its skylines in the north. However, society was dogged by social problems, such as the lynchings of thousands of African-Americans in the south, which contributed to their exodus to the industrial north. The first major banking crises occurred, as the finance industry naturally grew along with Capitalist investment. The financial Panic of 1893 set off a widespread economic depression in the United States and Europe, leading to the failure of many banks and thousands of companies, leading to a period of economic stagnation and industrial disputes.

Nevertheless, due to the industrial revolution, people who were not born rich could become rich for the first time, such as Ford, Carnegie and Rockerfeller, and the structure of regular paid wages made retirement accessible to the Working Classes. However, there was still a deep divide between North and South. For example, in the Deep South people still used the horse and cart, while in the North automobiles and gas-lit streets were commonplace. Buffalo had an International Exposition showcasing innovations in electricity, agriculture, forestry, and a new electric dam powered generator, while most people in the South had never seen a street light or indoor plumbing.

In the South, they were still recovering from the Civil War, and 80% of African-Americans worked as sharecroppers, in a situation which was criticised for not being very much different from slavery. They rented seeds, land, tools and houses from white land-owners who were not obliged by law to give a fair price for the crops they produced, nor declare their profits. White politicians brought in the 'Jim Crow' laws (named after the Black & White Minstrel shows in which they portrayed black people as simple and clownish). These laws created racial segregation in institutions such as restaurants, bars, cafes, public toilets, schools, public transport systems and hotels. In Birmingham, Alabama, it was even illegal for blacks and whites to play chequers together. Having won the right to vote, black Americans effectively lost it in the 1890s with these new State Constitutions promoting white supremacy, fuelling a mass exodus to the industrialised North in search of new jobs and lives.

In Asia, France colonised Indochina and made its capital Saigon, out of parts of Vietnam, Cambodia, and the Chinese territory of Guangzhouwan. The Qing Dynasty began to disintegrate over the issue of whether the Far East should industrialise to Western standards, or continue with traditional methods. But, Europe then had to deal with the rise of Asia, which occurred through industrialisation inspired by developments in the West, improvements in its military and reforms to the social system. However, a power struggle then emerged between China and Japan.

While Korea had been a tributary state to China, rising Japanese industrialism had occurred in line with Western models, giving them the power to negotiate a treaty with Korea which opened their ports to foreign trade, and prevented them from being dominated by any other nation. However, the traditionalist Korean government then asked for Chinese assistance during the 1894 peasant revolt known as the Donghak Rebellion. China sent 2,900 troops, but Japan responded by sending 8,000 and suggesting China and Japan should co-operate to reform the Korean government. When China refused, Korea asked the Japanese troops to leave. In response Japan captured Seoul in June, and installed a puppet government which then asked the Chinese troops to leave. When China refused, the First Sino-Japanese War (1894 –1895) began.

Japan won the land battle at the Liaodong Peninsula, and at sea at the Battle of the Yalu River. The Treaty of Simonoseki was then signed, which awarded the Liadong Peninsula and Taiwan to Japan. Subsequently, Germany, Russia and France forced Japan to withdraw from Liaodong, where the Russians built Fort Arthur and based their Pacific Fleet. It became an important Pacific port as Vladivostok could only function in the summer. Germany built a fortress at Jiaozhou Bay, where they based their East Asia Squadron.

After this, protests broke out in China, during the 1895 Gongche Shangshu movement, thousands of Beijing scholars and citizens protested against the Treaty of Shimonoseki. The Emperor responded with the Hundred Days Reform of 1898, as his regime admitted that weaknesses had been exposed in China, which had resulted from their failure to industrialise. Previously, China had only bought the latest technology, such as warships, weapons and artillery, without modernising itself to the extent where it could build its own.

His reforms included those at Peking University, encouraging members of the imperial family to study abroad, a naval academy, agricultural schools and colleges, a modern education system, trade schools for tea, silk and other traditional Chinese crafts, and rapid industrialisation using Capitalist methods in manufacturing and commerce. However, this was seen as too radical by the conservatives and a coup d'état put Empress Dowager Cixi in charge, leading to the belief that all hope of internal reform had failed and only a revolution could save China.

The subsequent Chinese Boxer Rebellion (1899–1901) was started by the Militia United in Righteousness (known in English as the Boxers, as many practiced Chinese martial arts). After several months of violence in Shandong and the North China Plain against foreigners and Christians, in June 1900, the Boxers converged in Beijing with the slogan 'Support the Qing government and exterminate the foreigners'. The foreigners themselves then sought refuge in the Legation Quarter. Eight nations: Austria-Hungary, Britain, France, Germany, Italy, Japan, and Russia sent troops to break the siege, while Empress Dowager Cixi supported the Boxers and, on June 21, issued an Imperial Decree declaring war on the foreign powers. Diplomats, foreign civilians, and soldiers as well as Chinese Christians in the Legation Quarter were subsequently besieged for 55 days.

During this time the Europeans brought 20,000 troops to China, defeated the Imperial Army, and arrived at Peking on August 14 to relieve the siege. However, plundering of the capital ensued, along with the execution of Boxers and government officials who had supported them. Foreign troops remained in Beijing, and a payment of 450 million taels of silver (approximately $10 billion today) was demanded over the next 39 years.

The Qing court initiated a series of 'New Policies', including administrative and legal reform, but young officials, military officers, and students debated both a constitutional monarchy and the creation of a republic. The emerging public opinion was created by intellectuals such as Liang Qichao and the revolutionary Sun Yat-sen. In 1911 The Wuchang Uprising overthrew the Qing dynasty, which had at one point a third of the world's population and one of the largest empires of all time. It created the Republic of China (1912–49) and ended 2,000 years of imperial rule. A new government was formed in Nanking, on 12 March 1912, with Sun Yat-sen as President, but he subsequently turned power over to Yuan Shikai, head of the New Army. Over the next few years, Yuan proceeded to abolish the national and provincial assemblies and declared himself the Emperor of China in 1915, creating a situation which led to civil war between the Nationalists and the Communists.

Russia also had its first major revolution in 1905, following defeat in the Russo-Japanese War (1904–5). The Balkan League (Bulgaria, Serbia, Greece and Montenegro) also rose up against the Ottomans in the First Balkan Wars (1912–13), losing the Turks 83% of their European territories. However, tensions then arose within the Balkan region, with regard to their relationships with the major powers.

Part 3: The World Wars which Ended the Modern Era

The assassination of the Austrian Archduke Ferdinand in Sarajevo, 1914 was just one event in a long line which led to the start of WWI. Behind it lies a vast web of relations between the European powers, nationalistic tensions over land, and international alliances. Although large, the war was quite simple in terms of its nature, causes and ambitions. It was a battle for territory between the European powers, which spilled over into the European colonies and their allies in the Far East. The U.S. and other nations in the Americas did not want to join, as they were not politically connected to the problem, but enough of the rest of the world became involved to drag them in.

It all started in Sarajevo, on 28 June 1914, when Gavrilo Princip assassinated Archduke Franz Ferdinand (heir to the Austro-Hungarian throne) and his wife Sophie (the Duchess of Hohenberg), as part of a plan by the Black Hand, a Serbian secret society, to end Austria-Hungary's rule over Bosnia and Herzegovina. They aimed to break away the South Slav provinces so they could be combined into Yugoslavia, but it led to a war between the two main groups of powers in Europe.

Firstly, Austria-Hungary went to Kaiser Wilhelm II of Germany for political support then, having gained it, issued an ultimatum to the Kingdom of Serbia which demanded all subversive elements within Serbia were neutralised. For several years they had been infiltrating the Serbian establishment and publishing anti-Austria-Hungarian propaganda, fuelling a political and military movement against them. Austria's ultimatum stated that these people had committed crimes against the state, including other murders, and both weapons and training had been issued by Serbian officials. It added they also had evidence that bombs and hand-grenades used in the attack had come from a Serbian army depot in Kragujevat. Serbia had two days to issue a satisfactory response.

Serbia's reply stated that it would attempt to co-operate to the best of its ability, involving any case in which Austria could provide evidence, but added that they failed to comprehend how they could be considered complicit in any such plan, if they did not have prior knowledge of when or where it might occur. Known as the July Crisis, Austria-Hungary broke off diplomatic relations with Serbia and began preparing for war, possibly hoping for a larger degree of co-operation. Russia, in support of Serbia, began to do the same. At this point, the British Foreign Office attempted to lobby Paris, Rome and Berlin, proposing a convention should be held to avoid conflict. The impetuous Kaiser Wilhelm II, however, opposed this and advised Austria to proceed immediately.

World War I

On July 28th, Austria-Hungary declared war on Serbia, and artillery divisions began a bombardment of Belgrade across the Danube. Russia, in response, ordered the mobilisation of its army on the Austria-Hungary front. After German demands to stop Russian mobilisation, Germany declared war on Russia on August 1st. France mobilised as Russia's ally and, on August 3rd, Germany and France declared war on each other. Germany then planned to invade neutral Belgium, which they needed to do as part of the Schlieffen plan to invade France, and Britain declared war on Germany as Belgium invoked the earlier Treaty of London.

Facing a war on two fronts, the German plan was to defeat France quickly, so they could transfer troops to the Eastern Front before Russia could fully mobilise. On August 23, Japan sided with the Entente powers (France, Britain and Russia), seizing German assets in China and the Pacific. In November, the Ottoman Turkish Empire joined the Central Powers (of Austria-Hungary and Germany), opening up fronts in Mesopotamia, the Caucasus and Sinai Peninsula. The war thus spread into European colonial territories and Africa.

By late 1914, the German advance into France had settled down into trench warfare, leaving both sides unable to break through. This was the most futile part of WWI, killing millions of soldiers for gains of only a few miles, on which war poets such as Wilfred Owen later commented, making parallels between the war and people's struggle to achieve representative government. However, the Eastern Front saw a much greater exchange of territory. In 1915 Italy joined the Central Powers, opening up a new front in the Alps, while Serbia fell to the Entente. Bulgaria and Greece joined the Entente in 1917, expanding the war in the Balkans, while Romania was defeated. The U.S. remained neutral, despite allowing the Entente access to supplies while denying the others. However, the sinking of American merchant ships by German submarines, especially the Lusitania, and attempts to incite Mexico to declare war on the U.S. forced them to act, in April 1917. Trained American soldiers did not arrive until 1918, but eventually they sent 2 million.

Meanwhile, the Russian 1917 Revolution ended their involvement, replacing the Tsars with a provisional government, allowing Germany to transfer huge amounts of soldiers to the western front. This led to the March 1918 offensive, but it was not enough to win the war and, due to the Entente's 100 Day Offensive, with new innovations such as tanks and aeroplanes helping ground troops to break through, Germany resigned. Bulgaria signed a peace treaty in September, the Ottomans in October and Austria-Hungary in November.

In total, it was one of the largest conflicts in history, involving over 70 million military personnel (60 million Europeans), with 9 million dead, plus 7 million civilians. In the aftermath of the war, combined with the 1918 influenza pandemic, another 50 to 100 million deaths occurred worldwide. Hence, it became known as 'The War to end all Wars', and is remembered to this day on November 11, as people across the world wear red poppies as a symbol.

The Russian Revolution

During WWI Tsar Nicholas II had taken control of the army and left his wife and her assistant, Grigori Rasputin, in charge of the capital. Hence, when Russia suffered losses, he took the blame directly instead of being able to spread it around in a way which would have been easier to manage politically. Rasputin was accused of corrupting the royal family and assassinated in 1916. Tsar Nicholas was also blamed for food shortages and war protests, which he sought to put down with his army, but the army joined the protestors. Russian generals called for his abdication and, when he did so in 1917, Russia formed a provisional government with its base at the Winter Palace.

Towards the end of WWI, the two sides were exhausted, and governments feared internal revolutions as much as the enemy. Labour strikes occurred in Britain, costing 17 million working days between 1915–8, and there was a protest at Tower Hill against conscription. The British Prime Minister, Lloyd George, used compromises such as introducing a State Pension. France similarly suffered stoppages and protests, many by women, due to price rises and lack of fuel while industrialists profited. In April 1917, the French Army tried to break through 7 miles of impenetrable German defences at Chemin de Dames, losing 40,000 in the first few days. Determined to press on, casualties rose to 150,000 by 5 May. By June, half the French army were refusing to man their trenches. However, this went apparently unnoticed by the Germans, one of the largest military intelligence failures of the war, as they were working on a plan to overthrow the Russians from within.

This involved returning communists such as Vladimir Lenin to Russia from their exile and supporting them with money and weapons. They had a plan to undermine the state parliament by setting up their own, the Petrograd Soviet. It called for the end of the war, and offered people food and land of their own. While the Russian army had run out of rifles, explosives and mortars on the western front, civilians suffered from harsh conditions and food shortages at home. Political agitators called upon the people to protest as the government refused to end the war, and Lenin's Bolshevik factions stood at the front of the protest when the army opened fire. Many leading Bolsheviks, such as Leon Trotsky, were arrested.

However, Trotsky did not spend long in prison, as the new Prime Minister, Alexander Kerensky, had appointed a new army chief, Lavr Kornilov, who marched his army on Petrograd after a dispute between the two. Kerensky released many of the Bolsheviks, as their military arm, the Red Guard, was the only thing that could stop him. They sabotaged Kornilov's army and it did not reach the city, but this did not leave the government in a strong position, and Lenin started calling for an armed rebellion of his own. After putting Trotsky in charge of the revolution and seizing the infrastructure of the city, Kerensky fled and the Bolsheviks took control of the Winter Palace. After this, Lenin issued three decrees: 1. An end to the war, 2. The end of private land ownership, and 3. A minimum wage for workers. He also introduced universal healthcare and education, increased the rights of women, and accepted Finland's declaration of independence. The Bolsheviks then announced free multi-party elections in the next month, which they lost. In response, Lenin controversially declared the elections illegal and moved his capital to Moscow.

In March, 1918, Trotsky negotiated a treaty with Germany and Austria-Hungary, which gave them a large tract of land in the west, which enraged Czechoslovakia, as they had been fighting on the side of the Russians in exchange for independence from Austria-Hungary after the war. They took up arms, inspiring other enemies of the Bolsheviks to join, and this started the Russian Civil War. As Britain, Japan and the U.S. became involved, the two sides became known as the Reds (Communists, Socialists and Anarchists) versus the Whites (Capitalists, Conservatives, Liberals, Nationalists and Tsarists). However, just when it looked like the Whites were winning, the Reds were actually stronger, as many of the White factions were fighting for their own cause. The Red's territory around Moscow was also equipped with better infrastructure, communications, a larger population, industry and food supplies. Deep into the war, the Red Terror policy took effect: as the former Tsar was executed to prevent his recapture by the Whites, and Trotsky held the families of his generals hostage to ensure their loyalty. When it became apparent the Reds would win, the Czechoslovakian fighters returned home, by which time their country was independent anyway, and a new order appeared in Russia.

Shortly afterwards Poland attempted to expand at the expense of Russia and invaded Ukraine. The Bolsheviks subsequently countered and pushed the Polish back to Warsaw. The Poles held their position, though, and this prevented Russia from directly bordering on Germany. Two puppet states then appeared in Ukraine and Belarus and the U.S.S.R. officially formed in 1922. Lenin suffered from a series of strokes and ill-health before he died in 1924, leaving the role open to two candidates: Joseph Stalin was the former editor of the Bolshevik newspaper and had become General Secretary, the highest political office in the U.S.S.R. He did not believe Communism was strong enough in Russia to yet export, and favoured policies of economic development and industrialisation. Trotsky, on the other hand, believed in the 'eternal revolution', one which must be continually taken to other countries to keep it alive. Stalin won the race and, in 1929, Trotsky was exiled (he was later assassinated in Mexico in 1940).

In Russia, Stalin strengthened his position through the use of secret police, purges of the government and army, and sending dissenters to political labour camps which were known collectively as the Gulag system. He also embarked upon five-year plans to improve output, and 'Collectivisation' turned Russian farming into a mass-scale industrial operation. Much debate has occurred over the years as to whether Stalin was ultimately a hero or a villain. He stated through Pravda in 1931 that the Soviet Union was fifty to one hundred years behind the major industrialised nations, and promised to catch up in ten. By 1936 he had collectivised 90% of the peasantry, which he saw as essential for creating the new state. Initially, grain production dropped, but gradually rose enough for exports to pay for industrialisation. In 1928 the first Five Year plan was created and doubled target levels in major industries, continuing until the 1941 German invasion.

The urban population grew by 30 million and a new generation of educated Russians emerged. Russia grew into a world superpower and was only threatened by the U.S. However, whole ethnic populations, such as the Chechens, were transported across Russia and many of them died. The collectivisation programme was chaotic and, when grain production dropped, the famine (1932–4) cost 7 million lives. Industrial targets were so important that quantity took precedence over quality, and the 1937 purge of the military led to half the army's leadership being imprisoned or shot. Many middle management figures were imprisoned for being spies or 'Wreckers'.

Parvus

There is also an aspect to the Russian Revolution which has only been publicly revealed in recent years, a man who was behind the German plan to overthrow the Russians. His real name was Israel Lazarevich Gelfand, and whose Communist alias was Alexander Lvovich Parvus (the little one, also known as 'Helphand' in literature on the Russian Revolution). Born into a lower Middle Class family in present-day Belarus, he studied Political Economy at Basel University (1888–91). However, when he returned to Russia he became subject to scrutiny by the secret police for his Marxist views and left for a career which would help fund his support of Socialism in the more industrialised Germany. While there, he joined the Social Democratic Party and became friends with German revolutionary Rosa Luxemburg. He met Lenin in Munich, in 1900, and they admired each other's theoretical work, after which Parvus encouraged Lenin to publish Iskra, his newspaper, which became the official mouthpiece of the Russian Social Democratic Labour Party.

Writing in the German press, he predicted Russia would lose the Russo-Japanese war and it would cause revolutionary unrest. At this point he developed Marx' idea of permanent revolution and the idea of using foreign wars to provoke internal discord. This idea was conveyed to Trotsky and further developed by Lenin and the Bolsheviks in his 1917 April Thesis, when Lenin returned to Russia and launched the Bolshevik uprising. Following the 1905 revolt in Russia, Parvus and Trotsky returned, and Parvus wrote an article in the Russian press which suggested their economy would soon collapse. He also co-ordinated agitation which made it look like there was a run on the banks, which caused hysteria and upset the Prime Minister, but did not cause the societal breakdown he had hoped for. For this, he and others such as Trotsky were sent to prison, where he was visited by Rosa Luxemburg.

After escaping, he published a book about his experiences there. Back in Germany, he made a deal with a Russian author, Maxim Gorky, to produce his play 'The Lower Depths'. He then moved to Istanbul, where he founded an arms-dealing business which profited greatly from the Balkan War. While there he worked with top officials, such as the Prime Minister, and the Ministers for War, Navy, and Finance. His company expanded to include food deliveries for the Ottoman army and he became the financial and political advisor to the Young Turks movement, while editing their newspaper.

By the time WWI had started, he was in a position to be more influential, and became close with the German ambassador to the Ottomans, Hans Freiherr von Wangenheim, who had previously established revolutionary fifth-columns among the Allies. Through him, he offered a plan to the German government to paralyse Russia with a General Strike, and Wangenheim sent him to Berlin, where he arrived in March 1915. There he presented a 20 page script for the Russian Revolution which combined money, sabotage, and the overthrow of the government. Entitled 'A preparation of massive political strikes in Russia', it proposed the political division of Russia, by supporting the Bolsheviks, authors who opposed Tsarism, and encouraging ethnic separatists in various regions to weaken state unity. A month later, the German treasury authorised 2 million marks ($500 million today) to support revolutionary propaganda in Russia.

He met Lenin in May and, while they agreed to this plan privately, they were careful not to be seen together in public. Parvus subsequently set up a financial network to get German money into Russia, by transferring it through several companies. Set-backs occurred, as he came to the attention of British Intelligence due to his revolutionary activities against the British, and he had to try to shut down his financial network. His plan to create a financial disaster in Russia also failed. However, the next plan worked better as, in 1917, a chartered train organised by Kaiser Wilhelm II and his Danish ambassador, Ulrich von Brockdorff-Rantzau (who had also co-ordinated his financial network), shipped Vladimir Lenin and 30 of his revolutionary comrades into Russia via Sweden and Finland, with the aim of starting the Russian Revolution. His arrival in Russia was a success, 'He is working according to your wishes' was the message sent by Germany's top army command to the foreign office.

With the additional assistance of arms smuggled in through a small village in Sweden into Finland, the Bolsheviks grew in power and military might. Lenin established the Petrograd Soviet upon his return as, when the time came, they had the resources and manpower to strike. The Communists then threatened to do the same thing in Germany, with Russian money. However, Parvus' work with the Imperial German government had ended relations with other revolutionaries, such as Rosa Luxemburg, and others who were engaged in the subversion of the German state. He then retired to a 32-room mansion on Berlin's Peacock

Island. After he died of a stroke in 1924, both Germany and Russia created a veil of secrecy over his involvement in the Russian Revolution.

The implications of this connection between the German government and the Bolsheviks is huge as, while Communism had existed as a doctrine for some time, it was actually Germany which enabled the Russian Revolution, hence the whole of the Cold War and the creation of Postmodernity. But, were they at the same time deceived to a certain extent by the Communists, as they did not know of the plan to subvert Germany with Russian money? As the Communist challenge to the established order in the West led to the subsequent rise of Fascism and WWII, it also means the way many events have occurred since need to be re-examined.

The League of Nations

The Great War led to the collapse of Russia, Germany, Turkey, Austria-Hungary and China. Shocked by its brutality, a new global initiative was launched, the League of Nations, based in Geneva, Switzerland. It was an international organisation designed to create a forum for resolving international issues, proposed by the U.S. President, Woodrow Wilson, as part of his 1918 Fourteen Points plan for peace in Europe (even though the United States did not join). The last of these points called for a 'general association of nations…formed under specific covenants for the purpose of affording mutual guarantees of political independence and territorial integrity to great and small states alike.' It represented the views of many officials who believed there was a need to create a lasting peace, involving both sides of East and West, and was hugely popular.

By this point, the U.S. had become an important global power. After the immediate reconstruction period an economic boom followed WWI in the U.S., known as the Roaring Twenties. In 1800, 95% of the U.S. lived in rural areas, but by 1920 this figure was only 20%. New modernist cultural trends appeared, such as Jazz and Art Deco. Automobiles became popular, along with telephones, motion pictures, radio, accelerated consumerism, and the media began to focus on celebrities, movie stars and sports heroes. Baseball stadiums and movie theatres became widespread. Walt Disney created Mickey Mouse, Gershwin wrote Rhapsody in Blue, and men started abandoning formal suits for sportswear. The electric razor was invented, the jukebox, frozen food, the liquid fuelled rocket, Thompson rifle, and the first flight was made across Atlantic. The discovery of Tutankhamen's tomb also occurred, along with Penicillin. It had taken 200,000 years for the world population to reach 1 billion, in 1804, and it arrived at the next billion in 1927.

Women and ethnic minorities, especially African Americans, began to enter the workplace in large numbers due to the skills they had acquired during the war, as many women worked in factories producing weapons and supplies while the men fought on the front lines. These people had access to mechanical engineering and book-keeping skills for the first time, which enabled them to set up their own businesses and work for others. However, the three major trading zones, the U.S., Europe and Asia, started acting independently of each other, and the competitive devaluation of currency became a problem as each sought to create a positive balance of foreign trade by making export goods cheaper. The economic boom did not sustain and the Great Depression of the 1930s followed the 1929 Stock Market Crash in the U.S. As a result of this, the position of the U.S. became weak and isolationist. In 1931, 4 million U.S. workers were unemployed, but this doubled in 1932. During that year the Communists led hunger marches, with 20,000 filling the streets of Chicago and clashes occurred with the police in Brooklyn.

President Herbert Hoover was seen to handle the crisis badly, as he sent the army to disperse a large group of war veterans who had descended upon Washington to seek early payments, and he was beaten in the 1933 election by Franklin D. Roosevelt. Shanty towns of tents and corrugated iron sheets had sprung up all over the U.S., known as Hoovervilles, millions became homeless, drifting from town to town, and people fought over garbage while others starved. Dead bodies lay in the streets. On national television, Roosevelt announced a programme of greater good for a greater number and said that this would go against those who were seeking to retain their privileges or achieve positions of power 'by a short cut'. He reformed financial institutions, and recruited the Middle Classes with policies driven by consumer prosperity, and a new country began to appear. By the next Autumn, around 40% of the people who were looking for work had found it. Appealing to the young generation to get involved, he set up the Civilian Conservation Corps, into which 2.5 million were recruited to fight fires, dig irrigation ditches and plant trees in the national parks.

A determined effort was being made, with First Lady Eleanor Roosevelt giving a speech about how willing women could support their neighbours and see it through. The Public Works Administration built highways, tunnels, ports and dams. Radio personalities held the country together culturally, and new social activities were created: Bridge became popular with the Middle Classes and jigsaw puzzles were sold in department stores. Pinball machines and one-armed bandits appeared, Bingo and Baseball became regular activities and Saturday became a public holiday. Before long, two thirds of people were going to the movies at least once a week. Also, magazines were popular and cheap, featuring stories on American Football, Baseball and the G-Men, while children read comics like Superman and Flash Gordon. Dance crazes also appeared, like Swing, Jazz, Jitterbug and Boogie-Woogie. In 1938, 20,000 went to a Swing carnival and 200,000 attended the Blues festival in Chicago.

By 1939, the U.S. had hope for the future. However, the recession remained a global problem as its effects had spread, and there was a new threat on the horizon, the rise of Fascism in Europe. Roosevelt said in at least two speeches that he had seen the horrors of war and wanted to remind people that he hated it. He hoped the U.S. would not get involved in any more wars, especially foreign wars, and believed the U.S. could stay out of this one.

The Rise of Fascism

In the 1920s Central Europe was in political turmoil, as it began to polarise between extreme right and left-wing ideologies. Meanwhile, Britain and France owed huge debts to the U.S. for war supplies, which they tried to pass off onto bankrupt Germany, leading to a French occupation of the Ruhr district which extracted raw materials such as coal. This led to the rise of the National Socialist Workers Party, who feared the French would break Germany down into regions of their own making. Russia was in civil war and, following the empowerment the Russian Revolution had given to the Communists, uprisings occurred in Berlin. Fascism arose in general as a force to counter the Communists, thus becoming popular with the monarchy, and there was nothing the Church could do to stop them.

By the 1930s, the League of Nations was beginning to fail, as the U.S. had not joined, Russia was not allowed in because of Communism, nor was Germany. It had no standing army, meaning that it could not enforce its sanctions. In 1921 it stopped a war between Finland and Sweden, but did not prevent the Polish from invading Lithuania, the Japanese invasion of Manchuria (1931), or the Italian invasion of Abyssinia. Britain and France were its only strong nations, and even they did not close the Suez Canal to Italy to prevent the invasion.

The Fascists also found support in the U.S. and other Western industrial powers, who were reluctant to lose their free markets to Communism. In some cases they combined with the racist element in society, as Socialism implied integration. For example, DuPont helped to finance the Black Legion in the U.S., an anti-Socialist group that used violence against Trade Union leaders and members, and were subsequently implicated in several murders. Reported to have over 1.5 million members in the U.S., it had links with the Ku Klux Klan. Many U.S. banks and businesses continued to support the Fascist regimes of Europe legally until the day Germany declared war on the U.S. and, despite this, some continued, such as Ford and General Motors, who supplied trucks and equipment as well as investing money in I.G. Farben plants. Standard Oil supplied the Fascists with fuel, while U.S. Steel and Alcoa supplied metals, and U.S. banks gave them billions of dollars in loans. At the same time, many U.S. citizens were protesting at events in Europe and the involvement of American companies. Along with the minority who supported the Fascists, there were also those who opposed them, including a group of American volunteer soldiers known as the Abe Lincoln Brigade, who went to fight against them in the Spanish civil war.

Germany had become genuinely terrified about the prospect of a Communist Revolution during the 1920s, as two political paths had emerged after WWI: social democracy and a council system similar to the Bolsheviks. A power struggle thus began between the ruling Social Democratic Party and the Communist Party of Germany (KDP), led by Rosa Luxemburg and Karl Liebknecht. This culminated in the Spartacist Uprising in Berlin (1919), which was mostly a series of street battles, with other similar incidents being suppressed in Bremen, the Ruhr, Rhineland, Saxony, Hamburg, Thuringia and Bavaria.

The Spartacists had concluded from previous experiences, as part of both the Socialist and Social Democratic Party of Germany (KSPD), that their goals could only be achieved through a party of their own, and founded the KDP, which was then joined by members of other left-wing groups. Rosa Luxemburg drew up their founding document and presented it publicly in December 1918, claiming that they would never win power without the support of the majority, but the KDP voted to continue along the lines of agitation and putting pressure on the government from the streets, in the hope this would cause a Communist Revolution like the one in Russia.

In January 1919, the USPD, KDP and Revolutionary Stewards organised a united demonstration, which turned into a massive political event, as hundreds of thousands of people came out onto the streets of Berlin, many of them armed. They gathered at the Police Headquarters and elected a 53-member 'Interim Revolutionary Committee'. However, unable to agree on a direction, they then called for a general strike, which attracted 500,000, and insurgents captured government buildings. But, when this led to talks with the government which broke down, the KDP resigned from the Revolutionary Committee, and the army did not take the side of the revolt. Subsequently, around 3,000 Freikorps (anti-Communist paramilitaries hired to suppress the revolutionaries) fired on the crowd, killing 150. Later that month, Rosa Luxemburg and Karl Liebknecht were discovered by a citizen militia hiding in a Berlin apartment and were subsequently executed.

From the paramilitaries, we can see there was already a defence mechanism operating against the Communists by the 1920s but, in 1922, Fascism emerged as a political movement in its own right. The Fascist Revolutionary Party (Partito Fascista Rivoluzionario) was founded in Italy in 1915. Mussolini then founded the Fasci Italiani di Combattimento in Milan, in 1919, which became the Partito Nazionale Fascista (National Fascist Party) two years later. King Victor Emmanuel II in Italy handed power to Mussolini in 1922 following his famous March on Rome, which led to the Prime Minister, Luigi Facta, attempting to declare an emergency, but the King overruled him and appointed Mussolini as Prime Minister instead. The term Fascist was derived from the ancient Roman 'fasces' (fascio littorio), a bundle of rods tied around an axe, which was a symbol of the authority of the civic magistrate, and could be used to enforce corporal or even capital punishment in defence of the state.

The Fascists rejected the notion that violence is absolutely negative by definition and proposed that the need to keep law and order, patriotism and even war were necessary for a nation's survival. Due to the dramatic growth of Communism, many people who were stakeholders in society saw it as a threat. Fascism sought to defend the state from its enemies, and build a strong nation with the power to act whenever necessary. To keep power, though, it meant the government must create constant progress to ensure popular support, thus keeping it active and dynamic. This appealed to many people who had secure jobs, those who owned businesses, and anyone else who did not agree with the Communist Revolution. The key factor in their success was that they enabled people to believe that society needed to improve in order to cope with the problems which had come with industrialisation. This was the exact opposite of the Communists, who proposed that the system needed to be entirely changed. While the Communists used social class the unifying factor which brought workers together, the Fascists used race as the factor which unified the people of a nation, and used it to forge a strong sense of national identity. Fascist political parties were generally appeased by the western European powers, who sought a strong buffer zone against the Soviet Union.

In 1923, Hitler appeared on the German political landscape. Born in Braunau, Austria, he had a troubled youth as his father was a violent man who beat his family and also a heavy drinker who died of a heart attack at the dinner table when Adolf was 13. By the time he was 17 his mother, who was also his father's niece, died of cancer and he was forced to move to Vienna as an orphan. While he was there he failed to pass the entrance exam to the Art College and stayed in a homeless hostel, making money by selling picture postcards and paintings he made himself in the street. According to various sources, he acquired a bitter hatred of foreigners during this time, as he believed they were taking German jobs, and especially of the Jews, who he would later accuse of controlling the country financially and corrupting its politics.

When the First World War came he joined the army and worked as a messenger to the front line. After being promoted to Corporal, he was hospitalised by a gas attack and devastated when he found out Germany had lost the war. Following this he served as a government agent, spying on new political parties. The German army was concerned that the German Workers Party (DAP) was a left-wing revolutionary group and sent Hitler, one of its education officers, to investigate. However, in one fateful moment, he discovered that the party's political ideas were very similar to his own, especially Drexler's German nationalism and anti-Semitism. When a member made a point he disagreed with, he stood up and made a passionate speech.

Drexler was impressed with Hitler's articulation and invited him to join. At first he was reluctant, but his commanding officer, Captain Karl Mayr, encouraged him. He was soon asked to join the executive committee and appointed as propaganda manager. Shortly after, Hitler brought several members of the German army into the party, including one of his commanding officers, Captain Ernst Röhm. The arrival of Röhm was an important development, as he had access to the army political fund and was able to transfer money into the party. Other early members included Rudolf Hess, Hans Frank and Alfred Rosenberg.

Hitler was often the main speaker at party meetings and it was during this period that he developed into a persuasive orator. His reputation attracted more people and this gave him tremendous power within it, as he became a valuable asset. In April 1920, he advanced the idea that it should change its name to the National Socialist German Workers Party (NSDAP), as Socialism had become popular in Germany after WWI, and it enabled them to compete with the German Social Democrat Party (SDP), which was the largest political party in Germany at the time. However, Hitler suggested they redefine Socialism, by placing the word 'National' before it, turning it into a hybrid concept which went beyond both. Members of the party referred to themselves as Nationalsozialisten (National Socialists), which gave rise to the foreign slang 'Nazis', which had been in use before the rise of the party as a colloquial or derogatory word for a backward peasant.

In February 1920, the NSDAP published its first program which featured the 'Twenty-Five Points.' These included a refusal to accept the terms of the Versailles Treaty, and called for the reunification of all German people. Equal rights were to be given only to German citizens, while Jews and other foreigners would lose their rights of citizenship. That year, the party announced that only people of pure Aryan descent could become party members and their spouses must also be 'racially pure' (Aryans). Party members could not be related either directly, or indirectly, to 'non-Aryans'.

At the time, France and Britain were extracting payments which were devaluing the currency and causing rising inflation, in order to pay back the U.S. money they had borrowed during WWI. It was the time of Germany's deepest humiliation, having been the mighty Holy Roman Empire. After WWI they were disarmed by the Treaty of Versaille and, while unable to defend themselves, France invaded the Ruhr district in 1923 and occupied various parts of the Rhineland. The French subsequently embarked on an intensive propaganda campaign, aimed at separating the Rhineland from the rest of Germany, and a French-backed separatist movement had already appeared in Bavaria by the Autumn. General von Lossow, the Bavarian chief of the Reichswehr no longer took orders from Berlin, and the Bavarian Prime Minister was set to announce an independent state on the eve of the Fifth Anniversary of the establishment of the German Republic, on November 9th.

The National Socialists became both organised and mobilised under Hitler, and staged a demonstration at the event which became known as the Munich Beer Hall Putsch. Hitler was accompanied by the famous WWI commander, Ludendorff, and attempted to create a national protest which they hoped the army would join. As the Prime Minister, Dr. von Kahr, started his speech, Hitler entered the hall, followed by Ludendorff, and broke up the meeting. The next day, storm battalions staged a mass demonstration in favour of national unity. However, the army opened fire as they reached one of the central squares in the city, killing sixteen. Hitler fell and broke his collar-bone. The firing only stopped when Ludendorff marched up to the soldiers behind the barricade.

After this failed attempt at a coup, Hitler was imprisoned in the Fortress of Landsberg am Lech, in April 1924. During this time he wrote Mein Kampf, the first part of which is dedicated to the 16 who died in the Putsch and were refused a common burial by national officials. It is written in 15 chapters, including one on his childhood, World War I, his early political activities, why the Second Reich fell, Race and People, Citizens and Subjects of the State, the first stage in the development of the German National Socialist Labour Party, the conflict with the Red forces, the nature and organisation of Stormtroopers, the Mask of Federalism, and the right to self defence.

From ''Mein Kampf' (My Struggle).

'German-Austria must be restored to the great German Motherland. And not indeed on any grounds of economic calculation whatsoever. No, no. Even if the union were a matter of economic indifference, and even if it were to be disadvantageous from the economic standpoint, still it ought to take place. People of the same blood should be in the same Reich. The German people will have no right to engage in a colonial policy until they shall have brought all their children together in the one state. When the territory of the Reich embraces all the Germans and finds itself able to assure them a livelihood, only then can the moral right arise, from the need of the people to acquire foreign territory. The plough is then the sword; and the tears of war will produce the daily bread for the generations to come.'

It seems to be very clear from this that he intended to return Germany to the rank of a major European imperial power. After Hitler's release from prison, the Party and its affiliated organisations were banned in Bavaria. However, at a meeting with the Prime Minister of Bavaria, Heinrich Held, in January 1925, Hitler promised not to seek political power through undemocratic processes and the ban was lifted. Then, after another inflammatory speech, he was barred from public speaking until 1927. During this time he appointed Gregor Strasser, Otto Strasser and Joseph Goebbels to enlarge the Party in northern Germany.

When the effects of the U.S. Great Depression spread to Europe, it reduced foreign exports and, when Germany was hit, millions lost their jobs and several major banks collapsed. Hitler promised to break the Treaty of Versailles, rebuild the economy and create jobs, something the moderate politicians were unwilling to do. Elections in September 1930 ended a political coalition, replacing it with a smaller government, with chancellor Heinrich Brüning (of the Centre Party), governing through emergency decrees from President

Paul von Hindenburg. The National Socialists won 18.3 % of the vote and 107 parliamentary seats, becoming the second-largest party.

Hitler then acquired German citizenship, which enabled him to legally run for public office, and he subsequently ran against Hindenburg in the 1932 presidential elections. He won support from Germany's powerful industrialists, through a speech to the Industry Club in Düsseldorf in January 1932, while Hindenburg's supporters were the nationalists, monarchists, Catholics, republicans and Social Democrats. Hitler won 35 per cent of the vote in the final election and, although he lost, became a powerful figure in German politics. Two influential politicians, Franz von Papen and Alfred Hugenberg, along with other leading industrialists, subsequently wrote a letter to Hindenburg, urging him to appoint Hitler as the leader of a government 'independent from parliamentary parties', which could turn into a movement which would 'enrapture millions of people'.

As chancellor, Hitler prevented opponents of the NSDAP from forming a majority government, and asked Hindenburg to dissolve parliament. Re-elections were scheduled for early March, but in February 1933, the Reichstag building was set on fire, and Dutch communist Marinus van der Lubbe was found inside the burning building. He was subsequently arrested and put on trial, despite claims that the National Socialists themselves had poured gasoline into the building before it was ignited. He was tried executed in January 1934. At Hitler's request, Hindenburg responded with the Reichstag Fire Decree (28 February), which effectively ushered in the dictatorship, as it suspended civil rights and allowed detention without trial. Activities of the German Communist Party (KPD) were suppressed, and around 4,000 of its members arrested.

New weaponry was provided to German troops (contrary to the Treaty of Versailles) and the majority of state powers were transferred from Hindenburg to Hitler and his cabinet.

Within a month, TIME magazine reported, nearly all the country's leading communists and socialists were in jail. Restrictions were put on personal liberty, the right to free speech, of the press, the rights of assembly and association, and the privacy of postal, telegraphic and phone communications. Additionally, the decree authorised the Reich government, which moved to Potsdam, to take over federal states completely, wherever necessary imposing the death sentence for crimes including serious disturbances of the peace by armed persons.

To achieve full political control, Hitler's government brought the 'Enabling Act' to a vote in the newly elected Reichstag. It gave his cabinet the power to enact laws without any other consent for four years. Since some of these laws would break with the constitution, it required a two-thirds majority to pass. To make sure it did, the National Socialists arrested all 81 Communist deputies and prevented several Social Democrats from attending. It passed by a vote of 441–84 in March 1933, as the Reichstag assembled at the Kroll Opera House. Ranks of Brownshirt Stormtroopers served as guards, while large groups outside protested. In this way, the Weimar Republic came to an end and the Third Reich began. On the 10 May, the National Socialists seized the assets of the Social Democrats and banned them on 22nd June. The SA also raided the offices of the German National People's Party, which disbanded on 29th, and the other political parties followed. On 14 July Germany became a one-party state as a law was passed which declared the National Socialists to be the only legal party in Germany.

The state parliaments and the Reichsrat (federal upper house) were abolished in January 1934, with all state powers being transferred to central government. When Hindenburg died in August from lung cancer, aged 86, Hitler had the cabinet pass a law which stated that the office of president would remain vacant, and Hitler would be entitled 'Führer und Reichskanzler' (Leader and Chancellor of the Reich). Hitler thus became both head of state and of government, thereby eliminating the possibility by which he could be legally removed from office. In a plebiscite vote, held on 19 August 1934, the German people were asked if they approved, and the Yes vote won with 90%. He publicly announced that the presidency was 'inseparably united' with Hindenburg, and it would not be appropriate for the title to ever be used again.

Civilian organisations, volunteer groups and sports clubs had their leaders replaced with National Socialist volunteers or party members, trade unions were dissolved and their leaders arrested. The Law for the Restoration of the Professional Civil Service was passed in April, and removed all teachers, professors, judges, magistrates, and government officials from their positions who were Jewish or whose commitment to the party was suspect. This meant the only institution not under control of the National Socialists were the churches.

They then abolished the symbols of the Weimar Republic and adopted the swastika flag of the Party, which became the sole national flag in 1935, while the Party anthem, 'Horst-Wessel-Lied', became a second national anthem. However, Germany was still in a difficult economic situation, with six million unemployed and a large balance of trade deficit. Forcing German client states to buy their produce, deficit spending and public works projects were launched in 1934, creating 1.7 million new jobs by the end of the year, and wages began to rise. But, in order to succeed, victories had to keep coming, and this led to Germany expanding its power internationally.

Countries such as France and Britain, which continued with traditional diplomacy and democratic government, opposed German expansionism as it destroyed the balance of power in Europe. But, Germany and Italy still pursued territorial gains, as Germany annexed Austria without bloodshed, and began the road towards hegemony over other German speaking people. In 1935–6 they recovered the Saar (pop 800,000) and remilitarised the Rhineland (governed at the time by the U.S. and France under a League of Nations mandate). Italy disagreed with German claims on Austria, but this changed after the 2nd Italy-Abyssinia war, as Germany became Italy's only ally. They then formed an alliance against Communism in 1936.

In 1937, when the Spanish Civil War started, Hitler and Mussolini sent tanks and troops to support Fransisco Franco, while the Soviet Union supported the left-wing Republicans. Franco later won and set up a Fascist dictatorship which lasted there until the 1970s. German speaking parts of Czechoslovakia were Hitler's next target and this nearly caused an international war, but the Munich Agreement of 1938 was approved by the British Prime Minster, Neville Chamberlaine, who said that 'peace, with honour' had been achieved. Others called it appeasement, and Chamberlaine was replaced by Winston Churchill after Germany later invaded Norway.

However, during the same year the assassination of a German diplomat, Ernst Vom Rath, by a German-born Polish Jew, triggered the Kristallnacht (Night of Broken Glass). In retaliation the Hitler Youth, Gestapo and SS attacked Jews in Germany and Austria, killing 91. 25,000 to 30,000 were arrested and sent to concentration camps. 267 Synagogues were destroyed and houses ransacked. From then on, genocide became a feature of the regime. Starting in 1939, they began to execute hundreds of thousands with death squads operating in occupied territories, including people with mental or physical disabilities in hospitals and asylums, Jews and other Holocaust victims. By 1941, millions were imprisoned, starved, worked to death, or murdered in concentration camps.

As the effects of the Great Depression hit Asia, it also caused a large downturn in exports. This led to a reaction from the right-wing, imperialist faction which had come to power in Japan, making it a natural ally of Germany and Italy at the time. At its height, it was led by the WWII Hideki Tojo cabinet of the Imperial Rule Assistance Association, under Emperor Hirohito. In 1931 the Japanese invaded

Manchuria and established a puppet state, Manchukuo. From 1931 to 1937, both Chinese Nationalists and Communists continued to struggle with Japan, leading to the largest Asian war in the 20th century, accounting for the most casualties in the Pacific War. Between 10 and 25 million Chinese civilians and over 4 million Chinese and Japanese military personnel died. When Italy invaded Albania in 1939, Victor Emmanuel III claimed the vacant royal title. Germany then invaded Poland, causing WWII, and this ultimately merged all the wars around the world into one, as virtually every nation ended up being on one side or the other.

World War II (1939–45)

During this time, the vast majority of the world's countries, including all the major powers, eventually formed two opposing military alliances: the Allies and the Axis. A state of total war emerged, directly involving more than 100 million people from over 30 countries. It was the deadliest conflict of all time, with 50–85 million dead, most of whom were civilians in China and the Soviet Union. As technology had developed since WWI, it was a new type of war, with huge radio-communication networks creating new levels of command and control. Flak towers defended cities from thousands of airplanes, while battleships with crews as big as small towns carried airforces halfway around the world. Developments in the armoured tank had led to the creation of motorised Armoured Divisions which, hundreds strong, could wreck cities in a few days. Whereas WWI was more about trench warfare, armoured tanks, supported by infantry and aircraft, created the Blitzkrieg tactics which enabled countries to invade each other in a matter of weeks.

War began on 1 September 1939, as the Blitzkrieg invasion of Poland by Germany resulted in France and the UK declaring war on Germany, who had signed the Tripartite Pact with Italy and Japan on 27 September 1940. This was a defensive military alliance which was also joined in 1940 by Hungary, Romania, and Slovakia. Bulgaria and Yugoslavia signed in early 1941. A coup d'état in Belgrade led to Germany, Italy and Hungary invading Yugoslavia, partitioning the country and creating Croatia, which also joined on 15 June 1941.

After invading North and East Africa, the fall of France occurred in mid-1940. The French army was large at the time, larger than WWI at 5 million, and the fighting was intense. During the Battle of France around 60,000 French soldiers were killed between May and June, while Germany lost 30 percent of its tanks and planes. Its death toll is estimated at 27,000 killed and missing in June, 21,000 in May. But, there was one main reason for the French defeat, the Germans took a decisive risk. They had anticipated the French response and concentrated their tanks in the Ardennes, getting themselves between the Maginot Line and the main body of the French army in the north. Hence they pushed through the Ardennes while the French army had gone north, to fight the Wehrmacht divisions they anticipated had gone through Belgium according to the Schlieffen Plan, which would try to cut from the north down to Paris, as it had in WWI. Hence, they cut off the French forces in the north, before heading south towards Paris.

By 1941, the Axis powers controlled much of Europe. Hitler made a pact with Stalin to partition the territories of their neighbours: Poland, Finland, Romania, and the Baltic. However, on 22 June 1941, the Axis powers launched an invasion of the Soviet Union, opening the largest land theatre in war history. Similar to Napoleon's campaign, after a series of victories, they encountered a Russian army who was embedded and, with neither boots nor coats to cope with the cold winter, millions perished. Additionally, in December, Japan launched a series of attacks on European colonies in Asia to create a perimeter in the Pacific, and struck Pearl Harbour in the United States, hoping the U.S. would sign a peace treaty while its navy was incapacitated.

However, due to the way U.S. politics worked, they could not tolerate such an attack and all-out war followed against Japan, supported by Great Britain. Gradually, the U.S. regained dominance in the Pacific, fighting various battles for strategic islands and outmanoeuvring the Japanese fleet while its navy was rebuilt. This culminated in victory at the Battle of Midway in 1942, in which the Japanese navy was decisively defeated. Germany and Italy were defeated by the British General Montgomery in North Africa and by the Soviets in Russia. By 1943, the Allies invaded Sicily and Italy, forcing the Axis powers to retreat on all fronts.

In February, 1944, the Allies met in Yalta, to discuss the re-organisation of post-war Europe. The Bretton Wood System, involving U.S., Canada, W. Europe, Australia and Japan, was established as a monetary order intended to govern financial relations between independent states. It addressed the lack of co-operation between free-market economies which had led to the competitive devaluation of currency, which in turn had caused the Great Depression. Each country would subsequently adopt a monetary policy which maintained its external exchange rate within 1%, by tying its currency to gold, with the International Monetary Fund (IMF) to bridge temporary imbalances of payment.

In 1944, the Allies launched a massive amphibious assault on the beaches of Normandy (D-Day) to liberate France from German occupation, while the Soviet Union started pushing westwards towards Berlin. Between then and 1945 Japan suffered losses in mainland Asia, Central and South China, and against the UK in Burma, while their navy was hunted down and defeated at sea by the U.S. In January 1945 the Allies pushed forward from Paris to the Rhine, while the Soviets began their East Prussia offensive. On 16 January Adolf Hitler took up residence in his Berlin bunker, before giving his last public radio broadcast on the 30th, announcing his belief that Germany could still win if they kept fighting.

On 17 January the U.S.S.R. occupied Warsaw and Hungary agreed peace with the Allies on the 23rd, followed by victory for Britain against Japan in Burma on the 30th. In February Venezuela, Uruguay, and Turkey joined the Allies, followed by Finland on 3 March. The Soviet Union also agreed to join the Eastern offensive against Japan, once the battle against Germany was won, while pushing across Europe and creating various Communist states along the way. Romania revolted on 28 February, before forming a Communist government under Radescu on 6 March, followed by Yugoslavia under Tito and San Marino later in March.

The last months of the war featured heavy bombing by Allied forces on Germany and Japan, destroying most of Dresden, Mainz, Wurzburg, Wesel, Tokyo and Kobe in Japan, and finally Berlin on 18 March. At this point, Hitler ordered all wartime industries in Germany to be destroyed, an order which was ignored, which Hitler then considered treason.

In March, Argentina declared war on Germany, the Arab League was formed in Cairo, and the Soviets pushed the Axis powers out of Hungary into Austria, while defeating the Germans in Prussia. The Concentration Camps, where millions of Jews were killed, were liberated along with the Allied advance, in some cases the prisoners revolting and killing the guards. On 12 April, Franklin Roosevelt died unexpectedly, leaving Harry S. Truman in charge of the U.S. However, it had no effect on the direction of the war, as the Allies captured the German gold reserves at Thuringia, Canada took control of the Netherlands, and the war in Europe concluded with an invasion of Germany by the western Allies and the Soviet Union, who met at the Elbe river on the 25th, dividing the country in two.

Goring sent a telegram saying he had assumed leadership and Himmler attempted to negotiate peace with the Allies. Both were arrested. Following the Battle of Berlin, the Soviets captured the city. Benito Mussolini was killed by Italian partisans on 28 April and, after privately admitting defeat to his generals two days later, Adolf Hitler and his partner, Eva Braun, committed suicide in their Berlin bunker. He was succeeded by Grand Admiral Karl Dönitz. This was followed by the suicide of Joseph Goebbels, his wife and six children on 1 May, and the former head of the S.S., Heinrich Himmler, killing himself while in British custody on 23 May. A mass-suicide also occurred in Demmin, after 80% of the town was destroyed, killing between 700–2,500. The German unconditional surrender was announced on the 7 May and took effect on the 8th (now known as Victory in Europe Day, or VE Day).

By June, the war had practically finished, with the Allied Control Council taking over Germany on the 5th, and the United Nations (UN) charter being signed on the 26th. Britain took over Syria and Lebanon and, on 1 July, Germany was divided into 4 parts, each to be governed separately by the French, British, U.S. and U.S.S.R. The Philippines were liberated on the 5th and the atomic bomb was approved by U.S. President Truman on 21 July, rather than face a lengthy extension of the ground war. On the 26th, the Potsdam conference called for Japanese surrender. However, Japan proceeded to sink the U.S. warship Indianapolis using submarines on the 30th and, on 6 August, the nuclear bomb was dropped on Hiroshima with 129,000–246,000 dead. The Soviets put additional pressure on Japan, starting their Manchuria campaign and pushing eastwards towards Japan itself, before a second bomb was dropped on the 9th, at Nagasaki, leading to Japanese surrender on the 10th. On 2 September, the war officially ended.

CHAPTER 14

Postmodernity

The term Postmodernity holds true as it applies to the period following WWII, as the world system underwent significant changes which continued into the 21st Century. During this period the United Nations began its mission and quickly moved the world away from the pattern of events which had dominated the early 20th Century. However, the Communist bloc declined to participate in the new system, instead creating its own, leading to the Cold War. Over time, this situation diffused itself across the world, eventually resulting in a mixed economy of private and public interests. By the 21st C the Internet enabled the globalisation of the world's industries and replaced political ideology as the main source of progress...

Part 1: The Cold War (1947–1991)

In 1945 the U.S. occupied Japan and South Korea while France, the U.S., U.K. and U.S.S.R. divided Germany into 4 parts. Berlin, in the Russian quarter, was subdivided into four zones in the same way. However, tensions began to quickly emerge between the West and the Communist bloc nations which had grown extensively since WWII, bringing with them their own political and economic system which was completely different from free-market Capitalism. The single-party government controlled the state and deployed resources between departments as was seen necessary. Hence, they had different ideologies and opposing ambitions. In 1946, attitudes in the West towards the Communist nations went into steep decline, mainly due to the plan for Soviet occupied Eastern Europe and the expansion of Communism.

Winston Churchill was invited by the U.S. President, Harry Truman, to give a speech in Missouri on his vision of the post war period. He called it 'The Sinews of Peace', as it was directed at building a new sense of lasting global security. After stating that he had achieved his own political ambitions and had no ulterior motive, he went on to talk about the current situation, which he described as the 'problems which beset us on the morrow of our absolute victory in arms, and try to ensure what has been gained through so much sacrifice and suffering shall be preserved for the future glory and safety of mankind'.

He stated that the U.S. had become the pinnacle of world power, but with that came a great responsibility and, therefore, 'a constancy of mind, persistency of purpose and the grand simplicity of decision shall guide and rule the conduct of English speaking people in peace as they did in war.' He spoke of the safety and security of society, in a period where people strove to guard themselves against poverty, and the importance of governments protecting society itself from war and tyranny. However, he added, while the U.N. organisation was already at work, national armouries should not be cast away until the situation was 'built on solid rock'. This included a recommendation that the U.N. should not be equipped with the atomic bomb, as it was still in its infancy.

He claimed that 'God' had willed the situation to be 'this way around', in the sense that the Communists did not yet have the nuclear device, something which shortly changed and gave the Cold War period a more serious dimension, even though he had a strong admiration for his wartime comrade, Marshal Stalin. Also that he understood the need for Russia to remove the German threat from its eastern border and welcomed Russia among the leading nations of the world. But, 'From Stettin in the Baltic to Trieste in the Adriatic, an iron curtain has descended across the continent.' He further added that ancient capitals were facing increasing pressure from Moscow and, while Greece was free to make her own choice, millions of Germans were being expelled from Poland as the Communist parties in those countries were being elevated beyond their numbers to the level of totalitarian control. He further stated that Turkey and Iran were alarmed by the pressure put on them by Moscow, and that the Soviets were trying to create a Communist government in their part of Germany. Putting German people up for auction between the two superpowers 'is not the liberated Europe we fought for', he said, nor does it contain the promise of permanent peace. Hence, the safety of the world required a new unity in Europe, one from which no nation should be outcast.

He blamed quarrels between the 'strong parent races' of Europe for the wars which had occurred, into which the U.S. had been drawn against its wishes. Hence, the post-war plan should involve working closely with the U.N. to secure a lasting peace. He additionally said, 'Until 1933 or even 1935, one shot could have spared us the fate Nazi Germany inflicted, but no one would listen and one by one we were sucked into the awful whirlpool. We must not let this happen again.'

However, as he spoke, the western Allies and Communist bloc were already manoeuvring in relation to each other. The Greek Civil War was being fought between the Nationalists and the Communists and, while the Soviet Union did not intervene directly, Yugoslavia and Albania sent supplies to the Communists. By 1947, Britain could no longer maintain its massive overseas commitments, having given independence to India, and Palestine to the United Nations, then withdrawal from both Greece and Turkey left Greece in danger of a communist takeover.

The Cold War 1947–53

Notified that British aid to Greece and Turkey would end in less than six weeks, U.S. President Truman met with the leaders of Congress, using the argument that 'apples in a barrel would all be infected by a rotten one', leading to the emergence of the so-called 'domino theory', which became important to U.S. foreign policy as it presumed that countries would fall one by one if the spread of Communism was allowed to gather momentum. In March 1947 he asked Congress to send $400 million in aid to Greece and Turkey, calling for the 'support of free peoples who are resisting attempted subjugation by armed minorities or by outside pressures'. His policy became known as the 'Truman Doctrine', and served as the beginning of the Western response to the Communist expansion into Eastern Europe.

In reply to this, the Soviet Union asserted its position was 'progressive' and 'anti-imperialist'. Stalin wanted to expand, seeking to secure oil rights on the Iranian border, but to get the oil out they needed to pass through Turkish waters. Subsequent measures put pressure on Iran for oil rights in a region which bordered on Turkey, and this put pressure on Turkey to grant them a military base and transit rights. Truman opposed this, as he sought an anti-Communist Turkey.

Relations further broke down in January 1948, when the U.S. State Department published a number of documents revealing a pact between Hitler and Stalin, which included a plan for the Soviets to join the Axis powers. A month later, the Soviet Union responded with a book re-edited by Stalin, 'Falsifiers of History'. It described the Western support for the German war effort, including aid the U.S. banks and industrialists had provided, while simultaneously encouraging Hitler to expand eastwards. The book stated that Stalin rejected Hitler's offer to divide the world between them, and the Soviet Union stood by this version of events until its dissolution.

The Truman Doctrine was then developed further, into the Marshall Plan, which extended aid to all of Western Europe. It was devised by George C. Marshall, a senior member of the U.S. military during WWII who became Secretary of State. From 1948–51 fuel, food, machinery and money were sent to Europe to help post-war recovery and build a strong resistance to any potential Soviet invasion. In 1948, the Organisation for European Economic Co-operation (OEEC) formed, led by Robert Marjolin of France, to help administer the Marshall Plan by allocating United States financial aid and implementing economic programs for reconstruction in Europe. It was perceived as a good deed, but also helped to build the U.S. markets for future trade. European businesses grew by 25% and exports increased massively. Stalin, fearing Western influence reaching into the Communist bloc, forbade Soviet satellite states from accepting this help. Eastern European countries suffered from political crisis during this time, with a dictatorship in Hungary and Czechoslovakia, non-communist politicians in Romania being executed and exiled, and a rigged referendum in Poland.

Meanwhile, Britain and the U.S. merged the zones they managed in Germany and, in March 1948, went forward with a plan for a separate West German state. This put an end to their co-operation with the Soviets, as they subsequently refused to discuss what they were doing. The allies wanted to introduce a new currency into their western half, while the Soviets wanted to use their own. The term 'Cold War' was invented at this point by Bernard Baruch, an adviser to the U.S. president, as it described the 'chilly' relations which had appeared between the two sides.

In June, the Soviets blocked access to Berlin, in their zone of Germany, citing technical difficulties. Gas and electric supplies were cut off in August and, with the Germans facing a harsh winter, the Western nations initiated the Berlin Airlift (Operation Vittles). Supply planes with fuel, food and medicine flew 2.3 million tonnes over 277,804 missions, to assist the two million inhabitants of West Berlin. They used three narrow air-corridors into the city from East Germany, which had been negotiated before the blockade took effect, entering by the northern and southern and leaving by the middle route, one taking off and landing every 30 seconds. Facing a no-win situation, by January 1949, the Soviets were prepared to negotiate.

During this period new states, constitutions and organisations formed on both sides, such as the People's Republic of Albania and Yugoslavia. Chinese factions fighting the civil war discussed peace, and war trials began in Japan. The state of Israel was created with help from the UN and declared independence in the Middle East, but shortly after was attacked by Arab forces, starting the Arab-Israeli Civil War, 1947–9. After an Israeli victory, Palestine was divided between Arabs and Jews under a Jewish occupation. Italy became a Republic, and women were allowed to vote there for the first time. The World Bank, Interpol and Bilderberg Group (an annual conference to foster dialogue between Europe and North America) were founded, along with the Central Intelligence Agency (CIA) in the U.S. However, the Group Areas Act in South Africa led to the repressive Apartheid laws, which created separate areas for white Europeans and coloured South Africans (1948–91).

When the Soviets developed their own nuclear bomb, in 1949, the West formed the North Atlantic Treaty Organisation (NATO). Eventually, 30 nations joined, including the U.S., its allies and their colonies. Already under the political and military hegemony of the Soviets, the Communist bloc developed their own post-war economic recovery strategy, COMECON (Council for Mutual Economic Assistance, 1949–91).

Joseph McCarthy (1908–1957) became the most visible public face of U.S. politics in 1950, when tensions fuelled fears of widespread Communist infiltration and subversion. He alleged that numerous Soviet spies and sympathisers were inside the government, universities, film industry, media and other institutions. During the 'Red Scare', which this caused, various prominent figures were accused of being communists or having communist connections, and 'McCarthyism' became a famous term for the persecution of individuals based on an alleged lack of patriotism or other personal traits.

As the two sides polarised politically, they created fundamentally different societies, each of which had its own type of freedom: the capitalists were free to make money, set up political parties, publish literature and write music which criticised the state, but they also lacked political unity, care for the poor, the willingness to involve each citizen and a common cause. In contrast, the Communist states were more united and organised, seeking to improve the lives of each citizen, and established a system which was (at least perceived to be) free from aggressive imperialism, corruption, and unnecessary internal competition. However, everything had to be regulated by the Communist Party. This required a very high level of government control and censorship of the press, plus private communications such as telephone calls and written letters. They were also less financially successful, and citizens themselves were under continual observation from covert government officials, often working in shops and other businesses. Millions of people were subsequently sent to prison camps for trivial offences against the state, where they were forced into 're-education' through hard manual labour. Shops had long queues for even basic foods, communication with the outside world was banned, and the system became the target of bribery and personal ambition, for better jobs, food and housing.

The Cold War 1953–62

As the situation developed, the second phase emerged as the most potentially explosive conflict of all time. Europe was heavily locked down by the Iron Curtain divide. However, trouble then flared up in Southeast Asia. As the U.S. had occupied South Korea since the end of WWII, it had established a provisional government there. The Soviets had done the same in the north, and set up a Communist regime. However, both governments wanted to be the sole legitimate government of Korea and, in June 1950, the North invaded the South.

Led by Kim Il-sung, it was supported by the Soviet Union and China, which had been led by Chairman Mao since the struggle between the Republic of China and its Communist Party (1927–1949) had ended with Communist victory.

The U.N. Security Council subsequently authorised the formation of a United Nations Command to defend South Korea, and 21 countries contributed, with the U.S. providing 90% of the military personnel. However, the combined South Korean Army of Syngman Rhee and the U.S. were nearly defeated in the first two months, before retreating behind the Pusan Perimeter. In September 1950, an amphibious U.N. counter-offensive was launched at Incheon to cut off the North Korean army in South Korea. A month later UN forces invaded North Korea and pushed up to the Yalu River on the border with China. However, in October, Chinese forces crossed the river and entered the war. Facing the problem of WWIII blowing up in their face, the U.N. forces fell back below the 38th Parallel by late December. During the course of the war, Seoul changed hands four times and North Korea was heavily bombed by the U.S. from the air (operation 'Rolling Thunder'). Jet fighters also fought each other for the first time, as Soviet pilots covertly flew missions on the Communist side.

It was also one of the most deadly conflicts of the post-WWII era, killing around 3 million. Nearly all of Korea's major cities were destroyed and thousands of massacres occurred on both sides. When the war ended in stalemate, in July 1953, the Korean Armistice Agreement was signed, creating the Korean Demilitarised Zone (DMZ) between the two countries. No peace treaty was ever signed, and the two sides remain technically at war.

In January that year, Dwight D. Eisenhower was sworn in as President of the U.S. and Stalin died in March, succeeded by Nikita Khrushchev. During this time, the UK and France obtained nuclear weapons. From 1952 the superpowers upgraded to the Hydrogen bomb, causing even more fears of nuclear conflict. The OEEC changed its name to Organisation for Economic Co-operation and Development (OECD) in 1961, becoming a forum for countries 'committed to democracy and the market economy', to compare policy experiences and seek answers to common problems. Through Cold War changes to the government system in the West, many issues were discussed which enabled it to move away from the problem which had caused Communism, increasing workers rights and representation. However, when West Germany joined NATO, the Soviets signed the Warsaw Pact to strengthen relations between Moscow and its western satellite states.

The growing divide in prosperity between the Soviet bloc and Western Europe also became an increasing problem for the Soviets during this time, owing to millions of workers defecting to the West via East Berlin, and the Soviets built the Berlin Wall in August 1961, to prevent East Germans from escaping. Agriculture was collectivised in East Germany, and there was a workers rebellion which caused the Soviet Union to order troops into East Berlin. There were also currency reforms which caused riots in Czechoslovakia, and coal mining areas of Poland. The Hungarian Uprising (1956) fought the Soviet army to a standstill, but was defeated after a second invasion killed thousands, and sent hundreds of thousands into exile.

All around the world, the European colonial empires lost their power, as Algeria fought for independence from France (1954–62), Libya (1951), Sudan, Morocco and Tunisia (1956), Ghana (1957) and the Belgian Congo won independence from Belgium. The Suez Crisis (1956) showed the extent to which the status of the European powers had been replaced by the superpowers, as Gamal Abdel Nasser overthrew the Egyptian monarchy, then joined the Non-Aligned Movement and nationalised the Suez Canal. It was previously a vital part of the British Empire's route to India and France, the U.K. and Israel invaded, but were forced to withdraw when the U.S. and Soviets objected. From then on it was generally regarded that Britain could not operate without U.S. consent, as it appeared they could not be allowed to interfere in the delicate balance between the superpowers. After Queen Elizabeth II ascended the throne in 1953, Britain embarked upon a new direction towards modernisation, combined with a large scale programme of decolonisation for Africa, Asia, Oceania and the Americas, which took place over the next few decades.

The 1950s also saw the 'Khrushchev Thaw', during which censorship and other extreme political measures in the Soviet Union were relaxed, and millions of political prisoners were released from the Gulag labor camps. Khrushchev replaced the hardline Stalinists in the Kremlin with more progressive thinkers. He personally met with Eisenhower, healed rifts with other nations and reformed laws governing international trade, education, the media (including the emerging national TV), cultural contact with foreigners, festivals, literature, movies, art, music, dance and clothing fashions. In Europe, social progress further developed, as the European Economic Community (EEC), predecessor of the European Union (EU), held its first assembly in Strasbourg, France, and the London Agreement cancelled 50% of Germany's war debts.

However, war broke out again, this time in Vietnam. In the French-Vietnam war (1946–54) the Communist uprising of the Việt Minh (led by Hồ Chí Minh) and the People's Army of Vietnam (led by Võ Nguyên Giáp) had fought the French, supported by Bảo Đại's Vietnamese National Army. This happened because the French Vichy government (under the Germans in WWII) had been forced to co-operate with Japan by allowing them better access to invade China but, in March 1945, the Japanese assumed complete control and destroyed the French colonial administration.

Vietnam, Cambodia and Laos were made independent states, within the Japanese sphere of economic interest, while the United States had supported the Viet Minh resistance fighters against the Japanese, who took control of the countryside. But, when Japan surrendered to the Allies in August, a state of chaos emerged as the French suddenly resumed control, combined with natural disasters to cause a famine in which up to a million died (1944–45), leading to an uprising against the French.

Most of the fighting took place in Tonkin in northern Vietnam, although the conflict then extended throughout Indochina into Laos and Cambodia. In February 1954, Eisenhower had authorised $385 million on top of the $400 million already allocated to military aid in Vietnam, but did not send troops to support the French. In the final battle the French attempted to draw the Vietnamese army out into the open and destroy them with superior firepower. But, after attempting to cut off enemy supply lines at Điện Biên Phủ, deep in the hills of northwest Vietnam, while resupplying the French position by air, the Viet Minh carefully positioned heavy artillery and anti-aircraft guns in a way which allowed them to pin the French down. In March, an artillery bombardment was followed by the French being overrun in May and, after a two-month siege, most of the French troops surrendered. The French government in Paris resigned, and the new Prime Minister withdrew all forces. At the International Geneva Conference, in July, the new Socialist French government gave the Việt Minh control of North Vietnam above the 17th parallel, while the South continued under Bảo Đại.

This was disapproved of by both the State of Vietnam and the United States and, a year later, Bảo Đại was deposed by his prime minister, Ngô Đình Diệm, creating the Republic of Vietnam. After the French withdrawal, the US had assumed financial and military support for the South Vietnamese, while the Việt Cộng, also known as the National Liberation Front of South Vietnam, continued fighting a guerrilla war in the south, on behalf of the North Vietnamese. North Vietnam had also invaded Laos in the mid-1950s to support the insurgency by establishing the Ho Chi Minh Trail to supply and reinforce the Việt Cộng in the field. U.S. involvement grew under President John F. Kennedy, from just under a thousand military advisors in 1959 to 23,000 by 1964. By this time, the North Vietnamese had sent 40,000 soldiers to fight in the south, while China was sending hundreds of PLA servicemen to the north to serve in air-defence and support roles.

After the Gulf of Tonkin incident, an encounter between the U.S. Navy and North Vietnamese fast attack craft, the U.S. believed they were justified in deploying their own troops, increasing their presence to 184,000. From then on, the U.S engaged in conventional warfare and used heavy bombing missions, Napalm and Agent Orange to defoliate forest areas, and conducted search and destroy operations against the Việt Cộng and their alleged collaborators. North Vietnam used booby traps and stealth tactics to contain Western forces in jungle areas. The war lasted 19 years, with direct U.S. involvement ending in 1973, and included the Laotian Civil War and the Cambodian Civil War, finally ending with all three countries becoming Communist in 1975.

Also under the Kennedy administration (1961–3), the most serious incident of the Cold War occurred, as the world came to the brink of thermonuclear war during the Cuban Missile Crisis. While the U.S. had increased their number of nuclear warheads from 1,000 in 1953 to 18,000 by early 1961, despite having overwhelming superiority, another one was produced each day. In 1955 they made the B-52 Stratofortress, the first jet bomber specifically designed to carry nuclear weapons. By 1962, the U.S. had over eight times as many bombs and missiles as the USSR: 27,297 to 3,332. They could also launch from nuclear powered submarines, which were undetectable to normal radar, and could appear anywhere in the world.

In 1961, the U.S. deployed 15 Jupiter IRBMs (intermediate-range ballistic missiles) at İzmir, Turkey. With a 1,500-mile (2,410 km) range, Moscow was only 16 minutes away. In response, the Soviet Union agreed with Fidel Castro, who had been president of Cuba since his 1959 revolution (and felt threatened by the recent U.S. Bay of Pigs invasion), to place nuclear missiles on the island only a few hundred miles from Washington. On October 14, 1962, an American spy plane discovered nuclear missile sites under construction in Cuba.

President Kennedy immediately called a series of meetings with senior officials and ordered a naval blockade around Cuba. Tensions increased and, as the Soviets brought their missile ships forward, people watched on televisions around the world as Kennedy ordered U.S. military forces to Defence Condition 2, warning that if the Soviets proceeded toward the blockade they would open fire. This is the closest the world has ever been to WWII. However, back-channels of communication were established between Washington and Moscow and they successfully negotiated the Soviet fleet turning around and sailing home. In October, Khrushchev announced the Soviet Union would withdraw all missiles from Cuba and, shortly after, the U.S. withdrew their nuclear missiles from Turkey in secret. Hence, the apparent major U.S. victory led to the downfall of President Khrushchev.

The Cold War 1962–79

Following this, the idea of a direct confrontation between the superpowers became untenable, due to its obvious implications, and the Cold War began to diffuse itself throughout developing countries on both sides. Both superpowers sought to spread their own methods into other nations, and ultimately to protect their own spheres of influence, but both sides also had their own internal problems to address. While the West was beset by competition between free-market Capitalist nations, Communist unity was shattered by a fall-out between China and Russia, which emerged as China obtained nuclear weapons and both wanted to be the leading Communist bloc power. A new type of conservatism appeared, as both sides had problems admitting their shortcomings, yet neither was capable of backing down, given the active threat the other posed. Additionally, this provoked the rise of radicalism, in order to create progress which could not otherwise be achieved.

Shortly after, President Kennedy was assassinated by Lee Harvey Oswald, and it was discovered that he had been assisted by Soviet agents in Mexico. He was succeeded by Lyndon Johnson, who immediately pushed through a large amount of social reforms against racial discrimination, and sought to eliminate the Ku Klux Klan using the Federal Bureau of Investigation (FBI). Leonid Brezhnev (1964–1982) succeeded Khrushchev in Moscow, leading to a new period in East-West relations. Brezhnev's conservative approach created political stability and a peaceful foreign policy, but allowed corruption and social stagnation, inefficiency, and a growing technology gap with the West. His regime also faced challenges to its authority, and had to approve the 1968 invasion of Czechoslovakia, and the Soviet–Afghan War which continued after his death. While accepting the no-win nuclear situation with the U.S., he achieved nuclear parity with the United States and maintained Soviet hegemony over Eastern Europe.

However, both sides then became heavily involved in a competition to influence world politics in order to advance their own agendas, leading to proxy wars, the funding of insurgencies, and creation of puppet governments. While the U.S. backed governments and political parties which supported Capitalism in return, the Soviet Union and People's Republic of China backed anti-colonial national liberation movements who wanted social change and reform, hoping that the creation of Socialist allies would deny economic and political resources to the West. It had mixed results, as both sides sought to overthrow each other, with the general trend emerging whereby countries which were in the closest proximity to the U.S. and Soviet Union tended to come under the most influence.

For example, the Soviets provided aid to the Arabs against Israel in the Six-Day War (June 1967), and the U.S. to Israel. U.S.-backed South Africans fought Soviet-backed Cubans in the Angolan Civil War (1795–2002). In the Somalia-Ethiopia War the two superpowers even switched sides as the regimes changed on both sides. The fundamental divide in politics caused massive instability in what are now known as developing countries, but at this point were described as the Third World, in which countries were struggling to establish their own governments (the Communist states were referred to as the Second World, and the developed West as the First). In Africa, the Soviets backed various armed independence movements, most prominently led by Communist parties which were part of the Conference of Nationalist Organisations of the Portuguese Colonies (CONCP). Pro-U.S. groups appeared in Angola, Mozambique, and Portuguese Guinea. 32 African countries gained independence between 1960 and 1968, marking the end of the European empires that once dominated them. However, a new type of problem began to appear in the developing world, mostly in the Southern Hemisphere, as governments were becoming increasingly resistant to their own internal opposition, meaning that terrorism became increasingly regarded as a method by which certain groups could receive public attention when they could not achieve their ends through political processes.

The result was often a military dictatorship on one side or the other, as the factions within nations themselves polarised. The nature of many opposition parties became highly radicalised towards governments with opposing values, and subversive guerilla warfare became commonplace. In the 1960s, military coups included ones against the democratically elected Brazilian government, South Korea, South Viet Nam, Greece, Peru, Iraq and Libya. However, it tended to work according to a particular pattern, as right-wing revolutions attacked Socialist governments, while left-wing groups tended to target dissatisfaction against colonial powers. The Naxalite movement in India, for example, began in 1967 with a tribal uprising against local landlords in the village of Naxalbari,

West Bengal, and was led by the Communist Party of India. It spread across tribal areas of Eastern India until counter-insurgency operations by the government caused it to fragment, but is still active in many districts. India acquired nuclear weapons in 1974.

Soviet states saw an opening of doors to foreign cultures and the liberalisation of consumer markets, allowing more types of goods to appear. However, they often lacked decorative qualities and were of poor quality, using advertising to increase the desirability of sub-standard products. China reacted to this with the Cultural Revolution (1966–1976), a period of widespread social and political upheaval initiated by Mao Zedong, who alleged that liberal bourgeois elements of society were infiltrating the party and seeking to restore Capitalism. It marked Mao's return to the central position of power in China following the Great Leap Forward (1958–1962, a period of mandatory collectivisation of agriculture, similar to Stalin's five-year plans). During this time a famine killed between 18 and 45 million. He insisted that revisionists sought to redefine the way events had occurred and they should be removed through a renewed class struggle. China's youth, as well as urban workers, responded by forming the Red Guards around the country and they took power from local governments and CPC branches, eventually establishing Revolutionary Committees in 1967.

The 1960s saw a massive redefinition of normality, as the reality of the situation changed. This period of the Cold War is known as the 'détente' period, a term which originated from diplomatic relations between France and Germany in 1912, a time when the easing of political tensions had occurred, but still no real solution had been found. The need existed for leaderships on both sides to guide progress away from direct confrontations and improve living conditions at the same time. The U.S. Civil Rights Movement, led by Martin Luther King and Malcolm X, established equal rights to employment, housing and education, as did a number of other movements across Europe. Traditional Christian values were relaxed as people began to explore ideas from other cultures.

By the 1970s many Western workers could afford a radio, television, refrigerator, and motor vehicles. Television programmes became more diverse as dramas, comedies and documentaries provided insights into everyday life. One major feature of postmodernity is that it became the period when people began to discuss themselves, and many started to explore alternative beliefs, lifestyles and, in cities in the West, practicing Eastern religions became more fashionable. Music festivals became popular, and 'pop music' brought a sense of openness in terms of common values. Bands like the Beatles sang about the moods and emotions of daily life; more serious social commentaries came from songwriters like Bob Dylan; The Who spoke to the 1960s young generation; and poetic social statements by bands like The Doors sought to give people an alternative to the type of socio-religious experience which they had previously only found in the Church. In literature, Betty Friedan published 'The Feminine Mystique' (1963), starting second-wave feminism.

Along with these more visible signs of change, political activism also spread into Western Europe and the U.S., as organisations such as Situationist International helped create avant-garde artists, intellectuals, and political theorists who criticised governments, arguing that while circumstances had changed since the time of Marx, the problem with outright Capitalism was that it stripped workers of their human dignity and subjected them to a type of existence which consumer goods could not possibly compensate for. Massive Socialist and Communist movements in most European countries (especially France and Italy) became popular with university students and, in May 1968, the student revolt in Paris worked together with a Trade Union to generate a strike of ten million.

In 1969 Richard Nixon became U.S. president and initiated better relations with China after a visit in 1972. China was becoming increasingly dissatisfied at constantly being seen as the second most important Communist country and, in the 1960s, an open split had developed with the Soviets which led to a series of minor skirmishes along the border. U.S. Foreign Policy then changed to the Nixon Doctrine, a willingness to participate in the development and defence of allied nations, but leaving the basic responsibility for the future of those nations to themselves. Nixon also signed the SALT I (Strategic Arms Limitation Talks) treaty with Brezhnev before resigning over the 1974 Watergate Scandal (in which five Republicans were caught breaking into the Democratic Party headquarters). He was replaced by Vice President Gerald Ford, who signed the Helsinki Accords in 1975, and also pardoned Nixon.

Meanwhile, the Central American crisis had begun. By the late 1970s, major civil wars and Communist Revolutions erupted, and the U.S. feared that these would cause the Americas to become bisected between North and South by pro-Soviet Communist governments. The cause of this was seen to be Western nations having exploited the need of developing nations for investment. In both Central and South America large multinational corporations had been granted massive influence in the region, which put formerly self-sufficient farmers and lower down workers into poverty. As Communist-backed Socialist parties challenged this, it led to an increasing need for U.S. hegemony over the governments of Central and South America themselves, rolling back regimes who became hostile towards them.

For example, the CIA poured substantial funds into Chile to help support the government against a Marxist presidential candidate, Salvador Allende. When he came to power through free elections, they gave more money to opposition forces which helped to destabilise his new government and, in 1973, the U.S.-backed military junta of General Augusto Pinochet was established. He persecuted leftists, executing between 1,200 and 3,200. As many as 80,000 were incarcerated and tens of thousands tortured. Thousands of people also mysteriously went missing. The C.I.A. also faked a pornographic film of President Sukarno who ruled Indonesia (1959–1966), who had been deemed pro-Communist, bribed journalists and editors, and planted paid operatives within the media to portray the U.S. in a favourable light. After this was banned they relied on volunteers. They infiltrated and spied on home affairs, including student groups, women's rights movements and the Black Panthers, looking for potential foreign influences. The worst accusations were made over Operation Pheonix, which ran during the Vietnam War (1965–72), as it involved the incarceration and interrogation of civilians who knew of Việt Cộng activities. Amongst accusations of torture, it was subject to 1971 Congressional hearings and replaced by program F-6.

Despite the Cold War settling down into a status quo during the détente period, it was argued that Nicaragua was the first 'domino' to fall in Latin America, and the U.S. increased arms sales to the surrounding 'friendlies': Honduras, El Salvador, and Guatemala, who were dealing with their own Communist-backed insurgencies. The same thing happened on the Soviet side, as Western backed insurgencies appeared. In 1979, the Soviet Union invaded Afghanistan, after a coalition of several Islamic tribes known as the Mujahideen (literally translated: Jihadists) were aided by the Pakistani, U.S., Chinese and Saudi governments, leading to a ten year war which was strongly condemned by the U.N. and killed one million.

Industrialised countries, except Japan (which overtook West Germany as the second largest economy), experienced a recession due to an oil crisis caused by oil embargoes by the Organisation of Arab Petroleum Exporting Countries (OPEC). The crisis saw the first instance of stagflation, a combination of stagnation and inflation, meaning that governments attempts to stimulate the economy only made it worse. Declining heavy industry, combined with rising computerised technology and growth of Asian manufacturing led to a redefining of Western economic theory, from the simpler Keynesian free-market theory to the neoliberal, which promoted the transfer of all possible resources to the private sector, ending the nationalisation of industries and minimal government spending as a method of increasing growth in markets.

Jimmy Carter was elected U.S. President (1977–81). Having earlier opposed racial segregation and supported the Civil Rights movement, he continued the détente foreign policies of the U.S. and signed the SALT II treaty in 1979 with Brezhnev. However, both U.S. and Soviet intelligence agencies continued to provide training, finance and arms to insurgent groups, governments and their armies, each seeking to install friendly governments. While coups and civil wars continued, the problem of terrorism developed in Europe and the U.S. European organisations such as the Red Brigades and Baader-Meinhof Gang were responsible for bombings, kidnaps and murders. Britain suffered attacks from the Irish Republican Army (IRA), while Loyalist and Republican paramilitary groups clashed in Northern Ireland. Radical U.S. groups appeared, such as the Weather Underground (originally The Weathermen) who called for the end of U.S. imperialism and launched a bombing campaign aimed at government buildings and banks. The Symbionese Liberation Army (SLA), whose logo was a hydra, called for a unity of all left-wing causes and killed a school superintendent for threatening to issue ID cards. In 1970 Palestinian terrorists hijacked four airliners and took over 300 people on board hostage (the hostages were released, but the planes were then blown up). Additionally, the Munich massacre took place at the 1972 Summer Olympics in Germany, where the Palestinian group Black September kidnapped and murdered eleven Israeli athletes.

The Cold War 1979–85

The election of Ronald Reagan as U.S. President led to the adoption of a more aggressive right-wing U.S. foreign policy, determined to rollback the influence of Moscow over the states of the U.S.S.R. He initiated a considerable buildup of U.S. military power to challenge the Soviet Union and accelerated the War on Drugs, which had become relatively popular with celebrities and fuelled various forms of counter-culture such as the Hippy and Beatnik movements. Hence, the U.S. was drawn into significant direct and indirect conflicts in Central and South America, both acting to oppose the spread of Communism and the illegal drug trade. This involved supporting Colombia's attempts to destroy its large scale cocaine-trafficking operations and providing support for the right-wing military government in the Salvadoran Civil War (1980–92), in which 70,000 people died. However, this became controversial due to the El Mozote massacre (1981), when U.S.-trained paramilitaries killed 1000 civilians a part of an anti-guerrilla campaign against Marxist-Leninist rebels. The U.S. also invaded Grenada in 1983, triggering a military coup which overthrew the revolutionary government, but this also became controversial due to accusations of American imperialism.

In the Soviet Union, Brezhnev, whose health had been deteriorating since 1975, died in late 1982 and was succeeded by two short-term leaders who both only lasted around a year. The first of these was Yuri Andropov (1982–3), who had served as ambassador to Hungary (1954–7) and was involved in suppressing the 1956 uprising, then became chairman of the KGB (1967) and cracked down on dissent through mass arrests. He was also responsible for the internment of numerous 'social undesirables' into psychiatric institutions. He then formed a ruling alliance with the Soviet Foreign Minister, Andrei Gromyko, and Defence Minister, Dmitry Ustinov, when Brezhnev's health deteriorated. As president, he sought to end corruption and inefficiency by investigating officials for long term violations of party policy. Faced with an economic crisis, he promoted a set of new reformers, including Yegor Ligachyov, Nikolai Ryzhkov and Mikhail Gorbachev. However, he then suffered from kidney failure and was succeeded by Konstantin Chernenko, who had been head of Soviet Propaganda in 1948. He became head of the General Department of the Central Committee when Brezhnev became First Secretary in 1964, but often could not fulfil his duties due to ill-health and Nikolai Ryzhkov recalls in his memoirs how Gorbachev would sit in his office 'like a little orphan' every Thursday morning, waiting to see if Chernenko would call in sick. Subsequently, Gorbachev frequently stood in for his boss at meetings when he was absent, thus securing his path to power. Chernenko appears to have returned to the conservative politics of the Brezhnev era, but also supported a greater role for the Labour Unions, reforms to education and propaganda, and dismissed Nikolai Ogarkov for putting military expenditure above the economy.

He also negotiated a trade deal with China and met with British Labour Party leader, Neil Kinnock, but did little work on Cold War relations with the West. When the U.S. boycotted the 1980 Summer Olympics over the invasion of Afghanistan, he responded by failing to attend the 1984 Olympics, along with 14 Communist bloc states who held their own 'Friendship Games'. Reagan found a firm ally in the British Prime Minister, Margret Thatcher, as Britain had suffered from strikes staged by the Labour Unions, which had caused widespread power cuts and school closures lasting several days, and train timetables disrupted. With her election in 1979, the Unions' power was curtailed as neoliberal politics and economics were brought into force in the UK.

The 1980s saw the rise of computerised technology, and a shift away from manufacturing industries in the West, with the rise of service industries such as banking, insurance and the dot.com bubble. Computers revolutionised the workplace, giving people free personal communication and increased social mobility. However, the computerisation of motor vehicle production and heavy industry caused a new type of structural unemployment.

During this time developing countries across the world suffered from multiple debt crises, and many applied to the International Monetary Fund (IMF) and World Bank for assistance. Ethiopia suffered from famine in the mid-1980s, resulting in a dependency on foreign aid and international events helped them to raise money, such as the Live Aid concert in 1985. However, the Asian economy improved as multiple multinational manufacturing corporations relocated to Thailand, South Korea, Taiwan, and China.

The Cold War 1985–91

As the Internet became a global system, Tim Berners Lee played a major part in its development, giving speeches promoting its use and extensive benefits. Both electronic and genetic technology made major advances, as Microsoft introduced the Windows operating system in November, 1985, which dominated the world's personal computer industry until 2014 when Android smartphones took over. It superseded the Apple Mac Operating System, which had been introduced in 1984. Television viewing became commonplace in developing countries, with the number of TV sets in China and India increasing between 10 and 15 times. The first genetic modification of 10 adult human beings took place in May 1989, and the first 'designer babies' were created in a laboratory in late 1989. Gestational surrogacy was first performed in 1985 with the first birth in 1986, making it possible for a woman to become a biological mother without pregnancy.

U.S.–Soviet relations finally improved as Mikhail Gorbachev assumed control of the Soviet Union in 1985. Reagan and Gorbachev began the first of four 'summit' meetings that year, to discuss the issues they faced as leaders. During these they signed the Intermediate Nuclear Forces (INF) Treaty (1987), which eliminated an entire class of nuclear weapons and, by 1991, 2,700 missiles had been decommissioned. Initially, a 50% reduction of nuclear weapons for both sides had been proposed by Gorbachev, at the second meeting in Reykjavik, Iceland (1986). However, negotiations broke down due to disagreements over

Reagan's Starwars Defence Initiative (SDI), a proposed space-based platform to shoot down incoming missiles.

Under Gorbachev, relatively young reform-oriented technocrats, who had begun their careers under Khrushchev, consolidated power, thus generating the momentum to create better relations with the West and internal reforms. Perestroika was a new set of economic policies which allowed joint Capitalist ventures with the West, while Glasnost was a new type of political openness which allowed the freedom of the press to criticise government, and other forms of free speech. Realising they could no longer maintain their empire by military force, they also allowed the East European states to choose their own destiny in free elections. On June 12, 1987, Reagan challenged Gorbachev to go further, by dismantling the Berlin Wall, in a speech at the Brandenburg Gate next to the wall.

However, at the same time, Reagan also encouraged Saudi Arabia to increase the world's oil supply and dramatically increased U.S. spending on arms. Since oil was the Soviet's main source of export revenue, they could not keep up with this new arms race, and were placed in a weaker position at the negotiating table. In the 1980s the Soviet Union took on a significant amount of debt from the Western banking sector, and these factors eventually contributed to the fall of the Soviet Union.

To many people, it seemed Hardline Communism had run its course; when it all started with Marx it was mainly about the exploitation of the worker, but now people in the West had leisure time, went to the movies and drove motor cars, and it was the communist worker who was being left behind. Communism had made its point globally, and now large Socialist movements existed in the West which had established social security systems, Labour Unions, race and gender equality and anti-discrimination laws. The world was not the same place anymore and there seemed little point in pursuing a divided society. In fact, opening up the Soviet Union had even helped to normalise Socialist values in the West, reduced the fear of Communism, and made left wing thought more acceptable.

1989 brought the fall of a number of Communist governments, such as Hungary, the Tiananmen Square protests of 1989 in China, the Czechoslovak 'Velvet Revolution', Erich Honecker's East German regime, Poland's Soviet-backed government, and the Nicolae Ceaușescu regime in Romania. Destruction of the Berlin Wall also paved the way for the Reunification of Germany.

After the end of the 1989 Revolutions, Gorbachev and U.S. President George Bush Sr. met in Malta to discuss the withdrawal of the Soviet military from Eastern Europe, and the future course of events. They publicly announced that they would work together on German reunification, the resolution of Third World conflicts and the promotion of peace, which was described by Bush as a 'new world order'.

However, the introduction of economic reforms into Russia were poorly handled by the Communist Party, which was not well positioned to oversee them, and the political chaos was condemned by Communist hardliners. The economy was struggling with low fuel supplies and high inflation, and the Chernobyl disaster in Ukraine led some to believe that these reforms were just a Western takeover in disguise. By 1990, Estonia, Latvia, Lithuania, Armenia and Georgia had already declared independence from the Soviet Union. Fearing complete fragmentation, on 11 December 1990, the KGB Chairman, Vladimir Kryuchkov, made a call for order over public television in Moscow, while asking his staff to prepare a plan of measures which could be taken in case a state of emergency was declared. Later, Kryuchkov recruited a number of high ranking officials into the conspiracy, with the aim of creating such an emergency state.

In January 1991, there was an attempt to return Lithuania to the Soviet Union by force and, within a week, pro-Soviet forces attempted to overthrow the Latvian authorities. At the same time, there were continuing armed ethnic conflicts in Nagorno Karabakh and South Ossetia, but Russia declaring its sovereignty, on 12 June 1990, had limited its ability to apply Soviet laws in other Russian territories. Following this, in March 1991, a referendum voted for a reform to the whole constitution, giving rise to the New Union Treaty which offered a less centralised federal system, but attempted to preserve the integrity of the Soviet Union. However, the conspirators then struck, as they feared it would lead to more states declaring independence, and they launched the August Coup.

On 23 July 1991, a number of party functionaries had published in the hardline newspaper, Sovetskaya Rossiya, 'A Word to the People', calling for decisive action to prevent a political disaster. They saw the new constitution leading to the break up of the Soviet Union, and wanted to solve the problem through a state of emergency, which they then created themselves. During this time Gorbachev, Russian President Boris Yeltsin and Kazakh President Nursultan Nazarbayev were discussing the possibility of replacing the hardliners with people who were willing to accept liberal reforms. However, they then found out they were to be targeted, as KGB head Kryuchkov had put Gorbachev under surveillance several months earlier. On 4 August, Gorbachev went on holiday to Foros, Crimea, planning to return to Moscow in time to sign the New Union Treaty on 20 August, but Baklanov, Boldin, Shenin, and Deputy Defence Minister General Valentin Varennikov flew down to meet him, demanding Gorbachev either declare a state of emergency or resign, and put Yanayev in charge. When Gorbachev refused, they detained him at his villa, cut its communication lines and placed KGB guards at the gates.

Additionally, they ordered 250,000 pairs of handcuffs and 300,000 arrest forms, in anticipation of a popular uprising in Moscow. Kryuchkov doubled the pay of all KGB personnel, called them back from holiday and placed them on alert, while the Lefortovo Prison was emptied in anticipation of civil unrest. When they flew back to Moscow, Yanayev, Pavlov and Baklanov signed the 'Declaration of the Soviet Leadership', and announced a 'State Committee on the State of Emergency' (GKChP) as Gorbachev was allegedly suffering from an illness and pronounced unable to fulfil his duty. To this group they added Vasily Starodubtsev, Chairman of the Peasant Union and Alexander Tizyakov, President of the Association of State Enterprises and Objects of Industry, Transport and Communications. These became known as the 'Gang of Eight'.

The GKChP also banned all newspapers in Moscow except for nine Party-controlled ones, and the only independent political radio station, Ekho Moskvy, was taken off-air. On 19th August (GKChP) documents were subsequently broadcast over the state radio and television, and armoured units of the Tamanskaya Division and the Kantemirovskaya tank division were called into Moscow, along with paratroopers. Four Russian SFSR People's Deputies were detained at an army base near Moscow. However, when the Russian President, Boris Yeltsin, arrived at Russia's parliament building, the White House, he issued a declaration that the coup was unconstitutional, along with Prime Minister Ivan Silayev and Supreme Soviet Chairman Ruslan Khasbulatov. The military was urged not to take part, and they called for a general strike which would allow Gorbachev to speak to the people. This declaration was distributed around Moscow in the form of pamphlets. By the afternoon, Moscow citizens began to gather around the White House and erected barricades around it. Major Evdokimov, chief of staff of a tank battalion of the Tamanskaya Division guarding the White House, declared his loyalty to the Russian leadership and Yeltsin climbed on one of the tanks to address the crowd, which was then broadcast all over the world.

On 20 August Yanayev declared a curfew through his military General Kalinin, from 23:00 to 05:00, and an attack was prepared on the White House. Planned by KGB General Ageyev and Army General Vladislav Achalov, it was supported by GKChP members and codenamed 'Operation Grom' (Thunder). Scouting began as they infiltrated crowds gathering around the White House, and group commanders reported back that it would cause civilian casualties and should be cancelled. However, it was announced that the attack would begin at 14:00 as planned. Around 13:00 on 21 August trolleybuses and street cleaning machines barricaded a tunnel against the Taman Guards' armoured personnel carriers approaching the White House and three people were killed trying to stop them. Dmitry Komar, while trying to cover the moving vehicles' observation slit, Vladimir Usov coming to his aid, and Ilya Krichevsky as the crowd set fire to one of the troop carriers and its crew escaped. After that, everything stopped. The army did not move on the White House and was ordered to pull out of Moscow.

The GKChP subsequently met in the Defence Ministry and decided to send a delegation to the Crimea to talk with Gorbachev, who then refused to speak to them. With his communications lines reconnected, Gorbachev declared the GKChP invalid and sacked all its members, and the USSR General Prosecutors Office immediately began an investigation. On 22 August Gorbachev and the GKChP members flew back to Moscow, where Kryuchkov, Yazov and Tizyakov were arrested. Pavlov, Vasily Starodubtsev, Baklanov, Boldin and Shenin were all caught within the next 48 hours. Pugo committed suicide the next day.

Gorbachev awarded the title 'Hero of the Soviet Union' to the three men who died in the coup, while Russian President Boris Yeltsin re-appointed the heads of regional administrations, as several of them had supported the GKChP. Gorbachev resigned as CPSU General Secretary on 24 August and Vladimir Ivashko replaced him until the 29th, when the Supreme Soviet terminated all Party activities. Yeltsin declared the transfer of the Soviet archives to the state archive authorities, and nationalised all CPSU holdings in Russia, including party headquarters, educational institutions and other assets.

On 25 August Belarus declared independence and, by 5 September, the Congress of People's Deputies had declared a transitional period, whereby the Soviet of Republics was replaced by the Soviet of Nationalities. Over the next few months Moldova, Azerbaijan, Kyrgyzstan, Tajikistan and Armenia declared independence and, by November, the only Soviet Republics that had not done so were Russia, Kazakhstan and Uzbekistan.

On 8 December the leaders of Russia, Ukraine and Belarus met with the prime ministers of the republics, in Minsk, and signed the Belavezha Accords, declaring that the Soviet Union ceased to exist 'as a subject of international law and geopolitical reality.' It rewrote the 1922 union treaty establishing the Soviet Union, and established the Commonwealth of Independent States (CIS).

Part 2: The Post Cold War Period

In the period following the breakdown of the Soviet Union, the world entered a new era, which some historians refer to as the period of U.S. Unipolar Hegemony, which replaced the bipolar phase of geo-politics. In 1990, political author Charles Krauthammer said it was a 'unipolar moment,' as 'the center of world power is the unchallenged superpower, the United States.'. The U.S. was in a strong position. Not only in terms of the military, politics and technology but also the strategic and cultural influence which it had built up throughout the Cold War. Capitalism spread, as many former Warsaw Pact countries moved from being single-party Communist states to having multi-party elections and private-sector economies.

Since then, attempts by both Russia and China to rebalance the situation in the other direction have backfired, and provoked reactions from the West which simply adapted to contain them. In other words, the world did not go back to the concept of the balance of power which had emerged during the Cold War. It moved on, but into a period of somewhat uncertainty. The 66th U.S. Secretary of State, Condoleezza Rice, said 'That we do not know how to think about what follows the U.S.–Soviet confrontation is clear from the continued references to the post-Cold War period.' She also stated that 'We knew better where we had been than where we were going'. As a result, the U.S. adopted both foreign and domestic policies which were designed to maintain its position in the world, while allowing it to adapt to changing circumstances.

Another term for this period is 'Pax Americana', similar to the time when the British Empire enforced hegemony upon its former territories in the 1800s. As such, the overall direction of politics in the 1990s leant towards rising material prosperity, at the expense of left-wing, Socialist government policies, resulting in economic growth, but also causing an increasing rich/poor divide. With the Technological Revolution in full swing, providing global communications, software for businesses and instantaneous online banking transactions, the speed of events accelerated and populations grew once more. The rise of computerised social networking also started a movement away from local groups and regional identities, towards private groups of special interests, hobbies, religion, sports and other activities.

Events in the Former Soviet Union

There is a large difference in the way former Communist bloc nations coped with the end of the Soviet Union. The Czech Republic, Estonia, Hungary, Latvia, Lithuania, Poland and Slovakia were integrated into the EU and experienced both political reconstruction and economic growth. However, in the short term, in Russia and its immediate neighbours, many people became poorer, there was a limited availability of products, crumbling streets and buildings, an overall decline in economic growth, and even a fall in life expectancy. In 1993, a severe political deadlock between Russian President Boris Yeltsin and the Supreme Soviet (Russia's parliament) led to Yeltsin ordering tanks to open fire on the Russian parliament building.

Additionally, this led to the sale of many advanced Cold War weapons systems, such as tanks, jet fighters and surface-to-air missile systems. This has further added to the problems of people in developing countries who found themselves with governments who were much more powerful militarily than their global position would suggest, meaning the rebels in those countries had to arm themselves to a higher level, and U.N. forces found they had problems intervening.

The First Chechen War (1994–1996) broke out between the Russian Federation and the Chechen Republic of Ichkeria, as Russian forces attempted to seize control of the mountainous Chechnya, but were held back by determined guerrilla warfare. This resulted in Boris Yeltsin's government declaring a ceasefire in 1996 and signing a peace treaty a year later. The Second Chechen War (1999–2009) was launched by the Russian Federation in 1999, in response to the invasion of Dagestan and the apartment bombings which occurred in Russia. Through this, Russian forces mostly recaptured the region of Chechnya, reversing the outcome of the previous war.

The Emerging Nations

The rise of other nuclear powers caused a restructuring of the U.N. and the relationship between nations. At the same time, various others have risen in importance by acquiring new roles, completing the shift to the new world order which was announced at the end of the Cold War. These became known as the 'emerging nations': China, India, South Africa, Nigeria, Malaysia, Indonesia, Canada, Australia, Japan and Brazil. All became major centres of economic power, while some provide military alliances, others add political and diplomatic stability to their regions. As the rest of the world followed along with this pattern in its own way, it caused a major cultural shift towards globalisation.

The Technological Revolution

Only about 20 million people (less than 0.5 percent of the world population at the time) were online in 1995, mostly in the US and other Western countries. Governments, the military and businesses were among the first users, before the home computer gained popularity. Hence, the 1990s featured a sharp rise in the globalisation of the world's industries due to an increase in their ability to communicate and co-ordinate their activities, plus online transactions made ordering and payments easier. Many banks began to view web-based services as a strategic advantage due to diminished transaction costs and marketing opportunities. By the year 2000, 80% of U.S. banks offered online banking.

Commercialisation of the Internet and the smartphone system followed, which made Internet access easier from any location, and replaced the general idea that progress was driven by political ideology. It is estimated that the entire written work of humanity up to 2003 contained around five exabytes of data. Since then, approximately that amount has been created every two days. With the ability of developed nations to develop computerised models of their strategic position and generate potential futures, statistical analysis has become of prime importance to influencing economic policies, winning political debates and elections. However, statistical methods also led to criticism of governments for being impersonal and unrepresentative of human values.

International Treaties and Trade Deals

During this time, increased international cooperation was seen as the key to progress in social terms, and several victories were won in terms of civil rights and laws controlling international governments. Greenpeace and Campaign for Nuclear Disarmament (CND) had been ongoing for many years, but this also led to the Organisation for the Prohibition of Chemical Weapons, the Universal Declaration of Human Rights, the Paris Climate Agreement, and the Convention on the Prevention and Punishment of the Crime of Genocide. Nelson Mandela was elected President of South Africa in 1994, becoming their first democratically elected President and ending apartheid. Israel and Palestine also signed the Oslo Accords (1993), which gave Palestine autonomy over the Gaza Strip and West Bank (but not official independence from Israel), and the Irish Republican Army agreed to a truce (1994).

Residual Instability

However, despite the situation moving forwards politically, new violence broke out in certain areas still finding it difficult to establish their own government. The First Congo War in Zaire (1996–7) resulted in the overthrow of their dictator, and the country was renamed 'Democratic Republic of the Congo'. The Second Congo War (1998–2003) became known as 'Africa's World War' and the 'Great War of Africa', involving nine nearby nations and around twenty other armed factions. It killed an estimated 3.8 million, mostly from starvation and disease. Millions more were displaced and sought asylum in neighbouring countries.

In the Rwandan genocide (April–July 1994), at least 500,000 of Rwanda's Tutsis and Hutu political moderates were killed by the Hutu government following the 'Hutu Power' ideology. Also the Kargil War (1999) occurred as Pakistan sent troops into Kashmir. A month later India retaliated, causing a Pakistani withdrawal to the Line of Control, and a military coup in October by Army Chief Pervez Musharraf. The Somali Civil War began in 1991 and, in Algeria, a long period of violence was caused by the cancellation of democratic elections. Large numbers of indigenous people in Mexico joined the Zapatista Army of National Liberation, and began a conflict with the government (1994), which continued through the 1990s. Also war between the Tajikistan government and the United Tajik Opposition (1992–1997) killed 50,000 to 100,000. The Colombian Armed Conflict which began in 1964 continued, as the FARC and ELN narcoterrorist groups took control of the countryside, while anti-terrorist paramilitaries grew in other places as businesspeople and politicians believed the government needed help. The Nepalese Civil War (1996–2006), between the government and the Maoist Party, killed more than 12,700. The Second Liberian Civil War (1999–2003) began with a rebel group, Liberians United for Reconciliation and Democracy (LURD), with support from the Government of Guinea, which took over northern Liberia through a coup. In early 2003, another rebel group, the Movement for Democracy in Liberia, emerged in the south, leaving the government with only a third of the country. The capital, Monrovia, was besieged by LURD, who bombarded the city, killing civilians and displacing thousands. The Algerian Civil War (1991–2002) ended with government victory, following the surrender of the Islamic Salvation Army and the defeat of the Armed Islamic Group, after more than 100,000 died. Additionally, the Civil war in Afghanistan (1996–2001) continued after the capture of Kabul by the Taliban, as the Afghan Northern Alliance then attempted to overthrow them. However, the Taliban continued to increase their territory and eliminated much of the opposition's leadership.

Terrorist attacks grew more frequent and deadly around the world, leading to them becoming a rising problem which represented a threat to all nations. These included the World Trade Centre bombing (1993), the bombing of federal offices in Oklahoma City by domestic terrorists (1995), bombing in Omagh, Northern Ireland, an unknown car-bomb at the AMIA Headquarters in Buenos Aires, Argentina (1994) and the IRA set off a car bomb in Manchester, England (1996), causing an estimated £700 million damage.

9/11 and The War On Terror

The issue of global terrorism came to a head on 9 September, 2001, as two large civilian passenger aircraft were hijacked and flown into the twin towers of the World Trade Centre in New York. Both buildings collapsed, killing thousands and provoking full scale war from the U.S. against nations deemed to be supporting, financing, or harbouring Islamic terrorist organisations. The attacks were caused by the Islamist jihadist group, al-Qaeda, which had emerged during the war against the Soviets in 1988, but was now taking the political stance that foreign powers, especially the U.S. superpower, were corrupting the Islamic values of the Middle East.

To understand how this situation arose, we must look at the history of the Middle East, especially that of its two main powers, Iran and Saudi Arabia. When the Ottoman Empire collapsed in Arabia after WWI the tribes in the region fought amongst themselves, before al-Saud (House of Saud) gradually took control and created Saudi Arabia (1932). Shortly after this they discovered they had vast oil supplies, and the money from this created roads and cities all over the country. This produced a totalitarian absolute monarchy, with the ultracon- servative Wahhabi religious movement (Sunni Islam) as its main faction.

Meanwhile, the Shi'a nation of Iran had a democratically elected government, led by Mohammad Mosaddegh, until it sought to audit the documents of the Anglo-Iranian Oil Company (a British corporation now part of British Petroleum), and limit the company's control over Iranian oil reserves. Britain and the U.S. feared a Communist takeover of the region and launched a coup which seized control of the government through the Iranian military. What they replaced the government with then became a Westernised secular society under the Shah monarchy of Mohammad Reza Pahlavi. However, it lacked the long-term legitimacy and power of the Saudis, terrorised its citizens with secret police, and this gave way to the 1979 Iranian Revolution of Ayatollah Khomeini. A populist, Shi'a Islamic, anti-Western cleric, he then proceeded to export the Islamic revolution to other Shi'a factions in the predominantly Sunni Middle East, something which deeply upset Saudi Arabian influence. A CIA report from 1980 says that it aimed to undermine the Sunni Western-backed governments in the Middle East by supporting rebel and insurgent groups, protests and demonstrations, and this led to Saudi Arabia securing its links with the West and other nations.

Ayatollah Khomeini had previous been expelled from Iraq, upon the discovery by Iraqi agents of a plot to take over the country and, after coming to power in Iran, he subsequently called upon the Iraqis to overthrow their government. As this threatened the position of the (Socialist) Iraqi Ba'ath Party, this led to the Iraq–Iran war (1980–88), during which Iraq attempted to exploit the chaos caused by the Iranian revolution. The war featured a number of proxy forces, with the People's Mujahedin of Iran siding with Iraq and the Iraqi Kurdish militias siding with Iran. The U.S., Britain, the Soviet Union, France, and most Arab countries supported Iraq, while Iran was largely isolated on an international level.

However, the war ended in a stalemate, leaving Iran in a position to continue its policy of supporting Shi'a Islamist revolutionaries across the Muslim world. Iraq was left with a strong military, having been supported heavily as a buffer state between Saudi Arabia and Iran. However, Iraq was financially bankrupt and subsequently accused Kuwait of flooding the oil market, preventing their economic rebuild, resulting in the 1990 invasion of Kuwait and the first Gulf War (1990–1), during which they were forcibly expelled by the U.S.

Border skirmishes between Iraq and Iran continued throughout the 1990s, as Iraq continued to host the Mujahedeen-e-Khalq, which launched attacks at Iran until the 2003 invasion by the U.S. Due to these ongoing wars, terrorist organisations on the revolutionary side had a rich supply of followers, and this is why the U.S. policy after 9/11 was to declare a general war against terrorism and invade various countries to stabilise their governments. This was criticised internationally, as al-Qaeda was effectively a jihadist movement within Islam, which had appeared in 1988 to fight the Soviet occupation of Afghanistan.

Shortly after the 9/11 attack U.S. President, George Bush Jnr., gave a speech outlining the fact that it would not be a single battle, but a long running series of campaigns which would eventually starve the global terror network of cash and resources, leaving them nowhere to hide. Hence, while it has been said that the subsequent war against Iraq and Afghanistan was just about the oil, it was really the attacks on civilians in various nations worldwide which caused the war on terrorism to appear in the form that it did.

This 2007 interview with [1]General Wesley Clarke, a former commander of U.S. forces in the Yugoslavian Wars, reveals how the U.S. saw the situation from a practical viewpoint,

'... I had been through the Pentagon right after 9/11. About ten days after 9/11, I went through the Pentagon and I saw Secretary Rumsfeld and Deputy Secretary Wolfowitz. I went downstairs just to say hello to some of the people on the Joint Staff who used to work for me, and one of the generals called me in. He said, "Sir, you've got to come in and talk to me a second." I said, "Well, you're too busy." He said, "No, no." He says, "We've made the decision we're going to war with Iraq." This was on or about the 20th of September. I said, "We're going to war with Iraq? Why?" He said, "I don't know." He said, "I guess they don't know what else to do." So I said, "Well, did they find some information connecting Saddam to al-Qaeda?" He said, "No, no." He says, "There's nothing new that way. They just made the decision to go to war with Iraq." He said, "I guess it's like we don't know what to do about terrorists, but we've got a good military and we can take down governments." And he said, "I guess if the only tool you have is a hammer, every problem has to look like a nail."

So I came back to see him a few weeks later, and by that time we were bombing in Afghanistan. I said, "Are we still going to war with Iraq?" And he said, "Oh, it's worse than that." He reached over on his desk. He picked up a piece of paper. And he said, "I just got this down from upstairs" — meaning the Secretary of Defense's office — "today." And he said, "This is a memo that describes how we're going to take out seven countries in five years, starting with Iraq, and then Syria, Lebanon, Libya, Somalia, Sudan and, finishing off, Iran." I said, "Is it classified?" He said, "Yes, sir." I said, "Well, don't show it to me." '

The plan was to neutralise those regimes who were responsible for causing the problem as a whole, and rollback their influence globally. He continues to say,

'Well, starting with Iraq, then Syria and Lebanon, then Libya, then Somalia and Sudan, and back to Iran. So when you look at Iran, you say, "Is it a replay?" It's not exactly a replay. But here's the truth: that Iran, from the beginning, has seen that the presence of the United States in Iraq was a threat — a blessing, because we took out Saddam Hussein and the Baathists. They couldn't handle them. We took care of it for them. But also a threat, because they knew that they were next on the hit list. And so, of course, they got engaged. They lost a million people during the war with Iraq, and they've got a long and unprotectable, unsecurable border. So it was in their vital interest to be deeply involved inside Iraq. They tolerated our attacks on the Baathists. They were happy we captured Saddam Hussein.

But they're building up their own network of influence, and to cement it, they occasionally give some military assistance and training and advice, either directly or indirectly, to both the insurgents and to the militias. And in that sense, it's not exactly parallel, because there has been, I believe, continuous Iranian engagement, some of it legitimate, some of it illegitimate. I mean, you can hardly fault Iran because they're offering to do eye operations for Iraqis who need medical attention. That's not an offense that you can go to war over, perhaps. But it is an effort to gain influence...'

The U.S., with the size of their economy and military, saw the problem more or less in practical terms. The Iranians, on the other hand, and other insurgent Shi'a groups, a tiny minority in a sea of Sunni Muslims, saw the situation differently. They would have to adopt revolutionary religious ideology to help them survive. As Islamic insurgencies created various war zones in the Middle East, their continued existence was al-Qaeda's main strength. The terrorist organisation continued to use fighters from these areas, and one of the main problems international governments had in terms of being able to prevent the 9/11 attack was due to the way the issue arose from within the fabric of global society itself. Even though they were watching the overt situation on the numerous battlefields, the covert movements of such organisations hid what was actually happening within their leaderships.

When Saddam Hussein's regime fell to the U.S. (2003), Iran claimed its agents had infiltrated and created numerous militias in Iraq, and built an intelligence system operating within the country. This became instrumental in terms of exercising Iranian influence inside Iraq during the Iraqi insurgency (2003–11), which was initially attributed to large numbers of old army factions being dissatisfied with the government the U.S. put in place. Iran had largely blamed Saudi Arabia for the Iran–Iraq war, and is also believed to be behind much of the Arab Spring, in which Shi'a minorities rose up against their Sunni governments across the region. Iran benefitted from the instability as it shifted the balance of power in the Middle East away from Saudi Arabia and high oil prices offset the sanctions put on its nuclear programme.

As such, several populations rose up against their autocratic dictators in a series of anti-government protests, uprisings, and armed rebellions which spread across much of the Arab world in the early 2010s. It began in Tunisia, in response to oppressive regimes which created and a low standard of living, and spread to Libya, Egypt, Yemen, Syria and Bahrain, where the rulers were deposed (Zine El Abidine Ben Ali, Muammar Gaddafi, Hosni Mubarak, and Ali Abdullah Saleh) and major uprisings occurred. Demonstrations took place in Morocco, Iraq, Algeria, Iranian Khuzestan, Lebanon, Jordan, Kuwait, Oman, Sudan, Djibouti, Mauritania, Palestine, Saudi Arabia, and the Moroccan-occupied Western Sahara.

The movement used digital technology such as social media to announce propaganda and events. Governments then responded by shutting down certain sites, or blocking Internet providers before a major rally. They also accused the perpetrators of various crimes, and thousands were imprisoned. As late as 2019, uprisings and protest movements in Algeria, Sudan, Iraq, Lebanon and Egypt have been seen as a continuation of the Arab Spring and, multiple conflicts lasted into 2020, such as the Syrian and Libyan Civil Wars.

The U.S. troops withdrew from the 2003 Iraq invasion in 2011, leaving security to the new army they rebuilt.

However, when the Syrian Civil War spilled over into Iraq, in 2013, it combined with the Iraqi insurgency to become a single conflict (often called the Arab Winter). During this time the Islamic State of Iraq and the Levant (ISIL) established itself in Syria in 2013. The U.S. subsequently returned as the head of a new coalition and the War in Iraq (2013–17), escalated into a full-scale war against ISIL, including the conquest of Ramadi, Fallujah, Mosul and Tikrit. Islamic State, a Salafi Jihadist militant group, can trace its origins back to the late Abu Musab al-Zarqawi, a Jordanian who, in 2004, pledged allegiance to Osama Bin Laden and formed al-Qaeda in Iraq (AQI) in response to the U.S. invasion. After Zarqawi's death in 2006 AQI created an umbrella organisation, Islamic State in Iraq (ISI), but was weakened by the creation of Sahwa (Awakening) councils by Sunni Arabs who were opposed to their methods. ISI was then led by Baghdadi, a former U.S. prisoner of war, who began rebuilding and, by 2013, it was launching dozens of attacks every month in Iraq.

It also joined the rebellion against President Bashar al-Assad in Syria, by setting up the al-Nusra Front. In April 2013, Baghdadi announced the merger of his forces in Iraq and Syria and the creation of Islamic State in Iraq and the Levant (ISIS). This move did not directly merge al-Nusra and al-Qaeda, but fighters loyal to Baghdadi split from al-Nusra and helped ISIS in Syria. In June 2014, the group formally declared the establishment of its own Caliphate, and demanded that Muslims across the world swear allegiance to its leader, Abu Bakr al-Baghdadi, and migrate into areas under its control. By September 2014, IS controlled much of the Tigris–Euphrates river basin (approximately the size of the UK) and, by 2015, it was estimated to have more than 10 million people. Many parts saw the strict implementation of Sharia law, where women are forced to wear full veils, public beheadings were common and non-Muslims were forced to either pay a special tax, convert or die.

Iran's involvement in Iraq eventually led to the assassination of their top military advisor, Qasem Soleimani, by the U.S. in January 2020. He was responsible for creating the Quds Force, an elite military organisation (the equivalent of both the CIA and the Joint Special Operations Command in the U.S.). With 10–20,000 members, it supported several groups which have been labelled 'terrorist' by Israel and the West: Hezbollah, Hamas and Palestinian Islamic Jihad in the Gaza Strip and West Bank, the Houthi rebels in Yemen, and Shi'a militias in Iraq, Syria, and Afghanistan. It has itself been classified as a terrorist organisation by the U.S., Canada, Saudi Arabia and Bahrain.

As the Middle East inherited the problem caused by the Cold War, the Syrian government was also supported by Russia, on the Iran/Shi'a side, but the world's major powers have all attempted to stabilise the situation from various directions. For example, the U.S. and Russia agreed to work together against ISIL. As such, the stand-off between Saudi Arabia and Iran did not become as serious as the one between the Soviet Union and the U.S., and they are still fighting complementary proxy wars in Yemen and Syria, as Saudi Arabia backs the rebels in the Syrian Civil War, while Iran supports the Houthi rebels in Yemen.

It has been called 'paradoxical' that we have had a global scale war against terrorism, due to the nature of the issue this raises, but if we also consider the way the world works, it makes sense how this has occurred. Obviously, in an ideal world, it would not have happened but, as we have seen how the situation evolved over time, it became inevitable due to the way Postmodernity was created.

Part 3: How Events are Progressing

While the first thing people in the West saw of this was the 9/11 attack and experienced the situation through the War on Terror, people in the East saw the events of the Islamic Revolution as being the product of the post Cold War era, and it has also been called the Third Great Revolution, after the French and Bolshevik, because of issues such as democracy, free speech and representative government once again becoming a problem. What does this say about the world today? We could say it is the product of the way the modern nations formed, as increasing pressure on them over time has combined with globalisation.

This would seem to indicate that, as of 2020, we are still in Postmodernity. But, things are changing. During the 2010s we saw the world largely moving out of the period when war in the Middle East was the main issue of global politics, with the Trump presidency in the U.S. signalling a new Arab-Israeli peace process, Xi Jinping in China launched the Belt & Road initiative and the West shifted to a new axis as Britain left the EU. The EU–Japan Economic Partnership Agreement was signed, the world's largest bilateral free trade deal, creating an open trade zone involving nearly one-third of global GDP. Overall progress also led to increased LGBT rights and female representation, particularly in the West and parts of Asia, Africa and South America.

The rise of China caused the biggest shift in the geopolitical balance of power between East and West as, by the 2010s, it had used manufacturing industries to create the money needed for investment in high technology, subsequently developing tech-Giants like Huawei. Able to then extend its influence into Southeast Asia and Africa, areas which the U.S. found difficult to reach, this counterbalanced the U.S. influence globally. However, this meant the United States sought to strategically 'rebalance' the Asia-Pacific region, leading to the Chinese response of strengthening its presence in the South China Sea and creating military bases on artificial islands to consolidate its position in Southeast Asia.

During this time, the issue of North Korea developing nuclear weapons became a gambit on the Asian side, which raised questions about the power of the U.S. in general, and was used to break down the initial relationship between the two sides before China stepped in with a stabilising influence. Dropping its support for Korea it announced that, if Korea was to act against the U.S., it would be doing so on its own. The Trump administration and North Korea then renegotiated the relationship between Capitalist and Communist nations, while the political axis of Russia and China shifted to a new norm, allowing state visits to stabilise relations.

Considering most of the world's land lies between them on one side, and its largest ocean on the other, what seems to have appeared in the nations in between is more like a natural balance between extremes. On one side the Far East mentality is reflected in Chinese Communism, while the Far West in U.S. Capitalism, and this is just part of the worldwide trend towards the radical left and conservative right in politics starting to balance out globally. The argument between the two sides now seems to have settled down into a trade war, with China accusing the U.S. of starting the 'largest in economic history' and announced retaliatory tariffs after the U.S. put them on $34 billion of Chinese goods. Google also withdrew support for Huawei phones, as well as the Google Play Store and Gmail apps, after the company was blacklisted in the U.S.

During the 2010s China also embarked on a massive multi-trillion dollar plan to revitalise the Silk Road trade routes with new infrastructure and connect with 60% of the world's population. Known as the Belt & Road Initiative (Belt, as it creates a trade belt around China, and Road because of the Silk Road), it looks set to become the biggest investment of the 21st Century, unless the U.S. responds by mining asteroids in space or minerals on other planets. This project includes loaning countries across Eurasia and Africa billions of U.S. dollars to build ports, roads and other infrastructure which will then act as parts of this network. The fact that the current breakdown of affairs in the Middle East was created during the period of U.S. hegemony, this has been appealing to many countries who are not on good terms with the U.S., and has allowed China to make political goals possible which might not have been otherwise.

So far, 60 countries have signed deals with China, including a rail link to London, gas pipelines to the Caspian Sea, mines, power plants, oil refineries, industrial parks, fibre-optic cable networks, a high speed rail network in Southeast Asia, a combined port, railway and highway network in Pakistan, a sea port in Sri Lanka and a major bridge in Laos. Also, the Maritime Silk Road consists of a string of sea ports from the South China Sea to Africa. For example, foreign trade with Pakistan was not popular due to political unrest and social problems, but the project there produced a $62 billion economic corridor and the country saw its first rise in GDP for 8 years. In Kazakhstan, Chinese leader Xi Jinping gave a speech saying that 'We should take an innovative approach and jointly build an economic belt along the Silk Road'. A month later in Indonesia he said, 'The two sides should work together to build up a massive Silk Road in the 21st century.' 6 economic corridors have been created across Eurasia, boosting opportunities for Chinese construction companies, which now include 7 of the world's 10 largest.

Countries that have found it hard to attract investment from the West, especially during the period of U.S. hegemony, such as Serbia, Azerbaijan and Belarus, have benefitted from this strategy, and China now also has economic ties with Afghanistan, Yemen, Ukraine and Iraq. For the reason that some of these countries have been fragmented by internal conflict, making the ability to pay back loans difficult, it has been called a risky policy but, when Sri Lanka failed to pay, China was able to take control of the port there on a 99 year lease. A similar 40 year lease exists on the strategic port in Pakistan, and China is now seeking another deal with Myanmar. The 'String of Pearls' theory has suggested they intend to protect and control trade routes in the Indian Ocean. As of 2020, India has said it has yet to respond.

Hence, while some people have questioned whether or not the world was entering the 'second phase' of the Cold War, this cannot be the case, as we have seen from the way international relations have already developed. This map of the world today shows the nations we have now are not so different geographically to where they were in the 1800s but, we are in a very different place now politically, economically, technologically and socially.

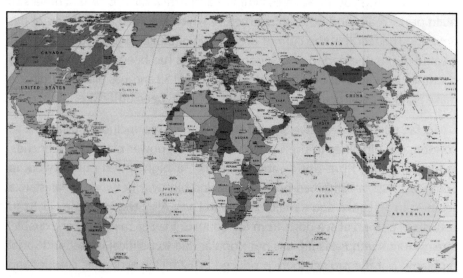

A Digital Age?

The 2010s saw a rapid creation of digital technology, with CCTV surveillance and facial recognition software becoming common throughout the world. Many cities such as those in China, for example, started operating largely without cash, using the Smartphone system to authorise payments. The Internet itself grew due to advancements in wireless networking devices, mobile telephony and cloud computing. Advancements in data processing led to the introduction of 4G broadband and later 5G, while cable television declined as users switched to lower-cost online streaming services such as Netflix, Disney Plus and Amazon Prime. Superhero films, notably featuring cyborgs, outer space, energy physics, computer-generated imagery (CGI) and alien encounters became box office leaders, with Avengers Endgame becoming the highest-grossing film of all time ($2.7 billion worldwide). Digital music overtook Compact Disc sales in 2012, while the video game industry became dominated by Sony, Nintendo and Microsoft.

The technological revolution began playing a major role in the world order, as it enabled governments to better organise themselves, giving an advantage to those who were connected online, restructuring both society and businesses. Through a faster transfer of information enabling an acceleration of events, this improved access to services, employment and interpersonal communication, creating a higher level of social mobility. As the Internet is continually spreading to new areas, this will improve skills and new jobs should be created as people are able to fill those roles. However, the problem with achieving this in practical terms is that the value of new goods must compete with existing markets, so it is not always profitable employing everyone. In other words, growth is limited by the structure of the economy itself.

New legal issues have come with the Internet, such as massive lawsuits and government investigations into the use of data by large companies, often used in the creation of marketing algorithms which select advertisements, leading to the declaration by Facebook owner, Mark Zuckerberg, that his employees did not have personal access to the information. More serious were accusations of governments spying on people using purpose-built software, especially in the U.S., where the National Security Agency (NSA) suffered massive leaks by former employee Edward Snowden, creating a website onto which thousands of documents were uploaded (Wikileaks). Other growing problems include ransomeware (which locks computers until a fee is paid), spyware (which searches for personal information such as bank account details) and D-Dos attacks (which can jam a website by rapidly sending it thousands of signals).

However, despite our new technology there is evidence that we need to get better at solving human problems. While Internet access in 2020 was available to an average of 53.6% of people worldwide, this was 86.6% in developed countries, but only 47% in developing nations. This means radically different political, economic and social conditions still exist throughout the world. In terms of education, Canada, Israel, Japan, the U.S., New Zealand, South Korea, Finland, Australia and Russia have the highest literacy rates, while South Sudan, Burkina Faso, Niger, Afghanistan, Mali, Chad, Somalia, Ethiopia, Guinea and Benin have the lowest.

Following the 2008 financial crisis, economic issues were prevalent in the West throughout the decade, such as austerity, inflation and an increase in prices, leading to political protests including the 15–M, Occupy and Yellow Vest movements. Similar to those of recent centuries, they focused on a lack of 'real democracy', control of the majority of the world's resources by a small minority (who have become known as 'The 1%'), and the apparent lack of tax regulations for the super-rich. With this came anti-corruption lobbyists looking for reforms to the existing system, such as the German newspaper, Süddeutsche Zeitung, publishing 13.4 million documents leaked from the law firm Appleby, which revealed the offshore financial activities of the rich and famous.

In certain places, protests spilled over into civil unrest, such as mass protests in Hong Kong against new Chinese laws, and the Black Lives Matter protests against police brutality which spread quickly across the U.S. and to other nations. In the U.S. a state of near emergency existed for weeks, as demonstrators entirely took over the centre of Minneapolis, burning buildings and looting shops. Eventually the national guard was called in to disperse them. Accusations that Antifa (anti-Fascist) and Anarchist groups had hijacked peaceful demonstrations were widespread in the media, with evidence being cited such as piles of bricks being found at several sites where no actual building work was occurring. In early 2021 Republican Trump supporters marched on the U.S. Capitol building following the allegedly 'stolen' 2020 election by Democrat Joe Biden, for which Trump was impeached for a second time for inciting the crowd (the only U.S. President to be impeached twice), but on trial was found not guilty of directly causing the incident.

Civil rights issues have also continued, such as the Rohingya persecution in Myanmar, the Chinese internment of a million Uighur Muslims in re-education camps (following the Xinjiang Conflict), and the crisis in Venezuela. Illegal Human Trafficking, especially into Europe from war zones in Africa and the Middle East, and into the U.S. from countries in South and Central America has been widely covered by news agencies and prompted U.S. President Trump to start building an enormous wall between the U.S. and Mexico.

Wars continued in Africa and the Middle East, with political unrest in Southeast Asia and South America. Conflicts which have continued into the 2020s include: the Syrian Civil War, the Second Libyan Civil War, the War in Donbass, the Iraqi insurgency, the Yemeni Civil War, the South Sudanese Civil War, the War in Afghanistan, the Somali Civil War, the Kashmir insurgency and the Israeli–Palestinian conflict. Notably, most of these are in either Africa or the Middle East, perhaps simply because of the way the world order has evolved.

The problem of terrorism continued, with Islamist attacks in Sri Lanka, Nigeria, Egypt, France, Britain, Germany, Finland, Iran, Turkey, Mozambique, Afghanistan and Somalia. White supremacist attacks also occurred in Pittsburgh (Pennsylvania), Christchurch (New Zealand) and Gothenburg (Sweden), mainly to retaliate for Islamic terrorism, but also because of bad relations with ethnic minorities. The shooting down of civilian aircraft additionally occurred, such as Ukraine International Airlines Flight 752 by Iran's armed forces, Malaysia Airlines Flight 17 by pro-Russian rebels in eastern Ukraine, and Metrojet Flight 9268 by a suspected Islamic State bomb. A school shooting and bomb attack in Kerch, Crimea, killed 20 people and 70 were injured. 36 people were also killed in an arson attack at an animation company in Kyoto, Japan. Numerous mass-shootings also occurred in the U.S., in Orlando, Connecticut, Colorado, Ohio, Texas and Florida.

While the Cold War was happening, it not only caused problems, but also prevented certain issues from being addressed on a national level, which has given rise to a new type of nationalism. The Trump administration and Brexit vote, for example, are cases where people have decided that the way the world moves forward should not be simply a continuity of what has happened before, as the way the world moved forward to start with was not perfect in the first place. However, what we are seeing increasingly from the right is a much more moderate approach than the irrational politics of Fascism, as it uses empirical evidence to back up its arguments, and does not claim to advocate imperialism or state-sponsored violence. The new left, likewise, questions what constitutes a good use of public funds, rather than simply demanding the transference of all private ownership to the state.

With the continuation of the war on terrorism, the structural issue within politics has reflected back into the West, causing a rise in far right groups and political parties. For example, the rise of the U.S. Trump administration, and the return of the U.K. Conservative Party to power in 2011 featured political ideas which were anti-immigration, reduced civil rights for the unemployed and favoured the rich over the poor, rather than being designed to promote social equality and mobility. Similarly, the 2016 Brexit campaign used images such as a tide of immigrants pushing Britain to breaking point, and was won on a mono-cultural, anti-immigration agenda, which pronounced Europe's institutions corrupt and controlling, while promising more money to the National Health Service. Perhaps while Western Europe and the U.S. wanted to attract more people during its long period of high economic growth, these groups are saying that period has ended and too many people from developing countries want to live and work in the West, taking jobs and housing away from Western people, whose governments should put their interests first.

The same type of national issues have appeared in many countries, for example, India favouring Hindus over Muslims with regard to the right to nationality. Far-right politicians with similar values increased their share of the vote in various European countries, and an international movement calling itself The Organisation was formed to help right wing parties win elections in Western countries. Most of them have existed for some time, such as those in France (National Rally), Greece (Golden Dawn), Hungary (Jobbik), Holland (Party for Freedom) and Germany (Alternative for Germany). But, in certain counties they even took power in recent years, such as in Italy (Forza Italia). Perhaps, though, the residual state of politics in the West is reflective of the East in broader terms, as Communism still exists in many Far Eastern states. However, it appears this period will give way to a more sophisticated vision of social integration, as governments are taking extensive action to denounce racism and encourage co-operation between communities.

Both natural and manmade disasters have continued to claim lives, such as dams breaking, explosions at chemical plants, widespread forest fires, plane, train and bus crashes, boats capsizing, and infrastructure collapses. The 2020 Beirut dockyard explosion, caused by over 2,000 tonnes of ammonium nitrate stored in a warehouse, caused at least 181 deaths, 6,000 injuries, U.S. $10–15 billion property damage, made an estimated 300,000 people homeless and caused a 3.3 magnitude earthquake. The media continued to report on increased climate change, with such evidence as glaciers melting, adding to evidence that some natural disasters are actually manmade, as extreme weather conditions and the fragmentation of the jet stream are being attributed to global warming.

These also include cyclones, tornadoes, hurricanes (especially ones in the Caribbean which frequently hit the southeastern U.S.), typhoons, monsoon related flooding (especially in Southeast Asia) and landslides. Additionally, the Intergovernmental Science-Policy Platform on Biodiversity and Ecosystem Services (IPBES) has said biodiversity loss is accelerating, with over a million species now threatened by human activity. Oil and chemical spillages, of sometimes thousands of tonnes, have ruined marine and coastal habitats, and poisoned people after leaking into the water table. Locust plagues and diseases have additionally damaged crops, causing famine in Yemen, Somalia, South Sudan and Nigeria.

Polio, Ebola, Zika Virus, Cholera, and SARS respiratory syndrome have all seen outbreaks in recent years. But, by far the largest has been the COVID-19 (Coronavirus) pandemic, which spread quickly to over 200 countries in early 2020. 500,000 cases and 23,000 deaths had resulted by March 26, growing to 10 million cases in June, with over 500,000 related deaths. By late August there were over 20 million cases and over 800,000 deaths. After a period of national lockdowns, a second wave grew by early 2021 to 25 million active cases and 2.5 million deaths before going into slow decline. Vaccines were quickly developed during 2020 and rolled out in early 2021, but the lockdown measures on public movement and the closure of businesses by governments caused the worst global recession since the Great Depression. All mass gatherings were banned, including sporting, cultural, political and religious events, panic buying ensued, and even services such as dentistry and medicine were suspended. As such, questions have been asked about the level of organisation the world lives at, and calls for a new period of political and economic history were made. The Great Reset, the name of the 50th annual meeting of the World Economic Forum, held in June 2020, brought together business and political leaders, with the aim of rebuilding global society in a more sustainable way following the pandemic.

How the World Works Today

A recent report stated that most people in the world have actually entered the Middle Classes, as they can afford a car, and have the ability to network outside the home. The traditional definition of 'Working Class' thus no longer applies to most people, and that seems to be a major reason why governments can now claim that they are getting on top of the situation. However, the same report claims it is more difficult now for people to get out of extreme poverty, due to the intense competition for resources. While large areas of the world are scarcely populated, those around major cities are severely overpopulated. In many cases they stretch out into miles of slums and shanty towns, which generate their own industries such as recycling and scrap metal. As cities can guarantee resources such as running water and food, easy access to employment, and civilising factors such as police services and electricity, their businesses and houses are worth so much more than outlying areas.

The problem is rooted in the structure of the global economy itself, because of the chaos involved in the way real events move forwards, meaning a need for a centralised government to manage the needs of society. Because of competition for resources like food, tools, education and jobs, life can be a slippery slope which some find impossible to climb. Hence, it has become the mission of most governments around the world to create a 'level playing field' for their citizens. However, while the structure of the nation is represented in its political framework of regional councils, this also means each society has a particular shape and, therefore, must work in a particular way. This is another reason why people are accusing the system of being corrupt, and unable to change. But, this is also why people who have a good understanding of social structure are more likely to climb the social ladder, as they will be aware of how the situation works.

Knowledge of economics, too, is the reason for many peoples' success, as certain market sectors are worth more than others, and this means more investment goes into them. Getting involved in a growth area means there are more jobs and opportunities for promotion. Major industries, such as oil, gas and coal emerge sporadically around where resources are found, thus requiring multibillion dollar sources of investment to fuel the shifting supply of these goods. This is one of the reasons why large multinational corporations have emerged, to enable companies to share their resources and direct them towards new projects where necessary. These have taken control of large sectors of the economy, such as food production and healthcare. It has been said that only around 1,500 companies now control most of rest, due to the need for secure supply lines, and they work through an economy of scale. Mixing top-down and bottom-up management styles, they succeed through strong middle-management, extensive research into product development, intensely targeted marketing, and have the ability to plan years in advance. They also invest in other businesses through hedge-funds, which indirectly help each other along and stabilise themselves (gold and silver, for example, are typical hedge-fund investment commodities as they tend not to crash completely during a recession).

However, money isn't everything. The World Happiness Report is an annual publication of the United Nations Sustainable Development Solutions Network. It ranks countries in terms of national happiness based on people's ratings of their own lives. In March 2020, Finland was ranked the happiest for the third year running, with Denmark, Norway, Iceland, and Holland coming next. Life expectancy at birth has risen globally, from an average of 31 in 1900 to 48 in 1950 and 72.2 in 2017. However, while being above 80 in the UK, South Korea, Australia, Hong Kong, Chile, Costa Rica, Cyprus, Canada, Singapore, Japan, and across the EU, it is still as low as under 55 in countries such as Nigeria, Sierra Leone, the Central African Republic, Lesotho and Chad.

The Global Peace Index is a yearly report produced by the Institute for Economics & Peace (IEP), along with experts from institutes worldwide. In 2019 it showed that Iceland, New Zealand, Portugal, Austria and Denmark were the most peaceful countries, while Somalia, Afghanistan, Syria, South Sudan, Yemen and Iraq were the least. Peace-building has been shown to provide monetary returns of 16 times the cost, while the global impact of conflicts in 2016, for example, was $14.3 trillion, 12.6 per cent of global GDP. It would thus seem the value of solving the problem of war far outweighs the cost and, now social sciences are explaining much more about the cause of much of the world's political instability, it may be possible to explain this to groups who may become less militant and more willing to negotiate.

As of the 2020 population, China and India are the largest with over a billion, then the U.S. with over 300 million. Indonesia, Pakistan, Brazil and Nigeria are next with over 200 million. Bangladesh, Russia, Mexico, Japan, Philippines and Egypt each have over 100 million. There are another 15 countries with 50–100 million, 63 with 10–50 million and the rest under 10 million. However, gross domestic product per capita (the value of all final goods and services produced within a nation in a year, divided by the average population) by far remains the highest in countries which industrialised in the 1800s. Those are in Western Europe, the U.S., Japan, plus Australia and New Zealand. Asia and South America come next, while African countries are the most economically disadvantaged. This seems to indicate that societies created later in history have become more technologically advanced, according to the manner in which the world globalised.

Perhaps the most telling statistic of all is access to safe drinking water, with around 4 billion people having access to fresh tap water, and another 2 billion having to use wells or public taps. A further 2.1 billion people lack safe drinking water, according to a 2017 World Health Organisation (WHO) report, a problem that causes 30,000 deaths weekly. The WHO says billions have acquired safe water since 2000, and 181 countries achieved 75% coverage of their total land area by 2015. However, many homes, healthcare facilities and schools still lack basic sanitation, such as soap and water for hand washing. The vast majority of these people live in developing nations, in Sub-Saharan Africa and Oceania. Quite clearly, the struggle for the most basic resources is still an issue. With demand for water expected to increase by 40% by 2025, UN Deputy Secretary-General Jan Eliasson stated in 2015, [2]'Water must never be a reason for rivalry or competition. Water must be a source of cooperation and of shared security and prosperity. Let us remember that water is our primary source of life. So this is also, fundamentally, an existential challenge and a moral obligation.'

Due to the number of countries, we can hardly say there is a single global paradigm, or one world government. The UN constantly adapts its mission, and we can see that between 1945 and the post Cold War era it was a case of encouraging international co-operation and avoiding a nuclear war. This has shifted over time to presently being more of a case of monitoring situations and advising governments, while assisting with diplomatic support and direct aid. The Treaty on the Prohibition of Nuclear Weapons, voted for by 122 states in 2017, indicates that nations are now working more closely together on the same mission.

Into the Future

Many important events during the 2010s were related to the exploration of outer space, with the Mars Science Laboratory landing a remotely controlled vehicle on Mars, NASA's Mars Reconnaissance Orbiter photographed evidence of liquid water on Mars, the first solar-powered mission to Jupiter was launched in the U.S., an unmanned Mars Orbiter was launched by India, and China landed the Yutu rover on the Moon. Elon Musk's SpaceX company ran various missions which included the first manned space flight since the retirement of the NASA Space Shuttle in 2011, and the U.S. Space Force was also founded, a branch of the Armed Forces dedicated to space warfare, indicating a shift towards large nations developing strategic interests in space. Some U.S. companies say they are ready to start mining resources in space, such as Platinum group metals which are found in large quantities on various asteroids.

The study of outer space continued through the CHEOPS space telescope, whose mission is to study the formation of planets beyond our solar system. Other discoveries included the first picture of a black hole, and water in the atmosphere of exoplanet K2-18b is the first to be found in a habitable zone around a star. By the Mid 2010s, the Swiss Solar Impulse 2 became the first solar-powered aircraft to circumnavigate the Earth, NASA's New Horizons spacecraft performed a close flyby of Pluto, and gravitational waves were detected.

Genetic research also made advances, with scientists announcing that they have created a functional synthetic genome, a living lab-grown ear made from collagen and animal ear cell cultures, and human embryonic stem cells were produced by cloning. Concerns over genetically modified (GM) food arose also, as the need to feed over 7 billion people is causing people to seek new methods of mass production. For example, crops which are resistant to disease are generally regarded as a breakthrough in terms of reducing losses, but ethical questions exist over whether we should modify the taste of a strawberry, and if doing so could affect humans. Scientists also concluded that they have sequenced enough of the Neanderthal genome to suggest that Neanderthals and Homo sapiens interbred. Additionally, physicists discovered the Higgs boson particles at the Large Hadron Collider at CERN.

However, as technological progress has come to affect the environment, many international agencies today are recording, reporting and speaking publicly about the damage human activities are causing. UN Secretary-General, Antonio Guterres, recently announced that nature is reacting with [3]'growing force and fury', to humanity's mismanagement of the environment, including a collapse in biodiversity, spreading deserts, and oceans reaching record temperatures. He noted that the continued encroachment of people and livestock into wild animal habitats risks exposing us to more deadly diseases. Additionally, whilst the economic slowdown resulting from the COVID-19 pandemic has temporarily slowed emissions of the so-called 'greenhouse gases', levels of carbon dioxide, nitrous oxide and methane are still rising, and the amount of carbon dioxide is at a record high.

Despite this, fossil fuel production continues to grow. The appropriate response, he said, is that we should flick the 'green switch' and transform the global economy, building a sustainable system driven by renewable energy, green jobs and a resilient future. Altogether, the post COVID-19 crisis period should be one in which we 'make peace with nature', and companies could adjust their business models to finance the rise of green energy. For example, pension funds manage around $32 trillion in assets, which they could easily invest for a long term profit, while most businesses have the problem of maintaining their cash-flow on a daily basis.

Additionally, the Intergovernmental Panel on Climate Change (IPCC) reported that the world faced 'severe, pervasive and irreversible' damage from global emissions of carbon dioxide, promoting concern that we need to take control of the situation. The 2015 United Nations Climate Change Conference (COP 21) held in Paris, France, was attended by leaders from 147 nations, and led to an agreement that all should reduce carbon emissions for the first time.

The actual amount of global resources has become an issue for governments, as consumption of fossil fuels (coal, oil and gas) is on the rise, while new deposits are becoming harder to find, and are becoming significantly smaller than ones already discovered.

16 of the world's 20 largest oilfields are at peak production, indicating that the industry is too small to cope with global demand. It is predicted that both oil and gas will run out in around 50 years. Coal has been given 150 years, but that does not take into account what will happen if we run out of oil and gas. As a result of this, it looks like we will see the left wing in politics try to create a swing towards questioning how resources are managed, adding pressure to the argument for more government regulation of private business to ensure demand is met. On the other hand, the right-wing argument will attempt to maintain private ownership of global resources and protect existing profits.

However, green energy is on the rise, especially solar, water and wind power. For example, water purification plants produce fresh water from sea water in places where it is scarce. The Three Gorges hydroelectric gravity dam, on the Yangtze river in China, is now the world's largest power station and is generally regarded as a massive economic and ecological success. Criticisms over the management of the project arose as floods occurred and a million people were displaced due to its building. However, learning from mistakes like these is essential, as pressure on governments to move to green energy will only increase as fossil fuels expire.

Ecologist Phil Gibbard said that, if the desire is there, we could achieve anything, but that his main worry is that not everyone has this desire, which is mainly an educational problem. Ideally, investment funds from developed nations putting money into green energy in developing countries could be the great economic solution the world is looking for, as it would also encourage political stability. French philosopher Bruno Latour has said that there are always plenty of options in terms of new technologies, the question is over how to choose the right direction.

Thus what should we expect to see marking the transition between the end of this period and the beginning of the next is governments becoming increasingly organised, especially when it comes to resources, selecting courses of action, efficient computerised administration, setting up peace treaties, trade deals, human affairs in space and protecting the environment. During this time, a shift in the practical management of the situation should show an increase in the use of computers to synthesise written records into a better functioning present. We can already see this happening in business, taxation, legal systems, passports, banking, social security, the housing market, education and many other areas.

The Anthropocene

The technological revolution is certainly having a similar influence to that which the industrial revolution had on the modern period, in the sense that it is accelerating established industries. However, can the 'Digital Age' actually become the new name for the period we live in? Periods are normally classified according to the impact of change on social conditions. Since 2016 some people have suggested that we are entering Post-Postmodernity, yet this is a bleak concept, considering the human need to create new ideas. Given the success we are having at taking over the planet, the 'Anthropocene' has arisen as an idea capable of surpassing the idea of Postmodernity, as it creates a shift towards a more scientific worldview and takes the world away from the subjectivity which has been the problem of the last period.

If we consider the initial problem of Postmodernity was to avoid WWIII, and the way we came into it led first to the Cuban Missile Crisis and then the problem of terrorism, people have realised that we never really considered where it all came from and this has led to the problems we have now. In other words, as we entered Postmodernity, the divides within politics were already there and took us very quickly into the Cold War. Subsequent events solved the previous crisis, but then caused another. However, because of the Internet, people are now waking up for the first time to the idea that we can see the direction events are going in, and take responsibility for the situation we are creating through our own actions. In other words, people are increasingly realising the need to move towards a world of our own making. Because of the way the current situation works, not everyone has the ability to entirely create their own narrative, but there is certainly more flexibility in terms of the way we can work, socialise, consume goods, and even practice religion. Therefore, there are more opportunities to evolve in directions of our own choosing, and in terms of what we can achieve. As this is reflecting back into society itself, we can also see more groups and organisations appearing which are concerned with the environment, global poverty, and other factors which contribute to human welfare.

Its dictionary definition is 'the period of time during which human activities have had an environmental impact on the Earth, such as to be regarded as constituting a distinct geological age'. Currently, scientists are looking for evidence on the grounds that the geological record must show some kind of 'golden spike' to prove the theory. That is, something which marks the point at which we could say the Anthropocene is definitely occurring. Some are claiming that it is there, in the measurable effect of the burning of fossil fuels on the atmosphere. However, it has also been proposed that the thin layer of radioactive material deposited in the environment since the nuclear age is enough to signify that we have arrived at this point technologically, regardless of our impact upon the environment.

The term Anthropocene has been around since the 1960s and was used in the 1980s by ecologist Eugene Stoermer, before being popularised around the year 2000 by atmospheric chemist Paul J Crutzen, who considered the impact of human activity on the Earth's atmosphere enough to constitute a new geological age.

In 2008, the Stratigraphy Commission of the Geological Society of London considered a proposal to make it a formal term. However, there were questions over the starting date. A March 2015 report suggested either 1610 or 1964, while other reports pointed to the physical strata of human activity, in a similar way to the strata of sedimentary rocks correlates with activity on the surface. That is, the Anthropocene is made up of huge layers of human activity which have built up over thousands of years, and thus both its onset and impact are spread out, not reducible to a single point in time. Hence, more recently, this two-step approach emerged:

1. An early phase with effects that began at a very low level thousands of years ago, such as those of organised hunting, large scale cattle grazing and small dams, but grew slowly during the pre-industrial revolution period.

2. A later industrial phase, during which we have created the need to realise the impact of our activities, in both practical and legal terms.

That is, both in terms of our total impact upon the environment as a whole, and specific instances such as the spillage of an oil tanker on the shoreline of an adjacent nation, which has led to changes in the law and an increase in legal regulations.

Logically, this seems reasonable, as the Industrial Revolution was the point when we began to mass produce the type of goods and industrial processes which affect the environment, such as the use of chemicals, huge open cast mines, and the use of oil in motors. Hence, we have acquired since then the need to regulate certain activities which did not exist before. Before the AD 1800s, the use of metals was not common and plastics were not invented, most houses and ships were made out of wood and there were no cars or airplanes. Therefore, most of what we created was biodegradable.

The Symbiocene, a term coined by Glenn Albrecht, Professor of Sustainability at Murdoch University in Western Australia, has evolved as the perfect concept to describe what will happen as we better adapt, as we achieve symbiosis with the planet. We can see the shift between the two periods as a time when humans realised the need to increase their knowledge of both the biosphere and the environment, marking the end of simply attempting to create human dominance.

Afterword

We are now moving beyond Postmodernity as our concept of the present, and we can see that the future is not entirely uncertain, it has a direction, but to see the way events are set to unfold in different areas we should be looking at the particular factors which are directly concerned. While I was researching and writing this, I realised it was very difficult to actually predict what was going to happen in specific terms, even though I could see a general pattern emerge, mainly because of the complex way the world works, but also because a multitude of different groups have control over important decision making processes, plus regular changes in governmental and other systems have become standard policy for reasons of security and updating methods. Thus I personally found the Internet news sites were very useful at helping me to follow the way events were occurring, and to recognise the rise and fall of political and other trends in various places. For example, CNN, BBC News, Russia Today and Al Jazeera cover between them large areas of the world's politics, economics and culture. Each state has its own news agency and, from them, we can also see a great deal about national states of affairs. This enabled me to function in the present for practical and discussion purposes, as I could relate the way events were moving forward on a daily basis to the world I could see evolving out of history. For this reason, I recommend keeping an eye on the changing perspectives within global news agencies as a method of keeping in touch with what is happening in the world, just be aware that the inherent bias in each channel is all part of the big picture!

Before I did this research, I often found it confusing how nations themselves behaved, especially the U.S. and China in relation to each other, and could not make sense of what was happening in the Middle East at all. But, all this changed when I could see the overall pattern in events emerging out of global history and that governments actually base their decisions upon very similar models, with advice from senior professionals. Now I am finding it quite easy to plug into the Internet and get my daily update, whereas it took a long time to build the overall picture, and I do not have to go back to understanding the whole of history all over again!

What I have also learned from all this is that the way global progress occurs is not an accident, it is based on very deep thinking on the part of governments and organisations, taking into account all of the available facts about how the present works. Because of this, we can see the part history plays as a subject is very important as it shows us how the situation is evolving over time. That is why it is taught in every school, college and university. Hopefully this book will stand as a record of how the people of their time saw their world.

BIBLIOGRAPHY

CHAPTER 1

1. O'BRIEN, P.K. (2002) Philip's Atlas of World History. Octopus Publishing. ISBN: 0 540 082597. Pages 16–17.

2. WELLS, H.G. (1920) The Outline of History. Cassell & Co. Ltd. London. Page 176.

3. DEAN, G. (1998) Signs Symbols and Ciphers, translated by Sophie Hawkes. Thames and Hudson. London. ISBN: 0-500-30087-9. Page 11.

4. MANKIEWICZ, R. (2000) The Story of Mathematics. Cassell & Co. London.

5. TRESIDDER, J.(1999) Dictionary of Symbols.
Duncan Baird Publishers. London. ISBN: 1-900131-62-5. Page 6.

6. C.F. TAYLOR, W.C. STURTEVANT (1991) Americans. Salamander Books. Page 123.

7. GHALIN, L. (2001) Egypt. Gods Myths and Religion. Lorentz Books. London SE1 8HA. Page 50.

8. Translated by FAULKNER, R.O. Edited by ANDREWS, C. (1985) The Ancient Egyptian Book of the Dead. British Museum Publications, London. Page xxiii.

9. SELEEM, R. (2001) The Egyptian Book of the Dead. Godsfield Press, David and Charles Ltd. Brunel House, Forde Close, Newton Abbott, Devon, TQ124PU. ISBN: 1-84181-109-2. Page 10.

CHAPTER 2

1. POLLOCK, S. (1999) Ancient Mesopotamia. The Press Syndicate of the University of Cambridge. The Pitt Building, Trumpington Street, Cambridge, CB21RP. ISBN: 052157568 0. Page 29.

2. ROHL, D.M. (1998) Legend. The Genesis of Civilisation. Century, a division of Random House. London. ISBN: 0 7126 7747 X. Page 33.

3. KRAMER, S.N. (1967) THE SUMERIANS. THEIR HISTORY, CULTURE, AND CHARACTER. University of Chicago Press. Library of Congress Catalog no. 63-11398. Pages 3–5; 4. Pages 171–3; 5. Pages 173–176.

6. BAHN, P.G. (1996) The Story of Archaeology.
Weidenfeld and Nicolson, Orion Publishing. London. ISBN: 0-297-83445-2. Page 142.

7. ROHL, D.M. (1998) Legend, The Genesis of Civilisation. Century, a division of Random House. London. ISBN: 0 7126 7747 X. Page 159.

8. SAGGS, H.W.F. (1967) Everyday Life in Babylonia & Assyria. B.T. Batsford Ltd. London, W1. Pages 30–35.

CHAPTER 3

1. SAGGS, H.W.F. (1965) Everyday Life in Babylonia & Assyria. B.T. Batsford Ltd. London, W1. Pages 37–40; 2. Page 42.

2. BAHN, P.G. (1996) The Story of Archaeology.

Weidenfeld and Nicolson, Orion Publishing. London.

3. DALLEY, S. (1991) Myths From Mesopotamia. Oxford University Press. ISBN: 9780192817891. Pages 233–74.

4. DALLEY, S. (1991) Myths From Mesopotamia. Oxford University Press. ISBN: 9780192817891. Page 1–35, Atrahasis.

CHAPTER 4

1. WELLS, H.G. (1920) The Outline of History. Cassell & Co. Ltd. London. Pages 177–9.

2. BUCKLEY EBREY, P (1996) China, Cambridge Illustrated History. Cambridge University Press. Pages 38–39.

3. Lao Tse — The Tao Te Ching.

4. IONS, V. (1992) Indian Mythology. Reed International Books. London. Page 12.

5. http://www.crystalwind.ca/mystical-magical/pantheons-and-myths/hindu/the-hindu-creation-story

6. BOWKER, J. (2002) Cambridge Illustrated History. Religions. Cambridge University Press. Pages 27–29.

7. Translated by GRIFFITH, R.T.H. (1896). HYMN XC, Perusa, Rig Veda. sacred-texts.com

8. VOIELS, V. (1998) Hinduism, A New Approach. Hodder & Stoughton, a member of the Hodder Headline group. London. Page 8.

9. HINNELS, J.R. (2000) Zoroastrian and Parsi Studies. Selected Work of John R. Hinnels. Research Professor in Comparative Religion. University of Derby. Ashgate Publishing, Aldershot.   ISBN: 07546 15014. Pages 253–254.

10. BOWKER, J. (2002) Cambridge Illustrated History. Religions. Cambridge University Press. Pages 27–29, 'Zarathustra and the Parsis'.

11. HOLLAND, T. (2005) Persian Fire: The First World Empire and the Battle For the West. Abacus, an imprint of Little, Brown Book Group. London. ISBN: 978-0-349-11717-1. Pages 1–15.

12. CURTIS, J. (2005) Ancient Persia. The British Museum. Pages 36–43.

CHAPTER 5
1. FREEMAN, C. (1996) EGYPT, GREECE AND ROME, Civilisations of the Mediterranean. Oxford University Press. ISBN: 0-19872194-3. Page 76.

2. MAGEE, B. (1987). The Great Philosophers. BBC Books. London. ISBN: 0 563 20583 0. Page 34.

3. THORNTON, A. (1970) People and Themes in Homer's Odyssey. Methuen & Co. University of Otago Press. Page x.

4. FORSTATER, M. (2004) The Living Wisdom of Socrates. Hodder and Stoughton. London. ISBN: 0340 73318 7. Page 9 paragraph 1.

5. CROSS, R.C. & WOOZLEY, A.D. (1964) Plato's Republic, A Philosophical Commentary. Macmillan Publishing. London and Basingstoke. Pages 206 – 7 & Page 69.

6. WOODFIN, R. & GROVES, J. (2001) Introducing Aristotle. Icon Books. Cambridge. ISBN: 1 84046 2337. Page 37.

CHAPTER 6
1. KERSHAW, S.P. (2013) A Brief History of the Roman Empire, Rise and Fall. Constable & Robinson Ltd. 55–56 Russell Square, London. WC1B4HP. Pages 1–2.

2. FREEMAN, C. (1996) EGYPT, GREECE AND ROME, Civilisations of the Mediterranean. Oxford University Press. ISBN: 0-19872194-3. Page 319; 3. Pages 325–328.

CHAPTER 7
1. PARKER, G. (1995 Third Revised Edition) The Times Illustrated History of the World. Times Books. London. ISBN: 0 7230 0671 7. Page 74–5.

2. DE LANGE, N. (1984) Atlas of the Jewish World. Phaidon Press. Oxford. ISBN: 0-7148-2724-4.

3. WRIGHT, N.T. (2001) Jesus and the Victory of God. S.P.C.K. Books. London. Page 296.

4. MORRIS, L. (1988) The Epistle To The Romans. Inter-Varsity Press. Leicester, England. Page 172-3.

5. POPE BENEDICT XVI. (2007) Jesus of Nazareth. Bloomsbury Publishing. New York, London, Berlin. ISBN: 9780747593782

CHAPTER 8
1. POTTER, D. (2007) Emperors of Rome. Quercus Publishing. 21 Bloomsbury Square, London WC1A 2NS. ISBN: 978-1-84724-166-5. Page 6 par 1.

2. PRICE, S. & THONEMANN, P. (2010) The Birth of Classical Europe. Penguin Books. ISBN 978-0-713-99242-7. Page 257-8.

3. POTTER, D. (2007) Emperors of Rome. Quercus Publishing. 21 Bloomsbury Square, London WC1A 2NS. ISBN: 978-1-84724-166-5. Page 66.

4. BISPHAM, E. (2008) Roman Europe. (Short Oxford History of Europe, General Editor: T.C.W. Blanning). Oxford University Press.
ISBN: 978-0-19-926601-2. Page 203; 5. Page 199.

CHAPTER 9
1. BRYCE, J. (1915) The Holy Roman Empire. Macmillan and Company Limited. London. Introduction.

CHAPTER 10
1. JOLLEY, K.L. (1996) Tradition and Diversity. Routledge Publishing.
ISBN: 978-156324468 1. Page 459.

2. WEATHERFORD, J. (2004) Genghis Khan and the Making of the Modern World. Crown and Three Rivers Press. ISBN: 0-609-80964-4

CHAPTER 12
1. WALLERSTEIN, I. (1974) The Modern World System. Academic Press. New York and London. Page 15.

CHAPTER 13
1. HITLER, A. (1925) Mein Kampf. Hurst and Brackett Ltd. London, Melbourne. Chapter 1, Page 1, Paragraph 2.

CHAPTER 14
1. General Wesley Clarke (2007). Democracy Now interview with Amy Goodman at the 92nd Street Y Cultural Centre, New York.

2. UN Deputy Secretary-General, Jan Eliasson. Speech at the Friends of Water Steering Committee. New York, September 2015. Reported by: https://www.un.org/press/en/2015/dsgsm896.doc.htm

3. UN Secretary-General, Antonio Guterres. State of the Planet interview with Professor Maureen Raymo. Columbia University, New York. Reported by: https://news.un.org/en/story/2020/12/1079032